THE STRUGGLE FOR THE PEOPLE'S KING

The Struggle for the People's King

HOW POLITICS TRANSFORMS THE MEMORY OF THE CIVIL RIGHTS MOVEMENT

HAJAR YAZDIHA

PRINCETON UNIVERSITY PRESS
PRINCETON & OXFORD

Published by Princeton University Press
41 William Street, Princeton, New Jersey 08540
99 Banbury Road, Oxford OX2 6JX

press.princeton.edu

ISBN: 978-0-691-24607-9
ISBN (pbk.): 978-0-691-24647-5
ISBN (e-book): 978-0-691-24608-6

British Library Cataloging-in-Publication Data is available

Editorial: Meagan Levinson and Erik Beranek
Cover design: Chris Ferrante
Production: Lauren Reese
Publicity: William Pagdatoon

Cover credit: Courtesy of Shutterstock / 4LUCK

This book has been composed in Arno Pro

10 9 8 7 6 5 4 3 2 1

For the Visionaries

Time itself is neutral; it can be used either destructively or constructively. More and more I feel that the people of ill will have used time much more effectively than have the people of good will. We will have to repent in this generation not merely for the hateful words and actions of the bad people but for the appalling silence of the good people.

Human progress never rolls in on wheels of inevitability; it comes through the tireless efforts of men willing to work to be co-workers with God, and without this hard work, time itself becomes an ally of the forces of social stagnation.

We must use time creatively, in the knowledge that the time is always ripe to do right.

—MARTIN LUTHER KING JR., *WHY WE CAN'T WAIT*, 1964

CONTENTS

ILLUSTRATIONS

Figures

Tables

PREFACE AND ACKNOWLEDGMENTS

> The difference between a dreamer and a visionary is that a dreamer has his eyes closed and a visionary has his eyes open.
>
> —MARTIN LUTHER KING JR.

WHEN I was growing up in the mostly White suburbs of northern Virginia in the 1990s, I was riveted by movies about the civil rights era. There are two in particular that I remember watching over and over again. The first was *The Long Walk Home*, a historical drama centered around Odessa (played by Whoopi Goldberg), a Black maid employed by Miriam (Sissy Spacek), an affluent White southern woman grappling with her feelings about the Montgomery Bus Boycott. When Odessa joins the boycott and refuses to ride the bus, Miriam starts driving her home each day after work. Eventually Miriam becomes an activist in her own right and joins a carpool group to help other Black workers. Miriam has an inspiring character arc as she breaks the chains of White supremacy by defying her racist husband, joining the civil rights struggle, and bringing her daughter (the film's narrator) along for the ride. The ending always left me feeling proud and joyous as the Black and White women, Odessa, Miriam, and Miriam's young daughter, stand side by side in resistance.

The second film was *The Ernest Green Story*, which is about the Little Rock Nine, who desegregated an all-White high school in 1957. I was captivated by the intense drama: the racist guards preventing the Black students from entering the school, the White students' leers and harassment, and the way White teachers look the other way during it all. Still, Ernest (played by a young Morris Chestnut) finds friendship with a White girl who gives us hope that White decency does exist. (All of these movies made sure to have a "good" White person or two to help in the struggle.) She is contrasted with Ernest's physics teacher, who is committed to failing him, which always made my heart race with rage, but Ernest works hard and passes the class anyway. At the end of the movie he graduates; his parents are so proud that we feel as though if he could beat racism, the possibilities are endless for Ernest Green.

That made-for-TV film received a Peabody Award for presenting "a story which reminds adults and teaches children about the courageous steps taken toward the elimination of discrimination in American society."[1] However, the nagging feeling I was always left with, after the joy of the triumphant conclusions faded, was that the endings didn't feel true. The mean racists weren't gone. They had not died with the past. And they didn't only live in the deep South. When red-faced angry White boys marched on my alma mater in the 2017 Unite the Right rally, tiki torches raised high in a terrifying expression of emboldened White supremacy, I witnessed the outpouring of public disbelief. "This is not who we are," wide-eyed people cried. "This is not what we stand for!" Again, that nagging feeling. After all, it was during my time on these very grounds that a Black woman running for class president was assaulted by a White man who slammed her head into a steering wheel and called her the n-word. Another Black student returned to her room to find a noose hanging on her door. This was most certainly who we were because it was who we had always been. These were, after all, the grounds of Thomas Jefferson's university where we walked with feigned innocence amid the hauntings of slave quarters.

One day when I was about five or six years old I was playing with friends—also Iranian American—outside their apartment complex in Cincinnati, Ohio. Our parents could see us on the playground from a balcony above, so they didn't feel the need to accompany us. I don't remember what we were playing or what I was wearing or what the weather was like that day. What I do remember is the White woman who yelled at us, "Go back to your country!" I think my friend's older brother yelled back at her, but I can't be sure. I'm not even sure we told our parents.

This is one of my earliest memories of having a troubling sense that my family and I did not belong here. My parents, with their accents, no matter how kind or hardworking or unassuming, were always a target for White people's disdain. I can still feel the way my heart would race and my stomach would lurch every time my parents had to interact with a White person—a waitress, a clerk, a friend's mother, my teacher, the police officer who pulled us over. I share these memories not for sympathy but because my experiences are not unique and because it is through this lens that I have come to this book with a commitment to sociologically analyzing the breadth of this social reality, however ugly and uncomfortable for my White readers. Racism does not have to look like White hoods and tiki torches to be consequential, and as I hope this book will show, ignoring its many faces poisons our soil and all that grows from it.

When I first began this research project, my interest had been sparked by the co-optation of civil rights discourse in the legal cases playing out in the news, what scholars call "color-blind constitutionalism." I had watched with rapt attention as Abigail Fisher, a young White woman who had been rejected from the University of Texas at Austin, took her case to the Supreme Court in a fight to repeal affirmative action. The legal argument was that affirmative action was a form of reverse racism, unconstitutional in its use of race-consciousness in college admission. I was appalled by the conservative co-optation of color-blind jurisprudence originally used by civil rights activists to challenge segregation, especially because it turned out that Fisher had been a mediocre college applicant. Still, the case unearthed debates about reverse racism that did not feel new, and I was especially interested in understanding how the protections against racial inequality could be turned on their head so explicitly.

As I began creating a data set to document color-blind constitutionalism in legal mobilization, these cases and their media coverage revealed another phenomenon. Color-blind constitutionalism was buttressed by a larger cultural pattern of misusing the memory of Dr. King and the civil rights movement to argue that affirmative action and social movements for racial justice were manifesting reverse racism. Black scholars and activists had been decrying these misappropriated uses of memory for decades, yet they only seemed to be growing in frequency and acceptance. Thus began a multiyear effort of collecting all the data I could to systematically examine the uses and misuses of Dr. King and the civil rights movement in the post–civil rights era. While my initial data collection ended in 2015, I supplemented the data collection to include the Trump presidency. The product of this multistage process was an ample data set tracing the collective memory of the civil rights movement from 1980 to 2020.

In writing this book I thought a great deal about what it meant for me to present this evidence as a non-White immigrant woman—a racially ambiguous one who, though born elsewhere, grew up in the United States. What does it mean for me to write about the misappropriation of Black history for White supremacy? In many ways, what brought me to this work was my own recognition of my place in White supremacy. I had long been troubled by the legal designation of Middle Eastern and North African people as White. Being White on paper meant nothing in my day-to-day life, where I was continually asked where I was *really* from. Yet it was only over time that I realized that although I was not seen as White, I still benefited from my ethnoracial obscurity and ambiguity and that I had internalized many of the racial logics that privileged appeasing Whiteness, conceding to power, staying small and out of sight. These recognitions also came through reading and sitting with the rich intellectual traditions of Black thought, some of the most formative being W.E.B. Du Bois, bell hooks, James Baldwin, Audre Lorde, and Frantz Fanon, as well as postcolonial theorist Edward Said.

To this end, continual self-reflection was essential throughout the research and writing of the book. I did not want fear and discomfort to pull me away from confronting the evidence before me, particularly when I was building on what so many Black activists, writers, and scholars had been declaring for centuries. I also worked to center activists' voices rather than my own, drawing heavily on their accounts to illustrate these case studies through their perspectives and subjectivities. I have written this book with the conviction that the evasion of social reality is its own violence, and I hope *The Struggle for the People's King* will be read with a spirit of curiosity, learning, and self-reflection. In the words of Dr. King, to confront these realities is to "merely bring to the surface the hidden tension that is already alive."[2]

I am grateful for the countless friends, family, colleagues, and mentors who have supported me and helped bring this book to fruition. *The Struggle for the People's King* took its greatest strides in the summer of 2021 thanks to the vision of Nitasha Sharma, Geraldo Cadava, and the inaugural book manuscript workshop hosted by the Council for Race and Ethnic Studies at Northwestern University. I thank Nitasha and Gerry for this invaluable opportunity, for their detailed, insightful feedback, and for connecting me with Meagan Levinson at Princeton University Press. I am also indebted to two of my academic idols, Joe Feagin and Vilna Bashi Treitler, for joining us at this workshop and providing such rich and perceptive commentary.

My colleagues—faculty and graduate students alike—at the University of Southern California and Equity Research Institute have given me a beautiful sense of academic community with kindness and encouragement during the long days and months and years of the pandemic. I am thankful for their engagement with my ideas at so many stages of the writing process, with particular thanks to my mentors Jody Vallejo, whom I hope to emulate in her spirit of generosity and deep and unyielding humanity; Manuel Pastor, who is a model of community-engaged scholarship; Mike Messner; Nina Eliasoph; Rhacel Parreñas; Paul Lichterman, my effusive chair Tim Biblarz; and so many wonderful and inspiring colleagues. In her first year at USC, my dear colleague Deisy Del Real generously brought me into a writing collective with Amy Zhou and Eli Wilson. This dynamic and encouraging group has closely read and provided feedback on nearly every chapter of this book. I am also thankful for the generous mentorship of David Meyer and Dina Okamoto, whose own field-defining work continues to inspire my own.

At so many stages along the way, I benefited from thoughtful feedback and the generous encouragement of brilliant scholars and friends including

Abigail Andrews, Ellen Berrey, Courtney Boen, Jennifer Candipan, Jeff Guhin, Nicole Hirsch, katrina quisumbing king, Elizabeth Korver-Glenn, Aliza Luft, Zakiya Luna, Neda Maghbouleh, Blanca Ramirez, Daisy Reyes, Josh Seim, Anna Skarpelis, Myron Strong, and the dynamic scholars of the Gender/Power/Theory working group. For the invaluable time and support they afforded in the writing of this book, I am grateful to the Ford Foundation Postdoctoral Fellowship, Haynes Foundation Faculty Fellowship, Turpanjian Postdoctoral Fellowship in Civil Society and Change, and Dr. Drusilla Lea Scott Summer Fellowship at UNC.

One of the most transformative experiences of my time as a junior scholar has been as a member of the WT Grant Cohort of the Institute in Critical Quantitative, Computational, & Mixed Methodologies. I owe the deepest well of gratitude to Odis Johnson, Ebony McGee, and Ezekiel Dixon-Román for creating this space and bringing me in community with the AQCM Cohort and so many like-minded and visionary scholars. ICQCM has expanded my imagination and conception of emancipatory futures in immeasurable ways.

I am also indebted to Charlie Kurzman, who not only provided feedback on the full manuscript but has been a cherished mentor. I am grateful to Chris Bail for his continued mentorship, inspiring research, and always thoughtful advice. For their helpful feedback on the early project, I thank Andy Perrin, Andy Andrews, and Neal Caren. I am indebted to my former colleagues in Camp Charlie, the UNC Race Workshop, and the 2011 Cohort. I am also grateful for the continued mentorship of Tamara Mose and Carolina Bank-Muñoz, who have seen me through from a master's student at Brooklyn College to an assistant professor at USC. For their meticulous research assistance, I thank Tomine Bergseth, Blair Buchanan, Bethany Cochran, Avery Nelson, and Avery Redfearn.

To my beautiful family and friends, far and wide, you are everything to me. To the ones who have known me since the days I said I was "from Germany," thank you Notorious 9 for loving me when I didn't know who I was yet, and later when I did. To my best friends from college, the carefree days in New York City, and beyond, thank you for the continued laughter and nostalgia. To my sweet and supportive in-laws Sharon and Woo, my "second-mother-in-law" Kim and Rich, Will and Ashley, thank you for the love and encouragement, and thanks to all the Ferrells from California to Georgia, the Groggs, Lundholms, and Marins. I'm also grateful for the love of the Nowers, whom I am so happy to claim as family. My deepest love and gratitude to my Irooni family around the globe; however rare our time together, you are in my heart always. To the Nourians and Salehis, we may not share blood but you are my first family, and my happiest childhood memories are with you.

For my sociological imagination and deep commitment to humanity, I am indebted to my parents, who were the first visionaries I knew. Maman and Baba, you taught me how to see, to never look away, and to keep asking questions. Thank you. To my brother-in-law, Brad, and my best-friend-sister-for-life, Solmaaz, thank you for the encouragement and cheerleading, for reminding me I was doing a very hard thing and it was okay to struggle. I could not have gotten through the home stretch without you and our beautiful Behrang. To my partner, Josh, you always said I could do it. You helped me persevere and find joy through it all. Thank you, I love you. To my son, JJ, and my daughter, Leila, you are my sun and my moon. I know you did not like mom working so much to finish this manuscript. Sometimes you sat on my lap while I wrote, and sometimes you slammed the laptop shut. I understood. I hope someday you will understand why I wrote this book. May your beautiful imaginations always run wild.

THE STRUGGLE FOR THE PEOPLE'S KING

Introduction

ON A humid day in late August 2010, right-wing Tea Party activist and Fox News television host Glenn Beck held a rally to "restore honor" at the steps of the Lincoln Memorial. It was the forty-seventh anniversary of the Civil Rights March on Washington, and Beck stood on the steps where Dr. Martin Luther King Jr. gave his famous "I have a dream" speech nearly five decades prior. In the months leading up to the rally, Beck used his television show to drive home the undeniable connection between the historic backdrop of the rally and the Tea Party's mission to safeguard American values, threatened by minority claims to "special rights." In this view, White Americans were the new victims under the Obama presidency, an idea Beck repeatedly espoused as when he warned viewers, "This president [Obama] I think has exposed himself as a guy, over and over and over again, who has a deep-seated hatred for White people and the White culture . . . this guy is, I believe, a *racist*."[1]

Earlier that spring Beck had proclaimed to his viewers, "We are the people of the civil rights movement. We are the ones that must stand for civil and equal rights. Equal rights. Justice. Equal justice. Not special justice, not social justice, but equal justice. We are the inheritors and the protectors of the civil rights movement."[2] Several days later, Beck warned viewers that King's vision had been "perverted," but he assured his audience that he planned to "pick up Martin Luther King's dream" and to "restore it and to finish it." He went on to declare, "We are on the right side of history. We are on the side of individual freedoms and liberties and damn it, we will reclaim the civil rights movement. We will take that movement because we were the people that did it in the first place."[3]

Beck's appropriation of the memory of the civil rights movement for the Tea Party's cause did not go unnoticed. Publics erupted in protest. Jon Stewart called the Beck rally "I have a scheme," satirizing its strategic connection to the "I have a dream" speech. Robert Greenwald, an activist and filmmaker protesting Beck's rally, created a website and video titled "Glenn Beck Is Not

Martin Luther King Jr." In the video, Greenwald juxtaposed "shock jock"-style sound bites from Beck with Dr. King's spiritual oratory in his "dream" speech, highlighting the absurdity of Beck's claim to Dr. King's legacy. At its conclusion, a message read, "Don't let Beck distort Martin Luther King Jr.'s legacy. Sign your name to virtually stand with Dr. King's vision on August 28th."[4] That petition received more than thirty thousand signatures. Civil rights activist Reverend Al Sharpton called Beck's event an "outright attempt to flip the imagery of Dr. King."[5] The day before the rally, political commentator Chris Matthews said on his MSNBC show, *Hardball with Chris Matthews*:

> Can we imagine if King were physically here tomorrow . . . were he to reappear tomorrow on the very steps of the Lincoln Memorial? I have a nightmare that one day a right-wing talk show host will come to this spot, his people's lips dripping with the words "interposition" and "nullification." Little right-wing boys and little right-wing girls joining hands and singing their praise for Glenn Beck and Sarah Palin. I have a nightmare.[6]

Still, on August 28 Beck stood, as had King, on the steps of the Lincoln Memorial and gave an impassioned speech to a crowd of over eighty thousand Tea Party supporters, declaring their work had "everything to do with God . . . turning our faith back to the values and the principles that made us great." He went on to describe an America at a crossroads, not unlike the country Lincoln faced during the Civil War. Referring to the Tea Party's struggle, he said, "It's the same story throughout history, all of mankind's history. Man finds himself in slavery and then someone appears to wake America up."[7] Through religious and historical imagery, Beck emphasized the power of American individualism in the face of oppression that he described as a sort of "slavery," driving home the analogy between conservative Americans' plight under multicultural  democracy and Black Americans' past enslavement.

Further down the National Mall, Al Sharpton and Dr. King's eldest son, Martin Luther King III, were leading a rival rally at the planned site for the Martin Luther King Jr. National Memorial: the "Reclaim the Dream" commemorative march. Avis Jones DeWeever, executive director of the National Council of Negro Women, pleaded with the audience, "Don't let anyone tell you that they have the right to take their country back. It's our country, too. We will reclaim the dream. It was ours from the beginning."[8] With Dr. King's son in tow as a living symbol, a gatekeeper of collective memory, the Tea Party's claims to King's legacy appeared illegitimate.

Yet the Tea Party organizers had prepared for this dilemma. Glenn Beck had arranged for another symbolic figure to speak. Alveda King, Martin Luther King Jr.'s niece and an outspoken right-wing activist, proceeded to

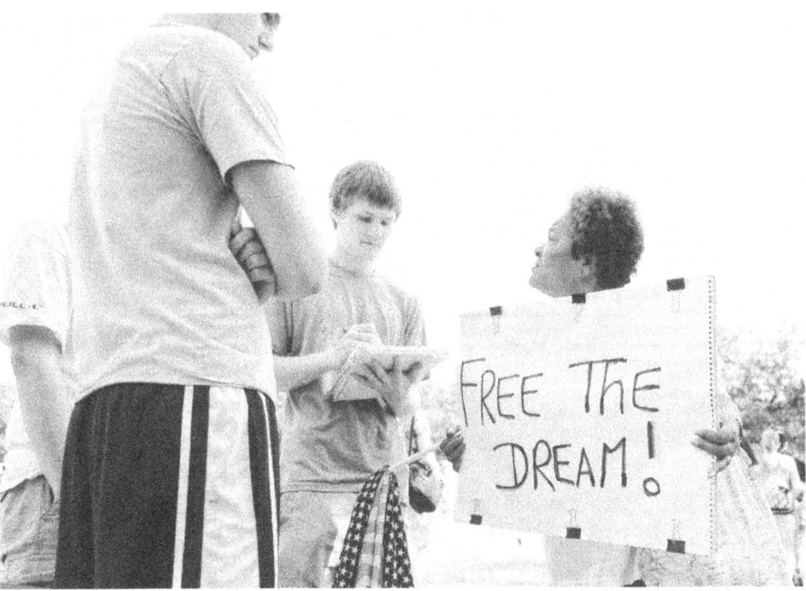

FIGURE I.1. Civil rights protester counters Tea Party's claim to Dr. King in 2011 "Rally to Restore Honor" in Washington, D.C. David Coleman/HaveCameraWillTravel/Alamy Stock Photo.

take the stage at the "Rally to Restore Honor." Alveda King called on the audience to:

> focus not on elections or on political causes but on honor, on character . . . not the color of our skin. Yes, I too have a dream. . . . That America will pray and God will forgive us our sins and revive us our land. . . . My daddy, Reverend A. D. King, my granddaddy, Martin Luther King, Senior—we are a family of faith, hope, and love. And that's why I'm here today. Glenn says there is one human race; I agree with him. We are not here to divide. I'm about unity. That's why I'm here, and I want to honor my uncle today.[9]

Here was another living inheritor of Dr. King, of the civil rights movement, lending credence to the Tea Party vision of color-blind individualism, where the acknowledgment of race, of racism, of racial inequality, could be named anti-White reverse racism.

From beyond the audience of the rally's conservative followers, there were vocal critics who worked to discredit the Tea Party's misuses of Dr. King. Yet Beck and the skilled Tea Party organizers had looked back on the political battles of the decades prior and had anticipated opposition. In the months leading up to the rally, they had worked tirelessly to thwart progressive activists' critiques by using Dr. King's own language, the imagery of the historic setting, and, now with Alveda King, the living progeny of the symbolic figure.

Historian Eric Hobsbawm wrote that social movements "[back] their innovations by reference to a 'people's past,' . . . to traditions of revolution . . . and to [their] own heroes and martyrs."[10] Yet Dr. King was not always a "hero and martyr" for conservatives. Just thirty years earlier, there were spirited congressional battles around whether to designate Martin Luther King Jr.'s birthday as a national holiday. Conservatives denounced King as a "communist traitor" and made public his alleged extramarital affairs to sully his reputation and question his morality. They declared King an unworthy figure for national celebration and commemoration. Although President Reagan signed the Dr. Martin Luther King Jr. national holiday into existence in 1983, statewide battles over the King holiday lasted into the 1990s. In many states like Alabama and Mississippi, the concession toward the King holiday came only with an agreement to merge the holiday with observances of Confederate "heroes" like Robert E. Lee, Jefferson Davis, and Stonewall Jackson. South Carolina was the last state to approve a paid King holiday, in the year 2000. Yet just ten years later, Glenn Beck, a brazenly radical conservative, would stand on the steps of the Lincoln Memorial to "reclaim" King's dream for the Tea Party. The next month, Tea Party activists swept the primary elections, and over the next few years they moved the Republican Party irrevocably to the right.

How did the collective memory of the civil rights movement, of Dr. King, become a ready-made political strategy for mobilization by groups with divergent, even antithetical aims? More importantly, what are the consequences of these (mis)uses of collective memory? How does misremembering the past matter for contemporary politics, and how does it shape the direction of our collective future? These are the questions this book explores.

At first glance, perhaps the Tea Party movement's invocations of Dr. King do not seem all that surprising. After all, scholars have shown that since the civil rights era of the 1960s, all sorts of groups including women, Latinos, Asians, the disabled, and LGBTQ coalitions have used memories of the civil rights movement to make claims to inclusion and equality. This period of widespread collective action by minoritized groups has been coined "the minority rights revolution,"[11] the "movement of movements,"[12] and the rise of the "civil rights society."[13] For historically excluded groups, strategic invocations of the civil rights movement seem like a natural mobilization strategy with a ready-made set of what social movement scholars call "repertoires of contention": the tactics, frames, and actions for mobilization against injustice.[14] More generally, the memory of Black Americans joining with kindhearted White Americans, mobilizing for and achieving legal recognition, has become central to the story of "who we are" as Americans, a shining beacon of the promise of American democracy. Dr. King is mythologized as the moral compass of American identity, reminding us of an unrelenting march forward, where "the arc of the moral universe is long, but it bends toward justice."[15]

However, increasingly since the 1980s, right-wing, majority-White social movements from the gun rights and family values coalitions to nativist, White supremacist movements have reshaped and deployed the collective memory of the civil rights movement to claim that *they* are the new minorities fighting for their rights. In these invocations, gun rights activists are the new Rosa Parks, anti-abortion activists are freedom riders, and anti-gay groups are protecting Dr. King's Christian vision. These misuses of the past are not merely rhetorical; these strategies have powerful effects. This book will show that as mobilizing groups remake a collective memory toward competing political ends, they generate new interpretations of the past that take on a life of their own. The proliferation of these interpretations of history, over time, changes the collective memory itself, shaping the way we make sense of the present and the way we direct action toward the future.

As social historians have shown, the domesticated memory of the civil rights movement has transformed into a vacated, sanitized collective memory celebrating color-blindness and individualism, as if racism is a figment of the past.[16] In the popular imagination, Dr. King was a widely beloved moral leader, preaching peace and nonviolence at all costs, invested in the dream of American exceptionalism. Rosa Parks was an accidental activist, a tired woman who did not want to give up her seat on a bus after a long day of work. These "Whitewashed" memories are not only bound up in the national holiday we celebrate once a year. They are also narrativized in children's textbooks, Oscar-winning films, political speeches, and popular media. Such memories amplify selective representations of particular figures—Dr. King, Rosa Parks, John Lewis—rendering other pivotal civil rights activists and their rich stories, struggles, and power invisible.[17] These flattened, "defanged"[18] memories are commemorated by rosy images of Black and White Americans joining, arms linked, in a quest for racial justice, through a particular conception of racism and violence as existing specifically in the South and—notably—in the distant past.[19] They are juxtaposed against memories of "radical," "threatening" activists like Malcolm X and the Black Panthers as "divisive" separatists, "a disruptive force to a beloved community."[20] These meanings are bound in commemorative structures and remain at the heart of American collective memory.

Why does it matter that the collective memory of the civil rights movement is remembered in this selective way? After all, collective memories generate a shared identity and connect us in a common narrative of our collective past. Why shouldn't the civil rights movement be remembered through ideals of unity, peace, and color-blindness? The danger of a sanitized reading of the past is that this selective memory evades social reality and enables the maintenance of White supremacy. While the story of racial progress can be a palatable one, the evidence tells a different story. The vestiges of a nation founded on the genocide of Native Americans and the violent enslavement of Black people live on in our institutions and our culture through systemic racism,[21] what Joe Feagin describes as the "complex array of white anti-other (e.g., anti-black) practices, the unjustly gained economic/political power of whites, the continuing economic and other resource inequalities along racial lines (unjust enrichment/unjust impoverishment), and the racial framing created by whites to rationalize privilege and power."[22]

For example, while one-quarter of White households have a net worth greater than one million dollars, this is true for only 4 percent of Black households. Even poor White people in the bottom 20 percent of the income distribution have a higher median net worth than all Black people. Working-class Whites have two to three times the median wealth of professional-managerial Black people.[23] These racial gaps are evident in every realm of social life at all stages of the life course; the inequalities across intersections of race, class, and gender are unending. They are reflected in, for example, infant mortality rates;[24] access to health care, food, housing, financial institutions,[25] and education;[26] hiring practices; wages and labor force participation;[27] incarceration rates; and violent encounters with law enforcement.[28] The system is deeply unequal, more so than it was in the hopeful years after the civil rights movement.

The Making of Societal Ignorance

Social change has not been linear, and scholars like Jennifer Richeson, Ivuoma Onyeador, Louise Seamster, and Victor Ray have argued that we must rethink our conceptions of racial progress as an undeviating movement forward.[29] The impulse to see racism and racial inequality as part of a bygone past, to see the legal gains of the civil rights movement as a final chapter in the story of racism, to see Dr. King's work as beginning and ending with the civil rights movement, is to ignore the complexity and regenerative character of social processes. When we evade social reality, we do not act in meaningful ways that change the unequal system. Worse yet, ignoring social reality means we reproduce the unequal system and then are shocked and confused when the system produces "unimaginable" violence. Scholars like Charles W. Mills and Jennifer Mueller describe the cognitive processes that make this thinking possible as an epistemology of ignorance that understands ignorance not in the traditional sense of "innocently unaware" or "unlearned." Instead, White ignorance is built willfully; it is created to preserve a way of thinking about the world around us and a way of life. Mills describes how the racial contract of White supremacy is characterized by this inverted epistemology of ignorance, which ironically means "whites will in general be unable to understand the world they themselves have made."[30]

The Pew Research Foundation's 2019 survey "Race in America" revealed just how divergent Americans are in their perceptions of social reality, largely along racial lines but also along partisan lines. When asked whether being White helps one's ability to get ahead, White Democrats were twice as likely as White Republicans and conservative-leaning moderates to say being White helps people get ahead (78 percent compared to 38 percent). More notably, 22 percent of White Republicans (compared to 3 percent of White Democrats) reported feeling that being White *hurts* one's ability to get ahead. Almost 30 percent of White Republicans (compared to 8 percent of White Democrats) said being Black *helps* one's ability get ahead.[31] This segmented perception of reality, that White Americans are the victims of minority "special rights" in the post–civil rights era, has been well-documented in studies of White resentment and White backlash, which helps explain the rise of Trumpism and the actions of emboldened White nationalists who stormed the Capitol on January 6, 2021.

Yet even among those who agreed that being Black hurts one's ability to succeed, perceptions diverged by race. While 84 percent of Black respondents attributed this to racial discrimination, only 54 percent of White respondents acknowledged racism as a cause. Almost 80 percent of Black respondents said the United States has not gone far enough in granting equal rights to Black Americans, compared to 37 percent of White respondents. Almost 20 percent of White respondents reported the country has gone *too* far in granting equal rights to Black Americans. Furthermore, of respondents reporting that the country had not gone far enough, half of the Black respondents said it was not likely the country would ever achieve racial equality. Of the White respondents who acknowledged that the country still has work to do, 80 percent said it was likely Black Americans will achieve equal rights.

These results demonstrate that Americans know that inequality exists. Popular media ensures a steady stream of representations of single welfare moms with a fleet of fatherless children, snaggle-toothed backwoods yokels, and gun-toting Black men in impoverished neighborhoods. Yet these representations rarely explain how these characters arrived here beyond their individual choices. It is the story of the inequality that matters for how we see it and what we do (or do not do) about it. As Eduardo Bonilla-Silva explains in his theory of color-blind racism, the post–civil rights era moved the explicit racism of the Jim Crow era beneath the surface. No longer was it legally acceptable—at least on paper—to discriminate on the basis of race. More

importantly for everyday people, no longer was it culturally acceptable to express outright hostility and violence toward Black Americans. Instead, racism took on a new form through color-blindness. Under color-blind ideology, to acknowledge racial difference was to perpetuate the "race problem," as if racism could be out of sight, out of mind. Social reality would be constructed by a White power elite across institutions from the economy to the media,[32] making sense of the world through what Joe Feagin describes as a "white racial frame."[33] Through this frame, Martin Luther King Jr.'s words about a dream of a world where his children would be judged not by the color of their skin but by the content of their character would be lifted out of its context and deployed time and time again to counter the ongoing realities of systemic racism.

Nowhere is the making of ignorance more evident than in the American educational system. Even before the contemporary battles over teaching critical race theory in schools, legacies of settler colonialism and slavery were intentionally evaded in curricula. A 2018 report by the Southern Poverty Law Center identified disturbing trends in youth knowledge of American history, specifically the racial past. Only 8 percent of high school seniors could identify slavery as a central cause of the Civil War. Many did not know slavery ended with an amendment to the U.S. Constitution. Less than half understood that slavery was legal in every colony during the American Revolution. Understanding racism as a blip in an otherwise fair system, an inconvenience quelled through the civil rights movement, is part of the construction of this willful ignorance that enables claims of innocence in matters of racial inequality and violence.

The story we tell ourselves as a society about how we arrived at this moment matters deeply. Our collective memories hold power for either justifying or challenging the way we collectively continue to go about the business of maintaining a society. It is the story that racism is a figment of the past that justified the repealed provision of the Voting Rights Act in 2013's *Shelby County v. Holder* decision. In that ruling, Justice Scalia called the provision protecting minority voting rights a "racial entitlement" standing in the way of the political process. The repealed provision had required jurisdictions with a history of race-based voter discrimination to "preclear" changes to their election rules with the federal government before implementing revisions. The provision had protected Black and Brown voters for decades, ensuring their democratic right to vote. Immediately after the 5–4 ruling, the floodgates opened with a swell of jurisdictions, particularly throughout the South, implementing stringent voting regulations, from strict voter ID laws to eliminating policies proven to expand voting rights, such as same-day registration. A 2018 study by the Brennan Center found that states previously covered by the Voting Rights Act provision purged voters from their rolls and disenfranchised voters at a significantly higher rate than jurisdictions that had not been covered by the provision.[34] In other words, the provision had served as a protective function as it was intended. Racialized disenfranchisement of voters was not a product of the past. The rollback of democracy has been enabled through a revisionist history that willfully evades the reality of racism, that understands the protection of minoritized voters as its own racism against White Americans. The stakes of confronting social reality are not only the strength of our social fabric and the viability of our democracy. The stakes are also our collective survival.

The Challenge of Reckonings

In late May 2020, just months into a global pandemic, waves of multiracial protesters left the safety of their homes and filled the streets to protest for the sanctity of Black lives. George Floyd had been suffocated under the knee of a White police officer in Minneapolis, his murder captured on a teenager's cell phone video. However, unlike so many prior similarly horrific moments, this one had the rapt attention of widespread publics. Though the Black Lives Matter movement had been active for seven years, for many Americans this was the first time the movement's name, message, and urgency had resonated. The phrase "systemic racism" moved to the mainstream, no longer a "radical" theory but for many an explicit reality. Even presidential candidate Joe Biden, who was known to cater to White moderates, posted on his social media, "We are having an important racial reckoning. This is our moment to address systemic racism, because it's clear our country has failed the Black community too many times. Black lives matter. But matter is the minimum."

Perhaps this was the moment when things would truly change. One longtime organizer, Fania Davis, director of the nonprofit Restorative Justice for Oakland Youth, was hopeful, noting, "In all of my 72 years, almost all of which I've been working as an activist, I've never seen anything like this." She said, "We are beginning to disrupt centuries of denial of our collective biography during this time. Whenever you have such an intense crisis, it also presents an opportunity for significant or revolutionary change."[35] In June 2020, an incredible 67 percent of Americans supported Black Lives Matter. Many progressives were hopeful through the summer of 2020, as books about racism flew off the shelves. White women's book clubs were discussing Robin D'Angelo's *White Fragility*, school administrators were assigning their teachers Ibram X. Kendi's *How to Be an Anti-Racist*, and in workplaces, there was a significant spike in formal Diversity, Equity, and Inclusion (DEI) programs and a sudden demand for hiring in-house DEI coordinators.

But as summer faded to fall, the burgeoning sea change ebbed and the fervor for systemic change seemed like a distant dream. As Hakeem Jefferson and

Victor Ray wrote of the so-called racial reckoning, "For a reckoning to occur, there has to be more than just an acknowledgement of injustice. There has to be action. Reckoning implied a reprieve for the Black Lives Matter activists who had spent the years since Trayvon Martin's killing protesting police violence. Reckoning implied transforming public safety. Reckoning implied support for policies to intervene in the yawning racial wealth gap, the perpetual employment gap, and the growing life expectancy gap. In short, a reckoning suggested the country was on the cusp of lasting change."[36] Of course, these changes, the acknowledgment of injustice, did not come to pass, just as the major wins of the civil rights era were never true societal reckonings. The significant legal gains of the civil rights movement were never coupled with honest societal reflection, acknowledgment of the deep roots of racism, its embeddedness in American social life, and its continued harms. The politics of appeasement had ensured no admission of systemic harm.

By September 2020, support for Black Lives Matter had decreased to 55 percent. More tellingly, *opposition* to the movement for racial justice had increased to 44 percent. Among Republicans, support for Black Lives Matter was even lower than it was before George Floyd's killing. The backlash was brewing, just as it had during the civil rights movement. Though the collective memory of the civil rights movement is characterized by unity, love, and a wide commitment to racial progress by morally apprehensive publics, there was powerful opposition to civil rights in its heyday. In 1963, 60 percent of White people had an unfavorable view of the March on Washington. In 1965, 68 percent thought civil rights were being implemented too quickly, and 58 percent believed that Black activists' strategies hurt their own cause. By 1968, the year he was assassinated, 75 percent of White people disapproved of Dr. King, up 25 percent from 1963. As the civil rights movement gained momentum, the White backlash was swift and violent. Jefferson and Ray have noted that racial backlash is its own racial reckoning.

Through *The Struggle for the People's King,* we will see how these dynamics take shape. In each chapter we will analyze rival social movements' strategic uses and misuses of the memory of the civil rights movement. In these battles to shape the direction of the societal future, the long trajectories of these reckonings and counterreckonings become apparent. Only by examining the deep and gnarled branches of these reckonings and the way they are mired in collective memory can we understand how we arrived at this moment and where we might go next.

These larger processes help us understand that the misuses of the past are not mere rhetorical blunders. This book shows that as invocations of the collective memory of the civil rights movement evolved into a political strategy, collective memory would be invoked to discredit movements' calls for social justice time and again. For example, when Black Lives Matter activists filled the streets to protest police violence, Republican presidential contender Mike Huckabee took to the twenty-four-hour news cycle to argue that Dr. King would disagree with their message and tactics. He said, "When I hear people scream, 'Black lives matter,' I think, 'Of course they do.' But all lives matter. It's not that any life matters more than another. That's the whole message that Dr. King tried to present, and I think he'd be appalled by the notion that we're elevating some lives above others."[37]

At the same time, grassroots activists have actively worked to counter the misappropriations of the civil rights movement, drawing on historical evidence and calling on its gatekeepers to correct the record, from Dr. King's daughter Bernice King to congressman and civil rights leader John Lewis. After Huckabee's invocation of King, sixty-six former civil rights movement activists from the Student Nonviolent Coordinating Committee (SNCC) issued a powerful statement in support of Black Lives Matter to emphasize the movement's continuation of the long struggle for Black freedom: "Fortunately, today, as in the past, the protesters who have taken to the streets against police violence will not be intimidated by slander or mischaracterization as 'racist' or 'terrorist sympathizers' born of the fear, ignorance and malice of their would-be critics. . . . We, the still-active radicals who were SNCC, salute today's Movement for Black Lives for taking hold of the torch to continue to light this flame of truth for a knowingly forgetful world."[38]

These oppositional forces, competing ideas of America's pasts and imagined futures, did not form in the civil rights era. Historians have shown that ideas about what the United States aspires to be, who "counts" as American, and whose voices ought to be heard have been contested since the founding. Moreover, as a country built on the institution of slavery and enduring through a system of racial capitalism, the meanings of race are embedded in the American project. As Dr. King himself said, "Our nation was born in genocide when it embraced the doctrine that the original American, the Indian, was an inferior race. Even before there were large numbers of Negroes on our shores, the scar of racial hatred had already disfigured colonial society."[39] While this book begins its analysis in the 1980s, acknowledging this longer history is critical for making sense of the deeper roots, and stakes, of the questions I explore here. The misuses of Dr. King and of the civil rights movement are part of a larger process. Examining the misuses of the racial past reveals how groups continually manipulate memory to challenge, or preserve, systems of power.

To take on these lofty questions, *The Struggle for the People's King* investigates the political career of the collective memory of the civil rights movement as it becomes bound into a symbolic cultural structure and is taken up, remade, and deployed by a range of political actors. These analyses help us make sense of our current social crises, the revisionist memories that divide us, and the seemingly eradicable roots of White supremacy. The chapters that follow will show how distortions of collective memory obscure the roots of our present-day systems of inequality, reproducing the very systems of inequality that many activists seek to dismantle.[40]

Key Concepts

Throughout this book, a number of key theoretical concepts undergird my larger arguments. First, I frequently refer to contentious politics, described by Charles Tilly and Sidney Tarrow as the conflictual processes generated by mobilizing groups that extend beyond formal social movements and trained activists. Contentious politics encapsulates the mechanisms that connect different actors—whether formal organizers or everyday people—engaged in different forms of resistance and conflict, contending with other groups, institutions, and culture.[41]

I also frequently refer to the concept of culture—as a set of meanings that constitute everything from identity to discursive frames, as a context, and as a set of symbolic resources. I draw on a broad definition of culture that understands the processes of meaning-making as mechanisms of power. As Stuart Hall explains, culture is a space of interpretative struggle where the hegemonic, or dominant, webs of meaning that shape society are created through ideologies, "the mental frameworks—the languages, the concepts, categories, imagery of thought, and the representation—which different classes and social groups deploy in order to make sense of, define, figure out and render intelligible the way society works."[42] We are socialized into these cultural frameworks for making sense of the world around us through institutions from family to church, schools to media. Yet on a more basic level, culture is made and transmitted through discourse, where power shapes accepted forms of knowledge, of identifying and naming and interpreting the world around us, schemas that we come to see as truth.[43] Through this lens, I conceptualize the cultural meanings assigned to the past through a second key concept: collective memory.

What does it mean to examine the civil rights movement as a "collective memory" as opposed to a historical event or even an individual memory? Put simply, collective memory is a socially constructed story about the past that emerges through a set of political and cultural practices. Collective memories tell groups "who we are,"[44] so American collective memories help constitute a collective national identity, shaping the symbolic boundaries between an imagined "us" as Americans and an imagined "them" as everyone else.[45] As Michèle Lamont and Virág Molnár describe, these symbolic boundaries are the conceptual distinctions that create classification systems, assigning meaning and value to different entities, whether objects or groups, places or times.[46] Though they are "only" conceptual, symbolic boundaries are consequential for social life, patterning the unequal distribution of power, resources, and status.

Symbolic boundaries are continually contested and reshaped. This means that collective memories are never a fixed thing, but some have more rigid boundaries than others, depending on how they are institutionalized and what role they play in the national story of itself. The more central a collective memory for national identity, the more power it holds in shaping the trajectory of the future. As a result, these collective memories become prized cultural resources that are all the more vulnerable to misappropriation. Collective memories are dynamic as different groups work to remake them for present-day purposes. At times, social change that shifts culture and how we think about social issues can also alter how we make sense of long-taken-for-granted collective memories. For example, the contemporary movements to remove Confederate statues emerged out of a larger cultural shift in understanding the continued commemoration of White supremacists as a social problem, as a symbolic means of maintaining White dominance through a sanitized memory of the past.[47] Sometimes marginalized groups mobilize specifically around forgotten, invisibilized, partial, or misrepresented memories, understanding the reclaiming of the past as a critical step in repairing deep harms that shape their present.[48] However, right-wing backlash to social progress can also set in motion memory-work centered on historical revisionism, alt-facts and histories used in the service of authoritarianism, social control, and violence that threaten democracy.[49] Such was the alt-history propagated by more than a dozen White extremist groups including the Proud Boys, Oath Keepers, and Three Percenters that shaped the January 6, 2021, insurrection at the Capitol.

The collective memories that result from these political efforts are powerful cultural structures that help legitimize "how things are," explaining why particular groups may have greater power or stature in society and why things ought to stay that way. It follows, then, that groups will use collective memories as political tools, legitimizing their political claims by connecting them to collective memory. However, mobilizing groups express different conceptions of "who we are" to make claims about "who we ought to be," using collective memory in competing ways to garner public support. Some of these uses of memory are effective; they resonate among multiple publics, generate broad-based coalitions, and drive mass political support—as we will see when Dr. King's wife and civil rights activist in her own right, Coretta Scott King, linked the memory of the civil rights movement to the LGBTQ movement to fight for gay rights. Other uses of memory are widely denounced and discredited—as when the animal rights group PETA compared animal slaughter to the lynching of African Americans to call for civil rights for animals. The uses of collective memory are bound up in a larger system of power that shapes not only the collective memory but also the groups who seek to use it.

The Study

This book uses a wide range of data and mixed methods to examine the strategic uses of the collective memory of the civil rights movement. Unlike historiographical works, this book does not delve into the extensive political, economic, and social contexts of each case study. I briefly summarize each movement's historical trajectory to situate the cases, but the particularities of the past are not the focus of this book. Instead, my goal is to take a series of past events and analyze them for generalizable patterns, for the social processes and the meanings that emerge and tell us something about how movements use memory and why it matters. To this end, to analyze the evolving uses of collective memory from 1980 to 2020 I use methods of historical sociology that examine events in a processual manner to develop explanations that can transcend the particularities of each historical moment.[50] This method is particularly useful for examining social change and transformation.

For the historical analysis in chapter 2, I draw on a unique data set of mobilizations using the memory of the civil rights movement in the post–civil rights era (1980–2020). This data set was developed by drawing on archival data from extensive primary and secondary sources to analyze trajectories of mobilization, including thousands of newspaper articles, organizational web pages and reports, blog posts, film and television transcripts, and press releases. I describe this data and methodology in depth in the methodological appendix. Having drawn out the eagle-eye view of the evolving branches of memory, the next three chapters analyze how these branches take shape on the ground. I examine case studies of three paired social movements (LGBTQ and family values; immigrant rights and nativist; Muslim rights and anti-Muslim), which were selected to represent a range of social positions (table I.1).

In pairing rival movements, I also included cases to represent other progressive and conservative movements, as well as old and new movements. From these dimensions of difference, I selected cases on one shared dimension:[51] movement strategy, specifically the strategic invocation of the collective memory of the civil rights movement. By holding the strategy constant but varying the social locations of the groups, I isolated the extent to which the messenger of collective memory mattered. Did the strategic uses of memory play out

TABLE I.1. Paired social movements comparisons

	Master Identity Group	Political Ideology	Strategic Use of Collective Memory of Civil Rights Movement
LGBTQ Movement	Sexual Orientation	Progressive	Yes
Family Values Movement	Religious	Conservative	Yes
Immigrant Rights Movement	Ethnoracial/ Nativity Status	Progressive	Yes
Nativist Movement	Race/Nationality	Conservative	Yes
Muslim Rights Movement	Ethnoracial-religious	Progressive	Yes
Islamophobia Movement	Religious/Nationality	Conservative	Yes

in comparable ways, no matter the group claiming the memory? Or were there varied dynamics and consequences for different groups that deployed the same memory? Could these dynamics be patterned, and could they tell us something about how power operates through culture? With the larger data set, I identified representative cases of major events from each of these six movements, from which I developed events databases to draw out the order of actions and counteractions. Using narrative analysis that centralizes meaning, sequence, and contingency, I examined how these interactions between movements shaped uses of memory on the ground and the patterns these dynamics unearthed.[52]

While chapters 3 and 4 use a comparative method to examine two events across two political contexts, chapter 5 takes a more holistic, long view from 1980 to 2020 through qualitative analysis of the retrospectives of interviews and focus groups with Muslim community members,[53] triangulated against a historical analysis of major events. Together, these data present detailed stories documenting the evolving interactions between activists, their rivals, and key stakeholders as they strategize to remake the past to attain their political goals in the present.

One of the most difficult negotiations of this book was accepting that I could not include every pivotal historical event, every contextual detail, and all the innovative and at times appalling invocations of civil rights memory. You may find yourself asking, "What about . . . ?" Despite the sheer breadth of data I collected and analyzed and the vast historical accounts I read, I could not include everything. For the patterns that emerged from the analysis, I aimed to include the most descriptive examples, but the work presented here is a conservative presentation of a much more significant phenomenon. Moreover, by bringing together a wide range of vast theoretical traditions, I found myself lamenting that I could not even scratch the surface on the breadth of interdisciplinary studies that guide this sociological study, from ethnic studies to Black studies and cultural studies. Though I could not include them all, I am indebted to the long traditions of critical thought that shape my own intellectual trajectory and that of this book.

Finally, despite its title, this is not a book *about* Dr. Martin Luther King Jr., nor is it a book about the history of the civil rights movement, although they both lend insight into various historical events picked up by activists. Work by scholars like Carol Anderson, Kenneth Andrews, Keisha Blain, Jacquelyn Dowd Hall, Elizabeth Hinton, Martha Jones, Aldon Morris, Barbara Ransby, and Belinda Robnett, among many others, offers meticulous historical research and a valuable corrective to sanitized histories of the Black freedom struggle. Particularly complementary to this book is *A More Beautiful and Terrible History* by Jeanne Theoharis, who deftly debunks the "Whitewashed" historical myths of the civil rights movement. Her book in many ways offers a valuable rationale for *The Struggle for the People's King* by showing that history has been remade in consequential ways. Yet rather than examining the past itself, this book focuses on how and why contemporary groups use interpretations of the racial past as a political tool and why it matters for our societal future.

Overview of the Book

This book has three goals: (1) to explore the trajectories of the collective memory of the civil rights movement as a political strategy among all sorts of groups over time; (2) to compare how groups with a range of collective identities across the political spectrum reshape the memory of the civil rights movement to make and contest political claims; and (3) to analyze the multilevel consequences of these (mis)uses of memory for political culture and the societal future. Across these chapters, I draw from theories of social movements, race and ethnicity, cultural sociology, collective memory studies, migration studies, the sociology of knowledge, and social psychology to build a critical theory of the strategic uses of collective memory in contentious politics. A critical perspective helps us understand three interconnected ways in which memory matters in contentious politics: the uses of memory unfold relationally and negotiate multiple and competing temporalities; they are perceptual; and these dynamics are embedded in and are themselves mechanisms of power.

In chapter 1, I examine how the collective memory of the civil rights movement was institutionalized in American memory through the Martin Luther King Jr. national holiday. I show that the congressional and public debates over the King holiday built the contentious groundwork for oppositional interpretations of the memory of the civil rights movement through ideological fractures. In one fracture signed into law by President Reagan, a dominant branch of memory remembered that King's dream of racial progress had been achieved, at a cost to White Americans, but the path forward required a commitment to neoliberalism and color-blind individualism. From a grassroots fracture, a branch of memory remembered a radical King murdered for his resistance to systemic racism, leaving a dream of racial justice unrealized. These intertwined branches of memory provided the foundations on which rival groups would draw, building on and expanding what would become the gnarled branches of collective memory.

To explore how these gnarled branches take shape and grow over time, chapter 2 takes an eagle-eye view of the strategic uses of the civil rights movement between 1980 and 2020. I explain how a critical theory of memory in contentious politics helps us understand how temporalities matter for movements and how they shape the pathways of collective action. Taking four decades of data on the strategic uses of civil rights memory, I describe the branches of memory that grew from the initial fractures of the King holiday. From a conservative branch of color-blind individualism grew the boughs of White victimhood, White nationalism, and eventually White rage. From the color-blind idealism of multicultural unity grew a commitment to minority rights and immigrant inclusion, challenged by the growing branches of White victimhood. A resurgent preservation of King's radical legacy brought anti-imperialist movements committed to global solidarities and transformational politics. By 2016, the gnarled branches of collective memory split into oppositional and deeply polarized social realities.

The next three chapters are close case studies that examine just how these dynamics take shape on the ground. By examining these battles between rival movements, we see the systems of power that enable and constrain how groups can use collective memory through moral, national, and racial boundaries. These chapters show how groups grapple with these symbolic boundaries and remake them, as well as the multilevel consequences of their memory work, cultural impacts that bear out at the individual, group, and societal levels. Chapter 3 examines the moral boundaries that emerge through mobilizations of collective memory, centering on battles between the LGBTQ rights movement and the family values movement. This chapter traces how the uses of memory evolved in battles over an anti-discrimination ordinance and an anti-gay amendment between the George W. Bush and Obama eras.

In these contests, the cultural attribution of morality became central to how groups claimed collective memory for themselves and discredited their opposition. Conservative groups' uses of Dr. King's legacy to claim moral authority became powerful tools for discrediting LGBTQ groups' claims to civil rights. Meanwhile, LGBTQ groups grappled with reclaiming the memory of civil rights while contending with internal recognitions of racism and classism.

Chapter 4 asks how these dynamics unfold when the mobilizing group is perceived as lying beyond the limits of American identity and examines the national boundaries of memory. This chapter analyzes how the dilemmas of cultural ownership—the widely held perception of who "owns" collective memory—shape a movement's claims to societal inclusion by focusing on the immigrant rights and nativist movements. The chapter also compares cases across two political contexts—the Bush and Obama presidencies—to illustrate an evolution of collective memory. By showing how the national boundaries of memory are activated in these battles, this chapter offers insight into collective memory as an unequally distributed cultural resource. As immigrant groups mobilize memory to make claims to American identity, latent perceptions of cultural ownership—to whom a memory belongs and is readily available—become the very grounds on which rival nativist movements seek to legitimize their exclusion. As immigrant activists witnessed the rise of emboldened nativism during the Obama presidency, they reimagined the boundaries of national inclusion and evolved their strategies to celebrate their multiracial and multicultural differences rather than to mute them.

Both chapters 3 and 4 reveal the moral and national boundaries of memory and their consequences. But why do groups use memory at some times but not others, in some ways but not others? Chapter 5 takes on an unusual puzzle. Although most minority rights movements deploy the memory of the civil rights movement to demonstrate that they are analogous to Black Americans and make claims to civil rights, the immigrant Muslim rights movement delayed their use of civil rights memory for three decades. What led Muslim activists to mobilize the memory of civil rights? This chapter examines the racial boundaries of collective memory and the trade-offs of claiming a racialized stake in American identity. In the wake of post-9/11 backlash, Muslim immigrants increasingly understood the impermeable boundaries around White American identity and created new ways "in" to American identity.

However, in doing so, they had to confront the anti-Blackness within their immigrant communities while also battling a powerful anti-Muslim movement that framed them as dangerous threats to homeland security. Through the racial boundaries of memory, this chapter shows that "who we are" shifts drastically from one branch of memory to another: Muslim activists contended with failed memory invocations as color-blind, White Americans and shifted instead to memory deployments as racialized minorities "like" Black Americans. The result is innovated branches of memory that recognize Dr. King's "inescapable network of mutuality" between groups.

These chapters show how the moral, national, and racial boundaries of culture play out through different movements' battles for their imagined America. They also show the consequences they hold for individual perceptions of identity, group conceptions of collective identity, and societal understandings of collective memory and social reality. But is society doomed to repeat these reckonings and counterreckonings ad nauseam in an endless loop? Is this deep contention all there is? In chapter 6, I show what happens when groups work to overcome a fractured past by examining two groups that are less rivals than parallel and intersecting forces in a larger quest for women's rights: Black and White feminists who mobilized in the wake of Black Lives Matter and Me Too. I show how, with the leadership of Black women, White feminists increasingly understood that shared power and an intersectional future required restoration of the past—namely, recognizing the pivotal role of Black women in the history of civil rights for all.

In the conclusion, I examine the consequences of these strategic uses of the racial past, showing how they have generated divergent social realities, for example, in the contemporary moral panic over critical race theory and the conservative movement to limit childhood education in America's history of slavery and settler colonialism. In summarizing the previous chapters, I demonstrate that movements from the far right have grown branches of civil rights memory that weaponize memory against itself, targeting and discrediting movements for racial and social justice. Through this new landscape, conservatives can argue that minoritized groups receive special treatment and that White Christian conservatives are the new oppressed minorities under multicultural democracy. These misuses of memory have wider consequences because they obscure public understandings of racial inequality and its roots through their evasion, their denial, of the past. This willful historical amnesia threatens and erodes American democracy. Still, glimmers of hope remain. I end by illuminating a burgeoning movement of visionaries arising from the gnarled branches of memory, reimagining societal futures, and embarking on a new emancipatory politics that could very well save us all if we would let it.

1

Making Collective Memory

THE CONTENTIOUS POLITICS OF COMMEMORATING KING

> History is written by the victors.
>
> —ORIGINS DEBATED*

> Who controls the past controls the future.
>
> —GEORGE ORWELL

> Nothing in the world is more dangerous than sincere ignorance and conscientious stupidity.
>
> —MARTIN LUTHER KING JR., "LOVE IN ACTION" SERMON, 1964

ON THURSDAY, April 4, 1968, at 6:05 p.m., Martin Luther King Jr. was struck by a sniper's bullet as he stood on the second-floor balcony of his room at the Lorraine Motel in Memphis, Tennessee. One hour later King, age thirty-nine, was pronounced dead at St. Joseph's Hospital. As news of his assassination spread, grief-stricken publics erupted in protest in over one hundred cities across the country. Hoping to quell the heightened emotions, President Lyndon B. Johnson called for a national day of mourning on April 7. The next day, Congressman John Conyers (D-MI) introduced legislation to commemorate

* The quote popularly attributed to Winston Churchill has a much longer and more contested history, embodying the very questions explored in this book of cultural meanings and their lineages, shaped by competing political projects over time. See Matthew Phelan, "The History of 'History Is Written by the Victors,'" *Slate*, November 26, 2019, https://slate.com/culture/2019/11/history-is-written-by-the-victors-quote-origin.html.

Dr. King with a national holiday. It would be another fifteen years before the King holiday bill was passed.

The contentious political and cultural debates that characterized those fifteen years would prove critical for the making of the collective memory of not only Dr. King but also the civil rights movement. As this chapter will show, the dynamics that shape the making of memory become its living roots, creating its boundaries as a cultural structure. To examine how collective memories are made through contentious politics, this chapter illustrates this process through the factious making of the King holiday.

How Collective Memories Are Made

Where memories are commonly thought of as individual, neurological manifestations, as varied as they are inconsistent, scholars of collective memory have complicated the way we think about memory. The rich field of memory studies shows that memory is in fact a social, collective process of meaning-making where even the way we recall the minutiae of our own childhood is shaped by the social world in which we are embedded.[1] But what is a *collective* memory? Jeffrey Olick and Joyce Robbins offer a useful definition of the study of collective memory as "a general rubric for inquiry into the varieties of forms through which we are shaped by the past, conscious and unconscious, public and private, material and communicative, consensual and challenged."[2]

Figure 1.1 demonstrates the way individual memories are nested within group memories, shaped within and in relation to collective memories. Collective memories have significant power in society because they teach individuals which groups they belong to, who they are relative to one another, and what status they hold in society. As a cultural manifestation of systems of power, collective memories delineate boundaries between "us" and "them," they teach us how to think about ourselves and one another, and they legitimize collective action in one direction over another. Groups do not just shape memory. Collective memory shapes groups. As a result, the way the past is commemorated tells us not only who the "heroes" and "villains" were "back then" but also who they still are today and what we ought to do about them.

This framework helps us accommodate the inconsistencies of collective memory by thinking of it not as a fixed thing but as sets of practices that connect the past to the present, evolving and often nonlinear.[3] What becomes clear when we focus on the *practices* of collective memory is that it is really a cultural process of meaning-making, of storytelling. Movements travel across space, emotions, social-cultural conditions, and memory[4] where the collective memory of a social movement can carry on at multiple levels, at once structural and cultural, collective and individual.

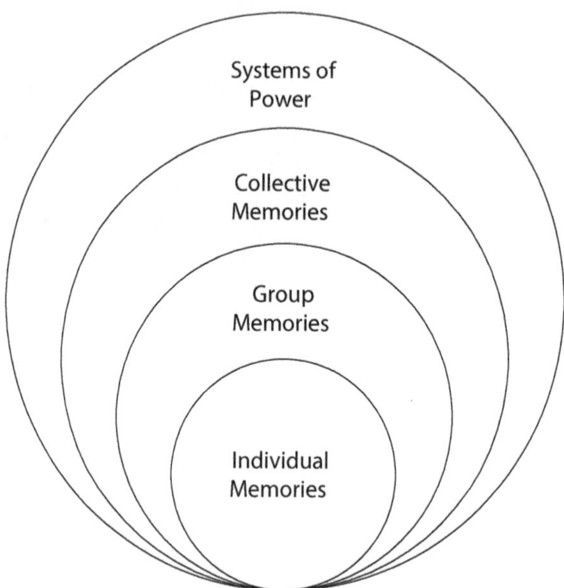

FIGURE 1.1. The nested dimensions of memory.

How Politics Shape Memory

To better understand how contentious politics shapes collective memory, I bridged accounts of how dominant cultural narratives, memories, and social realities are created. National myths, heroes and villains, are not only written from the top and handed down, although these elite actors hold outsized power in constructing dominant interpretations of the past. As shown in figure 1.2, the actors who battle over the memory of Dr. King, of the civil rights movement—the "Kingmakers"—reside in multi-institutional domains that are overlapping and often intertwined.

From above, there are the ruling elites, state institutions, and media conglomerates that work to shape a collective memory that upholds, legitimizes, and reproduces their power. Inside the bounds of memory, the mnemonic gatekeepers work to protect the memory from revisionism. These gatekeepers are the living bearers of the memory, as either direct participants (e.g., Congressman John Lewis) or those with direct lineage (e.g., Dr. King's children). From below, grassroots organizations and disparate publics can mobilize to either preserve or transform collective memory. Although dominant memories, those that are institutionalized and widely amplified, are handed down from above, grassroots publics are not mere pawns. Much of this book shows how grassroots contention from progressive groups dedicated to King's radical legacy holds the dominant branches of memory in constant tension.

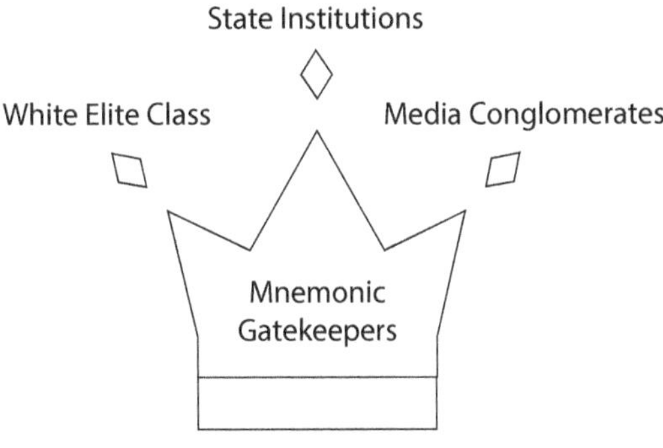

FIGURE 1.2. The Kingmakers of collective memory.

How, then, do these "Kingmakers" create collective memory together through contentious politics? One useful strand of research examines how groups battle over memory and why some memories prevail over others.[5] For example, Elizabeth Armstrong and Suzanna Crage explored why the Stonewall riots were central to LGBTQ collective memory whereas other similar events were not. They found that the memory of Stonewall became institutionalized because (1) activists perceived the event to be commemorable, made distinct through an annual gay pride parade; and (2) Stonewall had the "mnemonic capacity" to create a "commemorative vehicle," meaning the justification for commemoration and the strategic plan for how, when, and by whom a moment will be commemorated.[6] Other studies have shown that collective memories have less to do with contests over what *actually* happened and more to do with the series of events and cultural practices that constitute them over time, or their "trajectory of commemoration."[7] For example, Robert Jansen demonstrates how the Zapatistas and Sandinistas both invoked historical figures but in different ways, which were consequential for these figures' "reputational trajectories." In his path-dependent model of memory work, he shows that previous contestations around the memory of historical figures enable and constrain subsequent uses of historical figures.[8]

But as memory studies show, there can be substantial contention over the stories that get told about the past even after institutionalization. Difficult pasts in particular that leave cultural trauma,[9] from the slaughter of Native Americans to slavery in America, from the Holocaust to the Vietnam War, can generate what Robin Wagner-Pacifici and Barry Schwartz describe as less a symbol of national solidarity than an embodiment of "a nation's conflicting conceptions of itself and its past."[10] The perpetrators and those in their lineage may struggle with the perception of a "spoiled identity," the stigma of being marked by their relationship to mass atrocities. Rather than confronting the past, they may avoid it or remake it altogether. Christina Simko's analysis of the commemoration of terrorist events shows that some traumatic memories can become a bridge, uniting individuals through a moral universalism under a shared identity, while other forms of memory work can harden boundaries between groups.[11] Joachim Savelsberg documents how these conflicting conceptions can result in mnemonic practices that alternatively acknowledge, deny, or silence.[12] As Michel-Rolph Trouillot writes, the memories that win out for collective commemoration can silence others; history thereby becomes a process of "actively enforced silences."[13]

Beyond denialism and silences, historical revisionism can also take hold when ruling elites committed to maintaining or sedimenting their power set forth an alternative history, a process common among rising fascist leaders globally. Aleida Assmann's analysis of memory making after the fall of the Berlin Wall illustrates how Germans constructed a new collective memory of the Holocaust through a revisionist "false memory" characterized by denial and German victimhood.[14] Arlene Stein's analysis of the symbolic uses of the Holocaust in American politics shows that LGBTQ groups and Christian rights groups' battles over collective memory reshape the memory, particularly as the Christian Right's strategies generate historical revisionism.[15] These alt-histories can mobilize everyday people to violent action. Over time, they can become mainstream and accepted, where media may cite a revisionist version of the past under the premise of representing "both sides." The revisionist history can become so commonplace that it is taken for granted not as one story of the past but as *the* story of the past. When a revisionist history is created by and serves those in power, it becomes all the more difficult to challenge its hold in constructing social reality.[16]

These approaches are important in sketching out the contours of a theory of collective memory as embedded in a multi-institutional system of power that shapes its trajectories as an ongoing, collective process of meaning-making. By examining the collective memory's politics of institutionalization, its cultural traces and trajectories as it is made and remade over time, we can identify patterns that help us understand why the memory holds such significant power and how its uses matter for society.

The Contentious Politics of Kingmaking

After Congressman Conyers introduced legislation for the King holiday in 1968, days after King's assassination, the bill stalled. The civil rights movement and Dr. King were not particularly popular among the general public. Through the 1950s and 1960s, the civil rights movement had experienced challenges not only from outside but also from within. In a political landscape where organizers were contending with parallel movements—Black Panthers, Black Nationalists—publics frequently compared the civil rights movement against their counterparts in what scholars call radical flank effects—the extent to which radical activists generate positive or negative impacts for moderate activists. Memories of violence, militancy, and radicalism, often associated with Malcolm X and the Black Panthers, were juxtaposed against Dr. King's civility and nonviolence to highlight "appropriate" modes of protest and pit Black freedom fighters against one another.

Even within the civil rights movement, organizers frequently disagreed about the right path forward, whether incrementalism and the politics of appeasement were the way to go when they could no longer "turn the other cheek" and fight back. State-sanctioned violence against Black-led movements was not confined to the South. The FBI's surveillance tactics through its counterintelligence program (COINTELPRO) had devastating effects for social change movements throughout the country, particularly the Black Panthers. To destabilize and disrupt their operations, FBI agents sowed discord, disinformation, and distrust among organizers, which resulted in assassinations, imprisonment, and public humiliation that ultimately led to the Panthers' decline. Dr. King too was surveilled and blackmailed by the FBI, which wiretapped his hotel rooms, paid informants to spy on him, and sent him an anonymous letter written from a "close associate" suggesting that news of his infidelity would become public and he should kill himself. Under the guise of sniffing out communists and sympathizers, the state continually worked to limit Dr. King's power and credibility by threatening to sully his reputation and legacy.

The spillover effects extended beyond the movements themselves. Powerful contentious politics emerged from the gains of the civil rights movement, from desegregation mandates to the expansion of voting rights. Many White people saw desegregation as an oppressive practice that infringed on their own rights.[17] As historian Kevin Kruse writes, White southerners felt desegregation was intended "not to end the system of racial oppression in the South, but to install a new system that oppressed them instead."[18] These politics shaped a set of moral, national, and racial boundaries around how the civil rights movement would be remembered. While dominant collective memory invokes morality—good White people's moral convictions—as a central cause of growing support for the civil rights movement, the White opposition also rooted their claims in morality. Bishop John Shelby Spong famously recounted, "When I grew up in the South, I was taught that segregation was the will of God, and the Bible was quoted to prove it."[19] Dr. King himself had noted, "The church, by and large, sanctioned slavery and surrounded it with the halo of moral respectability. It also cast the mantle of its sanctity over the system of segregation."[20] Similarly, as Black Americans were arguing for recognition as equal citizens, their opposition painted Black people as unassimilable threats to the morally pure, racially White nation.

In the final year of his life, Dr. King's popularity reached its lowest point (75 percent disapproval rating), partly as a result of his public expression of frustration with the political establishment and White moderates' obstruction of progress. King had been taking what many White publics saw as a radical stance, speaking out against wealth inequality and the government's failure to care for its most vulnerable communities. In addition, in 1968 King had begun speaking out against America as the "greatest purveyor of violence" and against the American invasion of Vietnam.

In June 1968, two months after Congressman Conyers introduced legislation for a King holiday, King's widow and fellow civil rights leader Coretta Scott King founded the King Center in Atlanta. In the absence of official commemoration, she would continue her husband's work through the center, "the official, living memorial dedicated to the advancement of the legacy."[21] The civil rights movement's Southern Christian Leadership Conference (SCLC) circulated petitions in 1971 in support of the holiday, amassing three million signatures. With Representative Shirley Chisholm (D-NY), Congressman Conyers resubmitted the legislation session after session to no avail, although support for the bill began to grow. During the 1976 presidential campaign, Jimmy Carter promised to support the King holiday if elected, in exchange for the labor movement's support. In a written supplement to his State of the Union Address in January 1979, Carter wrote that "[King] led this Nation's effort to provide all its citizens with civil rights and equal opportunity" and pledged to "strongly support legislation" to commemorate King's birthday "as a national holiday." His statement mostly went unnoticed.[22]

Later that year, Coretta Scott King worked with the King Center to organize a new nationwide King holiday petition campaign. New, seemingly unlikely, sponsors for the bill emerged. Republican John Danforth of Missouri, a conservative Christian who saw in King a symbolic opportunity, urged Republicans to support the bill. As historian David Chappell wrote, "He did not want champions of the welfare state to have a monopoly on public claims of morality and decency. To Danforth, King's determination in the fight for equality symbolized the spirit of American freedom and self-determination," and Danforth wanted to extend King's moral symbolism to a growing sect of conservatives who sought to remake the GOP.[23] Danforth's stance was a new political possibility for conservatives: a potentially natural alignment with Dr. King's legacy built upon his Christianity, which could be deployed in the service of conservative causes on issues ranging from abortion to homosexuality.

From the Democrats, Robert Garcia (D-NY) championed the holiday "as an appropriate testimonial to an extraordinary individual who dedicated his life to the cause of human rights" that "would underscore the Nation's continuing commitment to alleviate the persistent and continuing effects of discrimination and poverty which Dr. King struggled to eliminate." The holiday would "indicate the kind of moral direction of our country in the coming years." Congress, he continued, "will have to make the most positive statement it can that the sectional and racial chapter of America's history has been closed forever."[24]

Still, the old conservative guard fought back with powerful attacks on King's legacy. Senator Strom Thurmond reconvened the joint hearing, calling forth author Alan Stang, whose account, "It's Very Simple: The True Story of Civil Rights," claimed that King had communist associations. Stang used King's own words against him, highlighting King's article on strategy in the April 3, 1964, *Saturday Review* as evidence that "the violence he got was not a surprise . . . he did not dislike it. He *wanted* it in order to pressure the Congress to enact still more totalitarian legislation."[25]

Thurmond also called on Julia Brown, a "loyal American Negro" and communist organizer who had joined the civil rights movement. Brown testified that she thought she was "joining a legitimate civil rights organization." Instead she found that she "was a true member of the Communist Party which advocated the overthrow of the United States Government." She described how members were "continually being asked to raise money for Martin Luther King's activities and to support his civil rights movement by writing letters to the press and influencing local clergymen, and especially Negro clergymen that he was a good person, unselfishly working for the American Negro, and in no way connected with the Communist Party." Brown concluded by drawing a powerful distinction between Dr. King and other African American leaders she deemed worthy of commemoration, proclaiming a "great many Negroes, such as George Washington Carver and Booker T. Washington, [provide American youth with a positive example]. . . . [King provided an example of] agitation and manipulation for goals dictated by hatred and envy. . . . [If a King holiday were approved] the memory of Carver and Washington would be dishonored . . . we may as well take down the Stars and Stripes that fly over this building and replace it with a Red flag."[26]

Next, Representative Larry McDonald highlighted what he saw as King's hypocrisy, pointing to the Supreme Court's 1978 *Bakke* decision upholding affirmative action. He asked whether "[King] really found racism repugnant in light of his support of discrimination in jobs and housing so long as the discrimination was in favor of blacks." McDonald pointed to King's affiliation with the "virulently racist Nation of Islam" to drive home his point, highlighting a 1966 quote from King staff member James Bevel, who said, "we need an army . . . to fight the White man this summer." In a written statement, John Ashbrook described the debate at hand as a question of "[supporting] the fictional assessment of Dr. King" and argued that "King's motives are misrepresented. He sought not to work through the law but around it, with contempt and violence. How soon we forget. When will politicians learn to accept history as it really happened instead of history as told by the *Washington Post*?" He warned against commemorating a man whom American children would "be misled into believing [was a great man] with the same reverence [as Washington and Lincoln]." Despite the vehemence of the opposition, a majority of House members voted to put the bill on the docket. However, as amendments were tacked on and the holiday began to lose shape, supporters led by Conyers moved to withdraw the whole bill and try again later with greater political support.[27]

In 1980, popular musician Stevie Wonder released a song called "Happy Birthday," a political call to commemorate King enveloped in cheery harmony and an unassuming song title. Wonder sang that there should be a law against anyone taking offense to celebrating King, that "Just because some cannot see / The dream as clear as he," we would all come to know what King stood for in due time. Although public support for the legislation grew, during the 1980 presidential campaign Ronald Reagan's increasing popularity caused concern among civil rights activists. Reagan was perceived by many as a politician who had gained support by opposing Black civil rights, from the Civil Rights Act of 1964, which he called "a bad piece of legislation," to the Voting Rights Act, which he called "humiliating to the South." Even during his campaign for governor of California in 1966, he had spoken in support of a proposition to nullify the fair housing law, explaining, "If an individual wants to discriminate against Negroes or others in selling or renting his house, it is his right to do so."[28] Following King's assassination in 1968, Reagan had suggested King was killed at the hand of his own tactics, "a great tragedy that began when we began compromising with law and order and people started choosing which laws they'd break."[29] The evening before the 1980 presidential election, Coretta Scott King confessed, "I'm scared that if Ronald Reagan gets into office, we are going to see more of the Ku Klux Klan and a resurgence of the Nazi Party."[30] Ronald Reagan defeated Jimmy Carter the next day in a landslide victory.

By 1982, support for the King holiday was steadily building, but President Reagan argued that the holiday would come at too great a cost to the federal government, minimizing the import of the commemoration by saying, "We could have an awful lot of holidays if we start down that road." At the 1982 hearings on the holiday, Coretta Scott King directed her testimony toward the opposition of years past, whom she referred to as a "traveling right-wing circus [specializing in] character assassination and infantile name-calling." She argued that King had opposed communism more vehemently than had his critics.[31] Still, returning to the forefront of congressional opposition, Representative Larry McDonald accused King of communist ties, pointing to the FBI's sealed files on King. He argued that a holiday commemorating an African American would be "racist." He said, "Why not a Chinese American? Why not an Hispanic? . . . We are supposed to be *e pluribus unum*."[32]

In testimony that would foreshadow conservative arguments for years to come, Black conservative writer J. A. Parker said, "[It's] unrealistic to rank King with Jesus and Washington." Parker listed those whom he deemed more appropriate figures for commemoration: Thomas Jefferson, Abraham Lincoln, Patrick Henry, Crispus Attucks, Booker T. Washington, General Daniel "Chappie" James, and Franklin Roosevelt. Then Parker argued that King's supporters were "unwilling to let history make its final judgment on the merits or demerits of Dr. King," pointing to King's criticism of America's involvement in Vietnam. He warned that overlooking King's "divisive" role was "to ignore the past and rewrite history" and warned that a King holiday would "further exacerbate the effects of a color-conscious society at the expense of the color-blind society, which should be our goal."[33] Parker went on to list five prominent African Americans who criticized King to further bolster his argument against the King holiday: NAACP director Roy Wilkins, Urban League director Whitney Young, Jackie Robinson, columnist Carl Rowan, and former senator Edward Brooke. As had Julia Brown in 1979, Parker's Black identity imbued his opposition to the holiday with symbolic power and credibility among his White conservative audience.

Stevie Wonder spoke out publicly against the opposition: "Allow me to quote one American leader who seems to understand the value of remembering Dr. King."

> There are moments in history when the voice of one inspired man can echo the aspirations of millions. Dr. Martin Luther King, Jr., was such a man. To America he symbolized courage, sacrifice, and the tireless pursuit of justice [*too long denied*]. To the world he will be remembered as a great leader and teacher, a man whose words awakened in us all the hope for a more just, more compassionate society. His time among us was cut tragically short, but his message of tolerance, non-violence, and brotherhood lives on. . . . Let us all rededicate ourselves to making Martin Luther King's inspiring dream come true for all Americans.[34]

The American leader that Stevie Wonder quoted was President Reagan. Meanwhile, Reagan had not expressed public support for the bill. Yet by Dr. King's birthday in January 1983, the tide was turning. Reagan made a public statement describing King as "the man who tumbled the wall of racism in our country. Though Dr. King and I may not have exactly had identical political philosophies, we did share a deep belief in freedom and justice under God." Reagan went on to describe the vulnerability of freedom as a constant struggle, how "freedom is never more than one generation away from extinction." Then he returned to Dr. King's example to describe the work of his movement as successfully completed, lifting the "burden" of racism. "History shows that Dr. King's approach achieved great results in a comparatively short time, which was exactly what America needed," Reagan said. "What he accomplished—not just for black Americans, but for all Americans—he lifted a heavy burden from this country."[35] By invoking racism not as a feature of American society but rather as an external force, a collective burden, Reagan absolved White Americans—including himself—of racism, leaving it as a resolved matter of the past.

On August 2, 1983, the Martin Luther King Jr. holiday passed the House with 338 members in support of the bill. However, once the bill reached the Senate floor the opposition had organized with renewed vigor. Conservative legislators led by Senator Jesse Helms and Strom Thurmond filibustered against the holiday, saying that Dr. King was a communist sympathizer and the bill would be too costly. Floor manager for the legislation, Senator Robert J. Dole (R-KS), argued back, "Since when did a dollar sign take its place atop our moral code? . . . To those who would worry about cost, I would suggest they hurry back to their pocket calculators and estimate the cost of 300 years of slavery, followed by a century or more of economic, political and social exclusion and discrimination."[36] Senator Helms countered, describing King's "calculated use of nonviolence as a provocative act to disturb the peace of the state and to trigger, in many cases, overreaction by authorities." Helms argued that a federal holiday should represent "shared values" but that King's "very name itself remains a source of tension, a deeply troubling symbol of divided society."[37]

The bill's supporters, led by Senator Edward M. Kennedy (D-MA), denounced Helms's claims. Kennedy retorted angrily, "I will not dignify Helms's comments with a reply. They do not reflect credit on this body." Republican senator Arlen Specter of Pennsylvania also rejected Helms's argument, arguing that Dr. King was a "Herculean figure on the American scene" and a "stabilizing influence"[38] who had prevented rioting in Philadelphia in the 1960s. Republicans and Democrats overwhelmingly supported the bill, and as many political analysts have noted, this largely stemmed from their awareness of strong Black voting contingents in their states. However, as Black Americans like Retta and Charles Gray of North Carolina wrote in a letter to the editor of *Time* magazine, the political contention over the holiday brought to the fore the continuing struggles through which the civil rights movement had initially emerged: "As supporters of the King holiday bill, we thank Senator Jesse

Helms for helping to secure the bill's passage. Helms reminded us by his behavior of the freedoms the Rev. Dr. King fought for."[39]

In an unexpected turn, Reagan threw his support toward the bill by year's end.[40] Many scholars have investigated Reagan's motives, including political scientist Robert C. Smith, who worked tirelessly to obtain Reagan's papers on the King holiday decision, although about 25 of the 4,811 pages known to exist are still confidential. Smith believes the secrecy reflects an effort to "Whitewash" Reagan's record on race.[41] Analysts have noted that the shift was not an effort to woo Black voters in the 1984 election, to whom Reagan did not expect to appeal, but rather a gesture toward moderate White voters.[42] Yet the two political strategies go hand in hand: Reagan's shift allowed him to signal support for civil rights, silencing critics like the NAACP, and to "Whitewash" King's memory for national commemoration through a selective interpretation of the civil rights movement: now racism was a product of the past and King's color-blind "dream" for America had been realized.

On November 2, 1983, fifteen years after the King holiday legislation was introduced, President Reagan sat amid a choir singing "We Shall Overcome," a powerful anthem of the civil rights movement, and signed H.R. 3706: "A bill to amend title 5, United States Code, to make the birthday of Martin Luther King, Jr., a legal public holiday." Outside of public view, Reagan maintained his oppositional stance toward civil rights, writing a letter of apology to Governor Meldrim Thomson Jr. of New Hampshire, who had vehemently opposed the holiday. Reagan reassured the Republican governor that his support for the legislation was based "on an image [of King], not reality."[43] This image was a sanitized commemoration free of King's political philosophies and the systemic racism and violence that shaped them. Instead, King's image would be characterized by a rosy rhetoric of color-blindness and individualism that Reagan would return to throughout his presidency to justify assaults on Black Americans' civil rights.

President Reagan's rollback of the civil rights movement's legacy was far-reaching. For example, protections for affirmative action hires were curtailed under a language of reverse discrimination, despite an uncooperative Supreme Court. Reagan's Justice Department also pursued cases that could set a foundation for banning affirmative action policy altogether. His administration restructured the composition of federal courts and their civil rights enforcement infrastructure, including the Justice Department, Labor Department, and Commission on Civil Rights. Reagan removed civil rights supporters from their positions and restaffed much of the Department of Justice and Commission on Civil Rights, replacing them with like-minded opposers of civil rights law who would weaken its efficacy. Reagan's Justice Department moved to no longer require entire school districts to desegregate, focusing instead on schools where there was evidence of intentional segregation. Although President Reagan signed a twenty-five-year extension of the Voting Rights Act, he also proposed making it easier for jurisdictions to become exempt from preclearance, a condition that had protected Black voters from disenfranchisement, and subsequently his Department of Justice ignored many violations of the act. Reagan proposed that enforcement of the act should require proof not only that a vote was denied but also that there was *intent* to discriminate.

Harold C. Fleming, a civil rights leader and president of the Potomac Institute, worried that President Reagan was going to "dismantle the whole apparatus" of civil rights enforcement. He explained, "If you look closely at what Mr. Reagan is doing, you see that he is trying to reduce the whole area of civil rights to a question of individuals."[44] By ensuring a particular institutionalization of Dr. King's civil rights legacy, Reagan could link his own anti–civil rights legacy to the great, Black moral leader. These efforts laid the groundwork for a national collective memory in which a revisionist history of King would be the protective coating around a political agenda committed to protecting White Americans' power. Conservatives could claim King's legacy for goals antithetical to the civil rights movement.

In 1988, fifty thousand people joined to commemorate the twenty-fifth anniversary of the March on Washington. President Reagan issued a statement characteristic of his selective adoption of Dr. King's memory, lauding racial progress made "toward fully achieving Dr. King's dream of a color-blind society." Though the event attracted a much smaller crowd than had the original march, attendees were more diverse and included Hispanic Americans and Asian Americans. In her public statement on the march, Coretta Scott King proudly proclaimed that her husband's "dream of justice, equality and national unity is not the exclusive property of any race, religion or political party." Some journalists noted a melancholy mood that day, as activists reflected on a decade that had turned back the clock on the civil rights gains of the 1960s and 1970s.[45] At the Lincoln Memorial, the historic site of King's "I have a dream" speech, civil rights activist Elena Rocha said, "If Martin Luther King could get up from the grave he would see that he'd have to start all over again raising hell."[46]

A Fractured Memory

The making of the King holiday illustrates the complex cultural and political processes that generated the structure of the collective memory. These foundational political debates would form the deep fractures at the roots of the collective memory. As the next chapters will show, these fractures enable all sorts of different groups to link their political causes to various interpretations of collective memory, splintering it into multiple branches over time. Through this new landscape of meaning, King's own detractors can now claim the mantle of the civil rights movement. Silencing racialized groups, they can claim that race-consciousness is antithetical to King's dream of a color-blind America while activating a captive audience through an increasingly established collective memory of Black and Brown progress as a threat to White Americans. Tracing the gnarled branches of fractured memory renders the rise of Trumpism a predictable extension of long-growing cultural forces. However, these trajectories also offer evidence of a growing resistance, a movement to not only reclaim but also restore a fragmented collective memory, to save a country from a dangerous historical amnesia.

2

Mobilizing Collective Memory

THE GNARLED BRANCHES OF CIVIL RIGHTS MEMORY IN CONTENTIOUS POLITICS

> You deplore the demonstrations taking place in Birmingham. But your statement, I am sorry to say, fails to express a similar concern for the conditions that brought about the demonstrations. . . . It is unfortunate that demonstrations are taking place in Birmingham, but it is even more unfortunate that the city's white power structure left the Negro community with no alternative.
>
> —DR. MARTIN LUTHER KING JR., 1963

NINE MINUTES and twenty-nine seconds. This was the amount of time it took a White police officer to kill George Floyd by kneeling on his neck as he begged for breath in the dying light of a late May day. Bystanders pleaded with police to let Floyd breathe as he lay stomach down, face twisted in terror against the pavement, calling for his mama in his final moments. Later we would come to learn that Floyd's mother had passed away two years prior, a devastating footnote. A doting Black father killed for allegedly using a counterfeit twenty-dollar bill to buy cigarettes.

Seventeen-year-old Darnella Frazier captured the horrific event on her cell phone. She posted the video on Facebook that night to share her grief, unknowingly setting in motion waves of irrevocable change. In the coming weeks, protests erupted in over two thousand cities in all fifty states and more than sixty countries around the world. Frazier's lawyer, Seth Cobin, said, "If it wasn't for her bravery, presence of mind, and steady hand, and her willingness to post the video on Facebook and share her trauma with the world, all four of those police officers would still be on the streets, possibly terrorizing other members of the community. . . . She's the Rosa Parks of her generation."[1]

Just one month prior, in April 2020, a much smaller series of protests captured media attention. Mostly White conservatives rallied in six cities around the country against the stay-at-home orders implemented in the wake of the deadly coronavirus, a pandemic the world had not seen since 1918. President Trump cheered them on, taking to Twitter in a series of emphatic tweets: "LIBERATE MICHIGAN! LIBERATE MINNESOTA. LIBERATE VIRGINIA, and save your great 2nd Amendment. It is under siege!"[2] Right-wing commentator and Trump advisor Stephen Moore also appeared on multiple media outlets to express support for the protesters as contemporary incarnates of a civil rights hero. "I call these people modern-day Rosa Parks. They are protesting against injustice and a loss of liberties," he told the *Washington Post.* On CBS News, he said, "It's interesting to me that the right has become more the Rosa Parks of the world than the left is." "We need to be the Rosa Parks here, and protest against these government injustices," he echoed on YouTube.[3]

Similarly, after violating a stay-at-home order by eating at a Houston restaurant, GOP-endorsed city council member Michael Kubosh reasoned, "Sometimes civil disobedience is required to move things forward, and so that's why we remember Rosa Parks." Explaining his strategy for countering public health recommendations by the CDC, conservative radio host Dennis Prager said, "Civil disobedience in the United States has a very, very, very noble history. . . . Rosa Parks wouldn't sit in the back of the bus because the disgusting law of blacks had to sit in the back of the bus in some Southern cities in the United States. Should she have obeyed the law?"[4]

In these invocations of the past, both a Black teenager catalyzing collective action for racial justice and White conservatives mobilizing against public health orders can be Rosa Parks. As journalist Eugene Scott wrote in the *Washington Post* of the paradox, "The response to the movement by some conservatives suggests that they are willing to wield the legacies of civil rights icons when it benefits them politically while blasting Americans whose activism actually aligns more closely with the work of those historical figures."[5] This chapter shows that these drastically oppositional interpretations of the past are not original, nor are they accidental. In fact, this chapter demonstrates that political uses of the civil rights movement are prevalent among mobilizing groups across the political spectrum, from conservative family values coalitions to progressive abolitionist groups.

Perhaps it is not that surprising that different groups would invoke memories of major civil rights figures like Dr. King and Rosa Parks. After all, as the last chapter showed, the memory of the civil rights movement has moved to the mainstream of American collective memory, the shared story of "who we are." The making of a King national holiday only solidified the idea that the civil rights movement was a collective American accomplishment, a moral triumph of American exceptionalism, a turning point in the arc toward equality for all to be celebrated by all Americans. Indeed, scholars of culture and social movements show that mobilizing groups routinely draw on recognizable, culturally resonant symbols—like historical figures—to make political claims and garner public support. Invoking popular figures like Dr. King grounds political claims in a larger story and provides a historical referent, an analogy, a moral foundation. Yet the invocations of Rosa Parks that opened this chapter complicate the idea that the political uses of memory are all comparable strategies *doing* the same thing. More importantly, as I will argue, these competing invocations of the shared past have deep and varied consequences.

Research in collective memory studies shows how political "memory work"—the strategic uses of the past—shapes "reputational trajectories," where prior uses of the past enable and constrain subsequent uses of it.[6] This research leads us to expect that the way groups strategically use the memory of the racial past will build on prior uses. Yet rather than existing along one reputational trajectory, memories of the civil rights movement are so multivalent that they obscure enduring systems of racism, upholding false narratives of American progress and the myth of a post-racial America.[7] What explains reputational trajectories that look less like long boughs and more like gnarled branches? How do these gnarled branches prevent us from charting a societal path forward collectively?

This chapter develops a critical theory of memory in contentious politics and its cultural consequences. These dynamics are embedded in systems of power and are (1) relationally unfolding, (2) shaped through temporalities, and (3) perceptual. As these contentious politics unfold, it is clear that those who remake collective memory, crafting and recrafting heroes and villains of the past for political purposes in the present, are not only politicians and media gatekeepers, although they play an outsized role in shaping dominant memories. The Kingmakers are also everyday people, lawyers, self-proclaimed moderates and radical activists, evangelicals and atheists, journalists and comedians, those who invoke historical figures like Rosa Parks or Dr. King to separate legitimate from illegitimate grievances, to frame collective action as peaceful rallies or violent riots. Kingmakers are the publics who show up in droves to support a movement as a moral obligation to stand "on the right side of history" or take to social media to decry lawlessness and thuggery.

This chapter lays the groundwork for making sense of these Kingmakers' present-day invocations of the past, how these invocations are patterned in meaningful ways, and why they matter for politics and racial inequality. Understanding the cultural trajectories of collective memory clarifies the deep roots of their political projects and their implications for the societal future, helping us make sense of not only *how* groups are polarized in their understandings of racial inequality but also *why* they continue to be so.

The Strategic Uses of Culture in Contentious Politics

A growing field of research at the intersection of cultural sociology and contentious politics attempts to explain why groups use culture in one way or another, why these strategies are received by audiences in particular ways, and why these strategies have particular consequences.[8] A common way to analyze the uses of culture is the widely adopted "framing approach" that draws from social psychological and linguistic theories—primarily Erving Goffman's work on the "schemata of interpretation"[9]—to connect processes of social reality construction with political processes.[10] Like a picture frame, a cultural frame focuses attention on a certain aspect or interpretation of the social world. The frame will filter, obscure, or even crop out other aspects of social reality, strategically shaping how the audience "reads" or understands an issue. It follows, then, that groups with different political goals can frame the same issue, say civil rights or climate change, in vastly different ways. Here, social movements are continually engaged in identifying and strategically directing cultural meanings "out there" toward particular audiences to make convincing claims and garner political support. The same frame, say human rights or family values, can also be adopted by groups with vastly different goals. For example, in *Come Out, Come Out, Whoever You Are,* Abigail Saguy shows that the "coming out frame" has been adopted by groups with all sorts of different identities and goals, from LGBTQ activists to undocumented immigrants.[11]

The framing approach seems to well explain the case presented here where widely different groups invoke the civil rights movement to legitimize their political claims. Through this approach, it is not particularly remarkable that all sorts of groups invoke the memory of the civil rights movement in contentious politics. Social movements scholar Sidney Tarrow has described how the movement produced a modular mode of action and discourse, a diffuse "master frame" on which movements draw:

> It was in the process of struggle that the inherited rhetoric of rights was transformed into a new and broader collective action frame. The lesson of the civil rights movement is that the symbols of revolt are not drawn like musty costumes from a cultural closet and arrayed before the public. Nor are new meanings unrolled out of whole cloth. The costumes of revolt are woven from a blend of inherited and invented fibers into collective action frames in confrontation with opponents and elites. And once established, they are no longer the sole possession of the movements that produced

> them but . . . become available for others to wear. . . . In the case of civil rights, as a result of the pathbreaking framing work of civil rights, "we began to see the heightened politicization of other groups, notably feminists, environmentalists, the elderly, children, the handicapped, and homosexuals organizing and demanding their 'rights.'"[12]

In this view, the civil rights frame is constituted by a relatively stable set of meanings, although the contexts in which frames are used may change significantly. But how do we make sense of the fact that both minority groups (e.g., undocumented immigrants) and majority groups (e.g., upper-middle-class White conservatives) invoke the same collective memory? Surely these uses of memory do not mean the same thing, nor do they reach and activate audiences the same way. And indeed, while social movement scholars have consistently employed the framing approach to evaluate the different ways groups position cultural meanings around strategic goals, there are growing critiques of this approach. Focusing on frames can obscure the complexity of cultural processes in contentious politics—the interactive, dynamic relationships between groups with varying levels of power, mobilizing in political and cultural contexts that are always shifting. Understanding these frames as static, as strategic tools that can be picked up at any point by anyone, can also obscure the larger systems of power and political ideology that motivate groups to use them and shape their consequences.[13]

Toward a Critical Theory of Memory in Contentious Politics

Understanding the strategic uses *and* consequences of the civil rights movement requires a critical theory of memory in contentious politics. This theory merges three central dynamics to make sense of the strategic uses of memory: (1) relationality; (2) temporalities; and (3) perceptions. This approach highlights the necessity of looking at not only the tools social movements use—frames, resources, tactics—but also *who* is using them, their relative level of power in society, and the way their identity is socially constructed and positioned in relationship to other groups. Figure 2.1 demonstrates how these three dynamics are interrelated to shape the uses of memory in contentious politics.

Relationality

The United States is built on entrenched systems of power including racial capitalism and settler colonialism, embedding relational forms of oppression, including White supremacy and heteropatriarchy.[14] The roots of these early

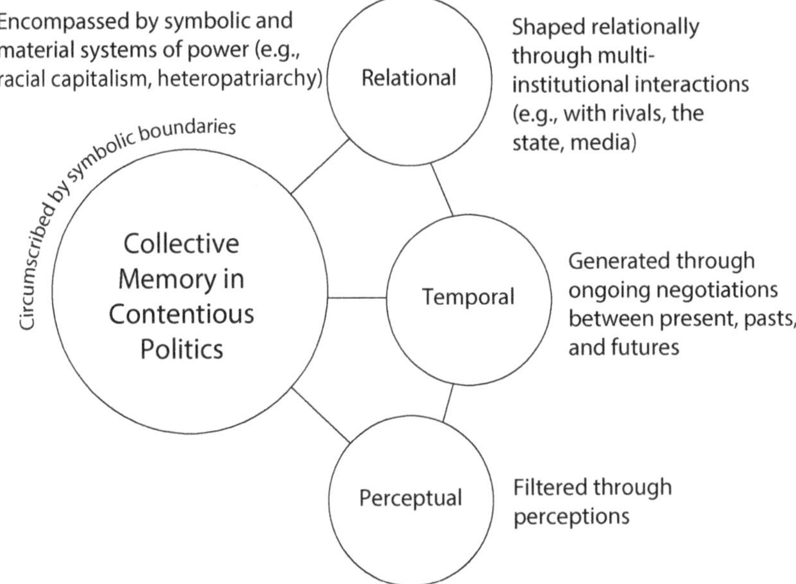

FIGURE 2.1. Critical framework for tracing collective memory in contentious politics.

systems did not die with the passage of time. Instead, they deepened their hold, evolving into the structures we know today through what Michael Omi and Howard Winant have called the system of racial formation. These projects that racialize individuals into relational racial groups are built not only into legal, political, and economic structures but also into cultural structures and the meanings ascribed to different groups.[15] For example, as Ange-Marie Hancock writes of the politics of disgust, "one's public identity is conditioned not simply by one's own speech and action but also by others' perception, interpretation, and manipulation—particularly for those citizens who lack political equality."[16] As a result, it is only by examining movements' cultural processes within the context of a relational, racialized system[17] that we can understand how power is distributed, organized, reproduced, and resisted.[18] Through this perspective, relational power structures[19] shape both the processes and consequences of collective action.[20]

As Elizabeth Armstrong and Mary Bernstein argue, a multi-institutional politics approach to making sense of culture, power, and institutions shows that movements are not only engaged with or resisting one source of power, commonly thought to be the state. Movements are continually in interaction with multiple forms of power—both material and symbolic—embodied by the state, media, other institutions, rival groups, and culture.[21] Relationality is central to these dynamics, and one clear pattern that emerges is the influential role of rival groups. These rivals are not only parallel competitors for power and resources but also direct threats that shape the contexts of mobilization.[22] Rival movements can both create and diminish opportunities for the other side, depending on the strategies they use.[23] Returning to the earlier example, if we understand disparate mobilizing groups as part of a shared political-cultural landscape rather than atomized entities battling in different political arenas, it becomes clear that gun rights groups claiming they are fighting for rights like Rosa Parks and gay rights activists claiming they are the new civil rights movement are relational strategies. These strategic linkages to the past are interrelated and have consequences for each other.

Temporalities

The relational dimensions of power also manifest through temporalities, in both their lived and perceived forms. Social inequality can both shorten a life span and make a life span drag on in seemingly endless pain and suffering. The time one has at their disposal to enact social change is also unequally distributed, where free time is a misnomer for those working around the clock for survival. Threats to one's survival, whether by racialized police violence or a disproportionate risk of death by COVID-19, can intensify the perceived urgency of now, limiting the capacity to imagine freely about the future. These are but a handful of ways time is shaped structurally, but time also matters as a cultural structure. Analyzing the strategic uses of the civil rights movement as a frame may miss a critical dimension of the strategy: its temporality; its imposition of *time*. In other words, when a mobilizing group makes political claims using collective memory, the invocation of time, of the past, is the point.

Integrating the dynamics of power with temporality, Crystal Fleming's analysis of activism around the racial past in France develops a helpful concept of "racial temporality," referring "to social actors' representations of race as a matter of time. Representing race as temporal involves making claims about the content of the racial past, present, and future, as well as the relationship among racial categories, relations, and processes in these different time periods. Racial temporality involves both 'time work' and cognitive labor as social actors attempt to describe race in the past, present, and/or future."[24] As Fleming shows, these claims can highlight the similarity and continuity between the past and present, as in activists' claims about trajectories of racism. These claims can also argue for dissimilarity between the past and present, portraying a post-racial society removed from the violence of the past.

Meanwhile, memories of the past are central in shaping how mobilizing actors make sense of the present and orient action toward the future. As the last chapter showed, collective memory constitutes more than a social history, or "things that happened in the past." Collective memory is the connection between the cultural past and the cultural present. These memories exist in a collective consciousness and are transmitted through communities, families, and institutions, generation after generation.

Perceptions

These temporalities are also taken up in the perceptual dimensions of social life. Social reality is filtered through an individual's socialization and cultural embeddedness, the cognitive frameworks and cultural frames individuals draw upon to make sense of the world around them. The same event can be perceived in vastly different ways by individuals in various social locations, interpreting the same circumstance through multiple frameworks. Most important for our conception of contentious politics is that these perceptions—of an urgent threat or a potential opportunity—play a powerful role in shaping social action. Constructing the perception of political threat is a cornerstone of political maneuvering for dominant groups working to maintain power, where the threat need not be real to *feel* real.

Similarly, perceptions are critical in the ongoing construction of social identity, the meanings that tell an individual who they are and where they stand relative to other people. Social identity is made and unmade through memory, where groups understand their "self" in relation to the cultural past: for example, what it means to be a Native American or a member of the Jewish diaspora or a White evangelical. When they mobilize, groups draw in collective knowledge from memories of what others in their social location—in the groups with which they identify—have experienced. These collective memories are shared through word of mouth and kept alive and transformed through storytelling, constituting social identities.[25] The past becomes a living ghost, haunting the present.[26]

Thus when groups develop strategies, these are not purely instrumental calculations based, for example, on what resources or political opportunities are available to the group. Strategies are *perceptual*, generated through the mobilizing actors' cultural understandings of the world around them, where they stand relative to other groups, the imagined stakes of enacting one strategy over another, and how time shapes who they are. For example, when sociologist Francesca Polletta analyzed invocations of Martin Luther King Jr. in congressional speeches between 1993 and 1997, she found that Black legislators' invocations of Dr. King were patterned by the institutional context and the legislators' status as "outsider-insiders." They did not use King in the same way within the congressional walls as they did outside in community spaces. In Congress, Black legislators understood themselves as occupying a precarious position as they "assimilated King into a pluralist framework by representing community service and institutional politics as the proper legacy of his activism,"[27] rather than highlighting King's radical extra-institutional collective action as they did elsewhere. Black legislators found themselves constrained by their conflictual identities as minority outsiders in a largely White political system, where racial progress had not been achieved yet. While they themselves saw the goals of the civil rights movement as unfulfilled, a living past, they understood that to many of their fellow legislators, their structural position as elected members of Congress reflected the seeming accomplishments of the civil rights movement. The stakes were too high to draw out Dr. King's radical legacy. To call out the unfinished work of the civil rights movement within Congress would jeopardize their already delicate position.

Strategic uses of memory, then, are not only about interpreting the past. They are also about anticipating the future and what *could* happen. Scholars have described these projective dimensions of decision making as future imaginations[28] or "protentions"[29] that shape how we take action and how we structure our choices.[30] Mobilizing groups from various social positions bring different forms of cultural knowledge to bear on these negotiations between past, present, and future. As a result, actors' orientations to the future may not be aligned, generating contention among groups with competing visions of the future.

Commemorative practices can also engage what Christina Simko calls "projective reversals," where powerholders will revise a "difficult past" by switching the roles of victims and perpetrators in the imagined future. Through this memory work, the victims of the past are reconstructed as the imagined perpetrators of the future, justifying policies, discourses, and actions that preemptively control against these possibilities and deny culpability.[31]

Despite the ways that power constrains future imaginations, creativity persists in the speculative visions and subjugated imaginations from below.[32] Afrofuturism is a particularly generative theoretical tradition that bends "time and space, merging both ancestral history and future possibility with the spiritual," that, as Myron Strong and K. Sean Chaplin write, "presents a world that both asks us to remember and acknowledge Africa as our root and understand social forces, like colonization, that have limited social progress."[33] By reimagining future possibilities beyond the constrained forces of the past, Afrofuturism allows actors to envision a different world. These fugitive imaginations can help heal deep traumas. They can be emancipatory.

As a result, when groups strategically draw on collective memory, they may come to the table not only with competing interpretations of the past. By

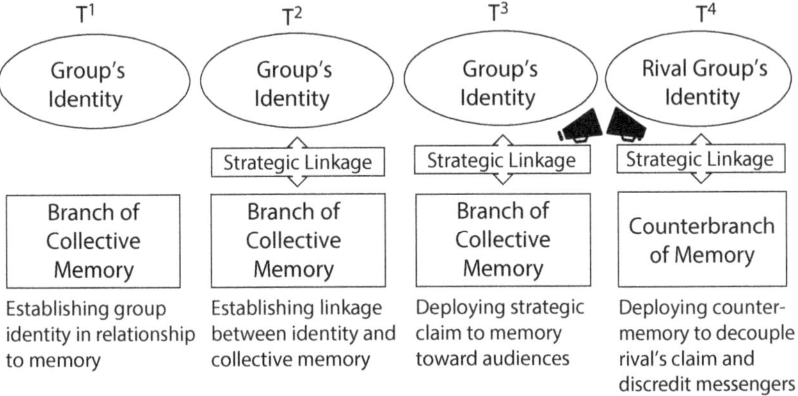

FIGURE 2.2. Strategic uses of collective memory in interaction.

affirming or contesting, expanding or contracting collective memories of the past, mobilizing groups may direct action toward opposing imagined futures. Thus in order to evaluate how groups want to enact change, they are always engaging with the dimensions of time, toggling between the perceived past, present, and future.[34]

To this end, when we examine how social movements use culture to make claims, we must consider the relational, temporal, and perceptual dimensions of the strategic work—where groups stand relative to one another and their relative power, their relationship to time, and perceptions of urgency, threat, and the time scape of action. As figure 2.2 conceptualizes, from Time 1 through Time 4, through interactions between movements and their opposition, actors can innovate strategies as rival groups work to offset one another's moves.[35] Through this process, rival groups draw on shared cultural meanings to discredit not only the opposition's message (the interpretation of memory) but also the linkage between the group that deploys the memory and the memory itself.

Without integrating these dynamics, we might see the invocation of civil rights memory as discrete uses of a common frame, simply evidence of a popular instrument in a cultural tool kit. We might miss the way these strategies are interconnected, not only patterned by a system of power but also maintaining that power over time by reshaping our recollection of the societal past. The earlier example of Polletta's study of Black legislators clearly illustrates that we cannot understand how movements use culture and why it matters without making sense of the structural position and collective identities of the actors and the way these positions shape their perceptions of time.[36] When different groups deploy the same memory to make separate political claims, they are embedded in a shared system of power that shapes their identities relative to one another, the perception of time through the political-cultural opportunities and threats they face at a given time, and their access to both material resources and cultural resources like collective memory.

As I will show in the next three chapters, the ways in which rivals discredit their opposition also reveal how power is distributed and remade through the strategic uses of memory. The memory of the civil rights movement is not only enabled and constrained by its prior uses. It is enabled and constrained by *who* uses it and their perceived position in society. Examining these battles between rival groups as relational, temporally interconnected processes brings to light the moral, national, and racial boundaries of culture. In this way, culture is not just a grab bag of easily utilized tools that any group can employ for their political goals. Through this lens, there is no false equivalence between the misuses of memory, no argument to be made about "both sides" being equally culpable in the distortion of social reality.

The Consequences of (Mis)uses of the Past

What comes of these strategic uses of memory? Why do they matter? After all, invoking Dr. King does not by itself change a law or implement a new policy. While the material consequences of these strategies may not be apparent, social movement scholars have shown that movements can also have profound, sometimes unintended, cultural consequences. These can take multiple forms, from slow and mounting shifts in public opinion and cultural attitudes, as was the case with the growing public acceptance of gay marriage prior to its federal legalization in 2015, to changes in discourse, the way we talk about an issue.[37] David Meyer argues that even when movements achieve no apparent gains, they leave traces along different domains in politics, policy, culture, and everyday people's lives.[38] Media coverage itself plays a powerful role in movements' cultural consequences.[39] Without news coverage, it is unlikely wide publics will learn about a movement, its strategies, and its goals. But the proliferation of "news" sources in the digital age means that media organizations are increasingly committed to covering news that is novel, sensationalist, "clickable." By amplifying disinformation, conspiracy theories, and alt-histories under the professed goal of representing "both sides," media have played a significant role in the cultural consequences of legitimizing and mainstreaming revisionist histories.[40]

In what follows, I will show that in the strategic uses of memory and its contestations, the continual interaction between group identities and memory produces a conflagration of interpretations of memory, gnarled branches that diverge in critical ways. Over the remainder of the book, I will show that these gnarled cultural branches have consequences at multiple levels. At the macro, societal level, the gnarled branches of memory contribute to a deeply divided culture dominated by what philosopher Charles W. Mills called an "epistemology of ignorance."[41] This willful ignorance about contemporary inequality and why it manifests in particular ways allows the system of power to maintain itself. Put simply, if we cannot see the problem, we do not have to do anything about it. Accordingly, scholars have shown that distorting the societal past—as in "Whitewashing" the collective memory of the civil rights movement—is a mechanism central to the maintenance of White supremacy.[42] If anti-Black racism is part of a bygone era, if King's color-blind dream was achieved, then racial inequality in the present must be a product of individual failings.[43]

Sociologist Jennifer Mueller describes racial ignorance as "a cognitive accomplishment grounded in explicit and tacit practices of knowing and non-knowing"[44] that helps explain the reproduction of systemic racism. Sanitizing and "Whitewashing" Dr. King, evading the knowledge of violence and racism that made and killed him, is a product of the mechanisms of "knowledge evasion and resistance."[45] Documenting how the manipulation of collective memory creates this larger cultural process of ignorance also helps explain growing research that shows that racial progress is not linear and that conceptualizing it as such mischaracterizes—is ignorant to—enduring patterns of racial inequality.[46] At the meso, group level, I show how the strategic uses of collective memory have consequences for shifting group identities and intergroup dynamics in chapters 3 through 6. At the micro, individual level, I show in chapters 4 and 5 how the strategic uses of memory have consequences for individuals' perceptions of who they are, their sense of empowerment and agency, and how they choose to create social change.

Bringing these threads together to make sense of not only how movements use collective memory but also why it matters, this book will show how social movements' strategic reconstructions of the racial past enable and constrain, reproduce or challenge systems of power in culture and politics. This integrated theory develops a critical analysis of memory in contentious politics that foregrounds power through mechanisms of relationality, temporalities, and perceptions. Through this conceptualization, when a mobilizing group invokes a collective memory for a political purpose, they tell a story about the past to make a claim about the present in order to shape action toward an imagined future. To understand the political uses of collective memory—how and why it is deployed in particular ways at particular times—we need to understand how this story links the group's identity to the past and to trace these linkages over time.

What is consequential, after all, is not merely that a group invokes collective memory. What matters is *how* memory is strategically invoked to make group claims. What and who is illuminated or obfuscated in this retelling of memory? What story does this memory of the past tell about "who we are" as a society and who counts as one of "us"? What social relations and modes of action (or inaction) does it legitimize? As different groups make strategic linkages between their identities and the collective memory of the civil rights movement, the interaction between identity and memory produces new sets of meanings. This chapter shows that these linkages generate competing interpretations of collective memory. Taking root, these divergent uses of the past grow into the gnarled branches of polarized social reality in contentious politics.

The Gnarled Branches of Collective Memory

To trace the political career of memory over time, this chapter takes the long view from 1980 to 2020 to analyze strategic uses of memory. I show how invocations of memory require strategic linkages between identities and collective memory that grow the fractured branches of memory. Dominant Kingmakers—the elite White class, state institutions, media conglomerates—become powerful purveyors of historical revisionism through their misuses of memory, strategies that are picked up by right-wing organizations and developed over time. The gatekeepers of civil rights memory and grassroots organizations are continually fighting to preserve the historical record, the critical and unfinished work of the civil rights movement. Yet over time, these gnarled branches generate divergent social realities.

By 2020, *all eleven types of social movements* (animal rights, anti-abortion, Christian Right, conservative, environment/conservation, gun rights, immigration, LGBTQ, Muslim rights, nativist/supremacist, police reform) had deployed civil rights movement memory. Although memory invocations were relatively rare in the 1980s, they increased in the 1990s, particularly among conservative groups throughout Bill Clinton's presidency. By George W. Bush's presidency and the subsequent aftermath of September 11, 2001, nearly 40 percent of the 110 organizations sampled had mobilized the memory of the civil rights movement. By the end of Barack Obama's presidency, 73 percent of social movement organizations had invoked the memory of the civil rights movement. While each movement deployed this collective memory toward competing goals, the framing approach would lead us to expect that the basic contours of the strategy would look similar. Comparable meanings would appear in these invocations, even if they were directed toward different targets.

However, a closer look at these memory invocations reveals markedly different results. The links between groups' identities and collective memory generate divergent but relational meanings, constructed in opposition to one

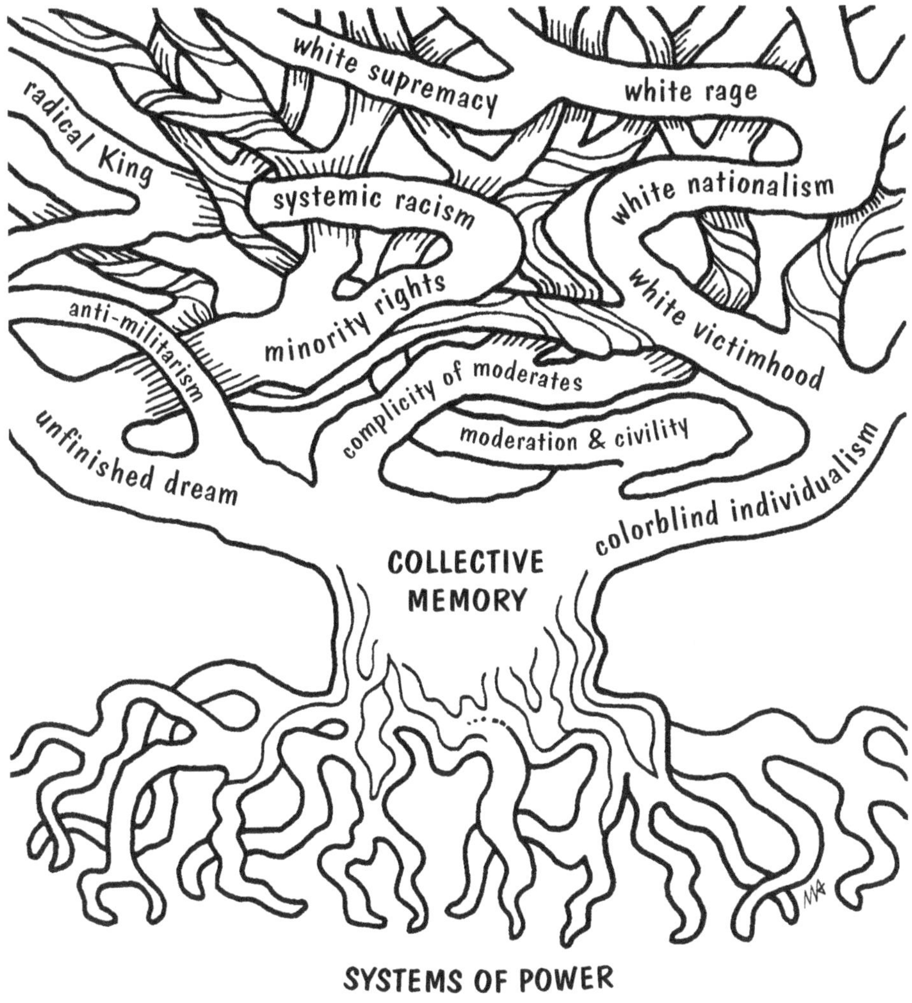

FIGURE 2.3. Gnarled branches of civil rights memory.

another and readily available to discredit the other. Yet the powerful Kingmakers who hold state power and control wealth and the media industries dominate the construction of social reality as political culture swings further and further to the right. The interaction between these linked sets of meanings generates branches of memory that, over four decades, have reshaped the collective memory of the civil rights movement and, by extension, the dynamics of contemporary politics.

The Civil Rights for All Branch

Injustice anywhere is a threat to justice everywhere.

—MARTIN LUTHER KING JR.

In the decade following the institutionalization of a national King holiday, strategic uses of civil rights memory were common among minority groups fighting for the unfinished dream of civil rights. LGBTQ groups were particularly prominent as they began shifting from a group celebrating sexual liberation to a political movement mirroring ethnoracial, interest-group politics.[47] Gay rights activists strategically linked the oppression of LGBTQ individuals to that of Black Americans in the decades prior, despite the frequent omission of recognition that Black people were also gay. For example, in a 1986 interview, a leader from the National Gay and Lesbian Task Force described the group's organizational strategies for countering growing anti-gay violence as a result of the AIDS crisis. He noted how the violence they faced was comparable "to the increase in violence against blacks in the 1960s at the peak of the civil rights movement."[48] Generating linkages between identity and memory to establish that their oppression was "like that of Blacks," LGBTQ groups claimed collective memory through shared experiences of violence and oppression.

Other minority groups similarly invoked the legacies of the civil rights movement to make claims to civil rights. For example, disabled people mobilized to demonstrate their relationship to other historically oppressed groups. With a growing sense of their linked fate, their "network of mutuality," they drew on King's memory to build coalitions and gain the support of publics. In a 1985 poll, 74 percent of disabled Americans said they shared a "common identity" with other disabled people and 45 percent reported they were "a minority group in the same sense as are blacks and Hispanics."[49] Activists fought against individualistic mindsets about disabled people overcoming challenges and increasingly pushed for societal, structural change that would alter how Americans thought about disability. They coined a slogan, "Disability Cool," as the news described, "the movement's equivalent of 'Gay Pride' or 'Black Is Beautiful'" and lobbied for a comprehensive civil rights bill in the Americans with Disabilities Act. Organizations like Americans Disabled for Accessible Public Transit (ADAPT) also adopted civil rights tactics to fight for lifts on buses, using civil disobedience tactics such as blocking traffic and participating in sit-ins at the Department of Transportation. Activists argued that separate transportation for people with wheelchairs was analogous to segregation. ADAPT leader Mark Johnson said, "Black people had to fight for the right to ride at the front of the bus. We're fighting for the right to get on."[50]

The Neoliberal Color-Blindness Branch: Whitewashing Memory through the Reagan and Bush Eras

> I have a dream that my four little children will one day live in a nation where they will not be judged by the color of their skin but by the content of their character.
>
> —MARTIN LUTHER KING JR.

The trunk of civil rights memory representing color-blind individualism grew through the Reagan era of the 1980s, characterized by political conservatism in the increasing White backlash to the civil rights era. The strategic use of Dr. King's legacy was central to the Reagan administration's rollback of Black civil rights gains and provided fertile ground for groups mobilizing to claim the collective memory of the civil rights movement for non-Black causes. President Nixon began the rollback a decade earlier, blocking the enforcement of the Fair Housing Act and calling desegregation a form of unfair reverse racism. The Republican "Southern Strategy" used dog-whistle politics to cloak anti-Black racism in "cultural" arguments for preserving the racial order. Reagan picked up these strategies to justify policies that emphasized individual responsibility while increasing White upper-class wealth and power through "trickle-down economics," effectively gutting the middle class. In late January 1986, during the week when the United States commemorated Dr. King, CBS aired a special news report titled "The Vanishing Family: Crisis in Black America" that focused on the changes in Black family structure and particularly the prevalence of unwed Black mothers. The program echoed the Moynihan Report of 1965, which explained racial inequality as a product of a Black culture of poverty, evidence that has been widely debunked by social scientists. While the *New York Times* reported favorably on the special as exhibiting "no negative stereotypes," it also described how the program was importantly "resuming the old discussion" of the Moynihan Report, amplifying questions like, "When does welfare assistance hinder rather than help? When does it destroy personal responsibility?"[51]

Activists such as Angela Davis critiqued the misrepresentation of the issue, which focused on flawed statistics and the attribution of blame to Black families. Others cited Dr. King's criticism of the Moynihan Report to warn of the negative consequences of the news special and its echoes in the Reagan administration's rationale for dismantling the social safety net: "Martin Luther King said, in effect, 'We are caught up right now in a struggle to end legal discrimination, and this report will give our enemies ammunition which they will distort.'" Activists tried to draw out the silenced memory of Dr. King's Poor People's Campaign, reminding publics, "But right before his death King started speaking to that issue, because he knew it was the one condition that could offset all the gains that had been made."[52] Still, the amplification of a neoliberal, color-blind King was far greater; King's color-blind dream was readily deployed to justify conservative policies. After all, if Black civil rights were now a matter of the past because Dr. King's color-blind dream had been realized, race-consciousness through civil rights era legislation could be framed as its own form of racism against White Americans. Conservative groups could garner political support as the new minorities.

In 1989, David Duke, a White supremacist and new Republican legislator, gave a speech at the Louisiana House of Representatives arguing against a bill to grant minorities a portion of state highway contracts: "I stand for equal rights, the rights of white people not to be discriminated against." In response, Black representative Raymond Jetson said, "Welcome to the fight for equal rights. I'd just like to ask where you've been all these years. Where were you when we were marching for equal rights for the past 20 years." Duke himself acknowledged the apparent shift in his stance toward civil rights and said, "Like most people, I have changed. I don't think I'm a racist." Still, as the reporter noted, "a few minutes later he expresses satisfaction at his new role in life. Mr. Duke maintains that blacks no longer suffer discrimination, but that whites are oppressed by the civil rights movement."[53]

Duke's contradictory behavior represented a growing branch of collective memory increasingly taken up by conservative groups into the 1990s.[54] Nativist groups linked White, majority-group identities to an interpretation of collective memory centered on color-blindness. Through this interpretation of the past, to acknowledge racial difference in the present, to institutionalize race-consciousness in any policy, would be to discriminate against White people. As Duke himself argued, affirmative action was "racist against whites," an argument echoed three decades later in ongoing challenges against affirmative action in higher education. These early uses of collective memory began generating a trajectory of meanings that strategically adopted the widely celebrated, sanitized memory of the civil rights movement while rejecting its historical context. The time scape was removed, anti-Black racism frozen in a distant past. These top-down strategies were powerful.

Civil rights leader John Jacob issued a warning call: "The rise of David Duke strips away the veil of American racism and exposes it to full view. Had Duke donned his Klan hood and waved *Mein Kampf* at election rallies, he would have been dismissed as a lunatic. But in his newly adopted guise of a populist conservative, he mouthed sentiments and code words made familiar through long usage by national leaders, making his sewer ideology appear respectively mainstream."[55] Public figures from the right strategically adopted the collective memory of the civil rights movement both to argue that civil rights legislation had enabled White oppression and to use its own branch of memory—as characterized by individualism, color-blindness—to justify overturning policies to remedy racial inequality. Much like the speculation around Reagan's initial motives for signing the legislation for the King holiday, for nativist groups appealing to general publics, civil rights memory deployments were a powerful tool for signaling non-racist intentions and cloaking racially coded strategies beneath a now widely adopted American collective memory.

In 1991, in an effort to strategize support for the Civil Rights Act of 1991, the Leadership Conference on Civil Rights, a coalition of civil rights, labor, and women's organizations, conducted a study to gauge support for the act among White voters. The study reported that "the civil rights organizations and proponents of civil rights were no longer seen as . . . addressing generalized discrimination, valuing work and being for opportunity. The proponents weren't seen as speaking from those values."[56] While there was significant support for egalitarian principles of equal opportunity, merit-based promotions, and workplace fairness, White voters also reported perceptions that civil rights activists' goals of equal opportunity were in fact cloaks for preferential treatment and that reverse discrimination in the workplace was prevalent. This survey reflected the changing tide of public sentiment after the wave of minority civil rights victories.

As one of the study's authors, Celinda Lake, reported in an interview with the *Washington Post*, civil rights advocacy was "seen as pressing the 'narrow' concerns of 'particularized' groups, rather than promoting a broad, inclusive policy of opposing all forms of discrimination."[57] Other public polls similarly showed that the majority of White Americans believed that African Americans and other racial minorities were no longer subject to discrimination or faced obstacles to equal opportunity. These conflicting interpretations of the relationship between the past and present reflected a divergent perception of social reality: one in which Black and Brown groups were still oppressed in a struggle for equality compared to one in which minority rights had been long achieved and civil rights policies paradoxically oppressed White groups.

These conceptions of reverse racism also spurred what many race scholars have identified as an era of color-blind racial ideology in which the very acknowledgment of racial difference is deemed a perpetuation of the "race problem." These arguments were not limited to conservatives: in 1992, presidential candidate Bill Clinton spoke out against the Black hip hop artist Sister Souljah for passionate lyrics in her song "The Final Solution: Slavery's Back in Effect." She decried the continuing violence against African Americans with lyrics like: "If your white great-great-grandfather / KILLED my great-great-grandfather / And your white great-grandfather / SOLD my great-grandfather

/ And your white grandfather / RAPED my grandmother / And your father stole, cheated, lied, and ROBBED my father / What kind of fool would I have to be to say, / 'Come, my friend!' to the white daughter and son?" Clinton denounced the lyrics, saying, "If you took the words white and black and you reversed them, you might think David Duke was giving that speech."[58] Later deemed the "Sister Souljah Moment" and a powerful tide-changing milestone in Clinton's campaign, the vilification of race-conscious discourse validated conservative arguments and appealed to moderates. When Sister Souljah defended her lyrics, arguing that they had been taken out of context, the opposition fought back by arguing that rhetoric that emphasized racial difference ran counter to King's ideals.

One characteristic op-ed read, "The temptation of a good old-fashioned hate isn't confined to any one race or creed or ideology. All these separate but equal demagogues have more in common with one another than each might admit. And all are most dangerous not to others but to their own cause—because they deprive it of moral legitimacy. That is why Martin Luther King Jr. preached nonviolence and why he was so successful in his time." A little over two decades after his assassination, the public memory of Dr. King had already erased how deeply unpopular he was. The op-ed went on to note, "Have you noticed how the very word racist has lost almost all meaning by its promiscuous overuse? It comes to signify nothing more than someone we strongly disagree with—just as Fascist and Communist once did. At one time or another, all these terms have been reduced to nothing more than generic cusswords. . . . Final note: Martin Luther King never had to claim that he was being quoted out of context or back away from his words in any other fashion. Because he always took the rhetorical high ground, he never had to explain away his presence in the fever swamps."[59] These strategies mirrored Reagan's initial intent in signing the King holiday bill: signaling color-blindness to acknowledge performative inclusion while obscuring the persistence of racial inequality. This tactical turn of meaning evolved into a strategy for other movements, both progressive and conservative, which sought to appeal to the White moderates Dr. King himself had warned against.

The Unfinished Dream Branch: Rival Branches of Memory through the Clinton Era

Let us realize the arc of the moral universe is long, but it bends toward justice.

—MARTIN LUTHER KING JR.

By the time Bill Clinton took office, progressive and conservative groups alike regularly used civil rights movement memory for their political purposes in predictable ways. With a seemingly progressive president in office, LGBTQ groups continued to receive attention around their growing movement for civil rights. By the 1990s, LGBTQ activists were calling themselves "the new civil rights movement." They deemed the 1990s their "civil rights decade—one future generations [would] liken to the 1960's battle for black equality."[60] (I describe this particular trajectory in greater detail in chapter 3.) At a 1992 march, Pat Hussain, co-chair of Atlanta's Gay and Lesbian Alliance Against Defamation, linked gay rights to the memory of the civil rights movement as the same inalienable rights.[61] At a 1993 protest in California, a gay business-woman described the change the movement was seeing: "There came a point even in little small Southern towns when black people stopped stepping off the sidewalk when whites walked by. We too have undergone that kind of sea change. It doesn't mean there are no more problems. It just means things will never be the same again."[62] LGBTQ organizations drew heavily on the imagery, symbols, frames, and tactics of civil rights memory to drive home the analogy between gay people and Black people. As a protester from the Gay and Lesbian Advocates and Defenders said in 1995, "It is very helpful for people who want to use 'street rhetoric' . . . the lifeblood of the civil rights movement. The importance of parades and street demonstrations is that it is the only form of speech available to poor people."[63] In the making of the "like Black" analogy, many Black activists noted the egregious invisibility of Black people in the mainstream movement and the violence of a language that distinguished between gay as White, and Black. Many of the movements that emerged around minority rights had to grapple with their anti-Blackness and classism, despite their progressive causes.

Progressive groups with historic roots in the civil rights movement, like the environmental rights movement and prison abolition movement, also highlighted their inherited connection to civil rights memory to build movement credibility and claim an unfinished dream. For example, the prison reform organization Citizens United for Rehabilitation of Errants invoked King to argue, "Justice too long delayed is Justice denied. Martin Luther King Jr.'s words have guided the efforts of the Petitioners since they first filed their lawsuit," aligning their efforts with those of the civil rights activists in the 1960s. Similarly the Prison Activist Resource Center, another prison reform group, linked the struggles of the civil rights movement to their organizational mission in the 1990s: "While many claim that the long tradition of racism in the United States ended with the Civil Rights Movement of the 1960s, the legacies of slavery and segregation continue to affect U.S. society on all levels." They cited the systems of racism that persisted: Black Americans were "disproportionately imprisoned by racist drug laws, denied access to the economic and educational benefits enjoyed by Anglo-Americans, and robbed of their civil rights and human dignity by a pervasive white supremacy that lurks just beneath the surface of our so-called democracy. This country's criminal justice system has not escaped the influence of, and is frequently the direct tool for, this racism."[64]

For these movements that stemmed directly from the civil rights era, developing links between past and present required less strategic work. Presenting clear evidence of their movement histories often sufficed to argue for the unfinished work of the civil rights era. Yet in a crowded field of memory uses across all sorts of groups, these strategies were less acknowledged by media gatekeepers, who increasingly covered and amplified the growing reactionary movements from the right.

Progressive movements for racial justice were recalibrating their strategies, understanding that the growing obfuscation of racism under the cloak of color-blind racism required reminding Americans of an unfinished dream. By the mid-1990s, popular media regularly rued the state of race relations. From the racial unrest following the beating of Rodney King by White police officers in 1991 to the acquittal of O. J. Simpson in 1995, racism and its discontents were unavoidable. Conservative backlash to the legacies of the civil rights movement grew during the Clinton presidency, embodied in the Contract with America, spearheaded by Republican leaders like Newt Gingrich and signed in 1994. The legislative agenda continued the rollback of civil rights, dismantling the social safety net and welfare protections for the poor under color-blind individualism and a language of "personal responsibility."

In October 1995, Martin Luther King III (Dr. King's son) joined Rosa Parks, Dr. Betty Shabazz (civil rights activist and wife of Malcolm X), and other civil rights leaders with an estimated 837,000 Black Americans for the Million Man March on Washington. The march was cofounded by Louis Farrakhan, the controversial leader of the Nation of Islam, who envisioned a march for unity among Black men and a call to uplift their communities. John Lewis himself expressed public opposition to the march under Farrakhan's leadership as a figure of "hate" and "division," but journalists noted the joyous tenor of the march and the spirit of unity and celebration of Black identity. When he rose to speak, civil rights activist and director of the Rainbow/PUSH Coalition Reverend Jesse Jackson Sr. invoked Dr. King:

> Why march? Father King said it was the shameful condition of the Negro. Today, it's disgraceful. Why do we march? Because our babies die earlier, infant mortality. Why do we march? Because we're less able to get a primary or secondary education. Why do we march? Because the media stereotypes us. We are projected as less intelligent than we are; less hard-working than we work; less universal than we are; less patriotic than we are; and more

violent than we are. Why do we march? We're less able to borrow money in a system built on credit and risk; San Diego, California, 30,000 mortgage loans; 29 to black. Why do we march? Because we're trapped with second-class schools and first-class jails. What is the crisis? Wealth going upward; jobs going outward. Middle class coming downward; the poor expanding rapidly.[65]

Challenging the growing revisionist history of an arc of racial progress, the Million Man March drew public consciousness back to the unfinished dream and the complicit society that enabled it. Black essayist and commentator Lester Sloan, appearing on NPR's *Weekend Edition,* remarked on the march's significance for the uphill battle for racial justice: "For African Americans, there are few that we claim for our very own. We got King after a fight, and there are those who want to take that back. We celebrate dates bestowed, but more often than not, they represent dreams deferred or promises broken. 'It brings a cool and serene breeze to an already hot summer,' Martin Luther King said of the 1964 Civil Rights Act."[66]

The White Christian Victimhood Branch

> If any earthly institution or custom conflicts with God's will, it is your Christian duty to oppose it. You must never allow the transitory, evanescent demands of man-made institutions to take precedence over the eternal demands of the Almighty God.
>
> —MARTIN LUTHER KING JR.

Minority rights strategies interacted with counterbranches of memory to discredit progressive groups and reclaim the mantle of memory. In response to the growing success of the LGBTQ "civil rights movement," for example, conservative backlash increased as organizers claimed the moral authority of civil rights memory. In 1993, Reverend Lou Sheldon, leader of the Traditional Values Coalition, argued, "The freedom train to Selma never stopped at Sodom . . . homosexuals have never been denied the vote. They have never been banned from public toilets. In fact, in some places, you have to watch out for your kids."[67] Decoupling gay activists' analogies to Black Americans was but one strategy for establishing minority rights as a threat to White conservatives and their families. Similarly, in 1994 the Eagle Forum, a conservative organization, issued a press release warning, "Just as the black civil rights movement produced calls for special treatment as a remedy for past injustice, so homosexual campaigners seem unlikely to stop at such mundane things as age-of-consent laws. As soon as they have scored those victories, it is said, they will move on to new demands."[68] Groups like the Christian Coalition, Eagle Forum, and Traditional Values Coalition increasingly deployed civil rights memory to link their Christian identities to the memory of minority struggle, arguing that gay rights were "special rights" that infringed on Christians' rights. These groups coalesced in a family values coalition led by evangelists like Pat Robertson, opposing a political context in which President Clinton expressed growing support for gay rights.

Anti-abortion groups like Americans United for Life also claimed that they were the new minorities being discriminated against, when, for example, Attorney General Janet Reno refused to meet with them in 1993. Reverend Patrick Mahoney said, "We have to believe clearly that we are being discriminated against. She's refusing to meet with us. We are nonviolent. We have committed to that on a personal level." Mahoney compared Reno's refusal to meet with the family values group to a refusal to meet with Dr. Martin Luther King and other civil rights activists "who were arrested in peaceful protests."[69] Conservative groups' claims to civil rights memory continued across organizations and movements, using faith to claim the moral center of national identity. In 1998, anti-abortion group Feminists for Life argued that "abortion is also a crime, a violation of human rights far more heinous than slavery," calling themselves "contemporary freedom riders, a courageous counterculture [that] will ultimately prevail over injustice just as the civil rights movement helped put a stop to segregation."[70] As the director of New York City's Christian Coalition argued, these interconnected movements were intended to bring Christian faith "back" to the center of society, invoking King to explain, "We're teaching about the fact that there is a God. I think Martin Luther King said that the church is neither the master of the state nor the slave of the state, but it's the conscience of the state, and what we're looking at here is that we need to have the church begin to speak so that the conscience can come back into the state institution."[71] Through these strategic uses of the past, family values groups claimed the moral legacy of the civil rights movement. This grew a branch of memory that bound collective memory to a set of symbolic moral boundaries that would be deployed in the battles to come over issues from gay rights to reproductive rights.

During the Clinton era, White conservatives maintained a growing trajectory of meaning establishing White Americans as the newly oppressed group, threatened by Black Americans' "preferential treatment" that, they argued, ran counter to King's dream of color-blindness. As one journalist wrote of the linked tropes, "President Ronald Reagan attacked 'welfare queens' in 1980. President George Bush used Willie Horton, a convicted black rapist, to scare the living daylights out of White America in 1990. And North Carolina Senator Jesse Helms, yet another Republican, kept it that way in 1990 with a hate-mongering TV spot that helped beat his black challenger." He went on to describe a commercial depicting a White, male hand adorned with a wedding ring, seemingly to represent a family man, ripping up a job rejection letter. A somber voice says, "You were the best qualified for that job, but you didn't get it. They had hiring quotas." The journalist concluded, "Message received. You've got to be a minority in order to get ahead in America."[72]

Strategic uses of civil rights memory during the Clinton era reflected growing feedback between political identities and culture, where different groups were contending with their social position in relation to other groups against a changing political climate. Groups drew on branches of collective memory through their perceived relationship to the past to renegotiate their position. They built on the trajectories of memory generated by identity-memory linkages of the decades prior, in evolving and deeply oppositional branches of meaning. Progressive and conservative groups alike increasingly enacted strategies that linked their identities to "Whitewashed" interpretations of collective memory: color-blindness, individualism, the American dream. Conversely Black Americans were constrained in their invocations of collective memory as the widely held, "acceptable" memory of the civil rights movement was increasingly narrowed, sanitized, and stripped of its power for resisting racism.

The conservative forces that countered progressive groups began to anticipate civil rights memory uses and to strengthen their tactical repertoires for discrediting these strategies. These counterstrategies were of two types: interpretations of memory that would discredit progressive groups' claims to memory; and new uses of memory that would frame conservative White groups as the unfairly oppressed group. The proliferation of competing branches of meaning continued to reshape the collective memory of the civil rights movement itself into the new century.

The Anti-militarist Branch: 9/11, New Minorities, and the George W. Bush Era

> I knew that I could never again raise my voice against the violence of the oppressed in the ghettos without having first spoken clearly to the greatest purveyor of violence in the world today: my own government.
>
> —MARTIN LUTHER KING JR.

By President George W. Bush's inauguration in 2001, the use of civil rights memory was common among many progressive and conservative social movements. A conflagration of linkages between group identities and interpretations of memory had produced a landscape of conflicting but relational branches of memory. These mobilizations of collective memory would only continue to increase after September 11, 2001. The attacks set into motion wide-reaching and long-lasting political and cultural shifts, from the Patriot Act to the War on Terror that would last nearly two decades, cost an estimated eight trillion dollars, and end at least nine hundred thousand human lives. For many anti-war activists, the unjust war recalled Vietnam in the 1960s and unearthed Dr. King's anti-militarist legacy in the last year of his life. King's critique of U.S. foreign policy, his solidarity with oppressed peoples around the globe, and his anti-militarism were some of the first strands of his legacy to be suffocated at the hands of his sanitized domestication in the 1980s. Almost four decades after his "Beyond Vietnam" speech, these words would be revived to challenge the Orientalism justifying the violence against Muslim people, including Muslim Americans.

Remarking on the vacated collective memory of the civil rights movement and its necessity for explaining anti-Muslim/Arab racism, James J. Zogby, president of the Arab American Institute, said, "Dr. King has been diminished in some ways by the way the day is celebrated, because many people have forgotten the country's long history of racism."[73] Dr. King's legacy was repeatedly invoked to call people to action against state-sanctioned anti-Muslim racism and foreign policy. In a speech at a 2002 rally for civil liberties, Al Sharpton compared the Bush administration's racial profiling and surveillance of Arab and Muslim Americans to the wiretapping and surveillance Dr. King experienced: "We cannot sit by and allow what J. Edgar Hoover did to Dr. King be done today to Dr. King's children. It's not enough to pack churches and sing hymns. Dr. King would have called us to take action."[74] In early 2003, thousands of anti-war protesters descended on Washington, D.C., to protest the likely war with Iraq. Organizers described the strategic plan to coordinate their "National March on Washington" with Martin Luther King Jr. Day. Organizer Eleiza Braun explained, "Martin Luther King took a strong stance against the war in Vietnam and fought for the same principles of health care and education that we stand for."[75] The march joined King's legacy with the anti-war movement, drawing on the anti-militarism King espoused at the end of his life.

The Multicultural Color-Blindness Branch

> Anyone who lives inside the United States can never be considered an outsider anywhere within its bounds.
>
> —MARTIN LUTHER KING JR.

Muslim Americans came together across ethnic and racial differences and mobilized in this new context. As chapter 5 will show, a growing Muslim rights movement relied on these branches of memory to challenge a powerful Islamophobia network. To fight the stigmatization of Muslims, they made claims to a civil rights memory characterized by color-blindness that allowed for unity and multiculturalism. In this branch of memory grown from Dr. King's dream but embedded not in Reagan's individualism but in minority rights activists' spirit of multicultural collectivism, color-blindness meant a shared American identity absent of race-consciousness.

For example, Yousef Al-Yousef, the chairman of American Muslims for Global Peace and Justice, called for Muslims to understand the post-9/11 moment through Dr. King's legacy. Framing the moment as one of hope and American exceptionalism, he said, "Not since the triumph of Martin Luther King Jr. and his Civil Rights movement were the newfound American values of fairness put to the test at such an enormous scale." Yet he suggested "good" Americans had prevailed as a critical mass "came to the rescue" to protect Muslims and Arabs from "extremist ideologues." Looking optimistically at Muslims Americans' capacity to cause Americans to remember their moral center in the march toward progress, he reminded them of their claim to the legacies of the civil rights movement: "The Civil Rights movement was not only an African American triumph; it was an American success. Few Western or non-Western societies have embraced reformers, who are not from the dominant class, with such swiftness."[76] This rosy reading of collective memory gave America, Americans, the benefit of the doubt through a memory of color-blind, multicultural unity that would hopefully ward off the erosion of Muslims' civil liberties.

Similarly, a new immigrant rights movement was growing, from an "Immigrant Workers Freedom Ride" in 2003 to nationwide protests in 2006 that would catalyze an infrastructure for a sustained movement. In the early years of these movements activists contended with the heightened nationalism of the moment and the heightened racism against immigrants. Activists drew on assimilationist ideologies purporting that the way out of exclusion was to be "in" through an unthreatening American identity that did not talk about race, that did not criticize American identity, and that held on only to safe and unthreatening aspects of cultural difference to maintain proof of patriotism. A branch of memory that celebrated color-blindness as the path toward unity made clear, "we are not different from you," and it would not critique the United States so much as draw on King's optimistic words to celebrate its promise. These movements felt the trade-offs of this color-blind strategy in subsequent years as nativism moved firmly to the mainstream and they understood their own deep and unavoidable racialization.

The White Victimhood Branch Grows into White Christian Nationalism

We want all of our rights, we want them here, and we want them now.

—MARTIN LUTHER KING JR.

Meanwhile, conservative groups celebrated a conservative, born-again Christian president who would protect their interests. At a 2003 gathering, the Pro-Life Action League lauded the Supreme Court victory of *NOW v. Scheidler*, effectively enabling abortion-clinic protests. Joe Scheidler described how King's dream was on its way to being recognized as abortion would soon be outlawed. He called on the movement to prepare for the day when the "impossible dream" would come true and "abortion will be as unthinkable as slavery is today."[77] The rising conservatism of the Bush era also witnessed growing efforts to quash LGBTQ civil rights gains through state and local referendums. Family values coalitions had developed powerful rival counterbranches of memory to challenge LGBTQ claims to civil rights, drawing on interpretations of Dr. King's religiosity to make moral claims to memory. In a 2005 marriage amendment challenge in Utah, conservative activist Gayle Ruzicka said it's "absolutely appalling" that gays and lesbians would equate themselves to the civil rights movement. She said, "I think it's an insult to try and compare what they're doing to the struggles minorities have gone through. What they're talking about is a sexual choice. They choose who they sleep with. . . . It has nothing to do with civil rights."[78]

In addition, in interaction with new movements like the immigrant rights movement and Muslim rights movement, conservative, nativist groups sought to discredit their use of civil rights memory while establishing their own linkages between identity and memory. For example, in 2003, the conservative group Accuracy in Media (AIM) reported on a rally marking the fortieth anniversary of the civil rights movement's March on Washington:

> The major media deliberately concealed the facts about how the "civil rights movement" has degenerated into a collection of political extremists, homosexual militants, Muslim activists, and anti-American Marxists. . . .
>
> Despite the cries of racism that roared through the nation's capital that day, dramatic evidence shows that the racism being practiced by the U.S. government consists of discriminating in favor of blacks and other designated minorities in federal hiring. . . . This may constitute massive reverse racism against white males. . . .
>
> Instead, it's the alleged "underrepresentation" of minorities that receives the press attention. . . . This is viewed by the press as evidence of racism

> against the minorities. So rather than focus on the harm caused by the over-hiring of minorities that may constitute reverse racism against white males, the media now push for even more hiring of preferred minorities in the senior ranks. . . . This is the reality of King's "dream" today.[79]

Like the uses of civil rights memory by nativist and conservative groups in the decades prior, AIM linked White identity to a collective memory of oppression, maintaining a divergent branch of memory in which King's dream necessitated color-blindness and "racial preferences" only enabled "reverse racism," counter to his dream. Through the proliferation of this conception of collective memory, Black struggle was a matter of the past, a symbol of how far we had come. King's color-blind dream warned against recognizing social difference lest White people become the new Black people. These strategies also highlighted an increasing distrust of "liberal" media, throwing the veracity of news into question and augmenting the power of right-wing news conglomerates like Fox News, which was founded in the midst of the conservative backlash of the Clinton era.

And then Barack H. Obama arrived on the political stage. The election of the first Black president marked a significant political-cultural moment, cited by many as the beginning of a post-racial era.[80] As many progressives and moderates erupted in joyful optimism, free of the racial tensions that characterized civic and political life, the brewing conservative and nativist backlash—coined by scholars as "Whitelash"—erupted above the surface. In early 2009, the Tea Party Movement emerged in vociferous condemnation of the Obama administration and its overreach, infringement on individual liberties and freedoms, and—notably—discrimination against White Americans.[81] The Tea Party would eventually move the Republican Party even further to the right through effective political strategies including uses of memory that established White groups as minorities, threatened by a Black president who allegedly favored Black and Brown publics to the detriment of White Americans.[82]

Among these far-right groups, gun rights activists were building on the growing perception of political and cultural threat to fight for the unregulated expansion of individual liberties. Gun rights groups leveraged the past for their own political purposes in the present by first discrediting gun control advocates and then developing their own claims to memory. In 2007, before Obama took office, the Citizens Committee for the Right to Keep and Bear Arms had made a public statement discrediting Reverend Jesse Jackson's twenty-five-city anti-gun protest. Jackson had timed the protest to coincide with the anniversary of King's March on Washington, but the Citizens Committee worked to discredit the effort as "a great hypocrisy." Chairman Alan Gottlieb said,

"Dr. King's historic march was to promote and defend civil rights. What Jesse Jackson is planning is designed to crush America's most important civil right. A right that Dr. King exercised by owning a handgun."[83] However, in the wake of the Obama presidency, the gun rights movement shifted from discrediting strategies to establishing their own linkages between past and present.

In 2008, Gun Owners of America argued that gun control was part of the system of Jim Crow still in operation: "That gun rights have played such a pivotal role in racial equality makes the historical correlation between gun control and discriminatory policies unsurprising. From their beginnings, gun control measures have worked to create legal disparities, granting unequal rights to members of various socioeconomic groups."[84] These strategies continued to build as calls for gun control grew. After the tragic Sandy Hook massacre of twenty schoolchildren and six adults, when public support for gun control hit a critical mass, the NRA announced a partnership with a new contributor to NRA News to increase Black support. Colion Noir, a Black gun advocate, was introduced through a strategic play to persuade Black Americans to lobby against gun regulation by linking gun rights to civil rights. The NRA posted a video on YouTube, in which Noir says, "The same government who at one point hosed us down with water, attacked us with dogs, wouldn't allow us to eat at their restaurants and told us we couldn't own guns when bumbling fools with sheets on their heads were riding around burning crosses on our lawns and murdering us." Noir emphasizes, "The only person responsible for your safety is you. Cops can't always be there. Obama definitely can't be there. Guy telling me to get rid of my guns when I need them the most, isn't my friend, isn't looking out for my best interests and doesn't speak for me or the community that I'm part of."[85]

Noir became a public face for the NRA, producing additional digital content invoking the civil rights movement to argue for gun rights. On January 20, 2014, the Martin Luther King Jr. holiday, the NRA released a video in which Noir connects the NRA's vision to King's dream, saying, "Let's not forget the first forms of gun control were created to keep people like me from having guns." Referring to Dr. King's denied application for a gun permit, he said, "Dr. King was a nonviolent man but even he understood the realities of self-defense and protecting his home and his family in the face of life-threatening violence. This is why he tried to apply for that gun permit . . . based on Dr. King's own actions, I don't believe that Dr. King would ever advocate leaving a family, or anyone for that matter, defenseless in the face of violent life-threatening danger."[86]

The repetition of these strategies strengthened a branch of memory that emphasized the threat to American liberties and freedoms under progressive multiculturalism. More notably, groups like gun rights organizations understood that their old uses of civil rights memory would be more credible, more powerful, coming from Black people. Who could represent Dr. King better than a Black messenger? These strategies emphasized that "true Americans" were the victims of this new administration and the multicultural progressives who elected him, and they would have to take their country back. In 2014, gun rights advocate Ted Nugent said, "In 1955, my hero, Rosa Parks, refused to give up her seat on a city bus. Good for her. In 2014, gun owners must learn from Rosa Parks and definitely refuse to give up our guns. As Rosa Parks once said, 'You must never be fearful about what you are doing when it is right.'"[87] Conservative groups were weaponizing the past against the present to claim that White conservatives were oppressed and under threat. White collective action was essential.

The Unfinished Dream Grows into the Systemic Racism Branch

> Law and order exist for the purpose of establishing justice and when they fail in this purpose they become the dangerously structured dams that block the flow of social progress.
>
> —MARTIN LUTHER KING JR.

Meanwhile, prison reform and abolitionist movements, encouraged by the increased publicity around the prison industrial complex, reinvigorated the linkages between their movements and the memory of the civil rights movement. With a growing movement for police reform, they drew on a branch of memory that remembered injustice as a systemic issue, manifesting now as a "New Jim Crow."[88] In 2010, the Sentencing Project highlighted the historical roots of the racial inequality embedded in the prison system: "Martin Luther King Jr., said we as a nation must undergo a radical revolution of values. A radical approach to the US criminal justice system means we must go to the root of the problem. Not reform. Not better beds in better prisons. We are not called to only trim the leaves or prune the branches, but rip up this unjust system by its roots."[89]

Similarly, in 2014 Families Against Mandatory Minimums drew on King's famous "Letter from Birmingham Jail" to highlight the ongoing struggle for racial justice: "As the Rev. Martin Luther King, Jr., wrote in his famous letter from the Birmingham jail, 'Injustice anywhere is a threat to justice everywhere.' Society should not ignore known injustices just because they may be few in number. Rather, society should correct such errors, especially when their number is small, because we can no longer, and should not have to, rely on the clemency process to rectify them."[90] These long-active movements for not only prison reform but also abolition would become foundational during the rise of Black Lives Matter, providing an organizational infrastructure and group of seasoned activists on the ground around the nation. The eruption of new waves of racial justice movements would give this branch of memory a louder voice to amplify King's radical legacy, to nourish it, and to watch it grow.

The White Nationalism Branch Grows into White Rage

> The principle of self defense, even involving weapons and bloodshed, has never been condemned.
>
> —MARTIN LUTHER KING JR.

In the last year of the Obama administration, White resentment had solidified in White rage, what Carol Anderson described as "the fear of a multicultural democracy. It is predicated on a sense that only whites are legitimate Americans."[91] Mobilizing conservative groups continued to deploy civil rights memory to generate perceptions of reverse oppression and justify civil rights appeals, from the repealed provision of the Voting Rights Act (*Shelby County v. Holder*) where Justice Scalia called the provision protecting minority voting rights a "racial entitlement" standing in the way of the political process to the repeal of affirmative action in college admissions (*Fisher v. University of Texas*).

In 2014, conservative politician Pat Buchanan was a guest on the *Steve Malzberg Show*, elaborating on his column in which he argued for the repeal of civil rights laws. He told Malzberg, "Everybody is claiming victim status. This isn't the same situation we had at Selma bridge, and it is time to move on. . . . Some of these civil rights laws in my judgment, once the job that they have been passed to do [has] been done, the reason they are continuing is because there is this gigantic bureaucratic empire that has been built up and erected to sit on top of all of us and oversee and police and monitor every decision we make in our corporate or personal lives."[92] The irony of Buchanan's comments was that conservative groups had become some of the most active messengers of civil rights, linking their group identities to collective memory to claim they were the new minorities.

Through public performances of White rage, the Tea Party had been mobilizing civil rights movement memory since Glenn Beck's 2010 "Rally to Restore Honor" on the steps of the Lincoln Memorial.[93] In 2013 at the Tea Party's "Audit the IRS" rally, Beck was quoted saying, "This is a civil rights movement, and it's time for us to start moving as a civil rights movement. We have to be willing to have the dogs be unleashed on us, because believe me—after what I saw today on the way they're handling things at the Capitol, you're not very far from having the same kind of oppression coming our way." Beck went on to cite the great figures of the distant past—"Harriet Beecher Stowe, Abraham Lincoln, Frederick Douglass, Booker T. Washington, Gandhi, Martin Luther King"—and then said, "Martin Luther King's time has passed. This is our time, and the long march towards civil rights is here."[94] In 2015 at the South Carolina Tea Party Convention, "Wild Bill" Finley announced that the Tea Party would rescue King's memory. To the cheering mostly White audience he proclaimed, "Martin Luther King had a dream, and it was a good one—a day when skin color wouldn't matter anymore. A time when character would be more important than skin color. But when we look at what's going on in America today, it's pretty easy to see that Dr. King's dream got hijacked." Accusing progressives of keeping racism alive, he posited, "Some people figured out that racism can be very profitable—both financially and politically. And now, those who are most vocal about Martin Luther King being their hero seem to be the most race-driven people in America." He went on to argue that if King were still alive, "the liberal left would spit in his face because he would be such a threat to their political agendas." Then he took the big leap and declared, "We are the people who practice Dr. King's dream. It is the Tea Party where people are not judged by the color of their skin, and it's Tea Party Americans who believe that character still counts. So today, I am officially announcing that the Tea Party is taking Martin Luther King away from the liberal left. And to you race-baiting promoters of division and hatred, you're not getting him back until you renounce your shameful skin-color politics and start practicing the politics of character."[95]

The Systemic Racism Branch Grows into the Radical King

> I submit that an individual who breaks a law that conscience tells him is unjust, and who willingly accepts the penalty of imprisonment in order to arouse the conscience of the community over its injustice, is in reality expressing the highest respect for law.
>
> —MARTIN LUTHER KING JR.

The Movement for Black Lives emerged from this landscape of divergent social realities, fighting to dig up the roots of King's radical legacy, to prove that the struggle for Black freedom had never ended. In response to the murder of Black teenager Trayvon Martin in 2012 by George Zimmerman, a group of organizations joined to protest systemic violence against Black communities, including that at the hands of the police. Many of these organizations connected their present struggles to the past to illustrate the *longue durée* of injustice against Black Americans. Deploying Martin Luther King Jr.'s dream, the Dream Defenders mobilized against policies of racial profiling, the school-to-prison pipeline, and "stand your ground" laws, which had legally sanctioned murders like Trayvon Martin's at the hand of White vigilantes. Phillip Agnew, one of the leaders of the Florida organization, explained, "When we first started mobilizing in 2012, I could have never imagined things would have happened this quickly. On the other hand, this really is something that, if you look back at history, was easy to predict." Citing the racism of police culture, the impoverishment of Black and Brown communities, lack of educational opportunities, and joblessness, he said, "This is a recipe for disaster. This is 1967. This is 1968, when cities around the country, including Chicago, Newark, Detroit, Oakland and Watts, began to explode."[96]

Similarly, an organization called Lifelines to Healing formed to bring attention to the disconnect between Martin Luther King Jr.'s dream and the experiences of Black Americans today. Drawing parallels between their work and the work of civil rights movement activists, Lifelines to Healing organizers coordinated a fifteen-city bus tour in 2013 leading up to the fiftieth anniversary of the March on Washington. Buses with Martin Luther King's image on the side, juxtaposed with contemporaneous images of Black Americans, traveled from Miami to Washington, D.C., with clergy, activists, and parents who had lost children to gun violence on board. After 2013, the Movement for Black Lives swelled around continued shootings of unarmed Black Americans by police officers, including eighteen-year-old Michael Brown, twelve-year-old Tamir Rice, and forty-three-year-old Eric Garner, a father of six. In response to the 2014 killing of Michael Brown, a coalition of civil rights organizations submitted a press release calling for police reform by invoking the unfinished work of the civil rights movement: "It has not gone unnoticed that the images of militarized law enforcement personnel surrounding peaceful demonstrations in Ferguson are eerily similar to those we equate with the inhumane and racist tactics used against protestors during the Civil Rights movement in the 50's and 60's." Calling for an honest reckoning, they said, "we are not and will never realize a post-racial society until we honestly acknowledge, confront and address the systemic structures that maintain the old vestiges of racial segregation and de-humanization in this country, particularly in law enforcement."[97] By 2015, Opal Tometi, a cofounder of Black Lives Matter and the executive director of the Black Alliance for Just Immigration, warned of the political landscape, "It takes me back to the time when black churches were burned with impunity in the '60s and

'70s. . . . Today we have the same type of domestic terrorism on the rise, we aren't supposed to call it that, but that is exactly what it is. We are seeing these white supremacist networks grow and become stronger."[98]

The Moderation and Civility Branch

Darkness cannot put out darkness; only light can do that.

—MARTIN LUTHER KING JR.

In backlash over the growing protests for racial justice, conservatives and moderates alike drew on a branch of selective, revisionist memories of King's ideology of nonviolence to discredit Black Lives Matter. These invocations drew on a memory of the civil rights movement characterized by nonviolent tactics and peaceful civility, one that "united" rather than "divided" Americans, that was characterized by blind optimism and faith in the "spirit" of American progress. In contrast, Black Lives Matter was framed as a violent, aimless movement of radicals espousing reverse racism against White people. For example, Fox News host Bill O'Reilly discredited the Black Lives Matter movement's tactics, calling them a "hate group" and arguing, "Dr. King would not participate in a Black Lives Matter protest."[99] Dr. King's niece, the conservative activist Alveda King and Fox News contributor, spoke out against the "inappropriate" tactics of Black Lives Matter activists as running counter to her uncle's dream. Of activists' efforts to take down Confederate monuments, she said, "We don't need to fight over skin color, eye color, hair color—all of those kinds of things. And we certainly don't need to tear up real estate and destroy things and decimate areas in order to get a point across." Later she would co-opt Black Lives Matter's claims for anti-abortion causes, arguing that "babies in the womb definitely matter as well."[100]

Yet conservatives were not the only detractors who drew on a revisionist memory to delegitimize Black Lives Matter. Although most of their protests were peaceful acts of civil disobedience, media coverage of rogue looters characterized the movement as unlawful and violent. On CNN, Wolf Blitzer criticized protesters in Baltimore for not acting "in the tradition of Martin Luther King." Democratic representative James Clyburn of South Carolina argued that Black Lives Matter's violence was hijacking the movement for racial justice: "Peaceful protest is our game. Violence is their game. Purposeful protest is our game. This looting and rioting, that's their game. We cannot allow ourselves to play their game."[101] Tactics drawn directly from the civil rights movement—marches down freeways, sit-ins, disruptions to the day to day that would garner public attention—were characterized as antithetical to King's legacy.

The Complicity of Moderates Branch

> First, I must confess that over the last few years I have been gravely disappointed with the white moderate. I have almost reached the regrettable conclusion that the Negro's great stumbling block in the stride toward freedom is not the white Citizen's Counciler or the Ku Klux Klanner, but the white moderate who is more devoted to "order" than to justice; who prefers a negative peace which is the absence of tension to a positive peace which is the presence of justice; who constantly says "I agree with you in the goal you seek, but I can't agree with your methods of direct action"; who paternalistically feels he can set the timetable for another man's freedom; who lives by the myth of time and who constantly advises the Negro to wait until a "more convenient season."
>
> —MARTIN LUTHER KING JR.

In reaction to the weaponization of memory against Black Lives Matter, activists worked to revive Dr. King's powerful words from his own acts of civil disobedience that landed him in a Birmingham jail. They reminded publics that Dr. King himself had been accused of inciting violence and hatred. Frequent invocations of the dangers of respectability politics and the White moderate were deployed against revisionist memories of a "civil" civil rights movement. Activists reminded publics that while King did not believe in the use of violence, he understood it within its larger social context when he said, "a riot is the language of the unheard." Organizers also looked to the gatekeepers of collective memory, original civil rights activists, to publicly remember how disruption was central to King's ideology and the larger civil rights movement. They called on memory to remind us of what was at stake.

The gatekeepers of civil rights memory responded. Cecil L. Murray, a former civil rights movement activist and Black Lives Matter supporter, wrote, "In 1964 and 1965, blacks won two massive legislative victories: passage of the Civil Rights Act and the Voting Rights Act, both historic victories for the cause of equality. But just a few years later—in 1968—the symbol of the movement that won those rights, Martin Luther King Jr., was assassinated." He went on to connect the moment to the present-day dismantling of the Voting Rights Act, ruing that "a half-century after our voting rights were secured, our jaws dropped when the Supreme Court turned voting regulations back to states that had long discriminated; we've had to battle new voter restrictions in more than a dozen states." He drew on collective memory not as a finished past but as a living and unfinished dream for an imagined future: "Looking back, I know much has been accomplished. Looking forward, I know much more must be done. . . . Some say we live in a post-racial, post–civil rights era. I say the era of civil rights isn't over. Like 1968, 2016 will be a decisive year. What future will we choose . . . ?"[102]

The White Supremacy Branch: Reclaiming White Supremacy during the Trump Era

> Let us therefore continue our triumphal march to the realization of the American dream . . . for all of us today, the battle is in our hands.
>
> —MARTIN LUTHER KING JR.

The time was ripe for a political candidate who could build on the growing perception that White Americans were victims of multicultural democracy and its movements for social justice, that the only way forward for White America was to return to the past. Who could make America White and Christian again?

In the weekend leading up to Martin Luther King Jr. Day in early 2017, just before his inauguration, president-elect Trump entered into a heated feud with famed civil rights leader and Georgia congressman John Lewis. Lewis had voiced his plans to boycott Trump's inauguration, perceiving the victory as illegitimate at the hands of Russian interference. Lewis was widely known as a civil rights icon: an original freedom rider and chairman of the Student Nonviolent Coordinating Committee (SNCC) who famously led more than six hundred activists over the Edmund Pettus Bridge in Selma, Alabama, where they met the violence of state troopers with billy clubs and tear gas and White citizens waving Confederate flags on what would be remembered as "Bloody Sunday." As journalist David Remnick has written of Lewis's pivotal role in American memory, "[Lewis] is the singular conscience of Capitol Hill. Lewis is a dismal institution's griot, a historical actor and hero capable of telling the most complex and painful of American stories—the story of race. That is his job, his mission. With Dr. King and Malcolm X, Fannie Lou Hamer and Ella Baker long gone, Lewis remains nearly alone in his capacity to tell the story of that era as a direct witness and, because of all that he has seen and endured, to issue credible moral judgment."[103]

It was all the more egregious, then, when President Trump took to Twitter to attack Congressman Lewis just before the King holiday:

> @realDonaldTrump: Congressman John Lewis should finally focus on the burning and crime infested inner-cities of the U.S. I can use all the help I can get! . . .
>
> Congressman John Lewis should spend more time on fixing and helping his district, which is in horrible shape and falling apart (not to . . . mention crime infested) rather than falsely complaining about the election results. All talk, talk, talk—no action or results. Sad![104]

Anticipating public outcries, Trump supporters and right-wing pundits immediately emerged to legitimize Trump's attack and to discredit John Lewis.

Right-wing commentator Dinesh D'Souza tweeted, "John Lewis is not a 'legend'—he was a minor player in the civil rights movement, who became a nasty, bitter old man."[105] Trump campaign operative Roger Stone tweeted that Lewis "negates his heroism on the Edmund Pettis [*sic*] bridge by acting like a partisan hack asshole, never to [be] taken seriously again."[106]

Others were aghast at the desecration of the civil rights leader. President of the NAACP Cornell William Brooks tweeted a photo of a young John Lewis, bloodied and beaten in Selma, writing, "By disrespecting @repjohnlewis, @realDonaldTrump dishonored Lewis' sacrifice & demeaned Americans & the rights, he nearly died 4. Apologize." Reverend Al Sharpton said, "If you can disrespect John Lewis on Martin Luther King Day, then what are you saying about the rest of us?" Lewis himself pointed out that he believed Dr. King would have boycotted the inauguration as well and that there would not have been a Trump presidency had Dr. King lived. Speculating on an alternative time scape, he lamented, "Dr. King would have been able to lead us to a different place and our country would have been different and the world community would have been different."[107] Four days later, on January 20, 2017, Donald J. Trump took office as the forty-fifth president of the United States. The rollbacks of civil rights began immediately with a series of executive orders that began limiting the rights of groups including Muslims, immigrants, prisoners, the disabled, and transgender Americans.[108] The Trump administration's cabinet appointees similarly pursued civil rights deregulation, from housing to health to education.

In February 2017, an editorial cartoon circulated depicting Trump's secretary of education, Betsy DeVos, as the new Ruby Bridges. Bridges was the six-year-old African American girl who desegregated an all-White New Orleans school in 1960, an image emblazoned in collective memory and made iconic in Norman Rockwell's 1964 painting titled *The Problem We All Live With* (figure 2.4). President Obama had displayed the painting outside the Oval Office in 2011, telling Ruby Bridges, "I think it's fair to say that if it wasn't for you guys, I wouldn't be here today."[109] Now, the 2017 cartoon depicted the controversial DeVos as a vulnerable victim of political forces, "Conservative" graffitied viciously behind her and tagged by the National Education Association (NEA), the largest union in the United States and a vocal opponent of DeVos's (figure 2.5). The symbolism was unmistakable, a commentary on the new political victims and their oppressors.

Controversy erupted over the equation of a White woman in a public, political office with an innocent Black child. Cartoonist Glenn McCoy apologized "if anyone was offended" and explained, "My cartoon was about how, in this day and age, decades beyond the civil rights protests, it's sad that people are still being denied the right to speak freely or do their jobs or enter public

FIGURE 2.4. Political cartoon depicting Trump's secretary of education Betsy DeVos as the new Ruby Bridges. Glenn McCoy © 2017 Distributed by Andrews McMeel Syndication. Reprinted with permission. All rights reserved.

FIGURE 2.5. Barack Obama talks with Ruby Bridges in front of Norman Rockwell's painting *The Problem We All Live With*. White House photo/Alamy.

buildings because others disagree with who they are or how they think." He said he was "speaking out against hate."[110] The implication was clear. The revisionist memory of civil rights had a stranglehold on the past, where Ruby Bridges and Betsy DeVos could be equated as analogous figures, but two sides of a coin on a political field voided of context, power, and time, where the mere perception of White victimhood was as good as reality.

Collective memory is a powerful symbolic resource that tells the story of who we are. By linking their identity to collective memory, a group makes clear their place relative to other groups in society, claiming a stake in collective national identity. Yet, as more groups make and contest these claims to memory, the meanings become tangled through competing branches of memory. Weaponized by those in power, revisionist memories take hold, evading social reality and becoming tangible through the repeated uses that legitimize them and their messengers. The next chapters take a closer look at how different groups—different Kingmakers—use and grow these gnarled branches of memory, telling stories of "who we were" to legitimize collective action toward divergent societal futures. More importantly, these case studies will illuminate how systems of power shape both the strategic uses and the consequences of struggles over collective memory as groups bump up against the moral, national, and racial boundaries of culture.

3

"Dr. King Would Be Outraged!"

LGBTQ and Family Values Activists' Contests over the Moral Boundaries of Memory

> Morality cannot be legislated, but behavior can be regulated. Judicial decrees may not change the heart, but they can restrain the heartless.
>
> —MARTIN LUTHER KING JR., 1966

> Twenty-five, thirty years ago, the barometer of human rights in the United States [was] black people. That is no longer true. The barometer for judging the character of people in regard to human rights is now those who consider themselves gay, homosexual, lesbian.
>
> —BAYARD RUSTIN, ORGANIZER OF THE 1963 MARCH ON WASHINGTON AND GAY RIGHTS ACTIVIST

ON JULY 11, 2017, the Trump administration's attorney general, Jeff Sessions, gave a rousing speech about the historical roots of American religious freedom to the Alliance Defending Freedom, a Christian rights group. He described how these pasts shaped the Trump administration's commitment to a "future of religious liberty." After proclaiming the "Western heritage of faith and reason," Sessions listed the founding fathers' manifold commitments to religious freedom and influential French political theorist Alexis de Tocqueville's deep admiration of American religiosity. Then he invoked another familiar figure, declaring, "And of course it was faith that inspired Martin Luther King Jr. to march and faith that truth would overcome. He said that we 'must not seek to solve the problem' of segregation merely for political reasons, but 'in the final analysis, we must get rid of segregation because it is sinful.'" Looking out at the rapt audience, Sessions continued, "It undermined the promise, as [Dr. King] described it, that 'each individual has certain basic rights that are neither derived from nor conferred by the state . . . they are gifts from the hands of the Almighty God.'" Sessions explained: "So our freedom as citizens has always been inextricably linked with our religious freedom as a people." He went on to describe a "cultural climate" that had become inhospitable to religious liberty, a powerful "inside-the-beltway crowd" that was disconnected from faith communities who were, in turn, "under attack" but that had turned out in droves to secure President Trump's election. Through the perception of Christian groups as the threatened minorities, Sessions reassured the room that "under this administration, religious Americans will be treated neither as an afterthought nor as a problem to be managed."[1]

The previous chapter showed how mobilizing groups across the political spectrum remake the collective memory of the civil rights movement by linking their group's identity with selected branches of collective memory. Here, the identity of the group matters for both how they use that memory and how audiences perceive their strategies. As this chapter shows, the perceived morality of group identity, as evidenced by Jeff Sessions's moral claim to Dr. King on the basis of Christian identity, is central to these linkages. The moral boundaries of memory—to whom it belongs and by whom it can be used—are one of the central grounds on which movements and their rivals battle for the direction of the future.

The Moral Boundaries of Culture

As I have argued, movements adapt, deploy, and generate cultural meanings to project their grievances to audiences, establish particular collective identities, and attract allies. In these processes, movements are enabled and constrained by symbolic systems, both in the availability of particular cultural meanings groups can deploy—as in, which meanings even exist for groups to draw upon—and in the extent to which these messages resonate with broader publics. Do audiences buy the messages movements are projecting? Are they credible?[2] Here, the core questions are: How much does a movement's particular construction of an issue match the audience's assumptions about the social world? Does it line up with their experiences of the social world, their sense of morality, their understandings of "how things work"? What does it tell us about society when certain ideas or symbols "resonate" more than others?

Communication studies show how audiences receive messengers from different social groups, along intersections of race, ethnicity, and sexuality, with widely divergent perceptions of their credibility and authenticity.[3] The same message can be interpreted and received differently depending on who is delivering it. It follows, then, that the same systems of power that ascribe groups with unequal levels of authority and credibility would also shape the ways their projected messages are accepted or contested. Understanding the identity of the messenger—in this case, the identity of the mobilizing group that invokes civil rights memory—is critical in making sense of how their message is received. After all, audiences are deciding not only whether the messages they receive make sense but whether it makes sense for a particular group to deliver the message.

Moral meanings—meanings that signify "right" from "wrong," "good" from "bad," "pure" from "impure"—are culturally embedded not only in particular behaviors, such as lying or stealing. They are also embedded in the social identities ascribed to groups in a system of power, such that two individuals may very well enact the same "immoral" behavior, but the perceived morality of the act will vary according to the ascribed identity of the group.[4] More specifically, within the racial capitalist system of power in the United States, studies show that immorality is ascribed to racialized groups like Black and Brown Americans and poor Americans, absent of any particular behavior or action.[5] By virtue of the sociohistorical system of racial formation under White supremacy, these identities are deemed "impure" and more subject to moral corruption. These embedded cultural meanings are often invoked in what is known as "dog-whistle politics" or "the politics of disgust," the racially coded appeals politicians use to generate perceptions of minority threat, as when President Reagan referred to the Black "welfare queens" allegedly draining the government through fraudulent use of the welfare state.[6] Politicians have similarly used morality to mobilize religious Americans to oppose LGBTQ rights, on the basis of "immoral" and "deviant" acts. These moral attacks inspired a countermovement by queer activists in the "Gay Is Good" movement, which hoped to use morality to generate support among progressive faith-based communities.

Given their powerful role in drawing symbolic boundaries between groups, moral meanings also become central in the politics of collective memory and the construction of victims and perpetrators. For example, in Anna Skarpelis's examination of the construction of collective memory after two different bombings during World War II, Dresden and Hiroshima, she finds these sites ripe for historical revisionism, where the German far right invokes moral equivalence among all war victims to deny war guilt, rehabilitate their image, and assert their own victimhood. As Skarpelis writes, "Collective memory is built around moral judgement, contesting the moral status of casualties becomes one of the primary levers in political projects of commemoration."[7] Yen Le Espiritu documents a similar process following the Vietnam War: the United States constructed a master "good war" narrative that depicted the United States as "triumphant and moral" where Vietnamese refugees were not the victims of U.S. imperialism but the grateful recipients of American refuge.[8]

TABLE 3.1. LGBTQ movement vs. family values movement

Year	National Context	Event	Movement	Master Identity	Political Ideology	Movement Goal
2002	G. W. Bush Era (R)	Take Back Miami-Dade (FL)	LGBTQ Movement	Sexual Identity	Progressive	Protect gay rights ordinance
2002	G. W. Bush Era (R)	Take Back Miami-Dade (FL)	Family Values Movement	Religious	Conservative	Repeal gay rights ordinance
2011	Obama Era (D)	Amendment One (NC)	LGBTQ Movement	Sexual Identity	Progressive	Reject anti-gay amendment
2011	Obama Era (D)	Amendment One (NC)	Family Values Movement	Religious	Conservative	Pass anti-gay amendment

Given the centrality of moral meanings in the strategic uses of culture, what happens when two different groups use the same collective memory to make oppositional claims? How do moral boundaries pattern these interactions? This chapter compares strategic uses of the civil rights movement between the LGBTQ movement and family values movement over two political eras through two major battles where the strategic uses of memory became central: the 2002 campaigns of SAVE Dade opposed by Take Back Miami-Dade and the 2011 campaigns of the Coalition to Protect All NC Families opposed by Vote for Marriage NC.

The Entangled Roots of the LGBTQ Rights and Family Values Movements

The contemporary LGBTQIA+ rights movement has a long lineage in the United States. Some accounts root the organized movement in the founding of the Society for Human Rights in Chicago, the first known gay rights organization. Others document the origins in the Mattachine Society, founded in 1951 by Harry Hay as the first national gay rights organization while the first lesbian rights organization, the Daughters of Bilitis, followed soon after in San Francisco. The conservative family values movement originated during the same time period with the shift toward a more pluralistic society that protected the rights of racial and ethnic minorities, women, and homosexuals. Laws were passed and policies enacted to protect individual rights rather than granting states the right to draw particular boundaries around morality. The era also witnessed such court decisions as *Stanley v. Georgia* (1969), which protected an individual's right to possess pornography, and *Roe v. Wade* (1973), which protected women's right to an abortion. To counter these waves of social change, the family values movement took on the courts and made early gains in southern states, many of which were later overturned.

Meanwhile, the 1969 Stonewall riots in New York City led by Black trans leaders like Marsha P. Johnson sparked the national gay rights movement as we know it today, turning small pockets of activists into a widespread movement for acceptance and equal rights. Though there were gay activists and leaders in the Black civil rights movement, the mainstream movement for LGBTQ rights led predominantly by White men did not initially consider itself an offshoot of the civil rights movement. However, there were important connections between civil rights and gay rights activists that would later become the grounds on which claims to memory would be made. One of the central organizers of the 1963 March on Washington was Bayard Rustin, a well-respected civil rights leader who was also gay. Further, many eventual gay rights activists participated in the March on Washington, learned from civil rights activists, and were inspired by the civil rights movement's repertoire of tactics and frames. One such activist, Jack Nichols, said, "We marched with Martin Luther King, seven of us from the Mattachine Society, and from that moment on, we had our own dream about a gay rights march of similar proportions."[9] In 1979 and then again in 1987 and 1993, there were LGBT marches on Washington modeled after the civil rights movement. Meanwhile, the family values movement was gaining prominence in the 1980s under the mantle of the "moral majority"; it became emboldened when presidential candidate Ronald Reagan placed family values at the center of his platform.

Using the collective memory of the civil rights movement was an early strategy for gay rights activists, who sought to draw parallels between the struggles of Black Americans in the 1950s and 1960s and those of LGBTQ individuals in the post–civil rights era. Scholars have argued that the LGBTQ movement shifted from a cultural movement centered on sexual liberation to a political movement analogous to ethnoracial interest-group politics.[10] Reflecting this view, in 1993, Robert Bray of the National Gay and Lesbian Task Force said, "Right now, gay people are the last minority against which it is socially acceptable to disparage, defame and discriminate."[11] Following the "minority rights revolution" that came on the heels of the civil rights movement,[12] many gay rights activists saw the 1990s as their "civil rights decade—one future generations [would] liken to the 1960's battle for black equality."[13] Prominent LGBTQ organizer Gregory King of the Human Rights Campaign Fund said, "The quest for lesbian and gay civil rights is the pre-eminent civil rights issue of this decade. I think Americans will look back with pride on the progress that will be made during the '90s."[14]

As the mostly White LGBTQ movement organizers began calling their work the "new civil rights movement," longtime gay rights activist David Mixner explained, "There were those who were reluctant to call us a civil-rights movement because they felt it would be offensive to African Americans, and for some it was, but we felt that until we really defined ourselves as a civil rights movement, beyond partisan identity, beyond political identity, and certainly not as a political interest group, we would not be successful."[15] There were, of course, Black Americans who were also gay, yet they often found themselves excluded from activist spaces wrought with the same anti-Blackness that infused society more generally.[16]

With their "new civil rights movement" in motion, activists turned their attention toward President Bill Clinton, described by Gregory King as "the Abraham Lincoln of the lesbian and gay community,"[17] organizing the 1993 March on Washington for Lesbian, Gay and Bi-Equal Rights and Liberation. As LGBTQ activist Tom Stoddard explained of the strategic timing, "The march marks the crossover of our movement, when we move from the political fringe to the mainstream. We have a movement that is ready. And we have a president who has finally endorsed our goals."[18] With the political opportunity in place, activists mobilized a multiprong agenda that included overturning anti-gay military policy, expanding the Civil Rights Act to protect homosexuals, and increasing funding for AIDS research.

While planning the march, organizers strategized to drive home the connection between gay rights and the civil rights movement, arranging for symbolic speakers like Reverend Jesse Jackson and NAACP chairman William Gibson. Torie Osborn, director of the National Gay and Lesbian Task Force, said, "We have a million Rosa Parkses in our movement who are all taking their own personal steps. After this march, the world had better get ready to talk about gay and lesbian people. After this march, these gay Rosa Parkses are going to go off and live their lives differently."[19] While the 1987 march had gone largely unnoticed with roughly 250,000 activists in attendance, the 1993 march outnumbered its inspiration, the 1963 March on Washington, with roughly one million attendees. Speakers like Senator Ted Kennedy compared the 1993 march to the 1963 march for Black civil rights, remarking, "We stand again at the crossroads of national conscience."[20] The immorality and injustice of denying gay Americans their inalienable rights was emphasized at every turn. As Linda Hirshman wrote in her history of the gay revolution, "They could ask the society to ignore or tolerate their behavior, immoral or not, in the interests of higher values like freedom or privacy," or they could assert their actions and identities were moral.[21] As the saying went, "Gay is good." Some organizers worried that in narrowing their focus to marriage equality, the movement was increasingly transforming from a countercultural force celebrating difference to an assimilationist movement emphasizing their normativity and traditional values, what Lisa Duggan called "homonormativity"[22] that echoes dominant norms of a White, family-oriented middle class and reproduces exclusionary power dynamics.

While LGBTQ activists grappled with these debates internally, a rival conservative movement under the banner of family values had been galvanizing to claim the moral high ground and public support. The Moral Majority had strategically morphed into a less threatening "pro-family" movement.[23] Reverend Lou Sheldon of the conservative Traditional Values Coalition explained, "Homosexuals are clearly winning the day. They are a viable political force. They are concentrated. They are committed to their cause in an unbelievable manner. But I believe they are beginning to peak and you're going to see a serious backlash."[24] In response to the tide of growing conservatism, LGBTQ organizer Robert Bray observed as much: "We're paying a price for all this newfound political visibility and power. That price is a backlash from the far right."[25]

Anti-gay legislation was emerging around the United States, from the repeal of ordinances protecting LGBTQ groups in Colorado to referendums linking homosexuality to pedophilia in Oregon, emphasizing the impure and immoral threat of gay civil rights. Gary Bauer, president of the conservative Family Research Council and former advisor to President Reagan, discredited the link between gay rights and civil rights, saying, "On principle, we're against extending civil rights protection to people based on what they do in bedrooms. If it passed, I don't see how you could avoid extending the same protections to transvestites or pedophiles."[26]

Family values organizers increasingly employed rival strategies to use their Christian morality to discredit the LGBTQ movement's uses of memory and, correspondingly, their emergent support among varied publics and growing coalitional base. In late 1993, Ralph Reed, executive director of the Christian Coalition, called for Christian conservative activists to use the example of the civil rights movement and its leaders to broaden their appeal and turn into "low-profile political professionals."[27] By 1997, Reed had developed a strategy called the "Samaritan Project," deploying civil rights memory to drum up political support among religious Black and Latino communities. Reed called on Republicans to make "racial reconciliation" the centerpiece of their legislative agenda and highlighted the project as a means for steering funding into minority communities. After quoting Dr. King, Reed said, "For too long, our movement has been primarily—and frankly almost exclusively—a white, evangelical, Republican movement, whose center of gravity focused on the safety of the suburbs. The Samaritan Project is a bold plan to break that color line and bridge the gap that separates white evangelicals and Roman Catholics from their Latino and African American brothers and sisters."[28]

Rival activists and civil rights leaders expressed skepticism about these strategies, which ran counter to the anti–civil rights stance of many conservative activists. Historian of the religious right William Martin noted the contradiction: "These are the circles that were once bastions of segregation."[29] Director of the ACLU Laura Murphy called the agenda "window dressing. . . . It is conceivable that black leadership could be siphoned off by Ralph Reed because this is a very slick and sophisticated snow job. . . . But it's a Trojan horse."[30] Michael Cromartie, director of an evangelical studies project at the neoconservative Ethics and Public Policy Center, confirmed Murphy's suspicions: "There is a huge untapped black evangelical constituency out there, and they don't have to be in the pocket of Jesse Jackson and the Democratic Party." Prominent social scientist Theda Skocpol noted that these strategies had power beyond submitting moral appeals to Black and Brown voters: "The Christian Coalition has always been very astute—especially Ralph Reed—about melding into the larger institution. I suspect the real goal is to make it look like they're not racist in the eyes of swing voters."[31] As President George W. Bush, a self-described born-again evangelical Christian, took office in 2001, the political stage was set for the rise of the family values movement.

The Take Back Miami-Dade Campaign

On September 7, 2002, the *Washington Post* published a story that sparked the notice of progressive activists nationwide. Regarding a local ballot measure in Miami-Dade County, Florida, the *Post* reported, "The election bears enormous practical and symbolic importance to national gay rights groups, which have sent dozens of volunteers to Miami in hopes of defeating the measure and discouraging repeals in more than 200 cities and counties that have laws prohibiting discrimination against gays and lesbians."[32] While anti-gay ordinances had gained popularity in the late 1990s, this 2002 political battle would become particularly consequential for the future of gay rights. Yet the campaign descended from an older conflict dating back to the 1970s, known as "one of the world's most famous gay rights battles."[33]

In 1977, beauty queen, singer, and orange juice spokeswoman Anita Bryant led an influential campaign to repeal an ordinance that protected gay and lesbian groups from discrimination in Dade County. Her "Save Our Children" campaign used Christian morality to stoke fear around homosexuality, proclaiming repeatedly, "Homosexuals cannot reproduce so they must recruit." Bryant's campaign was successful in repealing the anti-discrimination ordinance, a symbolic and instrumental victory for family values groups that shaped anti-gay measures across the country. As gay playwright Ronni Sanlo would explain later about her work *Dear Anita Bryant*—which laid out the devastating autobiographical consequences of Bryant's campaign—"Bryant was the catalyst that truly jump-started the LGBTQ civil rights movement in 1977. Her anti-gay crusade touched every state."[34]

Two decades later in 1998, the Dade County anti-discrimination ordinance was reintroduced to protect LGBT groups. Now, just four years later, the old battle was being fought again. Conservative Christian groups formed a "Take Back Miami-Dade" campaign to revoke the inclusion of sexual orientation in the 1998 "Human Rights Ordinance." The ordinance prohibited discrimination based on "race, color, religion, ancestry, national origin, sex, pregnancy, age, disability, marital status, familial status, or sexual orientation" in housing, employment, credit and finance, and public accommodation. Take Back Miami-Dade initially petitioned to get the issue on the ballot in 1999 but did not obtain enough signatures. After reorganizing and attracting a broader coalition, they were able to get enough signatures (over 59,000) to put the issue on the ballot in 2002.

However, unlike Anita Bryant's 1977 campaign, this battle took place on an evolved political and cultural terrain. Take Back Miami-Dade faced off against a coordinated LGBT rights campaign by Say No to Discrimination–SAVE (Safeguarding American Values for Everyone) Dade. Both LGBT and family values activists had fine-tuned their strategies over the preceding two decades as public opinion toward gay rights had warmed. Now, anti-gay sentiment required more measured, implicit expression. A poster in SAVE Dade's office highlighted this new context: "Undo Anita! Homophobia is soooo retro."[35] The executive director of the National Gay and Lesbian Task Force, Lorri Jean, described the SAVE Dade Campaign as "our version of the Freedom Riders. Anita Bryant wreaked havoc all over the country. We wanted to show the country that not only has Miami changed, but the world has changed."[36] To support the effort, the national task force contributed $100,000 and a trove of volunteers to SAVE Dade in Miami.

In the rival camp, the family values mobilization was led primarily by the Christian Coalition of Miami-Dade County, which attempted to gain the support of the local African American Council of Christian Clergy (AACCC) and civil rights group People United to Lead the Struggle for Equality (PULSE). While the Take Back Miami-Dade campaign was initially composed of mostly evangelical non-Cuban Latinos,[37] over time the LGBTQ rights SAVE Dade campaign had attracted many otherwise conservative Cuban Americans who were business owners and in positions of political power, including Mayor Alex Penelas.

For Take Back Miami-Dade, their failure to repeal the Human Rights Ordinance in 1998 resulted in a strengthened commitment to expand their networks to obtain the political support they needed. To oppose inclusion of

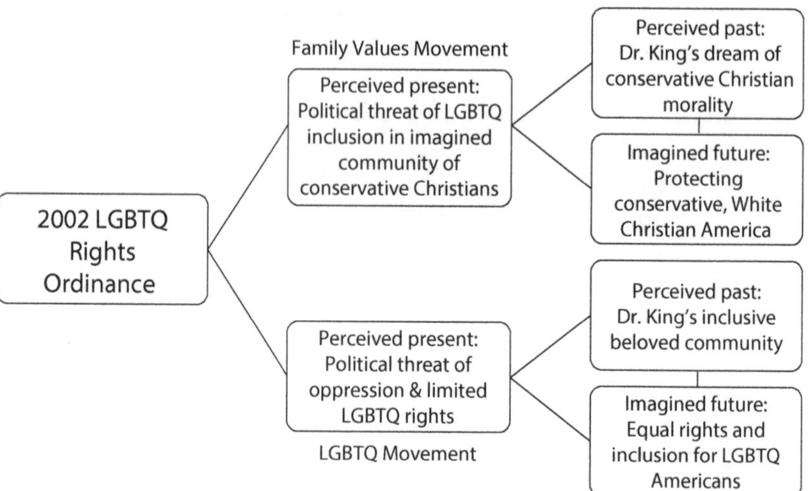

FIGURE 3.1. LGBTQ and family values movements' rivaling uses of memory in 2002 rights ordinance campaign.

sexuality in the anti-discrimination ordinance, they developed strategic linkages between the morality of family values and the memory of the civil rights movement to claim the moral high ground and discredit their opposition. Organizers contrasted LGBTQ civil rights frames with Black Americans' historical struggles to diminish claims of anti-gay oppression and discrimination. To establish the credibility of these strategies for the general public, they knew they needed the backing of Black community members. To rally this support, Take Back Miami-Dade targeted Black Christian organizations, first approaching PULSE at an April 2002 board meeting. The campaign distributed leaflets questioning the veracity of LGBTQ groups' claims of discrimination by drawing attention to their economic success. They read, "Homosexuals' income is nearly five times that of African-Americans!"[38]

Bess McElroy, the president of PULSE at the time, did not want to become an ally of an anti-gay campaign. She explained, "PULSE is a civil rights group that advocates justice and equality for all. Are we saying we're for justice and equality for some?" However, McElroy was outvoted and Take Back Miami-Dade gained PULSE's support. The AACCC's fifteen-member executive board also voted unanimously to support the repeal of the anti-discrimination ordinance.[39] The AACCC's support was particularly notable because the coalition represented 300 ministers and 250,000 parishioners from churches throughout the county. AACCC executive director Richard Bennett estimated that about 25 percent of the organization's members disagreed with the board and opposed repeal.[40] However, with the general support of Black leadership from these groups, the Take Back Miami-Dade campaign was well-positioned to develop a campaign that would receive public support.

Together, the leaders of PULSE, AACCC, and Take Back Miami-Dade developed a strategy that portrayed Martin Luther King Jr. as a historical symbol of Christian morality opposed to LGBTQ rights. Nathaniel Wilcox, former PULSE president, co-chair of Take Back Miami-Dade, and a Black American, led efforts to distribute campaign flyers displaying an image of Dr. King juxtaposed with an image of two men kissing, along with this message:

> Martin Luther King did not march or die for this . . . King would be OUTRAGED if he knew homosexualist extremists were abusing the Civil Rights Movement to get special rights based on their sexual behavior.[41]

The flyer went on to (falsely) quote civil rights activist Reverend Fred Shuttlesworth of Birmingham, Alabama, as saying, "Dr. King and I were not crusading for homosexuality. I've heard Dr. King speak out against homosexuality on many occasions. It is wrong to equate homosexuality with civil rights." AACCC executive director Richard Bennett was quoted on the back of the flyer as saying, "To compare the 'sexual preference' amendment to the Civil Rights Movement is embarrassing. It's nothing but a smoke screen. Our forefathers fought for us to ride the bus, be able to go to restaurants. The Civil Rights Movement has nothing to do with homosexuality."[42] Reverend Joe Silas, president of PULSE, said of gay rights, "Biologically it's wrong, spiritually it's wrong and with regard to civil rights it's wrong."[43]

An estimated fifty thousand flyers were distributed throughout Miami-Dade County to advance the family values cause.[44] Amplifying Take Back Miami-Dade's strategic use of civil rights memory to gain political support, Reverend Wilcox visited Black churches and preached, "I don't find gay slums. I don't find gay water fountains. I don't see gays riding the back of the bus. This thing isn't about discrimination, it's a smoke screen to mainstream the homosexual lifestyle."[45] Activating the moral boundaries of collective memory effectively required a two-pronged approach: (1) attracting public support to drive a wedge in the progressive base, *and* (2) discrediting the LGBTQ movement's claims to civil rights on the basis of their perceived immorality.

The pro-LGBTQ, Say No to Discrimination–SAVE Dade campaign had been busy implementing their own strategies to encourage voters to oppose the ordinance repeal. In response to the narrow passage of the Human Rights Ordinance during the 1998 campaign, the executive director of SAVE, Timothy Higdon, said, "Our support was not a landslide by any means, but when you really present the issue as discrimination, people see that. Also, people are very proud of living in a world-class [metropolis] where discrimination's not tolerated. So those are the core messages we're hammering on."[46] Similarly, George Ketelhohn, chairman of the campaign, said, "We're a world class city and we can't afford a small minority painting us as a community that favors discrimination."[47]

In focalizing cosmopolitan values like anti-discrimination and tolerance in their messaging, the LGBTQ movement had attracted wide support on the pragmatic basis that intolerance was simply bad for business. For a city economically dependent on tourism and LGBTQ nightlife, an image of a tolerant Miami was economically and politically advantageous.[48] Mayor Alex Penelas was outspoken in his opposition to the family values movement's campaign, saying, "We're trying to build an image of international metropolis, a bridge among cultures, but we would be saying, 'By the way, it's O.K. to discriminate based on sexual orientation.' That would just be wrong. We would be turning the clock back several years."[49] As part of his support for the campaign, the mayor recorded a phone message to residents urging them to vote against the repeal. The Say No to Discrimination–SAVE Dade campaign also had the support of prominent Black organizations like the NAACP and Urban League of Greater Miami. Politicians like Representative Carrie Meek, a Black woman, and local celebrities including singer Gloria Estefan similarly backed the "No" campaign, highlighting the family values movement's uphill battle against an increasingly progressive political and cultural context.

However, the family values coalition remained undeterred. As they developed strategic uses of memory based on their Christian claims to morality, they were drawing in conservative, Christian, Black supporters, and they were also unearthing divisions within Black and Brown communities, largely along class and ethnic lines. Their rallies were composed primarily of evangelical, poor, recent immigrants from Central America and Black Americans[50] while the gay rights opposition was supported primarily by business owners, wealthy community members, and political elites. Although the political and cultural tide moved in their favor, gay rights activists began to sense these tectonic shifts at the community level and knew they would have to face these moral claims head-on.

SAVE Dade's LGBTQ rights campaign reached out to national organizations for guidance in developing a counterstrategy that could challenge the family values coalition's claims to Dr. King's memory and, correspondingly, the moral high ground. Mandy Carter, a founding member of the National Black Justice Coalition, a gay rights group, reached out to Coretta Scott King to alert her to the campaign's efforts and the anti-gay flyer. King immediately issued a statement through the King Center in Atlanta calling for Americans to follow King's dream of equal treatment for gay men and lesbians, explicitly distinguishing Dr. King's position as one *in opposition to* the anti-gay movement, a position that would have included gays and lesbians in the "beloved community." Next, the American Civil Liberties Union created two new rival flyers for the SAVE Dade campaign, quoting Coretta Scott King: "If the basic rights of one group can be denied, all groups become vulnerable." Asked for comment, Take Back Miami-Dade's communications director, Eladio Jose Armesto, replied without a hint of irony, "Coretta Scott King is entitled to her opinion. She can't speak for her husband, though."[51]

Other LGBTQ organizers like Howard Simon, executive director of the ACLU of Florida, implemented a parallel strategy: invoking lesser-known figures from the collective memory of the civil rights movement to buttress King's support for LGBTQ rights. Speaking to the press, Simon described how King ignored repeated calls to remove Bayard Rustin, who was gay, from his inner circle. King refused to do so, and Rustin went on to organize the 1963 March on Washington that led to the Civil Rights and Voting Rights Acts. Simon said, "What King did with Bayard Rustin mirrors exactly what is happening in Miami-Dade. King gave Rustin probably the most important assignment in the Civil Rights Movement because he judged him on his abilities, not his sexual orientation. And that's all this battle is about today."[52]

In reaction to the gay rights movement's counterstrategy, Take Back Miami-Dade co-chair Reverend Wilcox distributed a second flyer using Dr. King's image and quoting Bible passages to reclaim the moral authority. However, simply discrediting LGBTQ activists' claims to civil rights on the basis of their immorality would not be enough; family values activists needed a more powerful moral claim of their own. Led by Armesto, Take Back developed a reverse-discrimination frame, using the language of "special privileges" to argue that by protecting sexual orientation under the Human Rights Ordinance, Christian conservatives' moral identities, their religious rights, were being infringed upon. Armesto argued:

> It [the ordinance] is being used to discriminate against institutions such as the Boy Scouts of America, who have decided that they're not going to allow avowed homosexuals to work as scoutmasters and leaders. We need to get rid of it because it establishes special privileges on the basis of sexual conduct, because it is used against institutions such as the Scouts that do not accept avowed homosexualists in their ranks, and because the promoters of this highly divisive amendment which is tearing our community apart are using the amendment to quash any criticism of any type of sexual conduct.[53]

The tactical innovation was a notable shift in strategy. Initially, the family values campaign had been focused on *discrediting* the civil rights claims of the LGBTQ movement as making illegitimate claims to the memory of the moral leader Dr. King on the basis of their perceived immorality. Now, family values activists were arguing that they were the ones experiencing discrimination, that Christian conservatives were the victims to be protected from gay immorality under the anti-discrimination ordinance. Through this processual interplay between rival movements battling over a human rights ordinance, the LGBTQ and family values movements were unwittingly shaping and reshaping the very memory of the civil rights movement.

Back in Atlanta, the King Center denounced Take Back Miami-Dade's newest flyer, but Reverend Wilcox retorted by noting that the King family allowed King's image to be used for a cellular phone commercial. He argued, "If [Coretta Scott King] can use his image to promote a telephone business why can't I use that image?"[54] Responding to the outcry from the LGBTQ side, Community Relations Board director Larry Capp said, "[Take Back Miami-Dade is acting] like it has special privileges over the King legacy. When did any one group copyright that strategy?"[55]

Meanwhile, news was emerging that the Christian Coalition had forged signatures on the initial petition to repeal gay rights. LGBTQ activists saw an opportunity to draw attention to the moral hypocrisy from a group self-identified through its Christian morals. The National Gay and Lesbian Task Force's executive director, Lorri Jean, commented, "In this campaign alone, they lied when they misrepresented the beliefs of the great Martin Luther King to the public; they lied when they said that Dr. King associate Reverend Fred Shuttlesworth supported them; and now it turns out they've lied about the signatures they've collected. It seems that these religious fanatics will break any Commandment in order to promote their hateful agenda of anti-gay bigotry."[56] The moral boundaries of memory were invoked once more: both groups knew that making a convincing claim to the memory of Dr. King was critical for legitimizing their cause and giving their group the cultural power it needed to win public support.

In September 2002, the Human Rights Ordinance went to a vote. Would the anti-discrimination clause that protected LGBTQ groups be repealed? As the news rolled in, activists erupted in cheers. The repeal did not pass, with a narrow 53 percent voting against it. Nadine Smith, executive director of gay rights group Equality Florida, credited Coretta Scott King's support in delegitimizing Take Back's Dr. King flyer as a major reason for the victory.[57]

Although the repeal did not pass, vestiges of the strategic uses of memory remained. The Miami-Dade campaign had set in motion new ways of thinking about and framing Christian identity and new ways of countering LGBTQ groups' civil rights claims. Family values activists increasingly deployed the memory of the civil rights movement to counter equal rights laws and amendments in support of LGBTQ groups, invoking Dr. Martin Luther King Jr. as a moral figure to counter LGBTQ groups' civil rights claims. In 2006,

Carolyn Garris, a research associate at the Heritage Foundation, a conservative think tank, wrote a widely shared report titled "Martin Luther King's Conservative Legacy." It read in part:

> It is time for conservatives to lay claim to the legacy of the Reverend Martin Luther King, Jr. King was no stalwart conservative, yet his core beliefs, such as the power and necessity of faith-based association and self-government based on absolute truth and moral law, are profoundly conservative. Modern liberalism rejects these ideas, while conservatives place them at the center of their philosophy. Despite decades of appropriation by liberals, King's message was fundamentally conservative.[58]

Garris's declaration was followed by a 2008 book by Clarence B. Jones, an old friend of Dr. King's, titled, *What Would Martin Say?* The book interpreted Dr. King's position on issues like diversity, the role of government, anti-Semitism, affirmative action, and "illegal immigration" through a conservative evangelical Christian lens[59] and provided a moral foundation for conservatives to "create a King in their own image."[60]

In 2008, the historic election of Barack Obama was perceived by the family values movement as an even greater threat. In his inaugural speech, Obama upheld the LGBTQ movement's claims to civil rights, invoking King's memory and connecting the Black civil rights marchers at Selma in 1965 to the gay rights protesters at Stonewall in 1969. He said, "We, the people, declare today that the most evident of truths—that all of us are created equal—is the star that guides us still; just as it guided our forebears through Seneca Falls, and Selma, and Stonewall; just as it guided all those men and women, sung and unsung, who left footprints along this great Mall, to hear a preacher say that we cannot walk alone; to hear a King proclaim that our individual freedom is inextricably bound to the freedom of every soul on Earth. It is now our generation's task to carry on what those pioneers began. . . . Our journey is not complete until our gay brothers and sisters are treated like anyone else under the law—for if we are truly created equal, then surely the love we commit to one another must be equal as well."[61]

By the end of Obama's first term, the family values movement had developed strategies specifically centered on discrediting the LGBTQ movement's claims to civil rights. In leaked documents, the National Organization for Marriage (NOM) detailed a strategy titled "Marriage: $20 Million Strategy for Victory." This was a plan to defeat Obama in 2012 by targeting religious Black and Brown voters to drive a wedge in the Democratic base. NOM's "Not a Civil Right Project" specifically targeted Black Americans and was detailed as follows:

> The strategic goal of this project is to drive a wedge between gays and blacks—two key Democratic constituencies. We aim to find, equip,

> energize and connect African-American spokespeople for marriage; to develop a media campaign around their objections to gay marriage as a civil right; and to provoke the gay marriage base into responding by denouncing these spokesmen and women as bigots. No politician wants to take up and push an issue that splits the base of the party.[62]

Bankrolled by major funders and crafted in conservative think tanks, these strategies were developed at the national level to discredit LGBTQ campaigns on the ground, and LGBTQ groups were being forced to reckon with this new political terrain where, among many conservative publics, conservative *Christians* saw themselves as the vulnerable minorities fighting for their civil rights.

The Amendment One Campaign

In North Carolina, the conditions were ripe for family values coalitions to take action. In 2011, with the first legislature with a Republican majority in both House and Senate since 1870, the North Carolina General Assembly began rallying support for Amendment One (SB514), a "constitutional amendment to provide that marriage between one man and one woman is the only domestic legal union that shall be valid or recognized in this State." The amendment would codify an existing ban on same-sex marriage, but the amendment's phrasing, "domestic legal union," left open its interpretation, potentially preventing the state from granting rights and benefits to committed but unmarried couples as well as same-sex couples.[63] However, given the obscurity of its aims and the proliferation of misinformation about the amendment, much of the public was unclear about what Amendment One sought to do. Just twenty-four hours before election day, polls showed that only 46 percent of voters understood that the amendment would ban both gay marriage and civil unions.[64]

Earlier in the spring of 2011, long-active networks of conservative organizations joined in coalitions to distribute advertisements, attract media attention, and lobby state representatives in anticipation of the legislative vote in September.[65] The initiative did not qualify for the 2011 legislative session, but the political move did not go unnoticed. In response to the proposed amendment, on August 30, 2011, House Speaker Joe Hackney accused Republican legislators of using the amendment as a political tool to mobilize conservative voters. He said, "This proposed constitutional amendment runs against the tide of history and has become a form of hate speech." Echoing the "bad for business" frame invoked in Miami a decade prior, he went on, "Modern corporations do not tolerate this kind of discrimination and neither should our state. But many of us recognize this unneeded amendment is not about rights or morality. It is part of the Republican political strategy to drive Republicans to the polls in 2012 while suppressing Democratic voting through voter ID legislation and cutbacks in early voting." Hackney emphasized that the discriminatory nature of the amendment and its underlying political motivations were "not about rights or morality" but about political power. However, in a special session in the fall of 2011 the initiative came to a vote once more, passing out-of-committee by only one vote.[66]

So began the campaign for Amendment One, scheduled for a public vote on the May 8, 2012, primary ballot. Family values coalitions coalesced under the Vote for Marriage NC campaign, while LGBTQ rights groups and progressive allies coalesced under the Coalition to Protect All NC Families. The ambiguity of the campaign names only contributed to public confusion. The pro-LGBTQ Coalition to Protect All NC Families was founded by the ACLU of North Carolina, which led the campaign, joining with local groups like Equality NC and allies at the Courage Campaign. The campaign hired a full-time organizer, whose team worked tirelessly to rally public support through a stream of campaign literature, statewide panels and community meetings, op-eds in newspapers, and grassroots efforts like the Know+Love Project, a website dedicated to sharing stories of committed LGBTQ families in North Carolina.[67] In the opposing camp, the family values Vote for Marriage NC campaign was composed of the Baptist State Convention of North Carolina, the Christian Action League, the NC Values Coalition, a coalition of African American pastors, the National Organization for Marriage (NOM), and several policy organizations and civic groups.

Amendment One was commonly perceived as a ban on gay marriage, a subject with indisputable moral valence for evangelical voters. As a result, LGBTQ activists grappled with how they would compete with rival groups to make clear moral appeals to constituents' values, particularly when their group was perceived as inherently immoral. As campaigns for and against Amendment One began unrolling through the fall of 2011, progressive coalitions framed the issue as a clear infringement on civil rights. Strategic uses of civil rights memory had been readily enacted by the LGBTQ rights movement in mobilizations across the country for over two decades and the central website for LGBTQ news was thenewcivilrightsmovement.com. The strategic groundwork for convincing linkages between LGBTQ rights and Black civil rights was already in place.

However, the opposing family values movement had learned to anticipate these strategies and had developed a repertoire of counterstrategies. Drawing from the national plan developed by NOM, the conservative family values coalition worked to discredit LGBTQ activists' claims to civil rights memory. As had happened during the Take Back Miami-Dade campaign nearly a decade

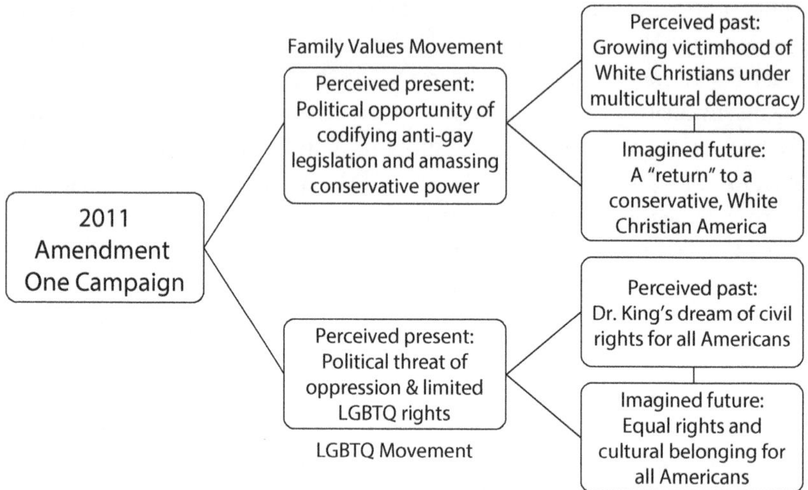

FIGURE 3.2. LGBTQ and family values movements' rivaling uses of memory in 2011 Amendment One campaign.

prior, invoking the moral boundaries of memory became tools by which family values groups would discredit their opposition, claim the moral high ground to attract support from religious Black voters, and drive a wedge in the progressive base.

In September 2011, legislators including House Speaker Pro Tem Dale Folwell gathered a group of Black pastors for a press conference in support of the amendment. The group invoked the memory of the civil rights movement to discredit the equation of LGBTQ oppression with that of Black Americans. Reverend Johnny Hunter of Cliffdale Community Church in Fayetteville said, "Blacks know what real discrimination is all about. [LGBTQ groups are] disrespecting . . . the foot soldiers of the Civil Rights Movement."[68]

In response, Reverend Dr. William Barber II, president of the North Carolina NAACP, issued an "Open Letter to Clergy Who Are Trying to Confuse African American Voters on Wedge Issue of Marriage Equality." He criticized the family values coalition, calling the wedge issue a "Trojan Horse trick." Calling out the family values campaign's moral hypocrisy, he wrote, "Those who insist on distorting and criticizing the President for doing his sworn duty insult the civil rights movement. These clergy ally themselves with the same extreme right organizations and people who have spent millions of dollars trying to overturn the 1965 Voting Rights Act, what most historians say was the most important achievement of the Civil Rights Movement." He continued, "These are the same extremists who are stirring the pot about 'gay marriage' and other code-slogans they dream up, all designed to divide and conquer the 99% who obviously can out-vote them. Their strategy is based on an arrogant assumption that we, the sons and daughters of the Civil Rights Movement, are too dumb to see through their Trojan Horse trick. They believe they can use wedge issues to seduce us into being a part of their scheme to deny LGBTQ brothers and sisters of their fundamental rights."[69]

Then Barber reclaimed the moral high ground, drawing on his Christian faith to emphasize the morality of standing with gay Americans as "efforts that clearly line up with the primary moral concerns of the Judeo-Christian faith." Of the anti-gay clergy standing with the family values coalition he wrote, "This intentional ignorance renders their critique suspect and void of credibility." Barber was not done. To drive home the moral legacy of the civil rights movement, he assured readers, "No matter our color. No matter our faith tradition. Those who stand for love and justice are not about to fall for their trick. No matter how you feel personally about same sex marriage, no one, especially those of us whose forebears were denied constitutional protections and counted as 3/5ths of extra votes for their slave-masters, who were listed as mere chattel property in the old Constitution—none of us—should ever want to deny any other person constitutional protections." Barber's open letter was shared widely and received significant attention from progressive groups nationwide, but the opposition was not ready to cede moral authority.

The strategic uses of civil rights memory continued through the fall and into the winter, as the pro-amendment coalitions continued to target Black churches. On January 17, 2012, Black pastor Patrick Wooden joined conservative activists Peter LaBarbera and Matt Barber in a rally against the Southern Poverty Law Center, which was considered a bastion of LGBTQ rights. The rally was organized by the conservative North Carolina Family Policy Council, which propped the Black pastor up as their main speaker. In a speech to the crowd, Wooden exclaimed:

> It's easy for African Americans when they're not thinking . . . to equate their beautiful blackness, their beautiful skin color, those of us who are darker than blue, it's easy for us to equate given the history of the country our plight with those who want civil rights status based on who they have sex with, and it's deviant, ungodly, unhealthy sex at that. I think that every African American ought to be appalled, ought to be angry, and should begin to wave their fist in the air and declare black power and say to the homosexual lobbyists, the homosexual groups, how dare you compare your

> wicked, deviant, immoral, self-destructive, anti-human sexual behavior to our beautiful skin color.[70]

The family values campaign rally also solicited the support of national backers in their efforts, including NOM president Brian Brown and the Family Research Council's national field director, Randy Wilson. A treatise called "Marriage Matters: Moral Wrongs Aren't Civil Rights—10 Reasons Why Homosexual '*Marriage*' Is Harmful and Must Be Opposed" circulated among conservatives on Facebook and online forums. The list, composed by the pro-amendment group American Society for the Defense of Tradition, Family and Property, read, "Homosexual activists argue that same-sex 'marriage' is a civil rights issue similar to the struggle for racial equality in the 1960s. This is false. First of all, sexual behavior and race are essentially different realities. . . . Same-sex 'marriage' opposes nature. Two individuals of the same sex, regardless of their race, wealth, stature, erudition or fame, will never be able to marry because of an insurmountable biological impossibility." The treatise made other arguments discrediting gay civil rights: "Inherited and unchangeable racial traits cannot be compared with non-genetic and changeable behavior. There is simply no analogy between the interracial marriage of a man and a woman and the 'marriage' between two individuals of the same sex."[71]

These "evidence-based" arguments, rooted in biblical texts, offered pro-amendment activists textual moral grounds on which to discredit the equation of LGBTQ rights with civil rights. As these arguments circulated in virtual spaces, a group of Black religious leaders traveled around the state speaking to audiences. Their racial identity and moral authority worked as a credible disruption of the strategic coupling of LGBTQ identity with civil rights memory. The message connected with many religious voters. At a city council meeting in February 2012, one resident rose to say, "They want to join themselves with the Civil Rights Movement? Martin Luther King would roll over in his grave. . . . To even in any way put that in the same context as the homosexual lifestyle is an abomination. Martin Luther King was struggling against racism. Homosexuality is not a race, but a disgrace."[72]

In response to these strategic claims to civil rights memory and its moral underpinnings, the LGBTQ movement needed a counterstrategy. In the spring of 2012, the LGBTQ rights group Every1Against1 began distributing a series of edited black-and-white images from the civil rights movement. In one image, segregated water fountains, mimicking the "White" and "Colored" water fountains of the civil rights era, instead distinguished the water fountains as "Straight" and "Gay." Another image depicted a restaurant window that read "We Serve Married Couples Only," while another, on the back of a bus, read

FIGURE 3.3. "Separate Is Never Equal" image counters Amendment One campaign. Every1Against1.

"Unwed Mothers Must Sit Here," with arrows ominously pointing down toward empty seats. In yet another image a sign next to a park listed prohibitions:

NO
Dogs
Lesbians
Gays
Bi-Sexuals
Single Parents
Bastards
Abused Women
Widows
Widowers

In the corner of each image, block letters read, "MAKE HISTORY. DON'T REPEAT IT. ON MAY 8, VOTE AGAINST AMENDMENT ONE."

On their website, Every1Against1 added text to the water fountain image that read, in large letters, "SEPARATE IS NEVER EQUAL." The campaign's website explained these images as follows: "Simply put, Amendment One is an unnecessary, thinly veiled attack on civil rights—a gross injustice to North Carolina's unmarried couples, children, families, seniors, women and businesses. If Amendment One passes, what's next? It would mark the first time the North Carolina constitution was amended in order to discriminate against specific individuals. This flies in the face of the state's tradition of amending the constitution to increase equality."

This strategy drew a parallel between oppressive Jim Crow practices, which discriminated against Black Americans and gave rise to the civil rights movement, and Amendment One, which was denounced as an act that oppressed citizens even beyond LGBTQ constituents. As legal scholars explained at the time, because of Amendment One's legal ambiguity it would not only ban same-sex marriage but also eliminate domestic partner insurance benefits in local governments, jeopardizing child custody and health care for unmarried couples and their children, and potentially invalidate unmarried women's domestic violence protections. The campaign emphasized the breadth of the amendment to issue moral appeals to voters who might not have mobilized for LGBTQ rights but were concerned about the plight of women and children. This strategy extended the analogy of minority struggle to a universal struggle beyond gay identity, circumventing the pro-amendment campaign's goal of discrediting LGBTQ rights as civil rights.

Some activists railed against this strategy, arguing that organizers were trying to "de-gay" the issue and obscure the religious community's targeted suppression of LGBTQ rights.[73] In defense of the approach, Jeremy Kennedy, campaign manager for the Coalition to Protect All NC Families, argued that focusing on gay marriage and religion would be a losing strategy. He said, "We're not asking you to make a religious or moral decision about marriage. We're asking you to make a decision about whether this amendment will hurt people, and it will." Governor Bev Perdue also spoke out against the amendment, focusing on its threat to women. In a campaign ad, she said, "Whatever your personal, moral, or religious views may be, writing discrimination into North Carolina's constitution is just plain wrong" and "dangerous to women."[74]

Other politicians sought to similarly avoid the question of the morality of gay marriage and, like the SAVE Dade campaign in the decade prior, emphasized the economic cost of such an amendment in a competitive global market. This group included officials like Harvey Gantt, Richard Vinroot, and Edwin Peacock III, who ran an ad emphasizing, "It is bad for business."[75] Similarly, corporate leaders like Bank of America executive Cathy Bessant and Duke Energy CEO Jim Rogers said if Amendment One passed, many businesses would reconsider working with North Carolinians. Rogers interlaced the morality of the issue with its costs for business when he spoke out at a meeting with business leaders: "If this amendment passes, we're going to look back 20 years from now, or 10 years from now, and we're going to think about that amendment the same way we think about the Jim Crow laws that discriminated against African-Americans. North Carolina is competing with the world for business," he said, and "we have to be inclusive and open."[76] Across other professional arenas, the North Carolina Pediatric Society and the North Carolina Psychological Association came out against the amendment on the grounds that it would threaten families and health care access. Debates played out in community forums, comment sections in newspaper articles, and on op-ed pages, not only in North Carolina but also on the national stage.

In May, former president Bill Clinton recorded a robocall phone message for North Carolinians, warning voters that "what [the amendment] will change is North Carolina's ability to keep good businesses, attract new jobs, and attract and keep talented entrepreneurs. If it passes, your ability to keep those businesses, get those jobs and get those talented entrepreneurs will be weakened."[77] Chelsea Clinton also spoke out against the amendment, as did numerous celebrities including Jeff Tweed of the band Wilco, actor George Takei, and musician Jason Mraz, who tweeted, "Yo North Carolina! On May 8, vote AGAINST Amendment 1. It's anti-gay, and takes away benefits from committed couples. Boo!"

In a viral video appealing to young voters, numerous indie rock musicians voiced their opposition to Amendment One for reasons ranging from "it is actually against my religion" to "it's the right thing to do." Musician Tom Barker cited a language of individualism, often invoked by conservatives, to explain his opposition to the amendment, saying, "This amendment doesn't just ban same-sex marriage, which is already illegal anyway, it also reduces the rights of all North Carolina families, giving the government more control over our individual liberties. I don't believe any government should have more power than the people it serves, and that is why I'm voting against Amendment One." The range of framings of the issue, often strategically avoiding the question of LGBTQ rights altogether (e.g., "same-sex marriage is already illegal"), revealed a campaign with great internal variation in where attention should be directed and the trade-offs of framing the issue in one way over another. What was clear among gay rights strategists was that conservative Christians would not be convinced that homosexuality was moral. Trying to sway these voters on the grounds of morality was a losing battle.

Yet the family values campaign for Amendment One was not without internal contestation. While the group of Black pastors, backed by the family values coalition, continued their cross-state campaign, some of the initial sponsors of the amendment withdrew their support. House Speaker Thom Tillis confessed he imagined the amendment would be repealed in a decade or two anyway and was not worth the effort. Conservative Democrat Jim Crawford, who initially voted to put the amendment on the ballot, withdrew his support in late April after listening to constituent concerns at a public forum: "I will definitely vote against it because I think it goes too far."[78] One resident fought back against Crawford's shift in position so late in the campaign, arguing, "It clearly didn't 'go too far' before that forum. What it goes to show is that even the people who wanted this on the ballot now, seeing the tide turning with conservatives and people of faith rallying against Amendment One, are running away from their decision to put civil rights of a minority on the ballot."[79]

By May, the anti-amendment forces of the LGBTQ camp had attracted a major political coalition: religious groups, libertarians, civil rights groups including the NAACP of NC and Southerners on New Ground, business groups, the governor and attorney general, and former Democratic and Republican mayors of North Carolina cities. With major political opposition to the amendment, broad multiracial coalitions, and the disintegration of Republican consensus over the amendment, the Coalition to Protect All NC Families seemed to stand a good chance of defeating the amendment. They had also outspent the conservative coalition, Vote for Marriage NC, by over $1 million, attracting popular celebrities and media attention to their cause. All signs pointed to a favorable outcome for progressive activists.

On May 8, Amendment One went to vote. In a shocking upset, Amendment One passed with 61 percent of the vote for and 39 percent against the amendment. The next day, the Protect NC Families Campaign wrote on their web page, "Together, we have proven to North Carolina and the entire country that fear tactics, discrimination, and division may compete with love, compassion, and solidarity in the short term, but we know that the time is coming for true equality. As Martin Luther King Jr. said, 'The arc of the moral universe is long, but it bends toward justice.'"[80]

Several days after the amendment passed, Governor Perdue shared her disappointment, likening the results to the violence of the civil rights movement: "People around the country are watching us and they're really confused to have been such a progressive, forward-thinking, economically driven state that invested in education and that stood up for the civil rights people including the civil rights marches back in the 50's and 60's and 70's. People are saying what in the world is going on with North Carolina, we look like Mississippi."[81]

In response, Black pastor Patrick Wooden, who had played a central role in the efforts to bring religious Black voters to the family values' side, discredited the governor's comments, saying, "We're not worried about it, to be honest with you, looking like Mississippi. We didn't shoot anybody. We didn't kill anybody. There was no bloodshed. No one was lynched or hung. We voted—one person, one vote. And the voice of the people was heard. I'm disappointed in the governor." Decoupling the connection between LGBTQ groups and Black Americans in the civil rights era, he said, "I've never seen a sign that says heterosexuals enter the front door, homosexuals go to the back."[82]

The Consequences

The battles between the LGBTQ and family values movement over the amendment had impacts that would shape political culture for years to come. At the group level, the Coalition to Protect All NC Families had developed an infrastructure for a coalition between LGBTQ groups and Black civil rights groups that continued to evolve after the vote. In response to the family values movement's moral uses of civil rights memory, the "Trojan horses" designed to drive wedges in the community, the NC NAACP's charismatic leader, Reverend Barber, drafted language for the national NAACP in support of marriage equality. The statement read:

> The NAACP Constitution affirmatively states our objective to ensure the "political, educational, social and economic equality" of all people. Therefore, the NAACP has opposed and will continue to oppose any national, state, local policy or legislative initiative that seeks to codify discrimination or hatred into the law or to remove the Constitutional rights of LGBTQ citizens.
>
> We support marriage equality consistent with equal protection under the law provided under the Fourteenth Amendment of the United States Constitution. Further, we strongly affirm the religious freedoms of all people as protected by the First Amendment.[83]

At the cultural level, the growing recognition of an increasingly anti-democratic political culture cloaked in evangelism also motivated new progressive religious movements to reclaim the moral legacy and mission of the civil rights movement. By 2013, Reverend Barber had spearheaded the "Moral Mondays" movement. Using grassroots organizing and civil disobedience to peacefully occupy the state legislature, Barber channeled the spirit of the civil rights movement to bring morality back into the civic sphere and to resist the growing swell of anti-democratic politics governing North Carolina and the nation. In his statement to the North Carolina General Assembly, "Why We Are Here Today," he explained, "As people of faith, we understand that we have been called to be the voice of the voiceless and the shepherd of God's beloved community. What we do here today is only what any responsible shepherd does to alert God's flock to the presence of the predators of democracy." Connecting the movement to its legacy he said, "Make no mistake about it; this is the beginning of something new in the Old North State. This is a new birth much as it was on February 1st, 1960 in Greensboro when four students from North Carolina A&T sat down at the Woolworth's lunch counter and a new generation rose up to freshen the wellsprings of democracy. It is a new birth much as it was in April of 1960 when the Student Nonviolent Coordinating Committee was born down the street at Shaw University, with students from colleges all over North Carolina and all over the South."

He issued a call to action: "We call on all residents of North Carolina who believe in the common good to pray and partner with us as we use the tools of protest and the tactics of nonviolent moral suasion to illuminate for the nation the shameful acts taking place here." Calling on Dr. King's words, he said, "We will become 'the trumpet of conscience' and 'the beloved community' that Rev. Dr. Martin Luther King, Jr. called upon us to be, echoing the God of our mothers and fathers in the faith. Now is the time. Here is the place. We are the people. And we will be heard."[84] Seventeen protesters were arrested that day. By summer, nearly a thousand had been arrested, and the Moral Mondays movement would only grow.

The traces of the rival movement battles extended into the legal arena as well. Family values groups developed new strategies to claim the moral and legal high ground on the basis of their own religious persecution. In 2014, back in Miami at the site of the SAVE Miami-Dade battle, gay couples had filed lawsuits seeking to overturn the ban on gay marriage in Florida. In response, PULSE president Reverend Nathaniel Wilcox, a central figure in the 2002 anti-gay campaign, compared the fight for marriage equality to Bull Connor's segregation campaign. As Commissioner of Public Safety in Birmingham in the 1960s, Connor had been responsible for the famously documented attacks on peaceful civil rights protesters by police attack dogs and fire hoses. Wilcox said, "Will Judge Sarah Zabel do to our voting rights what Bull Connor did to our civil rights? The blood of the martyrs cries out for justice. This lawsuit is hardly about the institution of marriage as much as it is about the constitutional right to vote and having our votes counted and protected."[85] Strategic uses of memory like these reflected an evolution of strategy focused not only on discrediting the linkages between LGBTQ identity and civil rights memory but also on establishing evangelical groups' own claims to oppression. These strategies emphasized the family values movement's marginalization as it sought to link the oppression of moral and religious values to racial oppression.

Similarly, earlier that year at a Utah rally against same-sex marriage, NOM president Brian Brown invoked the civil rights movement to claim family values were civil rights: "Throughout history, people of faith have stood up against gross injustices, stood up for true civil rights going all the way back to Rome . . . Christians stood up and said no. . . . We will organize, we will fight." Claiming the legacy of the civil rights movement, he said, "There is an attempt if we look forward in history to hijack and whitewash the truth of the Civil Rights Movement, and that truth is that leaders like Dr. King and others stood up precisely because of their Christian faith against overwhelming odds and were sometimes told it was wrong to bring their faith into the public square but they stood up and joined with other people of faith." He explained, "They knew that their arguments were based in reason. They knew it was unreasonable to treat people differently because of the color of their skin, but it was their faith that gave them the courage. Dr. King in prison, to have his home firebombed, to stand for the truth no matter what." Connecting the struggle for Black freedom to the fight against gay marriage, he declared, "It was faith, that courage to fight for the truth. . . . We are standing up for the civil rights of all when we stand up for the truth about marriage. . . . Blessed are you when you are persecuted!"[86] In claiming Christians were being persecuted for their moral values and religious identities, conservative organizers were establishing the family values movement as its own civil rights movement.

Meanwhile, at the grassroots level, LGBTQ groups mobilized a stronger coalition for the ground game. In April 2014, Equality NC and the NAACP worked together to hold a "Freedom Moral Summer" in honor of the fiftieth anniversary of the Mississippi Freedom Summer. Building on coalitions developed during the Amendment One campaign in North Carolina, activists marshaled Black, Latino, and LGBTQ groups in joint efforts for voter registration and community organizing. As conservative groups attempted to both discredit progressive groups' claims to civil rights memory and establish their own claims to memory, rainbow coalitions were forming to challenge the reactionary right-wing movements that were gaining popularity in the lead-up to the 2016 presidential campaign.

This chapter has shown how the political battles between LGBTQ and family values groups unearthed the moral boundaries of the collective memory of the civil rights movement and how these boundaries are continually contested and remade. Cultural constructions of morality shape both the meanings of the collective memory and the identities of the groups working to claim memory. These cases show how systems of power shape the cultural meanings ascribed to groups, namely how groups are perceived either as morally credible in their uses of collective memory or as illegitimate messengers by virtue of their immoral identities. As LGBTQ movements built claims to gay rights as civil rights, conservative groups anticipated these strategies, developed their own strategic claim to civil rights memory and the legacy of Dr. King's Christian morality, and discredited the analogy between gay and Black struggle. In turn, LGBTQ groups actively worked to discredit family values groups' moral claims to Dr. King's memory, recalibrating their focus by highlighting their historical links to the legacy of civil rights in figures like Bayard Rustin. By the 2010s, family values groups had developed new strategies to claim moral authority based on their perceived religious oppression. Where the remaking of the collective memory of the civil rights movement, of Dr. King's legacy, was a tool for conservative activists, shaping their strategies for attracting morally concerned publics, the strategic uses of the past enabled a powerful mode of cognition. By claiming King's Christian legacy and the moral authority of the "true," Christian America, it was possible to construct a social reality in which progressive gains for women and LGTBQ+ Americans were threats to evangelical Americans.

On January 20, 2017, less than two hours after President Trump was sworn into office, the official White House website erased all mentions of LGBTQ+ issues. With Attorney General Jeff Sessions and Education Secretary Betsy DeVos, the Trump administration's Departments of Justice and Education would revoke the Obama administration's school guidelines to protect transgender students under Title IX. Despite repudiation by celebrated generals and admirals, Trump moved to reinstate the ban on transgender people serving in the military and put forth a regulation to allow medical providers to refuse to provide services, including lifesaving care, to LGBTQ+ patients on the basis of their personal beliefs. These were but a handful of the rollbacks of LGBTQ rights that emerged during the Trump era, reverberating beyond his failed bid for a second term in office.

By 2022, the "Don't Say Gay" bills for parental rights swept state legislatures, whereby public schoolteachers were banned from teaching about or discussing sexual orientation or gender identity with students in kindergarten through third grade. Vic Basile, the widely celebrated LGBTQ rights activist and the first executive director of the Human Rights Campaign, reflected on the troubling rollback of rights after decades of hard-won gains. Having been at the center of mobilization efforts during the AIDS crisis of the 1980s, he recalled that the immense urgency of the political threat had driven everyday people to action. Drawing on Dr. King's famous promise, "The arc of the moral universe is long, but it bends toward justice," Basile offered, "The pendulum will eventually start to swing back. But God knows how long it will take for that to happen and how much more damage will get done in the meantime."[87]

4

"This Is the Beginning of Us Taking Back America"

IMMIGRANT RIGHTS ACTIVISTS' AND NATIVISTS' CONTESTS OVER THE NATIONAL BOUNDARIES OF MEMORY

> This I believe to be the privilege and the burden of all of us who deem ourselves bound by allegiances and loyalties which are broader and deeper than nationalism and which go beyond our nation's self-defined goals and positions. We are called to speak for the weak, for the voiceless, for the victims of our nation and for those it calls "enemy," for no document from human hands can make these humans any less our brothers.
>
> —MARTIN LUTHER KING JR., 1967

> When you are shut out of the process, you have to create new forms of entry. Whether or not they lock the front door to political participation because of our legal status, we will create a window and climb through it. They have left us with no other choice.
>
> —KEMI BELLO, UNDOCUMENTED NIGERIAN IMMIGRANT AND RIGHTS ACTIVIST

OVER A somber melody, a black-and-white image of a young Black woman flashes across the screen. With an anguished expression, she holds her head in her hands. In roll bleak images of impoverished Americans of all shades while a deep voice in the tenor of a Black pastor narrates:

> On Martin Luther King's birthday, we must ask, how would he feel about 20 percent of African Americans unemployed or underemployed, about giving amnesty and jobs to 11 million illegal aliens with so many jobless

> Americans; about admitting 30 million more immigrant workers when 17 percent of Hispanic Americans are having trouble finding work. About Americans of all races not seeing a wage increase in 40 years. *Was that Dr. King's dream?*

As the melancholy music fades out, the narrator quickly adds, "Paid for by Californians for Population Stabilization." The provocative 2014 ad ran nationally during CNN broadcasts, propagating the link between Dr. King's dream and anti-immigrant politics to wide audiences. In a public statement, Californians for Population Stabilization's media director, Joe Guzzardi, emphasized their claim to King's memory, saying, "As we mark the great Dr. King's birthday, it's safe to say, higher minority unemployment and no wage increase in 40 years were not part of his dream for Americans. So, why do so many of our congressional leaders today want to admit millions more immigrant workers to take jobs and depress wages when hardworking African American and Hispanic American workers can't find jobs? Have our leaders lost sight of Dr. King's dream?"[1]

As a well-funded nonprofit organization, Californians for Population Stabilization had been expanding its reach beyond state-level legislation to the national stage after President Obama secured reelection in 2012. Their expansion included working closely with John Tanton, the infamous White nationalist and founder of the contemporary anti-immigrant movement, and John Vinson, one of the founding members of the neo-Confederate League of the South. An organization with unapologetic White supremacists and neo-Confederates as members was claiming the memory of Martin Luther King for their anti-immigrant cause. As previous chapters have shown, this seemingly paradoxical strategy by a conservative group was not anomalous. In fact, framing immigration reform as a concern for minoritized American citizens was a long-standing political "wedge" strategy, generating confusion and dissension within otherwise progressive communities. This strategy was also a direct response to their rivals: the immigrant rights movement.

A decade earlier, immigrant rights activists had embarked on a nationwide civil rights freedom ride, linking their cause to the memory of the civil rights movement to great effect. In the years after, the immigrant rights movement built an infrastructure for strong rainbow coalitions with Black Americans, Asian and Muslim immigrant groups, and labor organizations. Nativist strategists had been observing and learning from these efforts. They could not simply discredit immigrant claims to civil rights. They had to reclaim the collective memory for themselves. After all, at the core of these battles over the strategic uses of collective memory are enduring questions about "who we are" as Americans. *Who* gets to claim and deploy American collective memory? To whom does culture belong?

Thus far, this book has shown how mobilizing groups make strategic links between their identities and collective memory. But what happens when mobilizing messengers hail from a culture beyond national boundaries, as in the case of immigrant activists? Is the collective memory still available to them as a cultural resource for political uses? How do immigrants establish their credibility as messengers of American collective memory, claiming a stake in "who we are" as a people? This chapter illustrates the dynamic process through which Latino immigrants, viewed by many American publics and policymakers as national outsiders, vie for inclusion using the collective memory of the civil rights movement. Comparing these strategies at two points in time across an evolving political context, these cases illustrate the cultural and political dilemmas that immigrant rights activists face when mobilizing American memory. They have to make critical strategic decisions about how to link their claims to the past. Who are "we" as immigrants and how do "we" fit into American identity (table 4.1)?

Through the Immigrant Workers Freedom Ride in 2003 and the Undocubus Ride for Justice in 2012, this chapter shows how immigrant organizers' understandings of "we" shifted as they came up against the limits of American collective memory as the path toward inclusion. As the nativist countermovement anticipates and discredits immigrant activists' strategic uses of collective memory on the basis of their perceived identity as national outsiders, activists have to innovate and reimagine their claims to national inclusion, what it *means* to belong.

The National Boundaries of Collective Memory

National identities are powerful social constructions, what Benedict Anderson famously coined "imagined communities," that bring disparate individuals together under a shared sense of identity. Institutionalized through laws, like citizenship and immigration policy, and culture, like dominant language and popular representations on television, these imagined communities become hardened in symbolic and material boundaries that distinguish between "us" as part of the nation and "them" as national outsiders in a way that *feels* natural and immutable to citizens. Holding these national identities together is the collective memory, the shared story of the national past, that gives the nation its distinctive character and boundedness in relationship to other nations and their peoples.[2] In his 1999 book *Myths and Memories of the Nation*, Anthony Smith describes how these myths of the past create the present through an "ethnohistory," a sense of shared origins that motivates collective loyalty over time and commitment to maintaining exclusive national boundaries.[3]

Yet these conceptions of national identity—the imagined community—shift over time in the wake of demographic change and waves of political,

TABLE 4.1. Immigrant rights movement vs. nativist movement

Year	National Context	Event	Movement	Master Identity	Political Ideology	Movement Goal
2003	G. W. Bush Era (R)	Immigrant Workers Freedom Ride	Immigrant Rights Movement	Ethnoracial/ Immigration Status	Progressive	Garner support for immigrant labor rights/reform
2003	G. W. Bush Era (R)	Immigrant Workers Freedom Ride	Immigrant Rights Movement	Race/Nationality	Conservative	Limit immigrant rights
2012	Obama Era (D)	Undocubus Ride for Justice	Nativist Movement	Ethnoracial/ Immigration Status	Progressive	Garner support for undocumented immigrants/ immigration reform
2012	Obama Era (D)	Undocubus Ride for Justice	Nativist Movement	Race/Nationality	Conservative	Close borders/deport immigrants

cultural, and economic transformation. For example, in the United States, the Immigration and Nationality Act of 1965, also known as the Hart-Celler Act, ended the long-standing national-origin quotas of U.S. immigration policy that had favored White immigrants from northern and western Europe. By 2018, the Pew Foundation reported that immigrants made up an estimated 13.7 percent of the nation's population, a fourfold increase since 1960. Fifty percent are American citizens. Many historians cite the Hart-Celler Act as a turning point for U.S. national identity, in concert with the hard-won legal gains of the civil rights movement to expand the boundaries of the imagined nation into a multicultural democracy. The expansion of boundaries was not without resistance and violent backlash, however. The legal inclusion of non-White immigrants in American democracy has motivated a deep resurgence of nativist movements. These anti-immigrant groups have policed national boundaries, whether through material force as in self-appointed militia groups near the U.S.-Mexico border or through culture, mobilizing publics by framing the expansion of national boundaries as a threat to their livelihood and existence.[4]

As a result, immigrants have long had to demonstrate their allegiance to the nation by holding on only to the "safe," "unthreatening" aspects of their ethnoracial identities, what Herbert Gans has called "symbolic ethnicity." Immigrants have been tasked with presenting their commitment to "assimilating" into dominant culture, melting into the rigid boundaries of the imagined community.[5] Even immigrants who reject this ideology behind closed doors have developed strategies of performative assimilation publicly to protect themselves and obtain a foothold in economic and social structures. Playing the part of "good Americans," performative assimilation, requires upholding the power structure, through both complicit acquiescence to Whiteness and pronounced anti-Blackness.[6] For nativists, this means that maintaining exclusive national boundaries requires making convincing cultural claims that the out-group will *never* "fit" or "assimilate" into the national identity and ensuring that the out-group does not have access to the imagined community.[7] As long as the collective memory of the nation is characterized by White Christian dominance, no level of acculturation will be enough for non-White immigrants to belong. Indeed, since the early waves of post-1965 migration, many immigrants and their children have learned that the "melting pot" model of White European migrants in the early twentieth century does not apply to them. No matter how "acculturated" and structurally integrated in workplaces and schools, many of these immigrants—Asian, Latino, Middle Eastern—are externally marked as non-White and continue to experience racism, xenophobia, and violence.[8] The persistence of a dominant conception of the United States as a White nation means non-White immigrants will be "forever foreigners."[9]

What does this mean for immigrants who have mobilized for better treatment, for belonging in the imagined community? This chapter illustrates the intra- and intergroup dilemmas faced by mobilizing groups positioned beyond dominant national boundaries. Specifically, this chapter analyzes the rise of the immigrant rights movement. To claim their place within the nation, immigrants must produce a convincing and credible identity claim to collective memory. Developing strategic alliances with groups who can grant immigrants legitimacy in their uses of memory becomes essential. In turn, the way the immigrant group makes this claim, the story they tell about "who they are" to gain allies, has significant consequences for the ways they either challenge or reproduce the system of power. These strategic claims to collective memory also shape how immigrant groups themselves understand and potentially remake the meanings of belonging.[10]

Forging Alliances across Cultural Boundaries

Studies of political communication and social movements show that to build strategic alliances across group boundaries, mobilizing groups draw on cultural meanings to generate bridges and a sense of commonality with other groups.[11] This can take the form of using strategic frames that emphasize a shared collective identity across group differences or frames that emphasize a shared ideology between groups.[12] When collective memory is the framing device, this can look like expansive interpretations of collective memory, as in Dr. King's "beloved community" that imagines a broad, multicultural collectivism.[13]

Within the Chicano/Latino immigrant rights movement, these strategic alliances have most often involved establishing commonality with Black Americans and highlighting related experiences of discrimination and oppression. Jennifer Jones shows that anti-immigrant political contexts generate a greater perception of "minority linked fate," shaping strong Black-Brown coalitions.[14] Still, as scholars like Vilna Bashi Treitler point out, anti-Blackness continues to trouble many immigrant communities committed to their own ethnic advancement, who may strategically compare their struggles to those of Black Americans while seeking the recognition, approval, and provisional acceptance of White Americans. As Bashi Treitler argues, "In their quest for increased racial status, ethnic groups with successful strategies did not threaten to bring down the racial status quo. Successful groups only sought to raise their own status within the hierarchy and did not question the legitimacy of racialized thinking or human hierarchies."[15]

In one study that looks specifically at how grassroots immigrant groups build alliances with Black Americans in Los Angeles, Sylvia Zamora and

Chinyere Osuji show that immigrant groups use "immigrant worker" frames focused on shared identity as workers essential to the economy and "social and racial injustice" frames centered on ideologies of social justice. The study shows that there are trade-offs to using one frame over another.[16] Emphasizing the strong cultural work ethic of immigrants, for example, can tap deeper ideologies of color-blind racism that pathologize Black "culture," positioning Black Americans as "lazy" counterpoints to hardworking immigrants.[17] These cultural strategies generate more division between groups than cohesion. Further, by positioning themselves within national boundaries as "regular Americans," immigrant movements can unintentionally propagate the ideological myth of meritocracy and the conception of a "model minority," one that positions industrious immigrants against "downwardly mobile" Black Americans.[18] Yet racialized communities can also deploy counterframes, either challenging the racialized cultural meanings ascribed to them—"we are hardworking, taxpaying humans, not criminals"—or amplifying their own ideas about who they are—"migration is beautiful, we are proud to be undocumented immigrants." In this sense, immigrants' uses of culture can—both intentionally and unintentionally—reproduce or challenge dominant systems of power.

For rival groups, disrupting immigrants' strategic alliances requires discrediting the immigrant group's claims to national culture and identity. The nativist group activates the national boundaries around culture to establish difference and opposition between groups. Nativist groups may also emphasize this cultural incongruity to claim that "special" rights for minoritized groups victimize other groups. For example, White Americans' claims that civil rights for Black and Brown groups disadvantage White Americans have been coined "White victimization" frames.[19] Similarly, nativist groups may use cultural incongruity to generate wedges between groups by heightening the perception of competition and threat between racial groups, as in the common argument that "immigrants steal jobs from hardworking Black and White Americans." How do these dynamics play out when the strategic device for immigrants' claims to belonging is the collective memory of the civil rights movement?

The Entangled Roots of the Immigrant Rights and Nativist Movements

Before turning toward the contemporary contests between immigrant and nativist activists that opened this chapter, it is helpful to understand how these battles are rooted in earlier social movements and enduring questions about American national identity. While popularly understood as a contemporary social movement, immigrant rights movements in the United States date to before the Cold War when working-class immigrants, predominantly from

Central America, Mexico, and Asia, allied themselves with labor movements. To thwart many of these efforts, the government targeted immigrant rights leaders for deportation. In the 1950s, the U.S. government deported over a million Mexicans while bringing nearly half a million Mexicans into the United States under temporary work visas for contract labor under the "bracero" program.

The Chicano civil rights movement emerged in the 1960s amid the wave of widespread social change. In 1964, prominent activists like César Chávez, Bert Corona, Ernesto Galarza, and Dolores Huerta worked to convince Congress to repeal Public Law 78, which sanctioned the bracero program. The next year, farmworkers went on a series of impactful strikes. Filipino farmworkers from the Agricultural Workers Organizing Committee began a grape strike, and Mexican farmworkers from the National Farm Workers Association founded by César Chávez followed suit. Given the common visions and ideologies of the two worker's rights organizations, they merged in 1966 as the United Farm Workers Union. With other activists, they lobbied Congress to pass the Immigration and Nationality Act of 1965, or the Hart-Celler Act, abolishing the National Origins Formula, which had established strict immigration quotas since 1921. Notably, the Chicano civil rights movement drew inspiration from a number of other social movements, including the civil rights movement, the Young Lords, the Brown Berets, and the Black Panthers. Student activists in particular were stirred by their Black counterparts. For example, at the University of Washington, the Black Student Union's radical efforts to promote campus diversity inspired Chicano student activists to join their efforts in collaborations toward joint civil rights. These early strategic alliances would be invoked later as evidence of the natural linkages between Black and Brown movements, Black and Brown solidarities.

Meanwhile, the ideologies of nativist movements are deeply rooted in American history, from the 1798 Alien and Sedition Act that deemed French peoples and culture enemies to the "American way of life," to the anti-immigrant movements against the Irish in the mid-1800s, to the forcible removal and incarceration of Japanese American citizens almost a century later. Nativism in the United States has rested on the social construction of "real" Americans as White Christians, drawing strict boundaries that exclude—with the support of law and policy, media, and state-sanctioned violence—anyone deemed "foreign," "alien," Other. Included in these threatening Others are actual Native Americans whose existence on these lands preceded White colonizers' occupation. Still, throughout U.S. history, these White-led nativist movements have played a powerful role in stoking fear of immigrants and the "threat" they pose as "foreign invaders," driving publics to batten down the hatches around "true" national identity.[20] The changing waves of immigration following the

Hart-Celler Act have inspired these movements of reactionary nativism, led by well-funded organizations warning of a "Great Replacement" of White Americans by non-White Others. These conservative groups include organizations like the Federation for American Immigration Reform (FAIR), NumbersUSA, and the Federal Immigration Reform and Enforcement Coalition (FIRE), with the support of militias like the Minuteman Civil Defense Corps (MCDC) and the Minuteman Project (MMP). The deep roots of these nativist movements and the well of resources behind them were consequential for the way immigrant rights activists understood the uphill climb ahead of them and the strategies they would demand.

Assimilative Inclusion through Collective Memory: The 2003 Immigrant Workers Freedom Ride

In 2003, immigrant rights activists declared they would embark on a nationwide freedom ride that would link the struggle for immigrant workers' rights to the Black civil rights struggle of the 1960s.[21] The original Freedom Ride had been organized four decades prior in the spring of 1961 to take on the continued segregation of the interstate bus system. Though the Supreme Court had ruled the segregation of buses and bus terminals unconstitutional in 1946 and 1960, southern states had yet to acknowledge the rulings and the federal government had not enforced them. The Freedom Rides were a powerful milestone for the civil rights movement, with over four hundred Black and White students on more than sixty rides through the summer months of 1961 and into the winter. The riders were ceaseless in their goals despite widespread violence against them, including attacks by KKK groups sanctioned by local officials. Publics watched in disbelief as media covered stories of riders dragged off buses and beaten by White mobs, buses firebombed, and hundreds of activists incarcerated for daring to exercise their constitutional rights. Outside the Greyhound Bus terminal in Montgomery, Alabama, freedom rider John Lewis was famously beaten and left unconscious, his blood pooling around him. The Freedom Rides left an indelible mark on the legacy of the civil rights movement, a testament to the young Black and White activists who were so committed to their cause that they would risk their lives for the promise of Black freedom.

In 2003, immigrant activists sought to remake civil rights memory in their own image. Generating a convincing link between the plight of immigrant workers and Black Americans' historical oppression would require a large-scale organizing effort, from gaining access to a collective memory that organizers understood was not their own to mobilizing immigrants of different backgrounds around a cohesive narrative and collective identity. Only then, with the linkage successfully welded, could the collective memory be deployed to garner public support for immigrant workers' rights.

Strategically Accessing Memory

The Immigrant Workers Freedom Ride was initially conceived in a brainstorming session among leaders of the Hotel Employees and Restaurant Employees (HERE) union in 2001. Thinking through strategies for garnering support for immigration reform, they understood the importance of generating solidarity among immigrant workers of different backgrounds with longtime labor activists. Union leaders received the backing of the AFL-CIO, and the organizing began.

Organizers first sought the support of Black civil rights movement leaders. Led by Maria Elena Durazo, president of HERE Local 11 in Los Angeles and chair of the Immigrant Workers Freedom Ride, they dedicated several months to setting up one-on-one conversations with Black community leaders. Durazo explained in an interview, "We wanted to be respectful. We had a lot of one-on-one conversations. If, in the end, people thought it was wrong, we wouldn't have done it."[22] The organizers of the ride understood that the collective memory of the civil rights movement was a cultural resource held by Black Americans and not to be accessed without their support.

The first strategy, then, was to enlist prominent Black civil rights leaders to endorse the freedom ride. One of the first leaders to sign on was Reverend Jim Lawson, a trainer for many of the original freedom riders. Lawson acknowledged that his endorsement was not shared by all Black community leaders: "There are some feelings in the Black community that immigrant workers are not a valid concern. This is a beginning. It's a step to launch a new conversation."[23] Organizers eventually won the support of the NAACP and the Congressional Black Caucus. Reverend James Orange, a civil rights activist beaten in Birmingham protests in 1961, was initially hesitant but after speaking to organizers he concluded, "When a worker is packed in the back of a truck and suffocates trying to get across the border, or when someone comes through the airport and gets detained just because his name is Abdullah, those are civil rights issues. The rights we fought for in the '60s are the same rights people are fighting for now."[24]

Forging a Collective Identity by Embodying Memory

By the 2003 planning sessions, organizers' main goals were solidarity among workers and broad-based coalitions. Maria Elena Durazo described the multilevel goals of the freedom ride in building multiple solidarities and coalitions

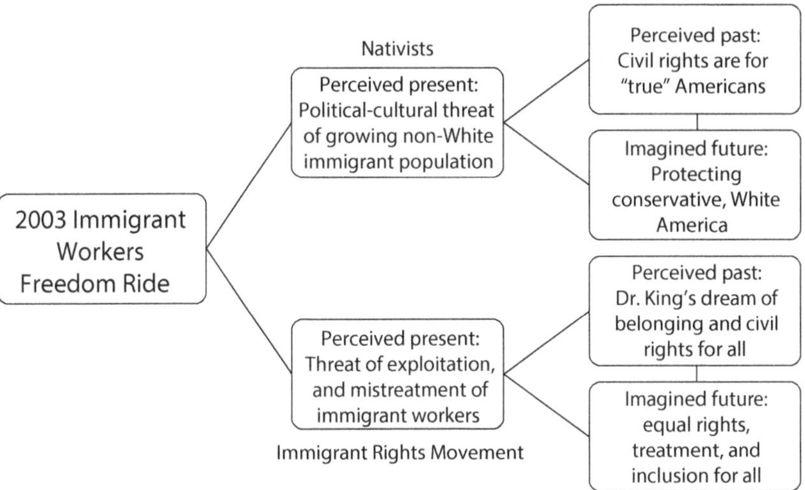

FIGURE 4.1. Immigrant rights and nativist movements' rivaling uses of memory in 2003 Immigrant Workers Freedom Ride.

across boundaries, organizing power in a new way: "We did it to work together on immigration, which had never been done before. . . . We wanted to strengthen the labor movement. We also wanted new opportunities to build relationships with the usual allies [grassroots organizations] . . . on immigration." Acknowledging the centrality of trust for these solidarity efforts, she explained, "We knew that there weren't enough experiences we could point to that built trust. . . . We needed to build trust so that whatever concerned us could honestly and sincerely come out into the open with positive discussion."[25]

Organizers knew that more than a rhetorical device—an invocation in a speech, an image on a poster—collective memory had to be *embodied* by activists to breach its national boundaries and generate a convincing link between immigrant workers' and Black civil rights struggles. To join participants together in an embodied whole, participants would need to understand civil rights history and its explicit connection to their lives and collective struggles. The organizers who were tasked specifically with rider education coordinated educational modules, including the history of the Black civil rights movement and its tactics. About the trainings and their impact on his understanding of Black struggles, one participant said, "To see how badly they were treated—one of the [original Freedom Ride] buses was even burned—it gives you a lot to think about. There's a lot to admire. It's not exactly the same for us. We don't have to go to the back of the bus. But still there is no respect at work, and we always, always live with fear."[26]

Strategically Deploying Memory toward Publics

Essential to the immigrant rights movement's strategy was framing their goals not as directed toward law and policy but toward the *soul of America*, the question of "who we are" and "ought to be." The chair of the freedom ride, Maria Elena Durazo, described it as a means to "wake up the consciousness" of the nation and direct public and policy action toward that consciousness.

So began the Immigrant Workers Freedom Ride on September 20, 2003. Nine hundred riders boarded eighteen buses departing from ten cities with over one hundred planned events at stops including the Memphis hotel where Martin Luther King Jr. was shot and all the locations in which major conflicts took place in 1961.

Generating credible links between Black Americans' systemic oppression and immigrants' experiences required thoughtful strategies that anticipated potential counterstrategies from rivals. After all, immigrant activists were mobilizing against a largely anti-immigrant context in which rivals had been long driving the narrative of "illegal," "system-draining" "free-riders." As David Koff, communications director for the Immigrant Workers Freedom Ride, told *Socialist Worker*, "This is allowing immigrants to tell their stories and put it into the context of national movement calling for drastic reform of the immigration system. There's no precedent of that, in the U.S. certainly. The debate has been dominated by voices that have targeted immigrants as the problem, rather than the system that has failed for years to function."[27]

Yet any old narrative would not do, and freedom ride organizers anticipated that competing and disjointed stories and images could derail the cause, allowing rivals to discredit their movement as a cacophony of alien voices. Approaching a scheduled stop, one staff member reminded riders of the importance of consistent and controlled images. She explained, "I want to clarify the ideology of the movement! That you don't carry flags of other nations. The reason I'm asking that you carry American flags is these people should see we want to be Americans so this is why we're demonstrating. . . . The idea is we are not less American than anyone else—we're all immigrants." Pausing to acknowledge the implications of suppressing their multicultural identities in the name of collective unity, she equivocated, "I'm not saying this as some dictadora. . . . The movement is mucho más grande than us being Mexicans or

from any other country. This is not a vacation, it's a civil rights struggle and we're not going to do it if we're not together. There's bus controversy and it's a distraction. . . . I just urge you all to keep it together! You have to give of yourself. Bottom line is we have to keep it together."[28]

Through repeated reminders of the necessity of cohesion, of minimizing ethnoracial difference toward a unified narrative of the riders as simply "American," riders had to forego their complex identities and layered cultural

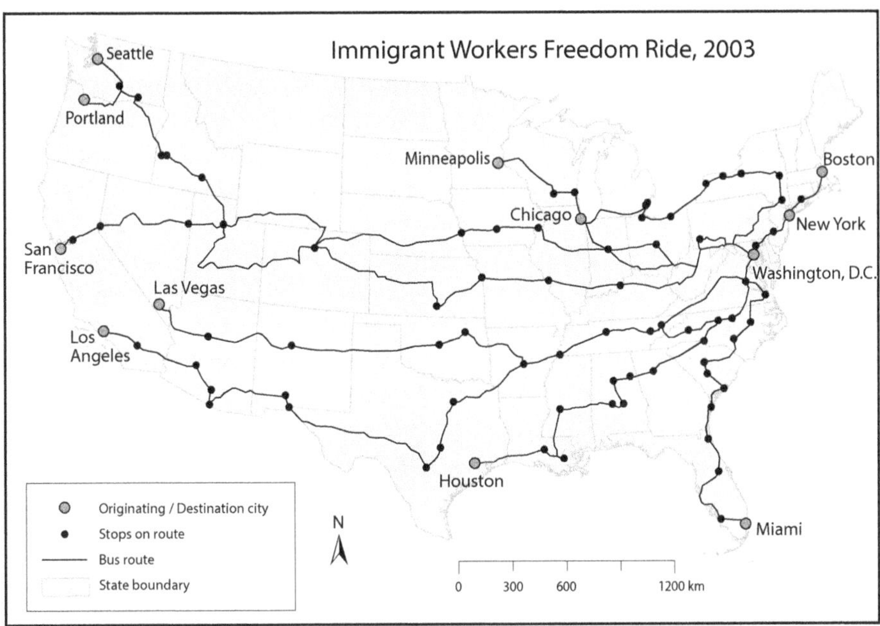

FIGURE 4.2. Immigrant Workers Freedom Ride route map. Kristin M. Sziarto, Eric Sheppard, and Helga Leitner, "The Spatialities of Contentious Politics," *Transactions of the Institute of British Geographers* 33, no. 2 (2008): 157–72. © John Wiley and Sons.

backgrounds. They were also continually reminded to frame their individual stories through a shared lens when speaking to the media so that publics could easily understand the links between immigrant experiences and the historical struggles of Black Americans. This strategic storytelling, however, also served another function among riders, beyond public view. As rider Jerry Atkin wrote:

> As we crossed the country in a bus dubbed Soul Power, I came to understand the importance of every story that we told each other, and of the beauty of every life revealed in the stories. I learned that these beautiful strands of life could be, and were, woven into something far greater than the sum of the stories. Taken together, these stories make up the true history of this country. As we traveled, I also came to understand that there was power in the telling itself, in the act of being listened to. We were breaking a silence and staking a claim to our history.[29]

The informal, individual stories shared on the buses among riders generated a sense of mutuality, of linked fate, trust, and collective identity in the imagined community.

These strategic linkages were also continually enacted through rider education and experiences as well as media coverage of public events. For example, during stops in Mississippi and North Carolina, labor organizers shared stories about how local retailers and hog-processing plants were generating wedges between Black and Brown groups to create racial tension and avoid contract negotiations. Bringing the shared experiences of Black and Latino Americans to the fore, the approach had some success in attracting Black unionists to support the immigrant riders. Willie Robinson, president of the Coalition of Black Trade Unionists in Southern California, said, "Since they are here, they might as well have certain rights. It might eliminate them from being scabs."[30]

Drawing important lessons from the civil rights movement, freedom ride organizers knew that stories would not be enough. Immigrants' claims to an American collective memory could not be merely stated; they had to be *demonstrated*. A credible claim to national inclusion, one that would grab media and public attention, would require some drama and emotional intensity. As a result, the bus routes included eight hundred miles along U.S. Immigration and Customs Enforcement (ICE) jurisdiction, including twenty hours at the border. With the support of volunteer lawyers, organizers prepared the riders for the high-risk action, training them as to their rights and the planned response should they be detained. They expected the bus to be stopped by ICE in Arizona and Texas. If stopped and asked about their immigration status, riders were directed to announce their right to remain silent. To further generate the connection between the immigrant ride and the original Black Freedom Rides, riders would sing civil rights era protest songs.

But not all the riders were comfortable with the high-risk strategy. Without any guarantee that they would not be permanently detained and deported, many riders were anxious, thinking of their families and children back home. The blanket strategy for inclusion, of making claims to American identity by demonstrating a wholesale image of unjust oppression analogous to that of Black Americans, entailed immense trade-offs for the riders.

Just as the organizers anticipated, as one of the buses pulled into the Sierra Blanca checkpoint on day four of the ride, ICE agents boarded the bus and began demanding identification and documentation from some of the riders. Everyone except the journalists on board followed their training and refused to comply, showing agents their name tags that said "right-to-remain-silent." Sociologist and rider Angela Jamison's field notes document the terrifying moment:

> After regrouping inside a low, beige portable building next to the highway, officers returned to the buses with dogs, ushering riders and staff alike—now singing in unison "We Shall Overcome" and many in wide-eyed

> tears—into cells inside. Each was separated from the rest and questioned, cajoled or mildly harassed. Many cried throughout the confrontation, but no one responded to officers. At around 10:30 officers released the detainees and ordered that most of them board the first bus; and they returned, stood cramped in the aisles while continuing to sing and cry. At 11:00 without explanation, officers ordered the buses to leave immediately. It was unclear if anyone had been left behind, or if they would be followed. "No one say a word!" Durazo, Gabriela and Luís each shouted as they drove several miles through the desert; everyone complied. They stopped at an exit and everyone stood between the two buses for a headcount in quiet shock. When Durazo shouted out that all were accounted for, staff, riders and most of the journalists broke into a sixty-minute euphoria of embraces, tears, some weeping and prayers of thanks. The interpersonal solidarity was total, and for once it coincided with an effective media portrayal.

Later, a rider would call the moment "the passion play that made us all American citizens."[31] Organizers also arranged for stops at historical civil rights sites to make explicit connections between the experiences of immigrants and Black Americans. The symbolic sites of civil rights struggle generated powerful emotions that both drew a movement together in shared collective identity and performed this identity to media and observing publics. Many riders were also expressing embodied connections to American history and one another. One rider wrote, "As we crossed state lines, generations, cultures, and languages, we came together in what Martin Luther King Jr. would have recognized as a temporary Beloved Community. Our signature chant changed from 'Si se puede!' ('Yes we can!') to 'Somos uno' ('We are one'). We were building the world we wanted, the world we deserved. We were making the road by riding."[32]

Particularly critical to the credibility of these claims to memory was the support of powerful Black leaders who legitimized the use of collective memory by non-Black immigrants. At a rally in Denver, the AFL-CIO arranged for civil rights leader James Orange to give a keynote. In Tucson, Arizona, Black Reverend John M. Fife said at another rally, "Then, as now, let the freedom buses roll. Then, as now, vigilantes terrorized and discriminated with guns. Then, as now, there is a moral and ethical issue that must unite church and synagogue and mosque and labor and civil rights and mainstream America in a movement to change the course of history."[33]

The ride was further bolstered by one of the most symbolic living gatekeepers of the collective memory, former civil rights leader John Lewis, who called the freedom ride "a movement that carries the struggle for civil rights for all forward into the new century." In an op-ed in the *Washington Post* on

September 30, 2003, he wrote, "Like the Freedom Rides of 1961, Freedom Ride 2003 calls on ordinary people to do extraordinary things . . . these new Freedom Riders are just like you and me—seekers after the American dream, makers of the American dream." Turning toward the past, Lewis wrote, "Just a little more than 40 years ago, on April 16, 1963, the Rev. Martin Luther King Jr. wrote from his jail cell in Birmingham, Ala., words whose meaning comes alive again in the Immigrant Workers Freedom Ride—words that fuel these new Freedom Buses as they travel across the ever-changing human landscape of America: 'Injustice anywhere is a threat to justice everywhere. We are caught in an inescapable network of mutuality, tied in a single garment of destiny. Whatever affects one directly, affects all indirectly.'" Lewis concluded with a call for Americans to "welcome the Freedom Riders, listen to them and join them in the continuing fight for civil rights and human dignity." The powerful words legitimized immigrant activists' strategic use of collective memory and drew public attention toward their cause.

Nativist Rivals React

As media coverage of the Immigrant Workers Freedom Ride grew, the rival nativist movement emerged in protest. Leaders of national organizations strategized how to discredit immigrant workers' claims to American civil rights. Dave Rey, associate director of the Federation for American Immigration Reform (FAIR), an organization that opposed "illegal immigration," said, "Civil rights have nothing to do with the opening up of our borders. . . . They are riding on the coattails of a completely different movement."[34] More nefariously, FAIR deployed an action alert to its members and followers, encouraging them to flood the Department of Homeland Security with demands to "arrest any illegal aliens" on the freedom rides.

Barbara Coe, head of the California Coalition for Immigration Reform, issued members an urgent "Action Now!" message: "These people are criminals. As such, they have NO 'RIGHTS' other than emergency medical care and humane treatment as they are being DEPORTED! We can only wonder how many in this group of foreign invaders have robbed, raped and possibly murdered law-abiding American citizens and legal residents." Discrediting the immigrant riders' very use of an American cultural resource, Mark Krikorian, director of the conservative Center for Immigration Studies, wrote in the *National Review*,

> If you wanted a way of persuading Republican congressmen to support something, the last thing you'd do is have the AFL-CIO organize a bus convoy of illegal aliens appropriating the rhetoric of the civil-rights

> movement. . . . And yet, this is just what the open-border crowd has done . . . the very fact that illegal aliens are hijacking the terminology of a brave struggle for liberty by American citizens is an abomination.

Comparing immigrants to the original civil rights activists, Rey continued,

> The real Freedom Riders traveled the South to challenge Jim Crow segregation in restrooms, restaurants, and other public facilities; a mob in Alabama attacked them, set one of the buses on fire, and beat some of the fleeing passengers. Other civil rights protesters, of course, faced police dogs, high-pressure hoses, and firebombs. The idea that lobbying for amnesty is in any way comparable to this is ludicrous.

Citing John Lewis's op-ed in support of the immigrant activists, Rey threw skepticism behind the racial commitments of the immigrant movement, arguing, "defending the interests of black Americans is not on the agenda of the open-borders movement."[35]

While the national leadership of the nativist movement worked to discredit the immigrant rights movement's claims to American memory, anti-immigrant protesters on the ground projected a disorganized cacophony of messages. A self-described "clearinghouse" for conservative, grassroots organizations "interested in immigration reform," the Million American March organized counterprotests called "welcoming committees" at every stop on the freedom ride. Protesting groups included conservatives, libertarians, nativists, White supremacists, neo-Nazis, and such organizations as Georgians for Immigration Reduction, 9/11 Families for a Secure America, the American Border Alliance, the Counsel of Conservative Citizens, Our Race Is Our Nation, Knights of the Ku Klux Klan, and the White Revolution. Protesters held a variety of signs with such slogans as: "Being Illegal Is Not a Civil Right," "Oppose Illegal Immigration and the Terrorism That It Causes," and "I Never Asked for Diversity." After a Chicago rally, one anti-immigrant protester wrote of the jarring sensation of finding herself among neo-Nazis with whom she did not associate, illustrating the lack of organization among the counterprotesters. Of the immigrant freedom riders' cohesion, the anti-immigrant protester wrote, "It broke my heart to . . . see their solidarity. Our fight is cut out for us!"[36]

Rival mobilizations were relatively small and contained at these stops, but nativist groups gathered for the largest counterprotest the day before the conclusion of the freedom ride on October 3 in Liberty Park, New Jersey. Hal Turner, a local radio show host known for posting tirades against Black Americans, Jewish people, gay people, and other minorities, was at the center of organizing efforts. On his show he said to listeners, "You have a bunch of illegal aliens boarding buses to demand amnesty, with the Statue of Liberty as a backdrop. I say we should lock them all up and send them back to the cesspools where they came from. People don't want them here."[37] Turner's nativist message attracted White supremacist groups, including the National Alliance, Aryan Nation, and Ku Klux Klan. The White racial solidarity of the nativist movement excluded otherwise receptive conservative audiences who were on the fence about immigrant rights. Instead of discrediting the immigrant workers' uses of American collective memory, the nativist countermobilization strengthened the linkages between immigrant rights and Black civil rights. Images of White nationalists yelling at nonviolent immigrant activists harkened to the very historical moment immigrant rights activists sought to project.

Most centrally, the rival movement failed to develop a counterstrategy to discredit the immigrant rights movement on the ground. In the grassroots arena, immigrant rights activists were actively embodying and performing collective memory, legitimized by speeches from civil rights leaders in rallies against the backdrop of civil rights monuments, singing "We Shall Overcome" amid throngs of journalists reporting on the cultural resonance of the moment.[38] While anti-immigrant leaders criticized the equation of immigrant rights with civil rights at the national level, these calls did not manifest in strategies on the ground. Instead, disparate anti-immigrant groups without a cohesive strategy joined in ad hoc counterprotests without a unified message.

Increasingly Gnarled Branches of Collective Memory

And, just like that, the ride was over, the media coverage faded, and the prospect of immigration reform receded from public view once more. While many White Americans' consciousness of the immigrant struggle would dissipate, replaced by the perceived threat of Islamist terrorism and a burgeoning war in Iraq, immigrant communities' political consciousness was irrevocably awakened. These new activists imagined their collective agency, political and cultural opportunities, for the first time, and their goals were not merely policy changes. As rider Jerry Atkin wrote, "So if the Freedom Ride was not a quick fix, perhaps it was a catalyst for change. As we rolled across the country, communities came together to support the Freedom Riders in a way that had not happened since 9/11. Everywhere we went people seemed hungry for justice, and we gave them a chance to remember the power of their vision, the goodness of this work. The ripples spread out from the Freedom Ride in our lives and the communities around us."[39] The consequences of the rides were felt among the group through a new sense of collective identity and linked fate, but they were also felt individually for immigrants who were learning the ropes of the American political system, gaining a sense of efficacy and empowerment in collective action, and understanding the potential limits of an assimilationist strategy.

The Immigrant Workers Freedom Ride may not have produced immigration reform, but through the successful embodiment of collective memory, the convincing story about "who we are," it built a durable multiracial coalition for subsequent mobilizations toward "who we ought to be."[40] Beyond the new sense of political consciousness, the ride generated concrete training in community organizing and activism. The foundation had been built for a sustained movement. Six months after the final stop on the freedom ride, thirty members of various immigrant rights organizations gathered for leadership training, nine of whom were former riders. Growing groups and coalitions continued to meet, from the newly energized Annual Caucus of the Rural Organizing Project to teach-ins about immigration the following year.

Driven by the efforts of the freedom ride, the Immigrant Workers Freedom Coalition, including the National Immigration Forum and National Council of La Raza, formed the Coalition for Comprehensive Immigration Reform (CCIR), supported by the AFL-CIO and with ties to the Center for American Progress. With the multisector support produced through the Immigrant Workers Freedom Ride, the CCIR obtained enough financial and organizational backing to continue an immigrant civil rights movement. For example, in 2004, the CCIR used grants from the Atlantic Philanthropies and the Evelyn and Walter Haas Jr. Fund to sponsor the New American Freedom Summer. Their organizing drew from the strategies of the original Freedom Summer of 1964, which sought to drum up student activism. CCIR organizers concentrated their efforts on key battleground states of Arizona and Florida. As one ride organizer, vice president of the Service Employees International Union Eliseo Medina, explained, "We need to organize and use the power of our vote. That's the next step in the struggle. It's not just about immigrant workers' rights, but about living wages, about decent education. This is the beginning of us taking back America."[41]

At the same time, the rival nativist movement was also developing new strategies after witnessing the outpouring of multiracial public support for the Immigrant Workers Freedom Ride. Leaked documents from conservative political strategist Frank Luntz indicated a strategic move toward emphasizing the criminality and illegality of immigrants to head off arguments about immigrant rights. The twenty-five-page strategic plan from 2005 titled "Respect for the Law & Economic Fairness: Illegal Immigration Prevention" highlights "Words that Work" as talking points for Republican politicians seeking political support. Luntz warned campaigning politicians, "Be careful of your language; words matter in this upcoming debate." These sound bites juxtaposed frightening language about terrorism and criminality with punitive language about border security and law and order. The strategic frames emphasized American values and the American dream and positioned "illegal immigrants" as threats to these core principles. More tellingly, the strategy emphasized the difference between legal immigrants who "played by the rules" and "lawbreakers," seeking to drive a wedge among immigrant, particularly Latino, voters. Luntz's plan read, "Republicans have made significant inroads into the Hispanic community over the past decade, and it would be a shame if poorly chosen words and overheated rhetoric were to undermine the credibility the party has built within the community. Communicating your position on illegal immigration will require a different approach among Hispanics and Latinos." To wedge the Latino base, Luntz prescribed trading the frame of punishment, which predominantly resonated among White conservatives, for a language of *accountability*, emphasizing hope and opportunity in an assimilative ideal of inclusion. "They believe in the American Dream," he wrote of Latino and Hispanic voters.[42]

As the new immigrant rights movement was growing in the 2000s, enacting powerful uses of civil rights memory to build coalitions and gain political support, conservative groups were organizing a significant political infrastructure in opposition, strategizing to both discredit immigrant claims to American civil rights and establish themselves as the credible protectors of American identity and its borders.

Intersectional Belonging through Cross-National Memories: The Undocubus Freedom Ride for Justice

As the 2012 presidential election approached, President Obama was poised to face off against Republican nominee Mitt Romney. Many Latino communities, feeling the reverberations of a covert "Deporter-in-Chief," felt unconvinced that President Obama and the Democratic Party deserved their unequivocal support. That summer, the Ruckus Society, a nonprofit organization dedicated to training activists in nonviolent action, joined with the National Day Laborer Network to organize a "ride for justice" among undocumented immigrants. The ride had multiple goals: mobilizing undocumented immigrants from fear into action; generating political support for immigrant rights (specifically undocumented immigrants' rights); and renewing political pressure on lawmakers to enact immigration reform. Like the Immigrant Workers Freedom Ride a decade earlier, organizers had to think strategically about how to access, embody, and deploy civil rights memory in a political context that had shifted significantly since the George W. Bush administration.

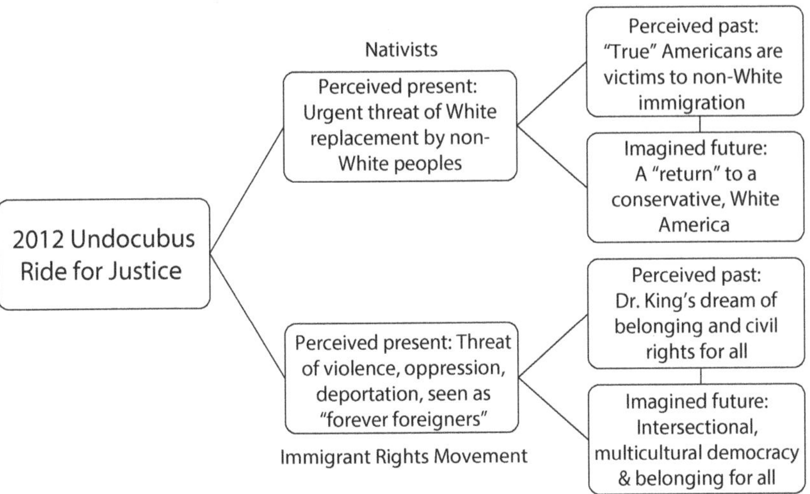

FIGURE 4.3. Immigrant rights and nativist movements' rivaling uses of memory in 2012 Undocubus Ride for Justice.

Strategically Embodying Memories

As deportations increased and anti-immigrant movements gained power, undocumented immigrants were coming to understand that their silence could pose a greater risk than activism. At least public visibility through action could garner some level of protection, where those in power might be less likely to take extreme punitive measures under the light of news cameras and public attention. But beyond the political threats that shaped the new rumblings of collective action, there was a deeper understanding of identity and belonging developing among undocumented activists.

Undocubus rider Kemi Bello recalled immigrating from Nigeria to Houston, Texas, at age six. She did not learn she was undocumented until she was applying to college. She recalled, "I noticed the third question was, 'Are you a U.S. citizen, are you a permanent resident, or are you an international student?' They were all check boxes, and there was no fourth box, no Other, no Miscellaneous."[43] That moment sparked a meaningful trajectory, a tectonic shift in her sense of self and belonging. She had long imagined inclusion would require shedding herself of the cloak of illegality to fold into some imagined American identity, playing the part of a model "Dreamer" to prove her worth. Now, she and many other young undocumented immigrants were seeing immigrants who were longtime citizens, exemplars of the American dream, being criminalized and othered in spite of their legal inclusion. Citizenship, assimilation, a legal status did not guarantee belonging. Bello explained that to be a Dreamer was to "pin all of our experience on one piece of legislation, and that piece of legislation doesn't define me."[44]

Countless undocumented activists shared this political awakening, of moving away from an understanding of belonging as being "folded in," "melted," assimilated to one American identity. Instead, they would proudly retain their complex and variegated intersectional experiences and fuse them with American memory. They would constitute a field of multicolored butterflies emerging from their cocoons to fill the sky in their undeniable existence, changing the very meaning of American belonging. Bello explained, "Survival as an undocumented person has reached a critical mass. It means pushing back against the entire political system itself, all while your lack of papers bars you from the most basic form of civic engagement: the right to vote." Connecting undocumented immigrants' struggles to those of Black Americans during the civil rights movement, she explained, "Voter suppression and anti-immigrant sentiment are rooted in the same unwillingness by those in power to yield to the political shift brought on by the nation's ever-changing demographics, whether through poll taxes and literacy tests in 1960s, Mississippi or Arizona's show-me-your-papers requirement in 2012. The same question remains: how do we force the political system to recognize and respond to the fact that we exist?"[45]

Organizers scheduled the bus to depart from Phoenix, Arizona, the site where the controversial anti-immigrant SB 1070 Act had been passed. The six-week route included scheduled stops at places known for anti-immigrant fervor and oppressive policing: New Mexico, Colorado, Texas, Louisiana, Mississippi, Alabama, Georgia, and Tennessee on the way to Charlotte, where riders would ultimately arrive at the Democratic National Convention. At each location, local committees organized widely publicized events and acts of civil disobedience such as sit-ins designed to block traffic to draw public attention to the issue of immigration reform.

In June, organizers held an Action Camp for Migrant Rights at the Highlander Center in Tennessee, a deeply historic and symbolic site of civil rights organizing and education. During the civil rights movement, Highlander Center trainings helped facilitate some of the movement's most impactful campaigns, from the Citizenship Schools to the Montgomery Bus Boycott to the Student Nonviolent Coordinating Committee (SNCC). At the Action Camp for Migrant Rights, sixty migrant rights organizers and fifteen activists from a swath of progressive movements joined for five days of side-by-side training in nonviolent direct action and solidarity building.

Forging a Collective Identity through Intersectional Memory

To generate a movement for recognition that would incorporate immigrants' complex identities and positions, ride organizers strategically emphasized their differences—across intersections such as legal status, race, and sexuality—instead of obscuring them like the Immigrant Workers Freedom Ride had done a decade prior. Rider Daniela Cruz emphasized the identity goals of the strategy: "We're excited to show people that we are not afraid. It feels different this time. We are painting the bus with the words: No papers, no fear. It's going to strengthen our community."[46] About half of the riders identified as queer, where their use of the "coming out" frame—out of the closet, out of the shadows—carried particular symbolic power.[47] Immigrant activists centered their dynamic journeys and stories in their collective identity, fusing them with American identity and its soul, the civil rights movement.

On the side of the bus, local artists and children painted the phrase "No Papers, No Fear, a Journey for Justice." Artwork and cultural expression was a central strategy for bypassing the contentious political battles that had characterized the previous decade's fight for legislative immigration reform. Instead, they would focus on the humans at the center of these battles and remind American publics of the beauty of diversity. Artist and activist Favianna Rodriguez explained the dual purpose of the strategy: "Art is beautiful. It speaks to more senses than press releases and newspaper headlines. The more we can turn a press conference into a performance art piece, by wearing butterfly wings, or showcasing our icon work, the better."[48] Despite strategizing through a less unified claim to collective memory compared to the 2003 freedom ride, the symbolism of the group's tactics was clear, reiterated through planned, publicized visits with civil rights leaders and historic civil rights sites along the route.

Strategically Deploying Memory toward Publics

The riders were nervous, but they were ready. On July 29, forty riders boarded the Undocubus and departed from Phoenix to begin the No Papers, No Fear Ride for Justice. In New Orleans, riders met with Black civil rights organizers from the Congress of Racial Equality (CORE), who described their experiences of mobilizing in the face of fear and police violence. In Memphis, riders visited the National Civil Rights Museum inside the hotel where Dr. King was assassinated and learned about student-led organizing and Dr. King's tactics. Reporting on the visit, one journalist noted how "activists embraced a Frederick Douglass quote they saw in the museum, 'If there is no struggle, there is no progress.' . . . Drawing inspiration from the 1960's Civil Rights movement, riders identified most with the Freedom Riders—a group of black and white activists who rode public interstate buses in the segregated South to test a Supreme Court decision to end segregation. These activists were beaten by violent mobs, arrested by local police and were almost killed when a Greyhound was firebombed. They seized national attention and inspired hundreds more to participate. Their eyes widened when they saw the Freedom rides crisscrossed the same states they were."[49]

In Nashville, riders talked to civil rights activists who had organized the lunch-counter sit-ins. Like the Immigrant Workers Freedom Ride a decade prior, the Ride for Justice educated riders about the civil rights movement as a central strategy for embodying American memory and forging a collective identity. While the freedom ride was more explicit about this educational strategy, the Ride for Justice facilitated experiences to ensure that riders would absorb collective memory along the way. The very process of riding on the bus, interacting with civil rights leaders, and visiting historic sites created links between Undocubus riders' struggles and those of African Americans in the past. On the public blog documenting the Ride for Justice, rider Mari Cruz described how she had heard about the civil rights struggle of the 1960s but had not realized that she could learn from it. She explained, "As an undocumented mother from Arizona, the more that I learn and think about organizing for my community, and what strategies we can use to fight for our rights, the more admiration that I have for the civil rights struggles of the African-American community in the United States, and the more that I want to learn from them." Comparing the anti-immigrant nativists to the KKK of the civil rights era, she described the chilling sense that history was repeating itself: "I feel like I am living those same moments right now. . . . It's similar to what we are fighting now," she wrote, reflecting optimistically that "without knowing, I think we are forging a similar path to the one fought for 50 years ago. African-Americans stood up for their rights, they came together with their White allies, and have been able to make gains. Although I understand that there is still a lot left to fight for, I believe one day we will all be equal, including immigrants." Describing the sense of transformation and empowerment she was experiencing through the ride, Cruz wrote, "[As] I have traveled on this bus I have learned so much and changed. I have been able to give more than I thought I could give to my community. I feel stronger every day."[50] This poignant reflection on the analogous experiences of undocumented immigrants and Black Americans illustrated the embodied connections through which activists were anchoring their diverse experiences in a shared collective memory.

Following the nonviolent tactics of the civil rights movement, riders and local activists engaged in civil disobedience at multiple stops along the way.

On August 19 in Alabama, protesters rallied outside a hearing on a controversial immigration law supported by Kansas secretary of state Kris Kobach. Undocubus riders attempted to testify, but when they were refused admittance they sat in the road and blocked courthouse traffic, then conducted a sit-in at the Sheraton hotel where Kobach was staying, where eventually they were removed by law enforcement.

On August 27 in Birmingham, the Undocubus riders parked and chanted outside the Commission on Civil Rights' Hearing on Immigration. Trainer Cesar Maxit had been working with migrant communities across Alabama for weeks prior in preparation for the Undocubus stop. He helped facilitate theatrical civil disobedience at the hearing to draw unavoidable attention to the cause, a strategy that specifically excluded undocumented riders to ensure their safety. He wrote later, "It was a powerful moment in various ways, but an important piece I thought was for folks to get a first-hand experience in escalating nonviolent tactics and building collective confidence."[51] The ride was, after all, as much for immigration reform as it was for building community power among immigrants. In Knoxville, Undocubus riders held a march against the local sheriff's proposed law to screen anyone who had been arrested for immigration status. Each stop mobilized immigrants and allies, and organizers arranged training workshops to sustain the activist networks long after the conclusion of the ride.

Finally, on September 3, riders arrived in Charlotte, North Carolina, for the Democratic National Convention. They blocked an intersection near the convention site, and ten undocumented immigrants held up signs that read "undocumented." They were immediately arrested. With immense media attention tracking the riders' fate, the ten undocumented immigrants were released the following day without charges. One of the arrested riders, Gerardo Torres, age forty-one, a handyman originally from Aguas Calientes, Mexico, said he had decided to get arrested the night before. During a meeting of activists at a local church, the importance of direct and unwavering action suddenly became clear, and he was tired of being afraid. He said, "I wanted to prove the point to the (undocumented) community that when we are together and we are united, we have a lot of power."[52]

Rivals Mobilize Countermemory Branches

The lack of sustained grassroots opposition to the riders was particularly notable. Without an explicit strategy making a claim to American memory, the riders bypassed counterstrategies for discrediting a link they never made outright. Steven Camarota, research director at the Center for Immigration Studies, an anti-immigrant think tank, said, "It's not clear to most Americans that this is analogous to the civil-rights movement. In the civil-rights movement, you had American citizens demanding equality. In this case, you have people who aren't supposed to be in the country demanding the rights of citizens, and to most Americans, or at least a large fraction, that is not roughly the same thing."[53] Echoing the nativist movement's strategy of discrediting the link between immigrant identity and American memory by emphasizing the illegality of undocumented immigrants, their lack of citizenship and claim to American identity, Camarota pointed out that in this case, the analogy was not even clear to bystanders. Though the counterprotests were few and far between, the backlash to Obama's presidency and the growing nativism movement were taking shape in powerful ways behind the scenes. Over the next few years, nativists would build a significant and foreboding perception of immigrant threat that would carry Donald Trump to the White House.

Meanwhile, in September 2012, the Democratic Party did not amend its approach to immigration reform. However, the Undocubus Ride for Justice had inspired, ignited, and mobilized undocumented immigrants and drawn public attention to their complex stories and undeniable humanity. One of the key organizers of the ride, Carlos Garcia, director of Puente Arizona, explained, "What it really comes down to is challenging the law itself and us being able to tell the stories of undocumented people and why they are risking everything."[54]

The Consequences

The consequences of the battles between immigrant rights and nativist activists were felt from the political-cultural arena, where policy debates took place, down to the group and individual levels, where immigrants and nativists alike grappled with their identities and what the past had to say about who they were as Americans. While the immigrant rights movement had been using the memory of the civil rights movement to develop dense grassroots networks and coalitions, the growing nativism of the 2010s motivated innovative counterstrategies for disrupting immigrant rights' organizers ground game. Nativist groups increasingly focused on disrupting immigrant rights claims to the memory of civil rights by attracting the support of Black Americans. Anti-immigrant organizations mobilized conservative Black leaders to speak out against immigrant rights as civil rights, drawing firm boundaries around collective memory as belonging to native-born Black and White Americans, not "foreign invaders." For example, the Federation for American Immigration Reform (FAIR), an anti-immigrant group, funded Black-led organizations like the Black American Leadership Alliance, a self-described nonprofit dedicated to "Protecting the Futures of Black Americans," to take on the cause of punitive immigration reform. In 2013, speaking to the House Subcommittee on Immigration and Border Security, Black organizational leader Dr. Frank L. Morris said, "African Americans have paid dearly for the long fight for equal citizen benefits. African Americans have long suffered in the past from the stringent enforcement of American laws such as those enforcing segregation, and when some of these citizen benefits evaporate because labor, immigration, and civil and criminal laws are not enforced against noncitizens, this breach against the American birthright should not be allowed to continue."[55] Morris's support for the anti-immigrant cause was notable. He discredited immigrant rights claims to civil rights by placing Black Americans' oppression in the *past* and by emphasizing the contemporary threat to civil rights as one generated not by the White supremacist state but by immigrants.

While Black support for anti-immigrant causes was negligible, the symbolic disruption of immigrants' claims to civil rights generated support among White moderates evaluating the political landscape in the lead-up to the 2016 presidential election. If Black Americans could be nativists, then nativism could not be racist. By reclaiming the legacy of civil rights as one inextricably bound to "native-born" American identity, nativists' strategic uses of the past sedimented a worldview and way of seeing that positioned them as the victims of demographic change. Through this lens, non-White *immigrants* were the threat to "real" Americans' civil rights, and their unenforced existence in the United States could be viewed as oppressing these "true" Americans.

As Donald Trump rode this wave of growing nativism, campaigning on the promise of a border wall between the United States and Mexico, he built the perception of migrant threat through racist constructions of Mexican immigrants as "bringing drugs . . . bringing crime . . . [as] rapists." Nativist ideology moved to the mainstream under the promise of oppressed White Americans "taking their country back," drawing tight boundaries on national identity that would reverse time, bring the past to the future, "make America great again." On Fox News, pundits like Tucker Carlson would warn of demographic change in the United States as a Great Replacement of White Americans by immigrants. A media analysis of Carlson's show revealed how he spread the threat of the Great Replacement over four hundred times, describing an alleged ploy by the Democratic Party to "import an entirely new electorate from the Third World and change the demographics of the U.S. so completely they will never lose again." Over and over, Carlson warned his nearly 3.5 million viewers ominously, "our country's being invaded by the rest of the world. . . . This policy is called the great replacement, the replacement of legacy Americans with more obedient people from faraway countries." This Great Replacement Theory built on the long-building branch of collective memory that remembered the gains of the civil rights movement as losses for White

Americans, as power they graciously "gave up" and had turned against them by minoritized groups claiming "special rights."[56]

The strategic uses of the past to claim a new White oppression, a White replacement or even genocide, had violent consequences. When a White supremacist warmly welcomed into a Black church in Charleston, South Carolina, murdered nine Black parishioners, he cited the threat of living in a town where White people were the minority, where White identity had to be preserved. When torch-bearing White nationalists marched in Charlottesville in 2017 chanting "You will not replace us! Jews will not replace us!" leading to one White nationalist driving his car into a sea of counterprotesters and killing thirty-two-year-old Heather Heyer, they called on the Great Replacement. When a White gunman entered a synagogue in Pittsburgh, Pennsylvania, and murdered eleven Jewish worshippers including a ninety-seven-year-old woman, he warned of White genocide and the Great Replacement. When a White gunman descended on a Walmart in El Paso, Texas, in 2019, targeting the predominantly Latino customers and murdering twenty-three innocent people, his manifesto cited the Great Replacement. By 2022, a poll by the AP-NORC Center for Public Research showed that 47 percent of Republicans agreed with the statement "there is a group of people in this country who are trying to replace native-born Americans with immigrants who agree with their political views." Instead of a wakeup call to conservatives to reject the emboldened violence of nativism and White supremacy, the alternative social reality had taken hold. The perception of White victimhood had only spread.

5

"Muslims Are the New Blacks"

MUSLIM ACTIVISTS, THE ISLAMOPHOBIA MOVEMENT, AND THE RACIAL BOUNDARIES OF MEMORY

I knew that I could never again raise my voice against the violence of the oppressed in the ghettos without having first spoken clearly to the greatest purveyor of violence in the world today—my own government.

—MARTIN LUTHER KING JR., 1967

If you're not careful, the newspapers will have you hating the people who are being oppressed and loving the people who are doing the oppressing.

—MALCOLM X

ON JUNE 19, 2018, the Council on American-Islamic Relations (CAIR) announced the launch of their "Alabama Civil Rights Tour Photo Journal Project." The campaign strategically coincided with Juneteenth, or "Freedom Day," the historic day in 1865 when news reached Texas that slavery had been abolished and the enslaved would be emancipated. CAIR's monthlong campaign, trailed by a documentary crew, would follow thirty Muslim American civil rights leaders and activists from around the country on a tour of symbolic sites significant to the civil rights movement. From the 16th Street Baptist Church to the Edmund Pettus Bridge in Selma, Muslim participants would share an image on social media each day with their personal reflections on the historic journey. As CAIR described in a press release, these Muslim American leaders would "walk the path of civil rights icons like Rev. Dr. Martin Luther King, Jr., learning about connections between slavery, the civil rights movement and Islamophobia."[1]

At the 16th Street Baptist Church where a firebombing by the Ku Klux Klan killed four African American girls in 1963, one activist connected the horrific violence to the firebombing of the Islamic Center in Fort Pierce, Florida, on September 11, 2016, and threats to mosques nationwide. In Selma, another activist connected the dehumanization of slavery to his family's displacement into refugee camps in Israel, acknowledging that he "may never fully be able to comprehend the precise scope of the suffering and enormous pain of enslaved Africans"[2] but that the shared pain of oppression and discrimination gave him a deep sense of empathy for the African American struggle.

The tour triggered many activists' raw nerves. The year prior, upon his inauguration in January 2017, President Trump had signed an executive order known as the "Muslim ban," which prohibited visitors from seven predominantly Muslim countries from entering the United States. Muslim travelers on their way back to the United States were shut out, visas for everything from life-saving surgeries to long-awaited reunions between families were canceled, visitors were detained and deported, and families were tragically separated. As Trump supporters rejoiced across the country, the trauma was palpable for Muslim communities. Since Trump's inauguration, CAIR had been working ceaselessly with organizations like the ACLU to challenge the series of anti-immigrant and anti-Muslim executive orders. Now, they hoped the Alabama Civil Rights Tour would help ignite the grassroots movement and generate coalitions and a powerful ground force to challenge the onslaught of political threats brought about by the Trump administration.

The civil rights tour culminated in the dedication of a memorial to the legacy of lynching in Montgomery. As the bus of Muslim civil rights leaders and activists approached the National Memorial for Peace and Justice, the executive director of CAIR's Michigan chapter, Dawud Walid, stood up to issue a prayer: "Allah, please have mercy upon our pious Muslim ancestors who gave their lives and shed their blood here on this land."[3] Remembering the violent enslavement of African Muslims, his voice wavered and broke. He stopped and choked back tears before continuing with the Islamic prayer: "Alhamd lilah rabi alealamin" (Praise be to God, Lord of the Worlds). As he finished the prayer, he wiped his eyes and walked solemnly to the back of the bus, a fellow passenger squeezing his arm as he passed.

The tour was wrought with emotion for the Muslim activists, many of whom were unfamiliar with the depths of terror and violence inflicted upon African Americans, including their Black Muslim brothers and sisters. The activists did not just take up the memory of the civil rights movement to strategically deploy it outward toward the public. Like the immigrant rights activists discussed in chapter 4, these organizers used collective memory to generate a new sense of consciousness and identity within the Muslim immigrant community. They climbed into and wrapped themselves up in the memory to embody their connection to American history and, more specifically, Black Muslims. As Nihad Awad, executive director of CAIR, wrote of the experience, "The legacy of enslaved African Muslims is a part of our history as American Muslims. As a community, we must uplift the narrative of the resilience of our Black brothers and sisters. We must use the lessons of the past to inform and shape the way we combat Islamophobia now and in the future." Awad emphasized, "It is only through both intentionality and solidarity, with arms linked, that we will be able to overcome the challenges of the future."[4]

This embodied solidarity, the symbolic work of constructing a collective identity not only analogous to but in this case *made up of* the experiences of African Americans, was part of a growing strategic direction for the Muslim rights movement. They would educate Muslim activists through a memory of "who we were" to strategize toward a shared conception of "who we are," as a group *made up* of African Americans rather than separate from them. In doing so, they would also work to eradicate the Muslim immigrant community's troubling history of anti-Blackness, transforming their long-held collective identity as emphatically *not-Black*. Their strategies would not go unnoticed by rivals. The dense network of anti-Muslim organizations emerging in the aftermath of September 11, 2001, would attempt to thwart these efforts by framing Muslim immigrants as threatening outsiders incomparable to Black Americans, antithetical to Dr. King's Christian vision. At the center of these battles was the question of racial identity and its inextricable relationship to societal belonging in the United States.

As the previous chapters have shown, for decades social movements across the ideological spectrum have strategically claimed the memory of the civil rights movement for competing political goals. Making the "like Black" analogy has given mobilizing groups a set of cultural and political tools for building coalitions with other minority groups to generate support and political power and challenge exclusionary attitudes and policies.[5] But the immigrant Muslim rights movement did not follow this common trajectory. Instead, Muslim immigrants have been fractured by internal debates over their relationship to Blackness, to a "like Black" analogy.[6] Such debates have been particularly complicated by a long-discounted reality: Muslim experience in the United States is *rooted* in Black history.[7] Why did Muslim activists follow this unexpected trajectory and what led Muslim activists to begin claiming the collective memory of the civil rights movement? How did anti-Muslim activists challenge these efforts, and what do these dynamics tell us about the *racial* boundaries of collective memory?

In this chapter, I argue that if we want to understand why movements use the collective memory of the civil rights movement at some times but not others, in some ways but not others, we must begin by understanding the racial boundaries of culture. It is through these boundaries that group identities

Time Period	Perceived Identity	Use of Memory & Imagined Future	Strategic Target	Rival Movement
1980s–2000	Not like Black	Avoidance of civil rights memory for assimilation	Institutional Engagement	Disorganized Orientalism
2001–2011	Stigmatized but not like Black	Color-blind memory for eventual incorporation	Public outreach/ cultural education	Growing Islamophobia Movement
2012–2020	Racialized like Black	Radical King for changing the meaning of belonging	Grassroots coalition-building	Organized Multi-Institutional Islamophobia Network

FIGURE 5.1. Muslim rights movement's shifting relationship between perceived identity and strategic use of memory over time.

are constructed, shaping how a group perceives itself and, critically, how these perceptions can change.

This chapter shows how Muslim activists progressed from using strategies that maintained their distance from Black identity, strategically avoiding alliances with Black Muslims and the collective memory of the civil rights movement, to those that use the memory of the civil rights movement as a cultural bridge, joining Muslim identity with Black identity in multiracial coalitions. Muslim activists' perceptions of collective identity recalibrate with changing political-cultural contexts, reshaping the way they understand their own racial identity and deploy the collective memory of the civil rights movement to challenge societal exclusion. What results from this new understanding of "who we are" through collective memory is a new conception of what it means to be not only Muslim in America but also American.

How Racial Boundaries Shape the Uses of Memory

How does a mobilizing group's perception of their identity shape the way they deploy collective memory? To arrive at a strategic decision, a group must share a conception of collective identity. Social movement scholars have shown that the process of collective identity construction is wrought with its own dilemmas as mobilizing groups make sense of their group's collective identity and position in relation to those of other groups.[8] For example, they might think, "We are most similar to that group" or "We are most definitely *not* like *that* group." Through their perceptions of their group's social location, they interpret the political landscape and their range of imaginable possibilities for action.[9] This is where a group might consider, "Given that we are similar to that group and they had this experience when they mobilized, we may be likely to have the same experience if we use the same strategy." Or they may think, "The political climate was less threatening to groups like us when that group mobilized, so we may not be as lucky since things are more hostile now." In short, perceptions of collective identity and its social location relative to other groups are at the heart of strategic decision making.

However, as social psychologists have shown, collective identities are not static but dynamic, changing through shifting political-cultural contexts and everyday interactions between movement actors.[10] This means that a group's perception of their identity can change as political and cultural conditions evolve and as the group learns more about the rules of the political game. Perhaps the political climate becomes particularly friendly to their group—whether through laws or politicians sympathetic to the group's interests—and the group no longer thinks of themselves as an excluded group. Perhaps a political event takes place that suddenly turns the public against the group and the group goes from feeling relatively good about where they stand to feeling targeted and excluded. It is also possible that through their experiences, the group learns more about society, where their perception of what it *means* to be included changes altogether. Perhaps they learn that inclusion does not have to mean changing their own identity but rather changing the system that deemed them outsiders to begin with.

The point of these insights is to show that a group's identity is shaped through perceptions of these social locations and the cultural meanings that constitute them, a process of meaning-making that is enabled and constrained by dynamic political contexts.[11] The way a group understands their identity is shaped through a constant negotiation between what society tells them they are (a set of meanings shaped by governments, laws, and policies), as well as cultural narratives and public attitudes, and what the group *feels* they are. In 1897, W.E.B. Du Bois explained this feeling as a Black man under the racialized system of White supremacy as a sense of two-ness, of a "double consciousness":

> It dawned upon me with a certain suddenness that I was different from the others; or like, mayhap, in heart and life and longing, but shut out from their world by a vast veil. . . . It is a peculiar sensation, this double-consciousness, this sense of always looking at one's self through the eyes of others, of measuring one's soul by the tape of a world that looks on in amused contempt and pity.[12]

And indeed, scholars of race and ethnicity have shown that these identities are rooted in ethnoracial formation processes; collective identities are shaped by sociohistorical processes and ordered racial meanings.[13] These ethnoracial formation processes shape the lenses through which groups understand their position in society and the constraints upon and opportunities afforded to these positions.[14] For mobilizing groups, these perceptions of group identity are harnessed to develop strategies to negotiate their position for inclusion. For example, in the United States, historians have described how groups who are now considered White (e.g., Irish, Jews) were once racialized and marked as "other." To vie for inclusion in the dominant category, these groups enacted a range of strategies to distinguish themselves from Black people and align themselves with White people.[15]

Yet increasingly scholars have acknowledged that the processes of integration into Whiteness have been less clear for non-White immigrants—the "other non-Whites"—for whom "hypodescent," physical markers like phenotype and hair texture continue to mark them as "other" beyond their structural incorporation into institutions and social systems.[16] Like that of East Asian and Latino diasporas, the experience of Muslim immigrants has been fraught with external contradictions and internal contestations, combining multiple ethnoracial groups with multiple legal racial classifications, including Arab, Middle Eastern, South Asian, and African immigrants and Black Americans, though notably erasing the latter. While the history of anti-Arab and anti-Muslim racism is extensive, post-9/11 laws, policies, and cultural discourses have been particularly instrumental in "racialized repression" that homogenizes Muslim immigrants as terrorists, perpetual non-White foreigners. Historically, Arabs understood the complexities of racial triangulation and strategically distanced themselves from not only Black people but also Asians to make claims to citizenship and inclusion. However, the post-9/11 "war on terror" tied Arab and South Asian immigrants together through what Louise Cainkar calls a "type of brown" terror threat.[17] For immigrants without particularly strong perceptions of group identity, post-9/11 backlash made a collective identity salient, politicizing some immigrants for the first time and mobilizing them to collective action against exclusion. As Vilna Bashi Treitler writes, "Since racialization cannot be avoided one (or one's group) must engage it. In their responses to ethnoracialization—a process that has most new ethnic groups enter at the bottom of the racial hierarchy—a group likely chooses to recreate their ethnicity in a way that can serve as a counterweight to the severely limiting racial characterizations they are assigned."[18]

As political contexts shift, enabling or foreclosing the available identity options, mobilizing groups must adjust their perceptions of their own collective identity as well as their perceptions of the larger system of inclusion. Perhaps the government creates a new category that links a number of groups who consider themselves distinct, as when pan-ethnoracial categories like "Asian" or "Hispanic" are created.[19] These disparate groups must then evaluate what new racial boundaries mean for their prospects of inclusion and then make strategic decisions about how to adopt or resist these ascribed collective identities.[20] The implications can differ, as one externally ascribed identity may grant a group protection and greater rights while another externally ascribed identity may enable mass racial profiling and limit their rights. As mobilizing groups come to understand the limits of these racial identity boundaries, their perceptions of the social world and their place in it are enhanced and they develop new strategies for inclusion. Understanding the relationship between shifting political-cultural contexts, the racial boundaries of culture, and mobilizing groups' perceptions of their racial identities can help us understand why they mobilize in particular ways, namely, how they see *themselves* in relation to collective memory.

The Entangled Roots of the Muslim Rights and Islamophobia Movements

Although there is a much longer history of Black Muslim activism and Arab American activism in the United States,[21] the immigrant Muslim rights movement has roots in the mid-1980s. This movement has been predominantly made up of South Asian and Arab immigrants who arrived after 1965 and their second-generation children.[22] American Muslims more broadly are a racially and ethnically heterogeneous group. According to the Pew Research Center, in 2016 Muslims were self-reported as 38 percent White, which includes Middle Eastern and North African Muslims, 28 percent Black, 28 percent Asian, 4 percent Latino, and 3 percent multiracial/other. Despite their heterogeneity, the social identity of Muslims as a "group" has been constructed as a homogeneous category through national laws, policies, and discourses that target Muslims and those who appear Muslim.[23] The dilemma, then, for activists is how to resist this homogenizing collective identity that lumps all Muslims together as a unified threat while also joining disparate Muslim communities in a unified mobilizing force. Do activists align themselves with the minority rights model shaped by the civil rights movement, following the trajectories of excluded immigrant groups that came before, or do they chart a different path? More critically, do the racial boundaries of culture allow for a different path?

To answer these questions, this chapter draws on archival data from 1980 to 2020 and focus groups with approximately two hundred Muslim community leaders and organizers in eight cities across the United States conducted between 2014 to 2015 (for details, see the methodological appendix). This chapter shows that Muslim activists' strategic uses of collective memory and anti-Muslim activists' counterstrategies reveal the relationship between shifting social contexts and the racial boundaries of culture.

Not Black: Institutional Engagement without Uses of Memory

When Dr. Faroque Khan founded the Islamic Center of Long Island (ICLI) in the 1980s, he and the handful of Pakistani and Indian Muslim families in the conservative, well-to-do suburb of New York City were mostly concerned with a space for preserving their religious and ethnic traditions. Like many of the affluent, well-educated Muslim immigrants in his community, Khan believed Muslim immigrants were model community members who ought to associate with those in positions of power. Drawn to the Republican Party for "its emphasis on family values, individual responsibility and small government,"[24] Khan developed relationships with local politicians, including a close friendship with local congressman Peter King. When the Islamic Center built a mosque in 1991, it was King who cut the ribbon. A seeming ally of the local Muslim community, King was one of the few Republicans to support President Clinton's foreign intervention to protect Muslims under siege in Bosnia and Kosovo in 1995. King contributed to Khan's 2001 book about the Islamic Center, *A Mosque in America*, writing, "My visit to ICLI was memorable. I couldn't help but be impressed with the work ethic, devotion to family and spiritual commitment so evident at the center. It has been gratifying for me to help build a political awareness in this, the fastest-growing religious group in America."[25] Years later, Khan would describe their relationship as merely "cordial, professional, he sometimes called me and sought my views regarding medical questions,"[26] but King also attended dinners at Khan's home and knew his family. King even attended the wedding of Khan's son in 1995. "It was like a family atmosphere with him," recalled Habeeb Ahmed, chairman of the ICLI board of trustees.[27]

Such relationships between Muslim immigrants and local politicians, law enforcement, and business leaders were not uncommon in the 1980s and 1990s, as Muslim immigrant-led organizations proliferated with the rise of immigration from Muslim-majority countries. Led by national organizations like the Muslim Public Affairs Council (MPAC) and the Council on American-Islamic Relations (CAIR), Muslim advocacy was largely made up of South Asian, Middle Eastern, and Arab immigrants and their children, to the exclusion of Black Muslims. Some scholars have argued that this exclusion was due to theological differences, while others have said it was because Muslim immigrant groups were wealthier and more well educated and had more economic organizing power than Black Muslims. After all, as one journalist described, ICLI was where "BMWs and Mercedes-Benzes fill the parking lot, and Coach purses are perched along prayer lines," where "young mothers in Burberry coats exchange kisses and chatter." However, some have argued that linking these explanations is an underlying thread of anti-Black racism in a strategic quest for a dominant status.[28] As Ibrahim Abdul Matin, a Black Muslim organizer, said, "Islam means Muslims aren't racist? That's a great idea but in application Muslims are some of the worst when it comes to racial dynamics."[29] Correspondingly, the early strategies of the Muslim rights movement were generated out of a perception of collective identity as integrating model immigrants who were distinctly *not*-Black, where Whiteness was perceived as a permeable category. Many immigrant organizers proclaimed, "We're just like the Irish," drawing on a classic example of immigrant incorporation to describe their strategic pathways toward inclusion into the dominant group.[30]

Like Khan's ICLI, many organizations focused on forging positive Muslim and American relations, both domestically and abroad, and establishing "Muslim American" as a social and political identity to be celebrated like other American symbolic ethnicities, such as the Irish or Italians.[31] Organizations like the Islamic Circle of North America described their early strategies as "educating its growing membership about Islam" and "establishing a place for Islam in America." Many of these Muslim organizations were not "grassroots" ones but rather relied on support from foundations and wealthy donors. Correspondingly, their strategies were mostly focused on institutions, although the Council on American-Islamic Relations' local chapters became pseudo-franchises that often embarked on their own place-based missions with diverse local constituencies.[32] National organizations strategized to build political and economic power for Muslims through a perception of their group identity as integrating model citizens, challenging discrimination when it cropped up.[33] The Muslim Public Affairs Council (MPAC) led a 1988 campaign to elect American Muslims to the Democratic National Convention, developing relationships with political and business leaders.[34] Yet the 1990s yielded greater political challenges for Muslim organizers as a result of growing anti-Muslim (and Muslim-"seeming") hostility, through foreign interventions like the Gulf War and domestic tragedies like the 1993 World Trade Center bombing and 1995 Oklahoma City bombing in which Arabs were initially implicated.

Like Faroque Khan, many American Muslim leaders maintained a commitment to "making friends in high places," as one focus group participant put it, generating a collective perception of model immigrant identity through connections with elites and institutional partnerships. Unlike other newly arrived immigrant groups that had used the memory of the civil rights movement to build multiracial coalitions and make claims to inclusion, organizers strategically avoided analogies to minority identity. In focus groups, organizers reflected on the ways these strategies were constructed through a perception of Muslim identity as not Black and, instead, aspirationally White. One Muslim community leader explained, "Here is the narrative of an immigrant community that wants to enter into all of the privileges of a somewhat smooth transition into middle-class American respectability and dare I say Whiteness, which assumes non-Blackness within itself." She went on to describe how Muslims had seen themselves as a model for the American dream. They organized with an eye to accumulating social and economic power to maintain their perception of collective identity, which another leader described in greater detail:

> Really our mindset is not a minority mindset. . . . How do you transfer that thinking of always feeling like you have the upper hand and you are privileged and . . . it's fascinating because we're not demanding our rights only because we believe in the justice system. We fight for our rights because we're a high-aspiring community, highly educated, well-placed, economically well-to-do, and we pay taxes, so we're not even sucking the system, we're not *those* people.[35]

Drawing on racialized meanings, she described how Muslims, as a high-achieving group, were not the sort of minorities society would describe as leeches on the system, and their strategies should reflect their group position. In her view, these strategies should engage key institutions and policymakers like city councils and police chiefs, leveraging what she described as the highly educated background of the Muslim community. Many discussions echoed themes of Muslims as a peaceful, law-abiding group compared to "other" groups. One organizer said, "You don't hear about Muslims . . . killing three people every weekend." These perceptions of Muslim identity were translated into rationales for not only how the Muslim community ought to be treated but also how organizers ought to pursue strategies for inclusion.

These narratives about the early Muslim rights movement, led largely by wealthy, well-educated Muslim immigrants like Khan, emphasized how Muslims constructed strategies through an understanding about who they were and more importantly who they were *not*. To use the memory of the civil rights movement would be to claim a minority identity that many Muslim immigrants worked hard to reject. Such divisions between Muslim immigrants and Black Muslims would become all the more salient during the 2000 presidential campaign as two massive Muslim American conventions—one immigrant-led, one Black-led—were held in Chicago. The result was a public endorsement of George W. Bush by the American Muslim Political Coordinating Council Political Action Committee (AMPCC-PAC), a powerful bloc of wealthy Muslim immigrants, infuriating Black Muslims who had not been consulted. Recalling the contentious moment, Imam Al-Hajj Talib 'Abdur-Rashid, a popular Black imam from Harlem known simply as Imam Talib, described a meeting the following summer when Black and immigrant

Muslims endeavored to sort through the friction. He described how a South Asian man turned to him and said, "I don't understand why all of you African-American Muslims are always so angry about everything." Drawing the most resonant analogy he could imagine, Imam Talib responded, "African-Americans are like the Palestinians of this land. We're not just some angry black people. We're legitimately outraged and angry."[36] Met with silence, the rift with Muslim immigrants felt irrevocable, a seemingly impossible alliance during that tense summer meeting in 2001.

Stigmatized but Not Black: Countering Islamophobia with a Color-Blind Memory

And then, thick black smoke clouded the clear blue skies and the Twin Towers fell in a violent spectacle. The terrorist attacks of September 11, 2001, were a significant historical moment, what sociologist Ann Swidler would call an "unsettled period," one of those times where social reality was up for negotiation.[37] Scholars documented the backlash, the vandalism, the racial epithets, and the violence, for those who were Muslim and those who appeared Muslim.[38] Around the country, many pro-American demonstrations turned into anti-Muslim protests. In Illinois, several hundred protesters gathering for a flag-waving show of support for the United States turned into angry marchers, descending on the Bridgeview mosque. In north Texas, six shots were fired into a mosque. A Pakistani cabdriver was dragged from his car and beaten by three White men. Vandals spray-painted messages like "No Forgiveness," "Terrorist," and "Go Home" on mosques and Muslim Americans' homes. In one account, a family of Muslim American citizens remarked on their growing fear in the wake of rising anti-Muslim hate. One family member woefully recalled his happy memories of being sworn in as a citizen, when "the judge said this is the only country built on immigrants and we should all be proud, we were all Americans." He went on to describe how fearful his family had been since 9/11, feeling like foreigners and staying hidden inside their home. Muslim parents around the country kept their children home from school as account after account of anti-Muslim backlash rolled in.

The FBI noted a 1,600 percent increase in hate crimes against Muslims that year alone.[39] The backlash was not only cultural but structural as new policies targeted Muslims as national security concerns.[40] President Bush called publicly for respect toward Muslim Americans, famously declaring, "Islam is peace," but behind closed doors, the Bush administration was working to implement the National Security Entry-Exit Registration System (NSEERS). The 2002 policy required non-citizens from twenty-five South Asian, Middle Eastern, and North African countries to present themselves to immigration offices for "special registration" and questioning, a program that led to numerous deportations, or as they were experienced by many Muslim community members, "disappearances." Through its amorphous aims, the "war on terror" would come to play a powerful role in institutionalizing the construction of Muslims—not particular political sects or foreign leaders—as objects of suspicion and purveyors of violence. As Khaled Beydoun wrote in *American Islamophobia*, "This war is dramatically distinct from its predecessors and unlike conventional wars in general. Its target is not a nation-state or empire, but rather the vague and amorphous concept of terrorism, conflated with Islam and the billions of its believers presumed to be sympathetic to or in cahoots with terror. The state has linked Muslims, whether immigrants or citizens, living in the United States or abroad, to the suspicion of terrorism, and has formally enacted a two-front war: the foreign war, and the surveillance, policing, and cultural wars deployed within the country."[41]

This Islamophobia would be further embedded in law and culture in the United States by a growing anti-Muslim right-wing movement. This tight-knit network, which included grassroots organizations, think tanks, and right-wing media groups, spread disinformation and conspiracies about Muslims as threats to national security and national identity, stoking the public's fears and racist Islamophobia.[42] One particularly effective strategy constructed a threat of Islamist extremists working to infiltrate the U.S. government and legal system to implement sharia law, mischaracterized as a violent Islamist ideology of hate and violence.

Back on Long Island, as in so many close-knit communities around the country, deep divides were forming, longtime friendships dissolving. Around 150 community members in Congressman King's district lost their lives on 9/11, among them one of the congressman's close friends. Meanwhile the ICLI mosque was receiving anonymous calls threatening imminent violence. Muslim children were terrified after rocks were hurled at them and slurs yelled at them from cars speeding down their neighborhood streets. Facing backlash and misplaced blame from neighbors, some Muslim leaders began calling for answers. Ghazi Khankan, ICLI's interfaith director, was quoted telling a journalist, "Who really benefits from such a horrible tragedy that is blamed on Muslims and Arabs? Definitely Muslims and Arabs do not benefit. It must be an enemy of Muslims and Arabs. An independent investigation must take place."[43] The subtext was that a conspiracy might be at play, that a foreign government like Israel might be involved. Faroque Khan saw the damage unfolding before his eyes and quickly embarked on a tour of local churches and synagogues, clarifying the comments and denouncing the attacks. But with Peter King, the damage had been done.

King turned against Khan and the Muslim community. Speaking to the media about Khan, he warned, "He's definitely a radical. You cannot, in the context of September 11, allow those statements to be made and not be a radical."[44] In interviews, he questioned Muslim Americans' loyalties, drawing on long-debunked statistics that "85 percent of mosques are being run by extremists." Khan and the ICLI remained steadfast in their support for their old friend, the congressman, contributing to his political campaign and requesting meetings to clear the air, but the outreach was met with silence. In 2004, Peter King published *Vale of Tears*, a fictional story about a Long Island congressman who investigates violent terrorist attacks stemming from a sleeper cell in a Long Island Islamic center under the leadership of a wealthy Pakistani heart surgeon who, as it turns out, is not to be trusted. The fictional congressman recounts, "It was dirtbags living here a few years. Right here among all of us." After bringing the terrorists to justice, a character tells the congressman, "Maybe this will show them that their real loyalties should be to America." He replies, "If it's a choice between some guy who's an illegal alien being deported or New York City being blown to pieces, I say fuck the alien."

Faced with a growing tide of anti-Muslim sentiment and Islamophobia, Khan began to reevaluate the community's limited alliances. As he noted of the increasing community fragmentation, "It's a challenge for the whole Muslim community, not just for me. United we stand, divided we fall."[45] Such revelations were commonplace among Muslim organizations across the country that found themselves abandoned by longtime allies and neighbors alike. Muslim activists reassessed their group position against this new hostile context and a growing understanding that their self-conception of Muslims as integrating model immigrants was being threatened as Muslim identity was being shaped externally by laws, policies, and a powerful anti-Muslim movement. The pathway toward inclusion was no longer clear. As one organizer said, "I think there's a common understanding that we're not seen as citizens," describing how the Muslim community, many of whom had lived in the United States for decades or who were born here, had to grapple with being seen as Other, as not American.

Many Muslim organizers acknowledged that in order to challenge this stigma and discrimination, they needed greater unity among Muslim communities: "Muslims are not that organized, and for that reason have not tended to speak out as a group. We haven't done this before."[46] Slowly, disparate Muslim immigrant communities and communities *perceived* as Muslim began to come together internally, under an umbrella collective identity. For example, the Arab American Association of New York and American-Arab Anti-Discrimination Committee, which had advocated for non-Muslim Arabs for

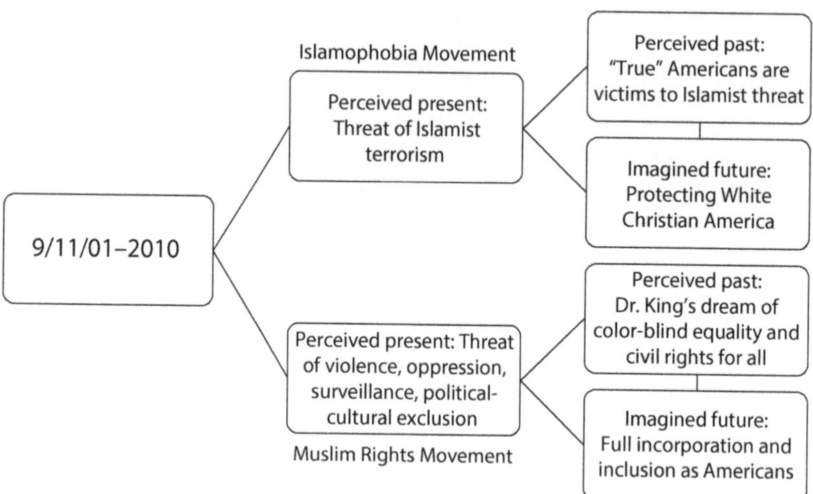

FIGURE 5.2. Muslim and Islamophobia movements' rivaling uses of memory from 2001 to 2010.

years, became two outspoken groups mobilizing for "Muslim rights." As one organizer explained, "For the Muslim community, 9/11 was a curse and a blessing. It forced people to now talk to one another and engage one another."

With greater hesitation, some Muslim organizers also began to reach out to the Black Muslims they had long ignored. Faroque Khan was among them. In 2005, he reached out to the charismatic Black imam from Harlem he had met five years earlier, in that tense 2000 convening of Muslim leaders in Chicago. He invited Imam Talib to speak at the mosque. Talib accepted. On a blustery day in February, the Black imam stood before the largely South Asian congregation and delivered a Friday sermon that combined Koranic verses with lessons from American history, powerfully linking the two. He called upon his immigrant brothers and sisters to learn from the civil rights movement.

However, many Muslim immigrants remained committed to a conception of their immigrant identity as exceptional, as unlike that of minority groups. They imagined that as quickly as the political tide had turned against them, as easily could it be turned back. To negotiate the growing gap between how society constructed Muslim identity and how Muslim activists viewed themselves, Muslim activists needed to transform a stigmatized identity into a positive one, reshaping public perceptions of Muslims to prove that they, while "not White," were Americans too. Such strategies were constructed through a growing perception that Muslims were stigmatized, but not like African Americans. Organizers rationalized that through education, Muslim immigrants would show the public that they were integrated model citizens "just like you," *you* being White, middle-class Americans. Furthermore, although there was a sense that federal policies were unjust, many Muslims operating in wealthy, mostly White spaces felt they were exempt from being targeted. As one affluent immigrant community leader explained, "We don't feel like we're the marginalized community. . . . We feel like we are part of America." Deploying Martin Luther King's words of religious tolerance and color-blindness as the true character of "who we are" as an American people, Muslim activists began developing campaigns to educate their fellow Americans about Muslim Americans, that they were like any other integrating immigrant group in the American patchwork. From "Meet Your Muslim Neighbor" events to "I'm a Muslim, Ask Me Anything" kiosks, CAIR even developed a widespread ad campaign showing Muslims as police officers, baseball players, attorneys: "I am Muslim, I am American."

When faced with publicized instances of anti-Muslim discrimination, Muslim activists remained committed to preserving their perceived identity as a respectable, high-status community, drawing on the mainstream, sanitized branch of collective memory of the civil rights movement centered on unity and color-blindness. As one community member explained, "Young people in our society need to remain calm and not respond with anger, and understand that tensions are running high. It's our job as good Muslims to inform the public that everything will be okay: we are on their side, we are American."[47] Organizers countered discrimination by coupling their collective identity with a memory representing the promise of diversity and equal rights for all. As one leader explained, "Both the message of Dr. King and that of Islam call for a world where all men are created equal and endowed by their creator with certain unalienable rights, with no real distinction between races, where every member of the human community loves one another as family regardless of what he looks like. This civil rights message, this human rights message, is an inherently and deeply Muslim message."[48]

In November 2006, after attending a conference of the North American Imams Federation, six imams boarded a US Airways flight at Minneapolis-St. Paul International Airport. Before the plane was scheduled to take off, several crew members and passengers reported their concerns regarding the imams' "suspicious behavior," and one passenger scribbled a note that a flight attendant delivered to the plane's captain:

> 6 suspicious Arabic men on plane, spaced out in their seats. All were together, saying ". . . Allah . . . Allah," cursing U.S. involvement w/Saddam before flight—1 in front exit row, another in first row 1st class, another in 8D, another in 22D, two in 25 E&F.

The pilot announced that the flight had been delayed while a U.S. air manager notified police. The imams were removed from the flight, arrested, and detained for hours. As it turned out, the imams had not posed any threat. As court documents would later show, all the matters of suspicion—"one-way tickets," "no checked bags," "loud prayers in the airport," "suspicious seating arrangements," "seatbelt extenders for thin men"—would prove to be false. Called the "flying imams incident," the event made national news, a public face to a common experience of racial profiling among Muslim Americans coined "flying while brown," an adoption of the Black experience of "driving while Black." The incident sparked a widespread debate over civil rights and national security. With CAIR's legal counsel, the six imams filed suit and settled out of court in 2009. In a widely read op-ed in *USA Today*, CAIR's then-communication director, Ibrahim Hooper, wrote, "Our nation's civil rights movement has been advancing steadily for decades, despite calls to maintain the status quo or suggestions to curtail the rights of certain citizens. That movement toward justice for all must not be put into reverse because of post-9/11 fears." Calling on Dr. King's words, he wrote, "When anyone's rights are diminished, all Americans' rights are threatened." Hooper went on to describe the beauty of a multicultural America and the importance of preserving its diversity through unity, community, and learning about one another.[49] He linked discrimination against Muslims to histories of discrimination against other immigrant groups and Black Americans, describing a "nation's civil rights movement" not specifically linked to Black history. Discrimination against Muslims was framed as a concern for "all Americans' rights," and Muslims were assimilated in this framework as "fellow Americans." Strategies like these drew on a branch of color-blind memory celebrating multicultural collectivism, projecting a collective identity that avoided racial distinction.

Despite these strategies in the decade after 9/11, external blows to Muslim identity kept on coming. Focus group participants described the proliferation of national news reports of global and homegrown terrorism, domestic reports of FBI entrapment and undercover informants, hate crimes, discrimination at airports, and the rise of a right-wing Birther Movement that spread a conspiracy that President Obama was foreign born and a "secret" Muslim. In addition, the 2010 mosque controversy reignited and empowered the anti-Muslim movement. A New York City imam proposed transforming an abandoned building in Lower Manhattan into a mosque and community center for interfaith dialogue, the Park51 Islamic Center. The proposal had generated significant debate locally and nationally, in no small part because the tight-knit network of anti-Muslim organizations had coined the project "the Ground Zero Mosque" and strategized a smear campaign against the Muslim developers as undercover extremists.

Over a decade, this Islamophobia network had grown with the backing of almost $40 million from seven foundations, distributed to right-wing organizations and think tanks like the Center for Security Policy, the Society of Americans for National Existence, the Middle East Forum, Jihad Watch, Stop Islamization of America, and the Investigative Project on Terrorism. These disinformation experts hawked conspiracies about Islam and Muslim Americans to attentive publics and distributed anti-Muslim legislation to politicians around the country in exchange for campaign donations.

Mobilized by the threat of the Ground Zero Mosque, anti-Muslim protesters descended on Lower Manhattan and the Park51 Islamic Center. While counterprotesters maintained support for the community center, the anti-Muslim message had been amplified, gaining traction around the country and leading to similar protests against Islamic centers across the nation. A decade after 9/11, anti-Muslim sentiment had only grown, and in 2011, Peter King held congressional hearings on "the extent of radicalization in the American Muslim community and that community's response." The controversial "radicalization hearings" reproduced much of the anti-Muslim discourse hawked by the Islamophobia movement, heightening the perception of a "homegrown threat." The moral panic was compared to the McCarthy hearings of the 1950s that worked to root out communists in their midst and turned communities against one another. With a coalition of more than forty groups, the ACLU issued a statement condemning the hearings by reminding publics of the dangers of the past, where "treating an entire community as suspect because of the bad acts or intolerant statements of a few is imprudent and unfair, and in the past has only led to greater misunderstanding, injustice and discrimination." The letter cited how theories of eugenics supported racist immigration policies and Jim Crow anti-miscegenation laws, how "misguided 'red' scares and racism drove abominable policies like blacklists, McCarthyism and Japanese internment, betrayed American values and did not improve security." Yet the hearings went on, and Peter King defended the decision by arguing that the Obama administration itself approved of his aims, that "the fact is the White House has said that the radicalization of the American Muslim community is a serious issue."[50] Among King's targets at the hearing was the Muslim civil rights group CAIR, whom he framed as uncredible co-conspirators to terrorists.

This onslaught of anti-Muslim organizing and public sentiment drove shifts in how Muslims viewed their identity and, subsequently, their strategic uses of memory. Muslim activists described a growing understanding that despite their perception of Muslims as a wrongfully stigmatized model immigrant group, the external perception of Muslims as foreign, criminal threats was more powerful. One organizer described her growing understanding that despite her best efforts at expressing her American identity, Muslims would continue to be seen as outsiders:

> This is colored by my own experience, but I think issues of race and immigration come up for me. What Muslims experience, broadly . . . the majority of us were raised in this country, seen as people of color, as different . . . so even when you're third or fourth generation, you still feel like I'm not completely from here . . . who am I? Who do I belong to? . . . Racism in general is a big challenge.

Her comments illustrated a perception shared by many other Muslim organizers that there was no pathway to inclusion through a color-blind articulation of multiracial Americans, arms linked in a shared vision of equal rights. The boundaries of American identity were impermeable and the identity options available to Muslims limited. They were not only seen as non-White but also seen as perpetual foreigners, a perception that "I'm not completely from here."

Like Black: Building Bridges through Memory

In 2011, the Associated Press (AP) released an alarming report that revealed extensive surveillance of Muslim communities by the New York Police Department (NYPD). Muslim community members knew there were surveillance programs. However, the AP report revealed surveillance that left no Muslim untouched. The report included hundreds of pages of internal police documents and indicated that undercover officers had infiltrated 250 mosques in New York and New Jersey, monitored Muslim student associations at colleges and universities, and identified hundreds of "hot spots," including restaurants and businesses, in the hunt for terrorists. The NYPD's strategies ranged from trolling through Facebook accounts to sending an undercover agent on a student whitewater rafting trip where he recorded students' names and noted in his files how many times they prayed. As reports later confirmed, they did not find one terrorist.[51]

Much of the Muslim community at large was shocked by the report and it made national news. Faroque Khan was quoted saying, "It's profiling and surveilling American citizens without any due process, without any reasons or validity." In focus groups, this event came up time and time again to highlight not only a reason to strategize but, more profoundly, a shift in how the community viewed its identity in relation to other groups and the legitimacy of the carceral system that targeted them. In turn, these sharpened perceptions shifted how they approached their uses of collective memory. One organizer explained, "When we have a police force that openly flaunts constitutional protections and creates a spying division that seeks out nothing but Muslim

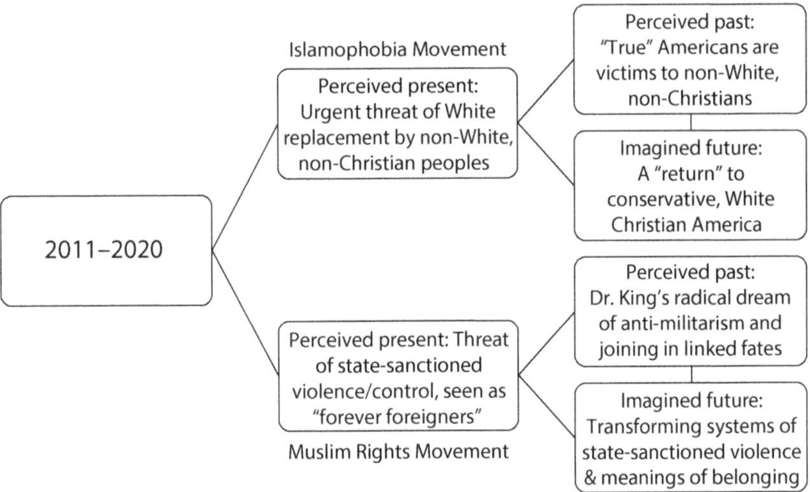

FIGURE 5.3. Muslim and Islamophobia movements' rivaling uses of memory from 2011 to 2020.

and Arab communities there's a problem with that and that's not the dream that Martin Luther King had." Another organizer described how the lessons of the civil rights movement highlighted the importance of mobilization: "Part of [Dr. King's] speech was about the urgency of now, and definitely in the Muslim community in these past two years it's got urgent. People finally realized you cannot afford not to be politicized because you're going to be targeted either way."[52]

Anti-Muslim practices were playing out at the national level as well, under the guise of homeland security. In 2011, President Obama issued a national strategy, "Empowering Local Partners to Prevent Violent Extremism," calling for law enforcement agencies to adopt community policing models to prevent terrorism. The plan specifically highlighted American Muslims "whose children, families, and neighbors are being targeted for recruitment by al-Qa'ida." Despite the lack of evidence that Muslims were any more likely to engage in terrorism than other groups, the public perception—fueled by post-9/11 policies, growing anti-Muslim movements from the right, and inordinate media attention—was that Muslim Americans were vulnerable to radicalization. The strategy's rationale was that by building trust with Muslim immigrant communities, community members would help police identify extremists and foil potential attacks.

These political realities were a catalyst for a recalibrated perception of group position for Muslim immigrants and politicized otherwise apathetic Muslim community members. However, the enduring dilemmas of collective identity reemerged as newly mobilizing immigrants perceived this surveillance as unique, aberrant injustice while those who had long been organizing and learning the history of civil rights struggle in America along the way understood its connection to a trajectory of state surveillance. As one organizer explained, "When you sit down with some leaders in the [local] African American community, they'll say 'why are you talking about this in terms of Muslims,' the government are using the same tricks from the COINTELPRO intelligence-gathering era and this is just the same game different name." He went on to say, "If law enforcement is engaging in tactics that members of the Muslim community find troubling, what's fascinating is how people find it troubling for different reasons. Some find it troubling because they're like, I'm part of a new community and we're being singled out, while others find it troubling because this is the same thing I saw thirty years ago. People are not finding it troubling for the same reasons."

Young, second-generation Muslims, growing up alongside Black classmates, learning about American history in school, and witnessing movements for social justice on their college campuses, also understood that their experiences were not unique. Through the collective realization of politically sanctioned discrimination, many young Muslims were also coming to see their collective identity as one that was not just stigmatized but also racialized. One young community leader said, "It's experiences where you find out that in your local [Muslim student association] where everyone was a good liberal, it comes out the cops were there [surveilling]. It's not unlikely for you to start critiquing the system overall . . . and to start identifying with other communities that have always had adversarial relationships with the police." Describing law enforcement agencies at large, one community leader said, "They're looking at everybody so no one is excluded anymore. It doesn't matter if you come from a wealthy family, live in an affluent neighborhood, they're looking at everyone." Another organizer added, "Latino and Black communities were the targets, then the target became the Muslim community after 9/11, like other communities before, and they surveilled our schools, restaurants, businesses, they sent informants, and paid informants to go after our kids." Shifting political contexts were forcing Muslim immigrants to reevaluate their collective identity and the imagined pathway toward societal inclusion. Through this back-and-forth process, as events and experiences accumulated to sharpen Muslims' perceptions of the constraints around their identity as well as the systems that construct these identities, their imagined prospects for inclusion shifted. Organizers were not only coming to terms with the unyielding constraints of an ascriptive "Muslim" identity as a racialized foreign threat but questioning the very legitimacy of the structures that deemed them as such, a *systemic critique*, as one organizer described.

Through this recalibrated perception of collective identity, Muslim organizers issued a call to develop strategies to ally with Black and Brown groups. Describing her realization that Muslims would always be marked as something other than White, one organizer suggested, "Maybe we need to reject that whole premise [of aspirational Whiteness] and embrace our solidarity with other people of color and also recognize we're privileged within that schema." Her comments highlight how Muslim collective identity was conceptualized in relational terms, where without the prospects of Whiteness, Muslim identity and experience were imagined as analogous to those of people of color. Through this shifting conception of group position, another organizer described how identity was coupled with strategy: "I think that what we need to do is . . . activate our connections to communities of color that suffer from police brutality, turn that into systematic militant action, militant like the civil rights movement." Organizers who had seen Muslim activism as best accomplished quietly, "respectfully," by using civil rights memory as color-blind inclusion, were now articulating a memory of radical struggle and adjusting their strategies accordingly.

Grassroots activism and coalition-building, long deemed the domain of racial minority groups, began to seem like the only way forward. As activists worked toward group understandings of this racialization, their strategies shifted toward building alliances across this new conception of Muslim identity as racialized, bound in the same systems of oppression as experienced by African Americans and Latinos. Many Muslim leaders began mobilizing community members toward this new conception of collective identity as one not superior to or separate from that of Black people but in solidarity with them. To produce this solidarity, Muslim activists began drawing on a branch of memory that focalized King's radical legacy, anti-militarism, and systemic critique of a racist society. One community leader explained the necessity of coalition-building through the collective memory of the civil rights movement: "The time of MLK was the time of a huge social movement that appealed to many people and it wasn't just one small group of people getting involved." Another community leader said, "Muslim families who immigrated to this country, in particular, must understand that we owe much to and have much to learn from the leaders of the civil rights movement." Muslim leaders deployed similar strategies in sermons and rallies, in op-eds and blog posts, a recurring theme of joining in solidarity with minority groups by deploying the memory of the civil rights movement to establish an analogous experience of Muslim identity as racialized.

Organizations formed to build bridges between non-Black Muslims and Black Americans, such as Muslims for Ferguson and joint grassroots efforts with local Black Lives Matter organizers. These alliances contrasted starkly

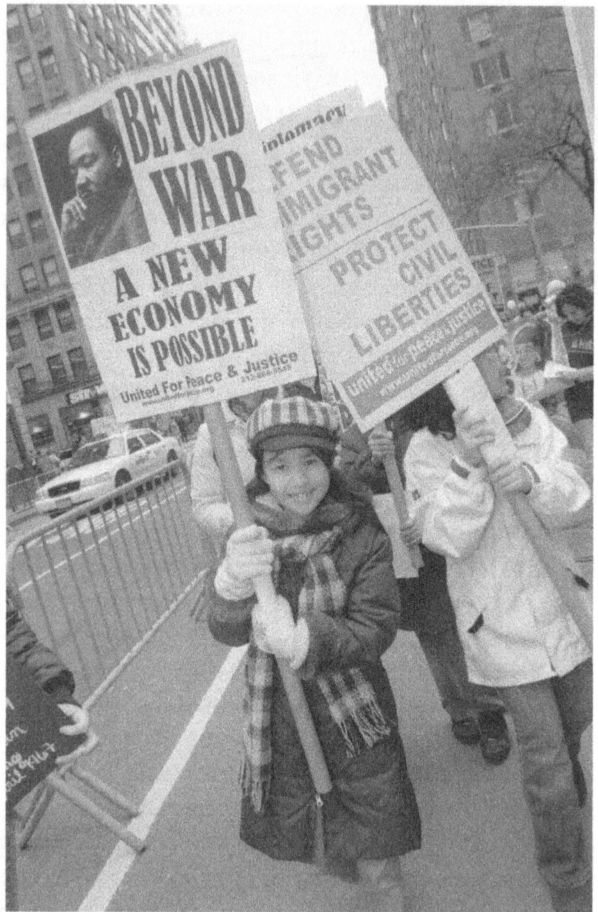

FIGURE 5.4. Anti-war protesters march in New York City. Richard Levine/Alamy Stock Photo.

with the strategies of Muslim immigrant activists just a decade prior. Muslim activists were contending with a growing understanding of the deep roots of racialization, which extended beyond individual interactions and attitudes and were hardened in institutional policies and systemic practices. Their experiences were not unique, nor were they new. Mustafa Abdullah, one of the leaders of Muslims for Ferguson, said, "I think that for the Muslims . . . we are really beginning to see that our experiences of racial profiling, our experiences of surveillance . . . the increasing militarization of the world and American police departments . . . we are really beginning to see that all of this is tied up with and connected to the experiences of African Americans, particularly black and brown youth in this country."[53] Through these strategic invocations and coalitions, Muslim organizers took the constraints of identity—as a racialized, criminalized group—and turned them into strategies for coalition-building in a new conceptualization of inclusion.

However, these strategies most often constructed Muslim identity as "like Black" rather than "also Black," often excluding Black Muslims. For example, in 2014, CAIR released a video called "Islamophobia and the Civil Rights Movement" in honor of their twentieth anniversary. The video opens with a historic shot of Japanese internment then segues into historic footage of the civil rights movement juxtaposed with present-day images of burning mosques, anti-Muslim vandalism, and interviews with non-Black Muslims about their experiences of discrimination. A woman's voice recalls, "Islamophobia is not much different from what I went through growing up in Selma, Alabama." Black Muslims are virtually absent from the video. At the Annual Muslim American Society and Islamic Circle of North America Convention, activist Khalilah Sabra called on the audience to mobilize, declaring, "Basically you are the new Black people of America." Although they had come to understand their collective identity as racialized, many organizers had yet to acknowledge that Muslims in America were not just *like* Blacks, they were *also* Black. But the movement was facing larger problems. As Muslim immigrant organizers worked to couple their identity with the memory of the civil rights movement, a backlash was growing.

Backlash and the Racial Boundaries of Memory

As the movement for Muslim rights gained steam, generating alliances through a conception of a "new civil rights movement" and grassroots membership, anti-Muslim groups took notice. A counternarrative actively worked to deconstruct memory deployments that framed Muslim rights as analogous to Black civil rights. On conservative forums, critics discredited the comparison between anti-Muslim discrimination and anti-Black racism, as well as that between religion and race. Anti-Muslim leader Daniel Pipes echoed prior claims that CAIR was "Islamists fooling the establishment," arguing that alleged links between Muslim civil rights organizers and terrorist organizations contradicted CAIR's self-identification as "like the Muslim NAACP."[54] On right-wing forums, one commenter wrote, "Rampant emotional rhetoric designed to fool the stupid. I fail to see how subjugation via religion is even remotely comparable to the Civil Rights Movement." Another commenter wrote, "CAIR has stated its grand jihad goal is eliminating and destroying Western civilization from within. Don't believe that's a civil right, they're a domestic terrorist org. period."[55]

Anti-Muslim organizers also discredited the crux of the memory deployment itself: the appeal to a collective memory of civil rights for legitimacy and cultural resonance. For example, commenter wrote, "This 'civil rights' thing has become as used and abused as the race card. Everything these days is falsely tied at the hip with civil rights. Killing innocent life is one, having a house is one, gay marriage, free everything is another . . . you can add to list infinitely." Similarly, another commenter wrote, "We know from the manuals recovered in raids that the Islamics have elaborately worked out how to use liberal guilt and its attendant panoply of signs, signals and portents—all based on state-of-the-art mid-20th century politics—to baffle and confuse the Politically Correct." Perceived as a strategic tool tapping into a repertoire of familiar cultural meanings, conservative critics railed against the memory deployment as a sort of conspiracy by Islamists.

As in many countermemory strategies, critics drew on alternative branches of the collective memory to discredit the use of memory. One commenter wrote, "The Muslim phonies hijack the name of Martin Luther King, Jr.—who was PRO-ISRAEL—and try to make the civil rights struggle of Black people (many of whose ancestors were sold into slavery by Muslim Arabs) into the same thing as defending a violent religion that commits terrorist acts around the world every single hour." Weaponizing memory in a projective reversal to identify Muslims as the threats to King's legacy, the commenter continued, "It's amazing that a religion whose US-based 'leaders' constantly claim that the 9/11 hijackers hijacked a religion (rather than what really happened—Islam hijacked them), is so consistent in its hijacking of things that stand counter to what Islam stands for. And, with Martin Luther King, Jr., they hijack the name and legacy of a man who stood with Israel and against them."[56]

Using one articulation of collective memory to counter another, this powerful backlash worked to decouple the strategic connection between Muslim identity and the collective memory of the civil rights movement. The Muslim rights movement was faced with a serious dilemma. The collective memory of the civil rights movement was not perceived as a cultural resource that belonged to them. Having come to understand their collective identity as racialized, Muslim activists needed to root themselves in a collective memory that would give them a claim to American identity.

Also Black: Reviving a Fringe Memory for a New Identity

For years, Black Muslims had reminded Muslim immigrants of their roots in a radical Black struggle, of the connection between their present experiences of discrimination and surveillance and those Black Muslims had faced in the past. They had been met with silence and, at times, disdain. When police fired forty-one shots at Amadou Diallo in 1999, killing the unarmed twenty-three-year-old West African Muslim immigrant outside his apartment building, Imam Talib could not find an immigrant mosque that would stand with him to challenge the police. "What we've found is when domestic issues jump up, like police brutality, all the sudden we're by ourselves,"[57] he recalled.

Now, some organizers were finally listening. Linda Sarsour, the outspoken Palestinian American activist and executive director of the Arab American Association of New York, passionately declared, "We are ready to fight harder than we ever have for Black sisters and brothers including our own dear Black sisters and brothers in the Muslim community. No more sitting on the sidelines. No more empty outrage. We got you."[58] One organizer identified the lessons learned in the shortcomings of earlier strategies, of learning to move away from anti-Black aspirational Whiteness as inclusion toward societal critique as a mode of inclusion: "We need to be American by making America live up to the ideas that it aspires to, versus being 'socially white' and aspiring to whiteness as our way of asserting our American-ness. . . . We need to examine our identities." She went on to describe grassroots activism and societal critique as fundamentally American. "We need to not have a problem with being the outsider," she wrote. "That is American. That's what it means to Black American Muslims to be American versus those of us who are immigrants, where our identities are more fragile and we're still negotiating them in the public space."[59]

This organizer's comments illustrate a dynamic through which activists were not only transforming collective identity to challenge how American society viewed their community but transforming collective identity to challenge their own community's internalization and reproduction of those systems of inequality. They were questioning the very rationales on which historical pathways of inclusion were built. Innovating their uses of memory, Muslim activists drew upon the very history of the Muslim rights movement in America, a Black Muslim movement of the civil rights era. To begin to forge genuine connections to Black Muslim communities, organizers deployed collective memory internally, unrolling educational campaigns like CAIR's Alabama Civil Rights Tour to teach Muslim immigrants the history of Muslims in America. In a speech at the Audubon Ballroom, where Malcolm X was assassinated, Imam Suleiman, the popular Palestinian American imam, said, "The world, and this country specifically, needs Malcolm's message now more than ever. With the deliberate attempts to erase him from history, we must push back. . . . When young Muslims exercise their right to not only live with dignity in this country, but also challenge the country to be more dignified, we owe Malcolm."[60] Back in Long Island, Dr. Faroque Khan acknowledged, "All of us need to learn from and understand the contributions of the Muslim indigenous community. Starting with Malcolm X."[61]

Muslim student associations across the country began implementing programs to educate themselves and community members about the history of Muslim struggle in the United States, rooted in Black civil rights history. For example, Muslim students at the University of Chicago invited Imam Talib from Harlem to speak on the forty-ninth anniversary of Malcolm X's death. He delivered a powerful lecture titled "Malcolm X: Reclaiming His Legacy." Opening with a discussion of a recent controversy, Talib described how fourth-grade students at a Queens elementary school were forbidden to give class presentations on Malcolm X. He explained, "There is a tendency in this country to hold Dr. Martin Luther King, Jr. on a pedestal when talking about Black history and about the Civil Rights Movement. But this point of view doesn't give attention to [Malcolm X], the giant at the other end of the fork."[62] He went on to describe the longer history of Muslims in the United States, rooting Muslim experience in American identity. The mostly second-generation Muslim audience listened with rapt attention. In 2015, with the Caucus of African American Leaders, CAIR sponsored a tribute to Malcolm X on what would have been his ninetieth birthday, celebrating his contributions to Muslim Americans and social justice more broadly.

Recognizing the vast internal work to be done to forge bridges between Muslim immigrants and Black Muslims, some organizers turned their efforts solely toward eradicating the anti-Black racism that had so long limited the Muslim rights movement. One valuable offshoot of these efforts, the Muslim Anti-Racism Collaborative, was launched by a Black Muslim woman and a Bangladeshi American Muslim woman. Their joint press release read:

> State violence against Black Americans does not bypass American Muslim communities. . . . Our faith mandates that American Muslims advocate for justice in the killings of all innocent civilians irrespective of whether it is the popular stance to take. Let us align ourselves with the countless others who are demanding justice by declaring that this stops today. . . . As Malcolm X noted in his Letter from Mecca after completing Hajj, "America needs to understand Islam, because this is the one religion that erases from its society the race problem."[63]

The organization coupled the memory of the civil rights movement and Black freedom struggle with Islamic theology, developing training and tool kits to use in sharing principles of anti-racism with other Muslim organizations. Muslim organizers were not only innovating strategies that situated Muslim identity within American history, giving Muslim immigrants a claim to civil rights memory, but also generating a new collective identity that was not just *like* Black but *also* Black. These strategies would have been unimaginable a decade earlier when Muslim collective identity was perceived as not Black, as inclusion through Whiteness.

Some activists pushed back against these memory deployments, questioning the credibility of the identity equation and the sincerity of the solidarity. One organizer argued:

> But the African American struggle is different from us who go to private schools and have banquets and go to the [local upscale] hotel and that's a different narrative than civil rights. For a Black youth to say I have a fear of police is different, but for Muslims who think they'll lead a revolution out of [city], I can't take you seriously. . . . Their history is not our present. . . . A third of Muslims are Black, I'm not saying they're not ours, but if you're going to co-opt and appropriate that struggle and use Malcolm X and MLK's words, then you have to be there at Ferguson and really own this, then do it all the way. If you're not there because of Mike Brown or Trayvon, where's your work with all the grassroots Black populations? You're working with Arab and Indo-Pakistani Muslims, it's schizophrenic, there's no consistency.

These comments highlight ongoing debates among some members of the community who negotiated competing perceptions of who they believed themselves to be and who society deemed them to be, generating fragmented perceptions of their collective path forward as Muslim Americans.

To be sure, there had been much progress since the 1980s. In that wealthy suburban community on Long Island, Dr. Faroque Khan would never have imagined in 1992 that twenty years later his Islamic Center would invite Black Muslims to celebrate Malcolm X's life alongside Muslim immigrants, as they did in 2012 with the event "The 'X' Factor: The Life and Legacy of Malcolm X." But how deep did the solidarities run? Would the Indian engineers in the BMWs show up to protest Eric Garner's death by police chokehold? Or would they simply issue tactfully worded public statements and maintain their positions on police commissioners' advisory boards?

In focus groups, some community organizers described these tensions as a "conflation of identity . . . these terms of 'house Muslim' and 'field Muslim,'" comparing the enduring dilemmas of identity among Muslim activists to Malcolm X's famous delineation of the "house Negro" and "field Negro." In his famous 1963 speech, Malcolm X describes the "house Negro" as the slave who defines himself through his master, upholds his system of power and violence, a false consciousness where the individual has internalized the power hierarchy and fails to recognize their relationship to the "field negro," those deemed inferior and brutalized outside the walls. Another organizer explained the comparison, saying, "Those who engage the government are the 'house Negroes,' good Muslims, and those who are the oppositional 'field Muslims' are righteous in their cause and opposition to the government." Malcolm X's conceptualization reflected the very idea that the way in which one perceives their identity, their social location, shapes the way they act and understand their capacity to act.

The Consequences

For Muslim activists without a shared understanding of this collective identity, it would be impossible to generate a unified front, a unified strategy for challenging the emboldened nativism and Islamophobia in the run-up to the 2016 election. At the same time, new alliances had been forged and new forms of political power generated, and for many of the young second-generation Muslim activists coming of age in the dawn of the Trump era, there was a reason to be hopeful that a real resistance was coming.

The consequences of these hard-learned lessons about the boundaries of racial identity in a racial capitalist society like the United States would shape not only the political and cultural discourses about Muslims but also Muslim activists' perceptions of identity and who they wanted to be. By focalizing activists' perceptions of collective identity and the political contexts in which they were shaped, this chapter has shown that the strategic uses of memory are shaped through activists' understandings of the racial boundaries of culture and their place in it. Mobilizing groups' collective identities are always in flux, dynamic and contested, internally and externally, within organizations, coalitions, and national movements. The inextricable link between collective identity and strategy can entail conceptualizing new forms of groupness and symbolic boundaries. It was the very experience of bumping up against boundaries, of learning their rigid, unyielding nature, that enabled a new mode of thinking and perceiving the world. The impacts of mobilization were not only the immediate material effects of identifiable political and legal changes. The impacts of mobilization were embodied, reshaping activists' modes of cognition and seeing the world.

As W.E.B. Du Bois described, while deeply constraining on the one hand, double vision also allows new ways of seeing.[64] With identity options constrained, Muslim activists were freed up to imagine new forms of belonging, new forms of groupness. A branch of collective memory representing the deep solidarities between groups united in a linked fate becomes a cultural bridge toward radical forms of groupness, challenging the racialized boundaries of American belonging. These bonds would be activated in the days after President Trump's 2017 Muslim ban, when broad-based Black, Brown, Asian, and Jewish coalitions came together to protest at airports, in the streets, and outside courthouses. One Black woman protesting at the Atlanta airport expressed her solidarity with Muslim Americans: "This nation was built on the backs of immigrants—those who came on their own accord and those of us who were brought here in chains." Calling on the legacy of the civil rights movement that preceded her she said, "It's a shame that 50 years later we're still doing the same thing."[65]

6

#MeToo, Black Feminism, and the Queenmakers

RESTORING THE INTERSECTIONAL LEGACIES OF THE CIVIL RIGHTS MOVEMENT

> One of the things that has to be faced is the process of waiting to change the system, how much we have got to do to find out who we are, where we have come from and where we are going.
>
> —ELLA BAKER

> What we must do is commit ourselves to some future that can include each other and to work toward that future with the particular strengths of our individual identities. And in order to do this, we must allow each other our differences at the same time as we recognize our sameness.
>
> —AUDRE LORDE, *SISTER OUTSIDER*

IN EARLY January 2018 at the Golden Globe Awards, Oprah Winfrey was called to the stage as the first Black woman to receive the Cecil B. DeMille lifetime achievement award. In her electrifying acceptance speech, Winfrey described the power of representation in her journey, her own transformative experience as a little girl watching Sidney Poitier, a Black man, accept the Best Actor award at the Oscars in 1964. She held up the particular importance of the moment, an evening when she and many of the actresses in the audience were wearing black in solidarity with the #MeToo movement as a testament to the power of stories, of truth telling. The speech Oprah went on to give was later coined the "#TimesUp speech," an impassioned call to collective action igniting headlines like "Oprah's Globes Speech Sparks 2020 Presidential Speculation."[1]

Oprah began her speech with these words: "I want tonight to express gratitude to all the women who have endured years of abuse and assault because they, like my mother, had children to feed and bills to pay and dreams to pursue. They're the women whose names we'll never know. . . . And there's someone else, Recy Taylor, a name I know and I think you should know, too." Oprah then told the story of Recy Taylor, a young Black wife and mother who, in 1944, was abducted by six armed White men on her walk home from church in Abbeville, Alabama. She was brutally raped and left blindfolded on the side of the road with their words ringing in her ears: they would kill her if she ever shared her story. Still, Taylor bravely reported the story to the NAACP, where a young investigator named Rosa Parks became the lead on her case. However, as Oprah explained, "justice wasn't an option in the era of Jim Crow. The men who tried to destroy her were never prosecuted." Oprah paused poignantly. "Recy Taylor died ten days ago," she said, "just shy of her ninety-eighth birthday. She lived as we all have lived, too many years in a culture broken by brutally powerful men. For too long, women have not been heard or believed if they dared to speak their truth to the power of those men. But their time is up. Their time is up."

Driving the words home, Oprah repeated, "Their time is up. And I just hope—I just hope that Recy Taylor died knowing that her truth, like the truth of so many other women who were tormented in those years, and even now tormented, goes marching on. It was somewhere in Rosa Parks's heart almost eleven years later, when she made the decision to stay seated on that bus in Montgomery, and it's here with every woman who chooses to say, 'Me too.' And every man—every man who chooses to listen." With the audience stirring in their seats at the moving speech, Oprah concluded, "So I want all the girls watching here and now to know that a new day is on the horizon! And when that new day finally dawns, it will be because of a lot of magnificent women, many of whom are right here in this room tonight, and some pretty phenomenal men, fighting hard to make sure that they become the leaders who take us to the time when nobody ever has to say 'me too' again."

Cameras panned to the star-studded audience as they rose in their seats, many with tears streaming down their faces, standing in ovation. Op-eds following the speech would compare Oprah's powerful oratory to those of civil rights leaders of the past. As one op-ed read, "Winfrey's words echoed those of Martin Luther King Jr., giving a voice to the voiceless and promising justice for the downtrodden. Without even mentioning him, she was able to bring the spirit of King's work to her speech that night."[2] But Oprah was not just channeling the memory of the civil rights movement to make sense of the present moment. Oprah was also *restoring* the memory of the civil rights movement. Oprah spoke Recy Taylor's name into public consciousness that evening, work that Black activists and historians had been doing for years to restore the pivotal role of Black women in Dr. King's legacy and civil rights memory.

Yet the year prior to Oprah's Golden Globes speech, it was a White woman, documentary filmmaker and producer Nancy Buirski, who released *The Rape of Recy Taylor* to tell Recy's story. The day after Oprah's speech, Buirski appeared on CNN to discuss the documentary and Oprah's speech with journalist Brooke Baldwin. Buirski described screaming out in excitement when Oprah mentioned Recy Taylor's name, explaining the importance of Taylor's work for charting the path of the contemporary #MeToo movement:

> BUIRSKI: She was so brave when her life was at risk. So you know, she's the start of this [#MeToo] movement. She's really the foundation for what we're celebrating today.
>
> BALDWIN: Say her name, Recy Taylor. . . .
>
> BUIRSKI: That's right. And so she's not only courageous on her own, but she is a symbol and a metaphor for so many women who didn't have the chance to speak out.

Two White women discussing a Black woman's historical leadership on a mainstream news outlet may not seem especially noteworthy. Yet, as some critics would write, White women representing Black women's histories spoke to the growing tensions of the moment: whose stories were being told and by whom? Whose voices were silenced in the process? Of the Recy Taylor documentary, the *New Yorker*'s film critic, Richard Brody, wrote, "Buirski's emotionally simplistic approach to her subjects in 'The Rape of Recy Taylor' is inseparable from her arm's-length, impersonal approach to it. She packages information, and she packages the responses to it, instead of conveying a lived, first-person relationship to the subject, to the place, to the people in the film . . . because the violence and the fear that the rape of Recy Taylor, and the impunity of it, depended on isn't over."[3]

The troubled remove between White women and the Black women they claimed to represent echoed the dynamics emerging through the #MeToo movement on social media just months prior. In October 2017, White actress Alyssa Milano took to Twitter and encouraged any women who had been "sexually harassed or assaulted" to "write 'me too' as a reply to this tweet." Within twenty-four hours, "me too" had been shared in more than twenty-four million posts.[4] While the outpouring of stories included women of all races and classes, it was largely influential White women's stories like those of actresses Rose McGowan and Ashley Judd that took center stage and consumed popular media attention.

Quickly, activists called on Milano to acknowledge the roots of the #MeToo movement as emerging from Black woman and longtime organizer Tarana Burke's 2007 movement of the same name for survivors of sexual harassment and assault. Black and Brown activists were particularly attuned to the

disparity in how these stories were being treated, both in whose stories were being amplified and in whose stories were being either discredited or ignored altogether.[5] After all, it was not just that Black and Brown women also experienced sexual harassment and violence. It was that these experiences were *also* raced and classed—they were shaped across intersectional social locations—meaning they experienced particular forms of violence, with fewer options for redressing harm compared to powerful White women. Yet these complexities were often obscured by White feminists focused on generating unified "women's movements."

Digital strategist and activist April Reign, a Black woman, began circulating a corresponding hashtag, #WOCAffirmation, as an affirmation of the invisibilized experiences of women of color. In an interview she explained, "White women have not been as supportive as they could have been of women of color when they experience targeted abuse and harassment. . . . We used it as a peaceful moment to say feminism should be intersectional. If there is support for Rose McGowan, which is great, you need to be consistent across the board. All women stand with all women." Reign went on to describe how White women had already erased the #MeToo movement's history: "Women of color are demanded to be silent and are erased. Like with Tarana." Actor and feminist Jane Fonda remarked, "It's too bad that [the #MeToo shift] is probably because so many of the women that were assaulted by Harvey Weinstein are famous and White and everybody knows them. This has been going on a long time to black women and other women of color and it doesn't get out quite the same."[6] Two days after her initial tweet, Milano reached out to Tarana Burke to join forces and grow the #MeToo movement together. These dynamics between White and Black feminists were not new, but their increasingly public face increased the urgency of their resolution. Many activists recognized that the future of feminism required a deep reckoning with the past—feminist pasts, racial pasts, and their intersections. It was no coincidence that Oprah focalized an overlooked Black woman in her speech.

As the previous chapters have shown, mobilizing groups understand that the way publics remember the past shapes the actions they pursue toward an imagined future. As a result, remaking the collective memory of the civil rights movement and its symbolic figures for present-day political goals is not a mere rhetorical strategy. These recrafted memories tell a particular story about America's racial history: its heroes and villains, whether racial inequality is a matter of the past or present, how much progress has been made and how far we have to go. These divergent stories about the past are consequential. They enable and constrain how groups imagine and pursue social change.

As these chapters have also shown, this work of "Kingmaking," of strategically recrafting collective memory for political purposes, requires making convincing linkages between mobilizing groups' political goals and collective memory. It is in this strategic work and its contestation by countermovements that deeper cultural meanings emerge, clarifying where power lies and for whom credibility and cultural ownership are assumed. Prior chapters have shown the range of strategies groups deploy to make these claims—from LGBTQ activists retrieving the memory of Bayard Rustin as a gay civil rights leader pivotal to Dr. King's ascendance to Muslim immigrant activists holding up the memory of Black Muslim civil rights leaders like Malcolm X to establish the long roots of Islam in America and make claims to American identity. Yet as this chapter will show, retrieving these "hidden figures" of collective memory is not only about remaking the past to make a more convincing political claim in the present. Remaking the past can also be a process of restoration, a process of truth and reconciliation.[7]

Where the prior chapters showed how the battles over collective memory reveal the moral, national, and racial boundaries of culture, this chapter shows how these intersecting boundaries are remade through contemporary feminist movements. Examining how these movements grapple with questions of identity, power, and the conflictual lineages of White and Black feminism, I show how feminists work to reconcile their present-day conflicts through the past, and specifically, the essential historic leadership of Black women in civil rights movements. What results is a process of Kingmaking—restoring the legacies of the civil rights movement—by "Queenmaking," lifting up the Black women whose activism, sacrifice, and leadership paved the way for contemporary movements. I also show how these intramovement challenges are further complicated by growing reactionary countermovements for "men's rights"—as in #HimToo—that work to discredit women's claims and frame men as the new victims. This chapter shows how collective memory can be recrafted strategically not only to reimagine "who we could be" but also to root these imagined futures in revelations about "who we have been all along," restoring the branches of the neglected past.

The Intersectional Boundaries of Collective Memory

Given its cultural power, the construction of collective memory is a contentious political process with high stakes. For mobilizing groups, strategic uses of collective memory often require resifting through history, looking for the branches of memory that can be upheld and grown as evidence of the group's claims.[8] Through this selective re-representation of the past, a group works to mobilize support and action toward their imagined societal future. There are patterns in how these claims to the past are made, how they are enabled and constrained by groups' relative levels of power in society, and the consequences of political uses of memory for how publics make sense of social inequality.

Yet resifting through history to remake collective memory can also serve another powerful function: restoration and reconciliation. As studies of gender and collective memory show, women have long been obscured in institutionalized stories of the past that center the "Kings," the prominent "great men" to whom sweeping social change is attributed.[9] Many of the case studies in this book have shown how Dr. King is so often the referent point for the collective memory of the civil rights movement, the inspirational leader upheld as *the reason*, the catalyst, for racial progress.

In response, feminist movements have done significant memory work to lift up the pivotal roles of women in history, from the women central to Holocaust resistance to the Black women who led apartheid resistance in South Africa.[10] These feminist movements imagine the restoration of the collective past, the correction of the historical record, as essential to the work of dismantling patriarchy. As Zakiya Luna and Whitney Pirtle write of a Black feminist sociology, "Black scholars have long understood that knowledge is a collective process."[11] Charting a path forward is impossible, after all, without being unequivocal about women's place in society—not as supporting characters behind the scenes but as central players, as leaders, as *queens*, at every turn. For example, Cheryl McEwan's study of memory processes in post-apartheid South Africa shows how Black women challenge the sanitization of collective memory and erasure of Black women, understanding that their societal belonging in the future is *contingent on writing their existence* into the past.[12]

Yet these feminist restorations of the past are not without their own conflicts and reproductions of inequality, specifically in the *longue durée* of western White feminism that has invisibilized indigenous, Black, and Brown women.[13] In the United States, Black women, activists, and historians have mobilized to center the pivotal role of Black women in American history including the long civil rights movement that precedes the 1960s back to the founding of the United States and proceeds into the present.[14] For example, historian Barbara Ransby has written extensively about Black women like Ella Baker and Fannie Lou Hamer, contextualizing their historic work to draw through lines to present-day inequalities: "Simple inclusion was not really what Hamer and her band of social-justice crusaders were demanding in 1964. They did not simply want brown faces in high places. Their demand was that elected officials take a long hard look at the lives of people like Hamer, people at the bottom of the social and economic hierarchy. They wanted these officials to develop policies that improve those conditions." Ransby explains the continued legacy of this unfinished work today: "It's sad to say, but today, those who live Hamer's pain are still with us. They live in migrant-worker communities, in soon-to-be-torn-down housing projects, prison cells, homeless shelters and cramped shacks. They exist with few resources and dwindling allies."[15]

These Black women—the "unsung heroes," "torchbearers," "hidden figures"—have been obscured through the intersecting constraints of systems of power that rely on Black women's bodies and labor but too often invisibilize their voices and humanity.[16] As political and cultural contexts have shifted toward greater receptivity of these retellings of the past, concealed "herstories" of "sheroes" have increasingly come to the cultural fore, both through specific movements to reclaim Black women's centrality in American history and through the rise of new public spheres that amplify grassroots movements. As media scholars have shown, the rise of social media has expanded public spheres of deliberation and meaning-making, where traditional institutions like the government and mainstream media are not the only "Kingmakers" shaping the boundaries of collective memory. Twitter, for example, is an emergent public sphere where alternative memories can take hold, reshaping stories about the past and uncovering untold histories.[17]

Through these virtual spheres contemporary feminist movements like #MeToo and #SayHerName have diffused rapidly, amplifying women's voices, stories, and histories. Yet these feminist movements have not escaped the old tensions about how to come together to challenge the power structure "out there"—patriarchy—while also grappling with the enduring power structure inside—racial capitalism—specifically across intersections of race and class.[18] What this chapter shows is that, increasingly, activists understand that these tensions cannot be reconciled to make forward progress without looking backward. To chart this path, feminist activists must restore the collective memory of Black women as central to King's legacy, as civil rights leaders, the queens who laid the groundwork for White and Black feminists alike, to unify feminisms toward an intersectional future.

Analyzing Digital Activism

With the rise of digital activism, many social movement scholars have considered whether contemporary movements coalescing around hashtags in virtual spaces are "real" mobilizations or simply an extension of the performative politics of virtual spaces. How can scholars study a phenomenon as diffuse as "hashtag activism"? Growing scholarly work in digital activism shows that these movements are not only real but have transformative power for reshaping public opinion and consciousness.[19] As communication scholars Sarah Jackson, Moya Bailey, and Brooke Foucault Welles write in their aptly named book, *#HashtagActvism*, "Ordinary African Americans, women, transgender people, and others aligned with racial justice and feminist causes have long been excluded from elite media spaces yet have repurposed Twitter in particular to make identity-based cultural and political demands, and in doing so have forever changed national consciousness."[20] These studies often use mixed methods—content analysis, virtual ethnography, computational text analysis—to examine questions about how digital activism takes shape and the extent to which it is influential.

Following this scholarship, to make sense of how the #MeToo, Black feminist, and rival #HimToo movements interact and pursue their goals, this chapter traces their dynamics between 2016 and 2020 combining three forms of data: social movement organizational documents from publicly available websites including website content, press releases, organizational publications, and archived interviews; newspaper data; and social media data from Twitter (see methodological appendix). These narrative analyses illustrate the processual, interactive nature of strategy construction, intramovement conflicts, and the strategic *re*construction of collective memory.

From White Women's Tears to "Black Women Will Save Us"

Despite popular ridicule of "the Karen" as a meme, an archetype of White women's entitlement, tears, and performative victimhood, White women's innocence has long been a cultural structure legitimizing White racism and violence. The dehumanization of Black Americans under slavery assembled Blackness as an animalistic, dangerous threat, such that enslaved Black men were constructed as sexual threats to White women. Communications scholar Apryl Williams explains, "White women are positioned as the virtue of society because they hold that position as the mother, as the keepers of virtuosity, all these ideologies that we associate with white motherhood and white women in particular, their certain role in society gives them power and when you couple that with this racist history, where white women are afraid of black men and black men are hypersexualized and seen as dangerous, then that's really a volatile combination."[21]

Unsurprisingly then, the public face of a sexual violence survivor has most often been a White woman. Social psychological studies have shown that "prototypical" women—largely characterized as White, "feminine-appearing" women—are perceived as more credible in sexual harassment claims compared to "non-prototypical" women.[22] Studies have also documented how television programs and films often depict White women as the sympathetic victims of sexual harassment and the heroic protagonists of battles against sexual violence, whether Charlize Theron in *North Country* or Carey Mulligan in *Promising Young Woman*.[23]

So while Black women are significantly more likely to experience sexual violence and harassment, they are also less likely to be believed when they report it. Black women are less likely to be upheld as courageous fighters when they speak out against sexual harassment or to have films devoted to their stories, told in their own voices. As Gloria Steinem, the White face of the feminist movement of the 1970s, said in a 2017 interview, "The problem, and what [many feminists today] are not saying, is that women of color in general—and especially Black women—have always been more likely to be feminist than white women. And the problem I have with the idea that the women's movement or the feminist movement is somehow a white thing is that it renders invisible the people who have always been there."[24] Black women have always been there. Yet when #MeToo set society into a reflexive tailspin, its public heroes were White women.

Using Memory Work for Solidarity Politics

As #MeToo was confronted with its troubling obfuscation of Black women in 2017, many Black activists felt the familiar echoes of the feminist movements of decades past. For too long, White women's movements had been able to thwart Black women's calls for recognition, for visibility, by virtue of their power as protected White women. Even the women's marches earlier that year, a massive wave of pink hats in the streets in reaction to Donald Trump's election, had been troubled by accusations that White women who had just woken up to the realities of racism and sexism were taking center stage, speaking over longtime indigenous, Black, and Brown activists. As the Palestinian activist and eventual women's march organizer Linda Sarsour explained of their initial reaction, "I'm supposed to go follow, like, a bunch of white ladies who never marched with us before?"[25]

Now, in a political-cultural landscape where a simultaneous mass movement was declaring that Black Lives Matter, Black women's voices could not be ignored. How could feminist activists reconcile these deeply rooted conflicts?

For many activists, it was clear the work would have to begin with a reckoning that acknowledged and *understood* the pasts that led to the present moment. To begin this messy work, activists would draw out the long trajectory of Black women's activism that made #MeToo possible. They would amplify Black women's histories. They would tell the stories of Black women's powerful resistance and how this work had benefited White women time and again.[26] After all, long before the #MeToo movement exposed workplace cultures of sexual harassment and assault, before "getting Weinsteined" became colloquial shorthand for being forced into nonconsensual sexual acts for fear of losing one's job, Black women had been leading the charge against racialized sexual

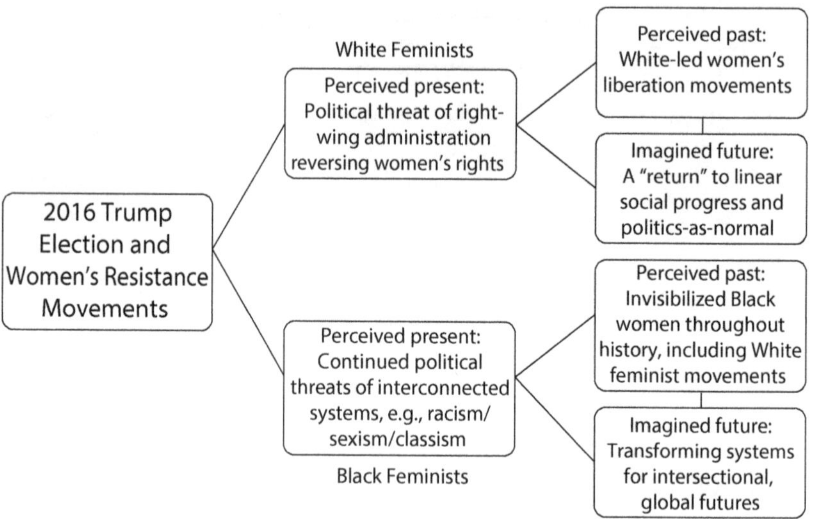

FIGURE 6.1. Black and White feminists' reactionary politics after Trump's election.

violence dating back to the anti-rape and anti-lynching movements of the 1800s.[27] In 1866, Black women, survivors of horrific gang rape by White men during the Memphis Riot, testified before Congress. The White men went free. Still, Black women continued to fight, to resist, the racialized violence that persisted. Ida B. Wells and Fannie Barrier Williams created campaigns against racialized sexual violence, and by the late nineteenth century, Black women had generated a framework for anti-rape movements.[28]

To make sense of the critiques of #MeToo's racism, some media outlets began amplifying these histories, explaining how the legal structures of sexual harassment law that we know today can be traced directly to Black women's resistance in the wake of the civil rights movement. These stories described, for example, how, in 1975, Carmita Wood, a Black employee at a Cornell University lab, resigned after experiencing ongoing sexual advances by her boss. With black civil rights lawyer Eleanor Holmes Norton and activists from Cornell's Human Affairs Office, Wood formed Working Women United. Norton drafted the initial anti-sexual harassment clause that would lead to contemporary sexual harassment guidelines.

In the years following Carmita Wood's case, Black women like Paulette Barnes, who worked at the Environmental Protection Agency, Sandra Bundy, an employee at the DC Department of Corrections, and Dianne Williams, an employee at the U.S. Justice Department, would take their traumatic experiences of workplace sexual harassment and assault to shape landmark sexual harassment lawsuits. As journalist Raina Lipsitz explained, "What these cases have in common is that they helped define sexual harassment as a civil-rights violation that harms women as a group, not a personal problem. . . . Because sexual exploitation was an element of racism for black women from slavery to the present, some scholars have suggested that they were quicker than white women to see sexual harassment as a form of discrimination."[29]

As these stories made their way to mainstream media, some #MeToo organizers were working to reconcile critiques of their own anti-Blackness. Heading into the winter of 2017, Tarana Burke was increasingly drawn into public appearances with Alyssa Milano to signal an acknowledgment of her leadership in the movement. Was it enough? Burke herself was skeptical. Having been an activist and organizer since 1989, her experiences told her otherwise. In an op-ed in the *Washington Post* that November, she wrote:

> What history has shown us time and again is that if marginalized voices—those of people of color, queer people, disabled people, poor people—aren't centered in our movements then they tend to become no more than a footnote. I often say that sexual violence knows no race, class or gender, but the response to it does. . . . Ending sexual violence [and harassment] will require every voice from every corner of the world and it will require those whose voices are most often heard to find ways to amplify those voices that often go unheard.[30]

2018: The Year of the Black Woman?

The new year rolled in, and the 2018 Golden Globe Awards—an annual event of Hollywood sunshine and sparkle amid winter's dreariness—looked different this year. On the red carpet, a sea of black gowns muted the typically vibrant affair. In symbolic solidarity with survivors of sexual violence, many stars had worn black. Supporting the new coalition to fight sexual misconduct, others wore pins that read "Times Up." More notably, a group of high-profile White actors walked the red carpet with unlikely partners: feminist activists of color. Meryl Streep accompanied Ai-jen Poo, director of the National Domestic Workers Alliance and co-director of the Caring Across Generations movement. Emma Watson accompanied Marai Larasi, executive director of the British organization Imkaan, which works to combat violence toward Black women and girls. Amy Poehler walked with Saru Jayaraman, the president of Restaurant Opportunities Centers (ROC) United and director of the Food Labor Research Center. Laura Dern accompanied Monica Ramirez, cofounder of Alianza Nacional de Campesinas, which promotes women farmworkers' leadership. Shailene Woodley walked with Calina Lawrence, whose activism targets police brutality against Native Americans.

In their brief interviews on the red carpet, these activists were well prepared to amplify their messages, their expertise, and their long histories of organizing. Monica Ramirez told a reporter, "We are leaders on this. We've been paving the way on this work for a long time. We offered our support to [Hollywood] to help work with them, to think through what a strategy could look like." Ai-jen Poo emphasized that the red-carpet strategy was not only a spontaneous performance but "an actual planned, organized act of solidarity. . . . It was not at all a one-off. It was part of a larger strategy that is gonna continue to build."[31]

And there was Tarana Burke, resplendent in black sequins, accompanied by actor Michelle Williams, who tried in each red-carpet interview to shirk the tedious queries about her dress and jewelry and turn the mic toward Burke. "I'm so much more interested in what you have to say than what I have to say," Williams said to Burke.[32] Burke understood the media attention would be fleeting and, during an interview with Ryan Seacrest, reiterated the importance of the moment for women's solidarities: "This is something that I started out of necessity, as something that I thought my community needed. It's grown over the years, but I could never have envisioned it growing like this. This moment is so powerful because we're seeing a collision of these two worlds—or a collaboration between these two worlds that people don't usually put together, and would most likely have us pitted against each other." Looking toward her celebrity date she said, "So it's really powerful to be on the red carpet tonight and for people like Michelle to be selfless enough to give up their time so we can talk about our causes." Later that night, Oprah would give her famous #TimesUp Speech, calling Recy Taylor into public consciousness. Several weeks later, many publics awaited President Trump's 2018 State of the Union Address, wondering whether he would address the #MeToo movement. After all, his 2016 campaign was riddled with accusations by at least seventeen women of Trump's history of sexual harassment and sexual assault. Pundits opined endlessly around the twenty-four-hour news cycle about whether the #MeToo movement would force Trump into a public reckoning.

Just hours before the State of the Union, House Minority Leader Nancy Pelosi called her fellow Democratic women to gather for a photograph. They were all wearing black. Following the Golden Globes red carpet, black would signify their solidarity with the #MeToo and #TimesUp movements to end violence against women. Representative Lois Frankel (D-FL) explained their goal of sending "a message of solidarity with those who are seeking economic security and a cultural shift that enables men and women to work side by side, in safety and dignity, free of sexual harassment, and be paid fairly for the value of their work."[33] Congressional Black Caucus members wore pins that read "RECY," commemorating Recy Taylor, who had died a month earlier without ever receiving justice. Representative Brenda Lawrence (D-MI) brought as her guest Danielle McGuire, a historian and expert on Recy Taylor's story. Representative Bonnie Watson Coleman (D-NJ) brought Rose Gunter, Recy Taylor's niece and caregiver. The State of the Union commenced, and President Trump did not mention #MeToo or women once in his hour-and-twenty-minute speech.

By the spring, cultural forces were in motion. At a March 2018 special convening of the House of Representatives, the Congressional Black Caucus declared they were reclaiming 2018 as the Year of the Black Woman. Commemorating the fiftieth anniversary of Shirley Chisholm's 1968 election as the first Black woman in Congress, also the forty-sixth anniversary of her historic run for the presidency, the caucus called for Congress to pass the Shirley Chisholm Statue Bill. If passed, the bill would commemorate Chisholm in the halls of Congress alongside the only other two Black women signified in stone: Rosa Parks and Sojourner Truth. During the sixty-minute congressional session, speakers rose to celebrate the power of Black women in American history. Citing influential Black civil rights activists from Ida B. Wells to Audre Lorde, Ruby Bridges to Tarana Burke, speakers urged their congressional colleagues to speak Black women's significance, their "Black girl magic" as Representative Barbara Lee proclaimed, into the official record.

Lee went on to remind Congress of Tarana Burke's foundational role in #MeToo and the violence of her erasure. "Last year," she began, "we saw the clearest indication of the influence that Black women have on our society through the emergence of the Me Too movement against sexual assault and misconduct. Many don't know this, but the Me Too movement was started by a Black woman 12 years ago to support victims and survivors of sexual violence. Tarana Burke's work and the phrase 'me too' have revolutionized the way we approach sexual assault in this country. But as has been the case throughout American history, Tarana's story, the story of Black women, is often lost in mainstream coverage of this movement, and what a shame it is."[34] As the session continued, speakers addressed this historic erasure head-on, highlighting not only the popular women of Black history but also the hidden figures who played critical roles in American history. Speakers emphasized the intersections of identity—race, class, gender—that rendered each of these women's experiences simultaneously unique and deeply common, embedded in a system of power that so easily muted their stories.

Amplifying Anita Hill through the Kavanaugh Hearings

That summer, President Trump nominated Brett Kavanaugh to the Supreme Court of the United States to succeed Justice Anthony Kennedy. Progressive groups began voicing concerns that the conservative justice, a member of the Federalist Society, would help overturn major legislation like *Roe v. Wade* (abortion), *Obergefell v. Hodges* (gay marriage), and *Lemon v. Kurtzman* (public religious expression). News outlets began publishing articles with headlines like "How Conservative Is Brett Kavanaugh?"[35] Kavanaugh's nomination grew increasingly contentious that summer as Democrats urged Republican leadership to release the expansive documents that detailed his judicial tenure, including his work for the George W. Bush administration. It would take time to review what was estimated to be over a million pages of records detailing Kavanaugh's juridical work. Yet it was just the day before the hearing when a critical 42,000 pages were released to the committee. The next day, on September 4, 2018, Brett Kavanaugh's confirmation hearing began. The overwhelming sound of protesters outside the Hart Senate Office building echoed in the hearing room, and seventeen protesters were arrested within just the first hour of the hearing.

Four days before the Judiciary Committee was scheduled to vote on Kavanaugh's confirmation, news erupted. The *Washington Post* reported that upon hearing of Kavanaugh's nomination, Dr. Christine Blasey Ford, a professor from California, had written a letter to Senator Dianne Feinstein in July describing how Kavanaugh had sexually assaulted her when they were in high school. Forced to confront the accusation, the committee postponed the vote. Instead, Kavanaugh and Blasey Ford would enter into a public hearing. The "Kavanaugh hearings," as they would come to be called, riveted publics and dominated the media cycle. Feminist activists tweeted hashtags like #BelieveWomen alongside #MeToo to highlight the link between the hearings and the larger movement against sexual violence. At the center of debates was the question of memory. Whose memories were credible, and even if the memory were real, to what extent did the past matter for the present?

During the public hearing, Blasey Ford would be remembered for a testimony so calm, her tears choked back painstakingly so that every word would land on the record, a testimony President Trump himself would call "compelling" and "very credible" in the moments after. Brett Kavanaugh would be remembered for emotional testimony alternating between frenzied anger and righteous tears, what Trump would describe as "powerful, honest, and riveting." In the media's coverage of the hearing, in the audience behind Kavanaugh's reddened face, was another familiar face: Alyssa Milano. An image of her glaring at Kavanaugh over her glasses, holding a booklet reading "I believe survivors," went viral. She explained that she needed to attend the hearings (as a guest of Senator Dianne Feinstein) to show public support for Blasey Ford. Media would later report that Tarana Burke was also in attendance, though she was not seated in plain view and did not receive viral attention. Burke connected the moment to the rise of #MeToo, saying of Blasey Ford, "She showed us what a hero actually looks like. Her coming forward is bigger than the Supreme Court." Burke went on to speak to the wide reach of sexual violence beyond White women in the public eye, describing the moment as "freeing for so many survivors around the world who are poised to tell their story."[36]

Meanwhile, Milano penned a guest column for *Variety* magazine in which she drew out a connection that many Black women had made right away. "I've thought about Anita Hill often in the past week," Milano wrote, "as the hearings to appoint Brett Kavanaugh to the Supreme Court advanced despite the multiple credible allegations of sexual misconduct against him. I think about how a panel of white men questioned Anita Hill about her sexual past and how despicably she was treated by politicians of both parties. I think about how far we've come in many regards. And at the same time, and in the same breath, I lament how much farther we have yet to go."[37]

As soon as news of Blasey Ford's accusations hit the news, Black women had said Anita Hill's name. The memory of what had happened to Hill had never faded. In October 1991, Professor Anita Hill testified before a committee of fourteen White legislators, headed by Joe Biden, during the confirmation hearings of Justice Clarence Thomas. During the hearings, Hill said that Thomas had sexually harassed her when she worked as an aide to him at the Equal Employment Opportunity Commission. As though she were on trial, the White senators grilled Anita Hill, forcing her to recount over and over the humiliating details of Thomas's sexual harassment from his repeated unwanted advances to a pubic hair placed on her Coke can. Clarence Thomas vehemently rejected the accusations and characterized the hearing as discriminatory, "a national disgrace . . . a high-tech lynching for uppity Blacks who in any way deign to think for themselves." Thomas invoked anti-Black racism to discredit Anita Hill's allegations, drawing out the intersections of race and class that shaped not only the dynamics of the sexual harassment but also the way different publics viewed the issue. Public opinion was against Hill, what some scholars would explain as "race trumping gender."[38] Later Hill would describe how alone she felt in those days, harangued in the hearing hall, a deluge of hate mail and death threats awaiting her at home. As scholars have shown, Black women have historically concealed the sexism and violence they experience in Black communities, what the playwright Loy A. Webb described as the community's sense that "black women are often told to put our pain on the back burner because the community has 'bigger fish to fry.'"[39] Anita Hill had violated these unspoken rules. Still, the Senate went on to confirm Justice Clarence Thomas after a narrow vote of 52–48.

Yet for many Black women watching the Kavanaugh hearings, remembering Anita Hill also harkened back to an even older collective memory.[40] At the Democratic National Convention in 1964, Fannie Lou Hamer, a sharecropper in rural Mississippi and civil rights activist, recounted the sexual violence she experienced after being arrested at a lunch-counter sit-in. Hamer's story would later be upheld as evidence of the importance of an intersectional lens, making sense of her experiences of racism and violence, the way she was treated by the public, the way she was minimized in the historical record, as distinctly shaped by her position as a poor Black woman in the rural South.[41] In the televised session she said, "I question America. Is this America, the land of the free and the home of the brave, where we have to sleep with our telephones off the hooks because our lives be threatened daily, because we want to live as decent human beings, in America?"[42] Her story was cut short, her voice muted when the broadcast suddenly cut out; President Lyndon Johnson realized the power of her testimony and the necessity of interrupting it. For so long, Black women had been cut off, muted, erased from the public record. But they had never stopped speaking.

Now, it was almost sixty years later, and after the Kavanaugh hearings in 2018, widespread publics from media outlets to activists alike wanted to hear from Anita Hill. With the platform she ought to have been afforded decades earlier, she publicly reflected on her experience in 1991, writing, "If the Senate Judiciary Committee, led then by Mr. Biden, had done its job and held a hearing that showed that its members understood the seriousness of sexual harassment and other forms of sexual violence, the cultural shift we saw in 2017 after #MeToo might have begun in 1991—with the support of the government." Hill went on to describe how political support for women, for listening to survivors, would have had a powerful "ripple effect. . . . People agitating for change would have been operating from a position of strength. . . . Instead, far too many survivors kept their stories hidden for years."[43]

The past was past, but the continued injustice of the system nearly thirty years after Hill's testimony, in the shifting cultural space of mass movements like Me Too and Black Lives Matter, opened up a space for historical reckoning. Society not only failed Anita Hill but had failed Black women. Where publics had turned away from Hill's testimony in 1991 in disgust or dismissal, now many publics—and importantly, the media that broadcasted to them—were listening. Media began highlighting the powerful impacts Anita Hill had in the years following her testimony, impacts that had not been properly commemorated. Hill's testimony in 1991 had opened up a space for women to have the uncomfortable conversations about harassment and violence they had experienced then buried in shame, realizing for the first time that these experiences were shared among women and that they were not acceptable.

At the National Women's Law Center, employees recalled phones ringing around the clock as women began to look for legal redress for the sexual harassment they experienced. At the EEOC, claims of sexual harassment skyrocketed, and Congress passed the Civil Rights Act of 1991 to give victims legal recourse. States began introducing additional legislation to protect women in the workplace, and there was a new institutionalization of anti–sexual harassment programs in workplaces across the country. The #MeToo moment would not exist without Anita Hill. The next year, a record number of women would run for Congress and win seats in what would be called "The Year of the Woman." One of these women was Senator Dianne Feinstein of California, who would receive that pivotal letter from Christine Blasey Ford twenty-six years later. After Anita Hill released her aptly titled memoir, *Believing*, in 2021, she described how she was "hopeful about student activism against sexual violence, about the rise of Black feminism . . . about teachers teaching truthful history."[44]

The Backlash: Playing Queens against Kings

Meanwhile, a swift backlash by conservative forces took on social media with hashtags like #BackBrett and #IstandWithBrett, circulating memes with ominous messages like, "As long as women who accuse men of sexual attacks are believed without evidence or due process, no man is safe. I'm not safe. Your husband isn't safe. Your father isn't safe. Your son isn't safe. Your grandson isn't safe. Your male friends aren't safe. #HIMTOO." President Trump rued, "It is a very scary time for young men in America, where you can be guilty of something you may not be guilty of." He somberly continued, "This is a very, very—this is a very difficult time. What's happening here has much more to do than even the appointment of a Supreme Court justice." Reflecting on the president's comments, Trevor Noah, a comedian and the host of the *Daily Show*, warned of the danger of Trump's remarks: "He knows how to offer victimhood to people who have the least claim to it, which is a really, really powerful tool. If you can convince men that they are the true victims of the #MeToo movement, you get men to fight against a movement that's really about holding men who are doing bad things accountable as opposed to making all men scapegoats for something that they're not doing."

This perceived victimhood of men—mostly White—as the targets of an "oppressive" movement by power-hungry feminists was a powerful strategy that riled up support among conservative men and White women alike by emphasizing the danger of this new world for their sons. Memes circulated among conservative circles, one reading, "Every mother of boys should be TERRIFIED that at ANY time ANY girl can fabricate ANY story, with no proof, & RUIN her boy's life." One viral tweet by a mother read, "This is MY son. He graduated #1 in boot camp. He was awarded the USO award. He was #1 in A school. He is a gentleman who respects women. He won't go on solo dates due to the current climate of false sexual accusations by radical feminists with an axe to grind. I VOTE. #HimToo."[45] Accompanying the post was a picture of her son in his crisp white navy uniform, knee up, grinning cheekily with his fist under his chin. A clear patriot and true American. The post went viral, both ridiculed by progressives for its melodramatic tone and unironically adopted as a rallying cry for conservatives. The hashtag #HimToo was shared widely with horror stories of men suffering at the hands of the #MeToo movement, of men allegedly falsely accused by women. Never mind that the tweeter's son took to Twitter to refute his mother's claims: "That was my Mom. Sometimes the people we love do things that hurt us without realizing it. Let's turn this around. I respect and #BelieveWomen. I never have and never will support #HimToo. I'm a proud Navy vet, Cat Dad and Ally. Also, Twitter, your meme game is on point."[46] He added a picture of himself casually dressed in a T-shirt and jeans with the same cheeky pose.

Despite the flimsy foundations of #HimToo, the countermovement was in full motion. Meanwhile, backlash was emerging from other directions. As many famous White men were taken to task for their decades of sexual harassment and violence, powerful Black men were also being called in to answer for misconduct that had long been swept under the rug as mere rumor. Russell Simmons, R. Kelly, Bill Cosby—if women were to be believed, Black women's stories should be heard too. Bill Cosby, the Black comedian and actor widely known as "America's dad," was accused of drugging and assaulting over twenty women. Despite his own troubling relationship with Black communities, having adopted a conservative stance of respectability politics and elitist moralism, Cosby was also seen as a cultural icon.

The Cosby Show had played a powerful role in maintaining the memory of a successful civil rights movement, of the Cosby family as evidence of racial progress achieved, Cliff Huxtable a doctor and his wife, Claire, a lawyer. Critics called out the whitewashed show for its rosy portrayal of Black life in the 1980s, diverting attention from the significant civil rights rollbacks of the Reagan era. Still, the show preserved a mainstream branch of memory characterized by racial progress and pride in Black excellence in the post–civil rights era. The show also demonstrated the intergenerational transmission of identity and memory through the Black family. For example, in one episode titled "The March," Cliff, Claire, and both sets of grandparents recount and pass on to the

Cosby children the powerful role the March on Washington played in their lives and their family trajectory. In another episode, family members file into the living room to watch Dr. King's "Dream" speech playing on the television. The characters sit in complete silence as King's words carry us into the end of the episode. Now Bill Cosby was under scrutiny.

Though public allegations of his sexual misconduct were rumored as early as 2005, Cosby was not taken to trial until June 2017. Of course, the resurgent #MeToo movement would not begin until October that year, so when the jury returned in deadlock, the mistrial did not bode well for the survivors seeking justice. Yet #MeToo did emerge, the cultural landscape palpably shifted, and when Cosby went back to trial in April 2018, jurors saw the case in a new light. With the increased attention on the trial, the judge also allowed for five additional women to testify against Cosby. After two days, the jury returned with a guilty verdict on all three counts of sexual assault.

While #MeToo celebrated one of the first major victories of the movement, Cosby's wife, Camille Cosby, spoke out against the perceived injustice against her husband. She reminded the press that "the #MeToo movement and movements like them have intentional ignorance pertaining to the history of particular white women—not all white women—but particular white women, who have from the very beginning, pertaining to the enslavement of African people, accused Black males of sexual assault without any proof whatsoever, no proof, anywhere on the face of the earth."[47] She compared Bill Cosby to Emmett Till, the fourteen-year-old Black boy who was lynched in 1955 after a White woman accused him of grabbing her in a lurid manner. In 2017 Till's accuser would recant the story, admitting to historian Timothy B. Tyson that it wasn't true.

Camille Cosby went on, "And by ignoring that history, they have put out a lie in itself and that is, 'Because I'm female, I'm telling the truth.' Well history disproves that, as well, and gender has never, ever equated with truth. So, they need to clean up their acts." She warned, "We know how women can lie." By invoking the history of racial violence against Black Americans, specifically Black men, she weaponized the critiques of the #MeToo movement's anti-Blackness against itself. Like Clarence Thomas's rhetorical work to discredit Anita Hill, Camille Cosby separated race from gender to position the White queens of the #MeToo movement as the villains taking down the heroic Black kings.

Picking up on the strategy, conservatives worked to discredit the growing coalition of #MeToo and #Black Lives Matter by testing the limits of the movement. Would they take down their own king? Strategists drew public attention to Dr. King's past infidelities and alleged womanizing. Historian David Garrow, a Pulitzer Prize winner for his 1986 biography of Martin Luther King Jr., wrote a long article in a conservative British magazine reporting findings from the newly released FBI files on Dr. King, detailing shocking allegations of sexual misconduct. The article, sensationally titled "The Troubling Legacy of Martin Luther King," ran against an editorial calling King "the Harvey Weinstein of the Civil Rights Movement." However, the claim against King—which took media by storm—was based on one FBI agent's note, a move both methodologically unsound for a seasoned historian and socially irresponsible. Barbara Ransby called out these "historical peeping Toms" and issued a scathing critique, arguing that "to accept highly suspicious evidence as fact and to dress it up with a litany of salacious anecdotes is to complete the job J. Edgar Hoover failed to do two generations ago, when he dedicated himself to denigrating Dr. King's life and work." She went on to write, "How unfortunate that the legitimacy of his entire legacy, and by extension the movement of which he was a part, is being called into question in such a sloppy manner today. How disturbing that the vitally important issue of sexual violence is being deployed and distorted in the process. All of this in this crucible moment, what Dr. King referred to in his own time as the 'fierce urgency of now.'"[48]

Despite wide critiques of the claims against King and their feeble foundations, the strategic backlash against #MeToo had its consequences. By using feminists' own moral claims against them to question their civil rights heroes, asking whether they would hold up as kings today, many feminist activists were divided once more as they reconsidered their commitments to the kings of the past.

In the years after Alyssa Milano's initial #MeToo tweet, the groundswell of feminist organizing increasingly interacted with the work of another major movement started by Black women: Black Lives Matter. Not only were Alicia Garza, Patrisse Cullors, and Opal Tometi Black women, but two of them identified as queer, and their commitments to an expansive, intersectional, and global vision of justice would shape the movement at every turn. Of the civil rights era of the 1960s, the Black lesbian feminist Audre Lorde had lamented, "The existence of Black lesbian and gay people were not even allowed to cross the public consciousness of Black America," where political participation for gay Black people was "not a guide for living but a new set of shackles."[49] But now, Black women led the way in holding up and demonstrating the intersections of systems of power across race, gender, class, and sexuality that rendered contemporary movements united in a linked fate.

Tarana Burke spoke out on these mutualities: "What we need to be talking about is the everyday woman, man, trans person, child and disabled person. All the people who are not rich, white and famous, who deal with sexual violence on an everyday basis. We need to talk about the systems that are still in

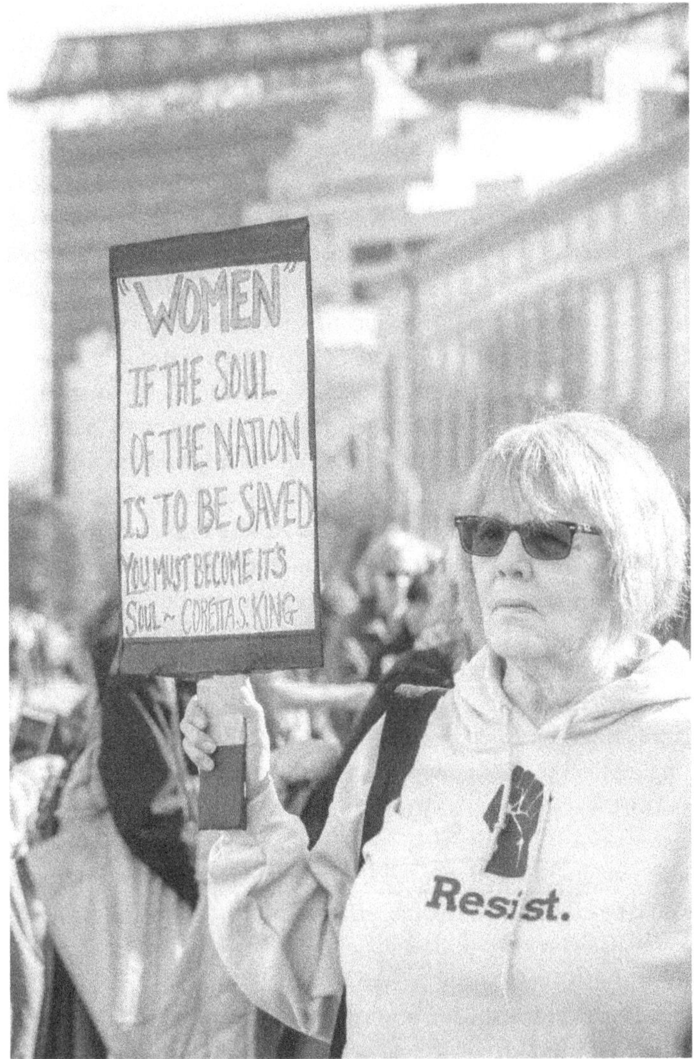

FIGURE 6.2. Women's March demonstrator holding sign with quote from Coretta Scott King. Shelly Rivoli/Alamy Stock Photo.

place that allow that to happen."[50] The consequences of the efforts to restore the memory of Black women's civil rights legacies would not be felt immediately, but they were shifting the cultural landscape for feminist activism toward one that required a global, intersectional imagination. As Coretta Scott King had told them, "Women, if the soul of the nation is to be saved, [I believe that] you must become its soul."

The Consequences

On March 13, 2020, just days before the United States would join nations around the world in lockdowns to control the spread of COVID-19, at least seven Louisville police officers broke into an apartment just after midnight as part of an investigation into a drug-dealing operation. The suspect did not live there. Without knowing who had entered their home, the residents jumped out of bed, terrified. One of them, Kenneth Walker III, fired a warning shot at the ground to defend the couple from the intruders. The officers fired thirty-two shots in return, killing Walker's girlfriend, a young Black woman for whom he had bought an engagement ring and to whom he planned to propose. Her name was Breonna Taylor. She was twenty-six years old, an emergency room technician, a loving human whom her mother described as an "old soul" "with big dreams." While small protests erupted afterward, Breonna's name slipped to the bottom of a news cycle increasingly dominated by updates on the unprecedented pandemic. Yet after George Floyd was murdered by police two months later and multiracial masses flooded the streets, Breonna Taylor's name was resurrected. Black Lives Matter organizers called on publics to say her name. With activist Tamika Mallory and the New York nonprofit organization Until Freedom, Breonna Taylor's mother, Tamika Palmer, helped organize a March on Frankfort, Kentucky, to call for justice.

This was not the first March on Frankfort. Fifty-six years earlier in 1964, an estimated ten thousand people joined Martin Luther King Jr. in a March on Frankfort, calling for legislation to end segregation and racism. Now, a 2020 March on Frankfort would continue this unfinished work, declaring that Black lives mattered, that *Black women's* lives mattered, and that without justice, there would be no peace. The march attracted celebrities like the musician Common, actress Jada Pinkett Smith, and her children, Willow and Jaden. Musician Alicia Keys hosted a virtual rally to complement the in-person rally. Black feminist thought was going mainstream, protesters holding signs with quotes from the Combahee River Collective's 1977 statement, "If Black women were free, it would mean that everyone else would have to be free, since our freedom would necessitate the destruction of all systems of oppression."[51]

In July 2020, Dani Ayers, a thirty-nine-year-old Black woman, became CEO of the Me Too movement organization. She told the press, "I think it's a testament and it's a representation of the fact that there are many movements that have been started by Black women. The Black Lives Matter movement was also started by Black women. It's an opportunity to shine a light. We are absolutely centering Black women and girls, people of color, queer, trans, disabled folks in our work because we know that solving and interrupting the issue of sexual violence in those communities means ending sexual violence everywhere."

Ayers went on to describe the importance of using an intersectional lens to understand the linked fate of seemingly disparate issues like anti-Black police violence and sexual violence. She explained, "We've seen money start to be pushed to Black-led organizations and it needs to happen, but sexual violence has not seen that same funding support. And I think it's because folks don't automatically understand the intersection of sexual violence and structural racism. And so we really have a lot of work to do."[52]

Ayers's vision, shared by Tarana Burke and many other Black organizers, enabled a wider coalition for more expansive collective action. Centering Black women was not only about remediating White feminists' harms of the past, which had only continued in the present. Centering Black women through an intersectional lens enabled a conversation about the larger carceral system, a natural segue to integrate public thinking about the connection between movements like #MeToo and #SayHerName and #DefundThePolice. Activists' strategic framing helped media outlets describe the interconnected movements and the systems that shape them. As one article noted, "History appears to be repeating itself as calls to #DefundThePolice intensify. This part of the current racial justice movement owes a tremendous debt to the grassroots organizing and scholarship of Black feminists and other feminists of color over the past few decades." The article cited Black abolitionists like Ruth Wilson Gilmore and Angela Davis alongside queer and trans activists like Marsha P. Johnson, Sylvia Rivera, and the Street Transvestite Action Revolutionaries "who knew they could not look to police or prisons to address violence against queer and trans people."[53]

With media increasingly receptive to these stories of silenced pasts, activists emphasized the interconnection between present-day movements and the historical activism of Black women who shaped the legacies of Dr. King and the civil rights movement. These representations of Black women as pivotal figures of American history and present-day progressivism increasingly took center stage, appearing in widely watched mainstream media and popular culture. On CNN, Black filmmaker Ava DuVernay appeared to promote her film with Oprah Winfrey. Given the platform in the interview with Van Jones, she described the importance of continued grassroots organizing through a historically informed and intersectional understanding of racial injustice. She explained, "It's about sharing information. That's what we tried to do in [the documentary] *13th*. There's more to do . . . you know, the 'Me Too' movements and the 'Time's Up' movements are directly correlated to Prison justice movements."[54] Discussions like these about the systemic roots of injustice, about an unrealized dream of racial justice and freedom for all, were taking place on a main stage.

Meanwhile, Kimberlé Crenshaw's 2015 #SayHerName report coauthored with Andrea Ritchie and the African American Policy Forum received renewed

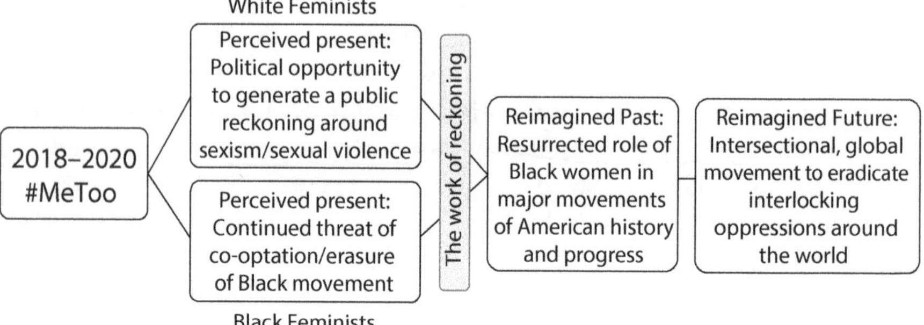

FIGURE 6.3. Black and White feminists' solidarity politics through memory after #MeToo.

interest among publics. As Crenshaw explained of the necessity of the movement, "Although Black women are routinely killed, raped and beaten by the police, their experiences are rarely foregrounded in popular understandings of police brutality." She went on, "Yet, inclusion of black women's experiences in social movements, media narratives, and policy demands around policing and police brutality is critical to effectively combating racialized state violence for black communities and other communities of color."[55]

As the 2020 election approached, activists wondered if these burgeoning waves of activism during the Trump era would bear out at the polls. After all, the backlash against the resistance had been powerful as conservative organizations co-opted news of growing intersectional coalitions as evidence of the victimized White man under threat in America. Even among Black and Brown feminists there was a sense of hesitation and protective skepticism about the true depths of their reconciliation, knowing that 52 percent of White women had voted for President Trump in 2016.

Still, many Black feminists, womanists, rising through the shared landscape of the #MeToo and #BlackLivesMatter movements, were working to restore collective memory—specifically the central role of Black women in American history—to remake a collective memory of a King by centering the Queens. By bridging the deep fissures between women structurally siloed across intersections of race, gender, sexuality, and class, the Queenmakers would keep working to enable intersectional solidarities for emancipatory futures. As Anita Hill pondered hopefully, "More and more I think the ability to take the long view, [is] to see—to measure progress, not just about in my lifetime, but to measure progress through the lifetime of women, to realize that we have moved forward, but also to take the long view in looking forward to thinking about what we can do for the next generation."[56]

Conclusion

> Our only hope today lies in our ability to recapture the revolutionary spirit and go out into a sometimes hostile world declaring eternal hostility to poverty, racism, and militarism. With this powerful commitment we shall boldly challenge the status quo and unjust mores and thereby speed the day when every valley shall be exalted, and every mountain and hill shall be made low, and the crooked shall be made straight and the rough places plain. . . .
>
> Now let us begin. Now let us rededicate ourselves to the long and bitter—but beautiful—struggle for a new world.
>
> —DR. MARTIN LUTHER KING JR., "BEYOND VIETNAM: A TIME TO BREAK SILENCE," APRIL 4, 1967

JANUARY 18, 2021: Twelve days after White insurrectionists stormed the U.S. Capitol in defiance of Joe Biden's election, two days before Biden would be inaugurated as the forty-sixth president, President Trump released the "1776 Report." It was Martin Luther King Jr. Day. The forty-five-page report was a direct response to the *New York Times'* widely lauded "1619 Project," launched in 2019 to commemorate the four hundredth anniversary of enslaved peoples' arrival on the shores of colonial Virginia. Developed by journalist Nikole Hannah-Jones, the 1619 Project worked "to reframe the country's history by placing the consequences of slavery and the contributions of Black Americans at the very center of the United States' national narrative." As Hannah-Jones explained, "It is time to stop hiding from our sins and confront them. And then in confronting them, it is time to make them right." Presidential hopeful Kamala Harris had tweeted, "The #1619Project is a powerful and necessary reckoning of our history. We cannot understand and address the problems of today without speaking truth about how we got here."[1]

But the conservative backlash had been swift, decrying the 1619 Project as "left-wing propaganda," "divisive" products of a "racial grievances industry." It was no coincidence when conservative strategists encouraged President

Trump to release the rejoinder, the 1776 Report, on Dr. King's birthday. King's legacy was woven throughout the report. On page 2 there was a black-and-white image of Dr. King waving to crowds at the March on Washington with a floating quotation from the civil rights leader amid a section titled "The Meaning of the Declaration":

> When the architects of our republic wrote the magnificent words of the Constitution and the Declaration of Independence, they were signing a promissory note to which every American was to fall heir. This note was a promise that all men, yes, black men as well as white men, would be guaranteed the unalienable rights to life, liberty, and the pursuit of happiness. —Martin Luther King, Jr.[2]

In a section titled "The Radicalization of American Politics in the 1960's," the 1776 Report describes Martin Luther King Jr. as a contrast to "more revolutionary groups [who] wanted to fight in terms of group identities." The report explains, "King refused to define Americans in terms of permanent racialized identities and called on Americans . . . to see ourselves as one nation united by a common political creed and commitment to Christian love." The report goes on to explain that during the 1960s, "many rejected King's formulation of civil rights and reframed debates about equality in terms of racial and sexual identities. The civil rights movement came to abandon the nondiscrimination and equal opportunity of colorblind civil rights in favor of 'group rights' and preferential treatment." Drawing out the argument about the foundational misappropriation of Dr. King's legacy by minority rights activists, the report says, "activists constructed artificial groupings to further divide Americans by race, creating new categories like 'Asian American' and 'Hispanic' to teach Americans to think of themselves in terms of group identities and to rouse various groups into politically cohesive bodies."[3]

The 1776 Report goes on to warn Americans of "the incompatibility of identity politics with American principles," using Dr. King to claim that the civil rights movement's goals, symbols, and Christian morals have been co-opted by conflict-ridden progressive groups that "propose to punish some citizens—many times for wrongs their ancestors allegedly committed—while rewarding others."[4] The report echoed efforts made by Trump throughout his presidency to draw on a revisionist memory that could cast movements for racial justice as themselves examples of anti-White racism, having even issued an executive order against anti-racism trainings in October 2020.

Among the most vocal publics denouncing the 1776 Report were historians who pointed out that it was not only saturated with historical fallacies but also neglected to engage research by actual historians. The American Historical Association put out a public statement condemning the 1776 Report, co-signed by dozens of professional scholarly associations. Rights organizations and activists also spoke out against the dangerous propaganda and its duplicitous release on a day celebrating the legacy of Black civil rights. ReNika Moore, director of the ACLU's Racial Justice Program, issued a reminder that these revisionist histories had loftier goals than a rosy retelling of the past: "Donald Trump has always attempted to use a fictional version of the past to justify racist policies. As such, it is only fitting that in the final days of his term as president, and on the day we celebrated the life of Martin Luther King Jr., his administration released a report that pushes a white supremacist version of our nation's history, justifies slavery as 'more the rule than the exception throughout human history,' and compares members of the opposing political party to fascist dictators."[5]

Although the report was largely dismissed as political propaganda, the strategic fervor behind it would grow, fueled by the resurgence of Black Lives Matter after George Floyd's murder by a White police officer the year prior. Trump was out of office, but the long branches of memory that made his election possible only grew during his administration with the strategic distribution of state resources—material and cultural—toward hardening a social reality committed to the maintenance of its own willful ignorance. These commitments would coalesce in the moral panic over critical race theory "recast by rightwing activists as an omnipresent and omnipotent ideology, one that is anti-American, anti-capitalist, and anti-white."[6] By summer 2021, nearly two dozen states had considered and some had passed anti–critical race theory legislation. Fueled by the powerful Kingmakers from above—the right-wing think tanks, politicians, and media—and set into motion by the grassroots organizations they funded like No Left Turn in Education, mostly White parents were arriving in droves at school board meetings to voice their opposition to critical race theory. The comparisons to the past were immediate. These White parents were not unlike those who protested the desegregation of schools during the civil rights era.

At a press conference of the all-Republican House Freedom Caucus, Representative Ralph Norman (R-SC) warned, "Folks, we're in a cultural warfare today. Critical race theory asserts that people with white skin are inherently racist, not because of their actions, words or what they actually believe in their heart—but by virtue of the color of their skin." The clear invocation of Dr. King's words was apparent, and an analysis by NPR showed that in a Republican news conference the month prior, roughly half of the conservative speakers deployed Dr. King's "desire to be judged 'by the content of their character, not the color of their skin.'"[7] Dr. King's daughter and CEO of the King Center, Bernice King, spoke out against the misappropriations of her father's legacy. "Daddy would never say excuse the history, and let's just start here," she

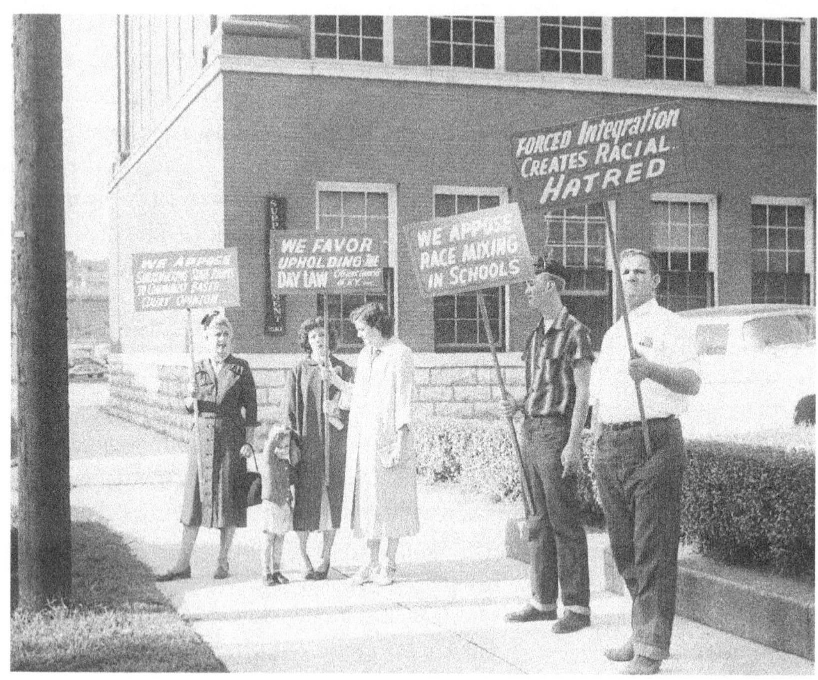

FIGURE C.1. White demonstrators protest school integration in 1956. Associated Press.

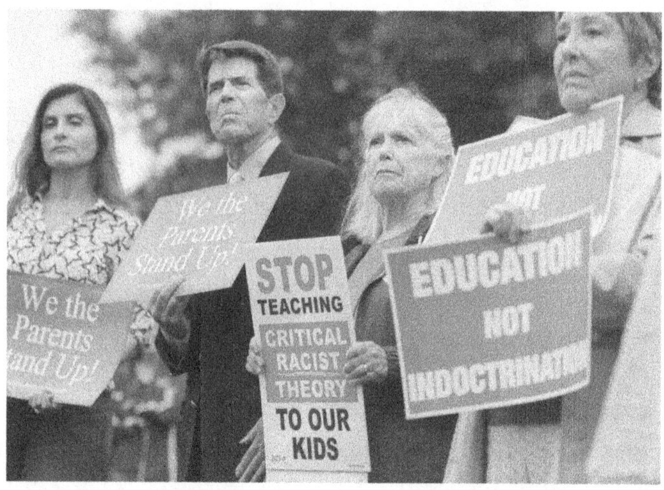

FIGURE C.2. White demonstrators protest critical race theory in schools in 2021. Evelyn Hockstein/Reuters/Alamy Stock Photo.

said. "He also said, if a nation has done something against the people for hundreds of years, then it must also turn around and do something for those people."[8] Yet the moral panic around critical race theory was galvanizing conservative voters.

In 2022, Ohio congressman and Senate hopeful Josh Mandel shared an anti–critical race theory video he filmed in Selma, Alabama, saying, "Martin Luther King marched right here so skin color wouldn't matter." Sharing the video with followers on Twitter, he tagged and thanked the King Center for the inspiration. Bernice King fired back, "Regretfully, I do not believe that I or @TheKingCenter legitimately motivated you to film this ad, as it is in opposition to nonviolence and to much of what my father taught. I encourage you to study my father/nonviolence in full."[9] Mandel retorted with an anecdote about Dr. King's attempt to purchase a firearm to protect himself, decontextualizing the story to claim Dr. King "knew the importance of the Second Amendment when he tried to exercise his right to self-defense and was wrongly denied a gun permit by anti-gun racists." Mandel went on, "Study your history better @BerniceKing."[10] Here was a White congressman from Ohio telling Dr. King's daughter, the CEO of the center dedicated to his legacy, that she did not know her father's history. With grace, Bernice King offered up the original text with her father's book, describing the incident and its full context. Mandel did not concede. His supporters were not deterred.

This book has shown that these misuses of the collective memory of the civil rights movement have long branches and deeper roots, dating back to the original ideological debates that planted White supremacy in the making of the King holiday. These gnarled branches of collective memory are the consequences of decades of political misuses of the past that have sedimented divergent social realities, that have made possible a society where citizens can believe that talking about systemic racism oppresses White Americans. Through this landscape, the memory of the civil rights movement can be weaponized against itself. White conservatives and moderates can simultaneously silence movements for racial justice for pulling a divisive "race card" allegedly countering King's dream, while also activating a captive audience through a revisionist memory of multiracial democracy as a threat to White Americans, the "true" America. The collective memory of the civil rights movement, increasingly removed from many of those who lived through it, has transformed. If collective memory tells the story of "who we were," it is not clear who "we" are anymore or ever really were.

Yet from these gnarled branches, another possibility has grown. Decades of contention over the memory of the civil rights movement in the struggle for the future has generated a deepening knowledge among young activists, a growing awareness that the old master's tools will not dismantle the unyielding power structure of the house.[11] If collective memory is a disfigured tree, in Angela Davis's words, a radical approach simply means "grasping things at the root." In the years after the Tea Party "reclaimed" the civil rights movement, young activists coming of age in the Obama era shared a widespread recognition, a rumbling consciousness. A Black president would not only fail to be the silver bullet to save the country from itself but also reactively bring to the fore its aggrieved White citizens defending a power structure that negated the full humanity of Black lives. The Movement for Black Lives would grow readily in this contentious soil, sparking a corresponding movement to reclaim the distorted memory of the civil rights movement. Organizers understood that there would be no path forward to a racially just future without remaking the past.

#ReclaimKing

In 2015, Black Lives Matter joined the Ferguson Action Committee to spearhead a #ReclaimMLK campaign. Ferguson Action spokesperson Mervyn Marcano explained, "We really feel that King's legacy has been clouded by efforts to soften and sanitize that legacy."[12] That year, in twenty cities across the country, Reclaim King demonstrations filled the streets, emphasizing the radical roots of the civil rights movement. In a press release about the effort, Ferguson Action wrote, "Martin Luther King Jr.'s life's work was the elevation, honoring, and defense of Black Lives. His tools included non-violent civil disobedience and direct action. Dr. King was part of a larger movement of women, and men, queer, and straight, young and old. This movement was built on a bold vision that was radical, principled, and uncompromising." The statement goes on to describe how "the freedom fighters who believed in this vision were called impractical, rash, irrational, and naive. Their tactics were controversial. Some elders distanced themselves from what was then a new movement for change. Some of the older generation joined in. Our movement draws a direct line from the legacy of Dr. King."[13]

By 2018, the Reclaim efforts had generated a strong intersectional infrastructure. The Anti Police-Terror Project had developed a powerful alliance with groups like Third World Resistance to build coalitions for reclaiming King's legacy and tackling a range of interconnected global struggles including abolitionism, anti-imperialism, and immigrant rights. On their organizational page, the San Francisco–based Alliance of South Asians Taking Action (ASATA) described joining with these groups in ninety-six hours of direct action. The multifold efforts included a "Political Education session on Martin Luther King, Jr.'s radical internationalism facilitated by the Center for Political Education and Haiti Action." Activists learned how to screen print "art carrying messages of international solidarity to carry at the Reclaim MLK Day

March." And activists would go on to "[march] under a common banner to show solidarity for the black liberation struggles in our cities and stand up for immigrant rights, and self-determination for all."[14]

Railing against incrementalism and respectability politics to reclaim a radical legacy of civil rights, these movements were also acknowledging the *limitations* and unfinished work of the civil rights movement. The queer Black men and women who drive Black Lives Matter work to dismantle not only the systems of power they see in the present but also those within the histories they restore. As founders Opal Tometi and Gerald Lenoir wrote in an op-ed in *Time* magazine, "As black activists from two different generations, we understand that the black liberation movement in the U.S.—from its inception as an anti-slavery movement, through the civil rights era, and up to now—has never been only for civil rights. The movement is a struggle for the human rights and dignity of black people in the U.S., which is tied to black peoples' struggle for human rights across the globe." They go on to quote Dr. King: "Since we know that the system will not change the rules, we are going to have to change the system. . . . This vision is critical to our work, as it highlights that this struggle is beyond just, 'Stop killing us, we deserve to live.' We deserve to thrive, and this requires the full acknowledgement of the breadth of our human rights."[15]

The Revival of the Poor People's Campaign

Movements to restore King's radical legacy have taken on other forms as well. In 2017, Reverend William Barber II, the Black civil rights and religious leader and president of the North Carolina NAACP, stepped down from his post. He had a new mission. With theologian Liz Theoharis, Barber would revive Dr. King's unfinished work in the Poor People's Campaign, a national movement challenging "the interlocking evils of systemic racism, poverty, ecological devastation, militarism and the war economy, and the distorted moral narrative of religious nationalism." Just months before he had been assassinated in 1968, Dr. King had announced the Poor People's Campaign as the next chapter for the civil rights movement, one that would draw national attention to economic inequality and poverty. King envisioned the campaign as one that would be "the beginning of a new co-operation, understanding, and a determination by poor people of all colors and backgrounds to assert and win their right to a decent life and respect for their culture and dignity." It gained the support of a wide coalition including leaders of Native American, Puerto Rican, Mexican American, and poor White communities. The SCLC had continued this work after King's assassination, under leaders like Coretta Scott King and Ralph Abernathy. Still, the campaign's goals had not been realized, as poverty only increased during the Reagan administration when the working middle class became the working poor. As Dr. King's daughter Bernice King had argued, "Today's church must take the lead in social transformation and in eradicating racism, poverty (and the third evil of the Triple Evils that my father often mentioned, which is militarism); and commit to doing justice, loving mercy and walking humbly with our God."[16]

Now, the Poor People's Campaign was being picked up again. Barber issued "A National Call for Moral Revival," a series of direct actions across the nation for forty days of civil disobedience to build solidarity among the poor and working classes. Barber explained, "Only by joining together and asserting our authority as children of God can we shift the moral narrative in this nation and create a movement that will challenge those in power to form the 'more perfect union' to which we aspire. Now as in 1968, this notion looks impossible. Except, again, there is no other way."[17]

"Where Do We Go from Here? Chaos or Community?"

In his 1967 book, the last book he would write before his assassination, Dr. King addressed the question so many of us ask in the wake of moments of possibility and transformation. He wrote, "Now, in order to answer the question, 'Where do we go from here?' which is our theme, we must first honestly recognize where we are now." We must *recognize* where we are now. This book has shown that willful ignorance through the strategic mystification of social reality, the evasion of uncomfortable truths about our society, will not allow us to move forward. The distortions of our collective past are but one manifestation of a system of power that is committed to reproducing itself. While there are powerful people at the helm of this system, deeply resourced with the extreme wealth built on the backs of others, we are all complicit. There is no easy set of policy solutions to extract us from this reality, and worse yet, time has shown that under the current system, the political will to pursue a transformative agenda may not manifest. Yes, we must vote, but voting is not enough. However, the grounded knowledge of communities long in the trenches of this system offers ideas for where we might go from here.

First, this book has shown that the United States has not experienced a true racial reckoning that honestly faces, accounts for, and pays for its past. Reparations are but a minimum. Transitional justice organizations and scholars of truth and reconciliation have long argued that with sustained effort, truth commissions can help heal deep cultural traumas. However, truth and reconciliation require relinquishing willful ignorance and denial. If anything, the movement against critical race theory that opened this chapter indicates a grim likelihood that this reckoning will take place collectively and without violent backlash. After all, the maintenance of ignorance requires an absence of knowledge. If children are not taught about the violence of American history, the pathways that lead them to where they are, then they will not have to do anything about racial inequality. They can maintain the myth of American exceptionalism and reproduce the "natural" racial order. Yet the damage runs deep and the dismantling of an epistemology of ignorance requires more than education. Too often, well-meaning people point to a lack of quality education as the explanation for our present-day state of affairs. "They don't know better," people will say. "You just need to teach them." Our sociological evidence suggests otherwise in that no amount of formal education has eradicated White supremacy. Many well-educated, well-credentialed people, conservative and progressive alike, cannot and willfully do not see the systems of power that shape our social world.

Still, we must hold our institutions—political, educational, and cultural—accountable for perpetuating the alternative histories that distort the past. Many activists, educators, grassroots organizations, and Black communities have been working for decades to correct the record. From Coretta Scott King's leadership through the King Center to preserve Dr. King's true legacy to contemporary efforts like the SPLC's Teaching Tolerance project and the Zinn Education project, to the intergenerational stories of Black resistance passed down through families, there are living branches of memory that actively counter revisionist histories. Media institutions are particularly overdue for a reckoning, for radically rethinking the standards through which they evaluate social reality, amplify disinformation and egregious misuses of history for clickbait, and represent false equivalences between groups with vastly different histories and levels of power in society. Deeply rooted revisionist memories die hard, and the path forward will require a systemic, multi-institutional reckoning with the past.

Second, as we witness an accelerating climate crisis amid the rise of anti-democratic forces all around the globe, we are reminded of Dr. King's urgency of now. White supremacy does not only hurt non-White people. As Jonathan Metzl shows in his book *Dying of Whiteness: How the Politics of Racial Resentment Is Killing America's Heartland*, right-wing policies also devastate the lives of the White people who vote for them.[18] From the erosion of the social safety net to conceal-and-carry policies that lead to high rates of White death, Metzl demonstrates how White supremacy also shortens White people's lives. We are overdue for a broad-based multiracial grassroots revolution. Democratic institutions are dismantled under our noses as mainstream progressives committed to the old institutional processes wait for their conservative colleagues to play fair. This old guard decries the "leftist" wing of the party for their "radical" tactics, their "impatience," for "not understanding how these things work."

Grassroots activists in the spirit of Dr. King have long understood that these rules were meant to placate them, that social change will not come from waiting patiently for their turn. Interest convergence will not be the way forward. As Vanessa Williamson and Dana Fisher noted in a recent op-ed, "Progress in America has rarely occurred without disruption. The movements for civil rights, workers' rights, and women's rights all required coordinated campaigns that interrupted the regular action of government and business and were often against the law."[19] The moment requires a confrontational politics that disrupts quiet acquiescence to institutions and a corrupt political system, that puts sand in the gears to trouble the status quo and demand attention.

Finally, before we can initiate collective healing, we are overdue for self-examination at the individual level. If the COVID-19 crisis and the widespread death, suffering, and long-term isolation ought to have taught us anything, it is that we are fundamentally social beings. The system of racial capitalism alienates us not just from one another but from ourselves. Widespread public health crises, from mental health to heart disease to the opioid crisis, manifest through a system that forces us to elude truth and feeling, our inner conscience, and sense of human morality. Reverend Barber's calls to save the heart and soul of America ring the alarm on our collective moral crises. We are inclined to evade reality and to buffer ceaselessly, to numb ourselves from this troubled world. But what are we living for if not one another?

Although I am skeptical that formal education is the only way out of our current state, on the other hand the legacies of the civil rights movement show us that a critical education and a spiritual education can be transformative. A critical education teaches individuals how to build a sociological imagination that evaluates and interprets their own experience within a larger sociohistorical context. This imagination can be a lifeline, illuminating our interconnectedness to one another across boundaries, borders, and time. A spiritual education reminds us of our connection not just to other humans but also to the natural world and beyond, to feel pain and joy together as part of the experience of living, and to activate our sense of morality as social beings. Joined together, this education can enable a fugitivity of imagination, resisting the world we've been given to imagine together a world that could be. Writer and activist adrienne maree brown describes how it is by reactivating our connection to one another, remembering our interconnectedness, that we reclaim our agency and build power together. Through fractals, these small interactions, an "adaptive, relational way of being," we can develop "emergent strategy for building complex patterns and systems of change."[20] Building relationships takes time, but it works. Sitting together, listening to one another, deliberating, problem-solving, negotiating and conceding, are the building blocks of a solidarity politics that give us a sense of purpose and belonging, that build power from the ground up.[21]

Only time will tell if the legacies of the civil rights movement will be remade by the visionary king- and queenmakers, if these innovative uses of collective memory by new social movements will lead to a true reckoning to reshape our deep systems of power and allow us to see the liberating possibilities of alternative futures. For now, hope is in the long-overdue clarity with which a new generation is seeing and rejecting the futility of the old strategies, the violent politics that have brought us to this societal impasse. We cannot even envision emancipation from the violence and inhumanity of our present world if our eyes are closed, if we cannot see the forest for the trees. As James Baldwin wrote, "We made the world we're living in and we have to make it over." Let us begin.

METHODOLOGICAL APPENDIX

THIS BOOK relies on a mixed methods analysis that draws on a wide range of evidence to capture the interconnected relationship between political-cultural contexts, movements engaged with a range of actors and institutions including rivals and media, and cultural impacts. To begin, I wanted to identify how social movements used the collective memory of the civil rights movement. I initially drew from social movement scholars Edwin Amenta and Neal Caren's data set of Political Organizations in the News (published in their 2009 *American Sociological Review* article). The data set documented over six hundred social movement organizations mentioned in news articles in the *New York Times* in the twentieth century, disaggregated between movement sectors.[1] I selected this data set as a representation of the breadth of the *types* or sectors of social movements covered by a mainstream media source over time, following a tradition of longitudinal social movement studies that examine protest events in the news.[2]

Rather than analyzing all six hundred organizations as data points, I wanted to draw out a sample of movements to examine their strategic processes in depth to better understand not only whether they used memory but *how* they used it and what happened next. From their extensive data set of social movement organizations, I randomly sampled ten organizations per movement sector for a total of 110 organizations across eleven movement sectors: animal rights, anti-abortion, Christian Right, conservative, environment/conservation, gun rights, immigration, LGBTQ, Muslim rights, nativist/supremacist, and police reform. Because I was interested in invocations of the civil rights movement after 1980, commonly known as the post–civil rights era, I did not include organizations that were defunct after 1980. If the organization was defunct, I randomly selected another organization. For the purpose of my study, this sample meant that I was getting a conservative estimate of invocations of the civil rights movement. As a result, when I found that organizations from every movement sector had strategically used the memory of the civil rights movement, I knew the actual breadth of the strategic uses of memory was much more significant than the counts identified through these organizations.

TABLE A.1. Number of articles per movement sector

Movement Sector	LexisNexis Articles
Animal Rights	470
Anti-Abortion	1,254
Christian Right	303
Conservative	825
Environment	855
Gun Rights	633
Immigration	699
LGBTQ	1,136
Muslim Rights	246
Nativist/Supremacist	310
Police Reform	922

To identify whether, when, and how organizations used the memory of the civil rights movement, I used LexisNexis as a reliable archive of "over 36,000 global business and legal sources, including newspapers, newswires, transcripts, magazines, trade journals, blogs, forums and more." I searched for the co-occurrence of the organizational name with keywords from the civil rights movement identified by historians as the mainstream interpretations of civil rights memory ("Martin Luther King Jr.," "civil rights movement," "Rosa Parks," "freedom ride"). I sorted results by oldest to newest to locate the organization's first publicized invocation of mainstream civil rights movement memory. Although this limited my data set to mainstream invocations rather than all invocations of civil rights figures (e.g., "Diane Nash" or "Ella Baker"), at this point I was interested in narrowing the focus to systematically document the trajectories of the institutionalized memory. Later during the coding process, evidence of these "fringe" memories would emerge. I downloaded the resulting articles in text format; the counts presented are presented in table A.1.

Based on research that documents social movements' struggles in gaining media coverage, I anticipated that many organizations would not have newspaper articles pertaining to their strategies. To also account for invocations of collective memory that did not appear in the news, I used the same search terms on each movement organization's website to download organizational documents with invocations of the civil rights movement. This generated a large data set that included organizational news, press releases, flyers, brochures, reports, and blogs. I supplemented this organizational data with archived web pages from these organizations using the web archive the Wayback Machine, taking screen shots and/or copy-pasting when possible the relevant web pages. This was a time-consuming step but important for documenting as much of the movement organization's history of invoking the civil rights movement. Of course the Wayback Machine is a partial record and included only selective dates, so again, this data provided a conservative estimate of an organization's invocations of memory. Additionally, this method of data collection could not account for invocations of memory that preceded the internet. For chapter 4's case of the Immigrant Workers Freedom Ride, I also visited the Archive Research and Study Center at UCLA, which houses the Immigrant Workers Freedom Ride Documentary Project. With over 450 hours of footage shot during the two weeks of the ride, these archives include hundreds of stories and interviews with the riders as well as documentation of the hundreds of events and rallies held across the country.

As a final check to develop as systematic as possible an account of strategic uses of the civil rights movement, I compiled secondary sources for each movement sector. Social movement scholars describe how political and cultural contexts guide movements' perceptions of opportunities and constraints, shaping strategy construction, so given the influence of political-cultural climate on social movement processes, I wanted to evaluate the extent to which invocations of memory differed not only between movements but also between political contexts over time. I studied histories of these movements to analyze the extent to which their strategic uses of memory were related to or emerged out of larger political and cultural changes, and the extent to which each movement was rooted in the civil rights movement (as, for example, the prison reform movement was). Thus I could account for movements that were not just invoking a national collective memory but also invoking their own movement's memory. Through these secondary sources, I also identified occasional footnotes that directed me toward primary resources I had not yet identified, for example, a congressional hearing or a popular culture event that indicated an invocation of collective memory.

Drawing on methods of comparative-historical sociology, I wanted to generate a chronological accounting of events within each social movement compared along axes of similarity (social movement strategy; political context) and difference (master identity category; political leaning; grievances). I was initially interested in identifying whether there were common conditions under which movements used the memory of the civil rights movement as a strategy. I coded all of these newspaper and organizational descriptions of memory invocations and quotes from organizational members using Atlas.TI, using a deep analysis of cases to move between generating and applying concepts.[3] I wanted to account for the context of the mobilization event (why the group was mobilizing), the description of the movement event, and how each movement organization used the memory of the civil rights movement, removing articles that did not meet the criteria (e.g., an article about a protest taking place on Martin Luther King Avenue, rather than about a group using the memory of Dr. King). These early codes highlighted how movements were drawing analogies between their identities and interpretations of collective memory, as in describing themselves as "the new Blacks" or as "color-blind like Dr. King."

It was from the breadth of these original codes that I began clarifying that while there were recurrent themes in interpretive concepts, there was much more fragmentation than coherence in the conditions under which particular strategies emerged. These themes mirrored the fractured meanings of collective memory described in the making of the King holiday: invocations directed alternatively between establishing racism as a matter of a finished past or an unfinished dream continuing into the present. These were strategies that deployed memory toward a conception of "who we are" as a country, whether on moral, national, or racial terms, and made claims about the appropriate modes of resistance. Yet these arguments took very different shapes depending upon the group deploying the strategy. For example, an animal rights group claiming animals were the newly oppressed minorities received different public responses compared to a family values group decrying unborn fetuses as the newly oppressed minorities, despite their shared code within a coding scheme. In other words, there was no clear set of contextual conditions that explained the strategic uses of memory. There was more going on under the surface of the strategies.

Because of these complexities, I conducted a narrative analysis of these fragmented meaning structures,[4] focusing on examining the "scenes," or series of actions coalescing into meanings, through which the strategic invocations took place as described in the newspaper and organizational accounts.[5] From this coding scheme, I built a chronological events database to catalog these strategic uses of memory over time. I compiled a spreadsheet that listed the date of each mobilization event; the group that mobilized, their identity (e.g., religious, ethnoracial, nativist), and ideology (progressive or conservative); prominent actors and rivals that emerged through the event (e.g., politicians and countermovements); and any reported outcomes including public responses, coalitions that resulted, movement perceptions of their impacts, and subsequent strategies. This data set became the foundation for the macroanalysis of the competing branches of memory over time in chapter 2 and aided in case selection for chapters 3–5.

Having established a sketch of each movement sector's trajectory of uses of memory, I narrowed in on three paired cases to represent a range of identity positionalities (see table I.1). I held the cultural strategy constant—meaning, all six of these groups use the memory of the civil rights movement. I also held the political context constant in the selection of events, but I varied the group's identity. This way the question was not "Does the strategy work?" but rather "How do the dynamics of using this strategy play out for different groups that are battling for power and what emerges from these battles?" Chapters 3 and 4 analyze these rival movement battles in depth by narrowing in on representative cases from each movement. These cases were selected based on three conditions: the well-documented strategic use of the civil rights movement (more than a single quote in a speech, this is a documented strategy for the social movement); notable national media attention on the movement event (at least fifty articles); and a countermobilization by the rival group. While the macroanalysis in chapter 2 covers many invocations that have no explicit backlash, the close case studies are meant to document the branches that emerge from strategic uses of memory. The outcomes investigated here are cultural—what meanings, discourses, identities, and perceptions emerge from these strategic contests over the battleground of collective memory?

Chapter 5 takes a holistic view to analyze shifting strategies over time with retrospective data. From late 2014 through 2015, with a research team, I conducted forty focus groups with approximately two hundred Muslim organizational leaders and community organizers in eight cities across the United States to investigate perceptions of policing and discrimination as well as the strategic question of what ought to be done. Focus groups are a particularly fruitful tool for generating debate, identifying competing assessments of the same subject, and examining different framings and constructions of meaning to explain divergent evaluations of reality.[6]

Participants represented a range of age groups, genders, ethnicities, and levels of religiosity, as we sought to generate conversations about a range of experiences and perceptions. Most participants were South Asian, Arab, or Middle Eastern, with the exception of several Southeast Asian and African American participants. As the participants were not randomly selected, they cannot be generalized as representative of all Muslim activists in the United States.

To triangulate participants' accounts of community history, I combined focus group results with archival data. With the addition of this historical trajectory, these conversations clarified ongoing debates and patterns of meaning-making in Muslim American activism. I complemented participants' perceptions of events with historical accounts of those events. To analyze each event, I constructed an event catalogue using archived organizational materials, press releases, and publications, as well as secondary historical accounts and the population of newspapers articles mentioning each event. The first interview module centered on community histories to lay out context, and it was through these semi-structured discussions of the relationship between past and present that clear connections emerged in how perceptions of "who we were" were consequential for how activists pursued strategies in the present toward "who we ought to be." In these focus groups, participants' individual perceptions documented the micro-level outcomes of this strategic work.

Finally, to examine where these strategic uses of memory may be leading us, I identified a case prominent in the data from 2017 to 2020: Black and White feminist activism during the #MeToo and #BlackLivesMatter era, countered by a backlash by #HimToo. These groups are not oppositional so much as parallel in a long lineage of contention between White and Black feminists. These cases document how progressive movements increasingly grapple with their own intragroup inequalities by reckoning with the past (in this case the historical exclusion of Black women) to pursue a justice-oriented, intersectional future. During my second wave of data collection between 2017 and 2020, I replicated my method of data collection using LexisNexis to include #MeToo, #BlackLivesMatter, #SayHerName, and #HimToo in my search terms, supplementing with organizational documents downloaded from organizations identified in newspaper articles. I added an analysis of Twitter data to account for the dimension of hashtag activism. In initial analysis, I hand coded a sample of Twitter data (n = 1,000) from a data set of millions of tweets gathered by Pablo Morales Henry and Jennifer Weintraub in the #metoo Digital Media Collection hosted by the Harvard Dataverse.[7] In chapter 6, I drew from this analysis the tweets that helped triangulate events identified through news and organizational articles. Together, these data sets provided a rich set of multimedia data that tell a patterned, deeply complex story about the trajectories of civil rights memory in American politics.

NOTES

Preface

1. "Peabody Awards: Ernest Green Story," https://peabodyawards.com/award-profile/the-ernest-green-story/.

2. King, *Letter from Birmingham Jail*, 14.

Introduction

1. Calderone, "Fox's Beck."

2. Zernike, "Where Dr. King Stood, Tea Party Claims His Mantle."

3. Glenn Beck, *The Glenn Beck Program*, Fox News, August 2010.

4. Greenwald, "Glenn Beck Is Not Martin Luther King Jr."

5. Sisk, "Glenn Beck."

6. Chris Matthews, "Let Me Finish" segment of *Hardball with Chris Matthews*, August 27, 2010.

7. Beck, "Keynote Address at the Restoring Honor Rally."

8. Thomas-Lester, Harris, and Thompson, "Sharpton's 'Reclaim the Dream' Event Brings Thousands to Honor MLK."

9. Dolak, "Alveda King Speaks at Glenn Beck's D.C. Rally."

10. Hobsbawm, *The Invention of Tradition*.

11. Skrentny, *The Minority Rights Revolution*.

12. Fraser and Gerstle, *The Rise and Fall of the New Deal Order, 1930–1980*.

13. Bumiller, *The Civil Rights Society*.

14. Snow and Benford, "Master Frames and Cycles of Protest"; Tarrow, *Power in Movement*; Tilly, *From Mobilization to Revolution*.

15. Dr. Martin Luther King Jr., "Remaining Awake through a Great Revolution," speech given at the National Cathedral, March 31, 1968.

16. Hall, "The Long Civil Rights Movement and the Political Uses of the Past"; Hill, "Sanitizing the Struggle"; Romano and Raiford, *The Civil Rights Movement in American Memory*; Theoharis, *A More Beautiful and Terrible History*; Terry, "MLK Now."

17. Barnett, "Invisible Southern Black Women Leaders in the Civil Rights Movement"; Robnett, "African-American Women in the Civil Rights Movement, 1954–1965"; Collier-Thomas and Franklin, *Sisters in the Struggle*; Glasrud and Pitre, *Southern Black Women in the Modern Civil Rights Movement*; Greene, *Our Separate Ways*.

18. Cobb, "William Barber Takes on Poverty and Race in the Age of Trump."

19. Morris, *The Scholar Denied*; Theoharis, *A More Beautiful and Terrible History*; Hall, "The Long Civil Rights Movement and the Political Uses of the Past."

20. Bell, *The Black Power Movement and American Social Work*, 9.

21. Baker, "The Historical Racial Regime and Racial Inequality in Poverty in the American South."

22. Feagin, *The White Racial Frame*, x.

23. Addo and Darity, "Disparate Recoveries."

24. Greenwood et al., "Physician-Patient Racial Concordance and Disparities in Birthing Mortality for Newborns"; Vilda et al., "Structural Racism, Racial Inequities and Urban-Rural Differences in Infant Mortality in the US"; Slaughter-Acey et al., "Skin Tone Matters"; Boen, "The Role of Socioeconomic Factors in Black-White Health Inequities across the Life Course."

25. Perry, Aronson, and Pescosolido, "Pandemic Precarity"; Odoms-Young, "Examining the Impact of Structural Racism on Food Insecurity"; Massey and Denton, *American Apartheid*; Korver-Glenn, *Race Brokers*.

26. Ewing, *Ghosts in the Schoolyard*; Stovall, *Born Out of Struggle*; Rich, Candipan, and Owens, "Segregated Neighborhoods, Segregated Schools"; Owens, "Unequal Opportunity"; Jabbari and Johnson, "The Collateral Damage of In-School Suspensions"; Jabbari and Johnson, "The Process of 'Pushing Out'"; Byrd, *Poison in the Ivy*; McGee, *Black, Brown, Bruised*.

27. Royster, *Race and the Invisible Hand*; Gaddis, "Discrimination in the Credential Society"; Tomaskovic-Devey and Avent-Holt, *Relational Inequalities*; Ray, "A Theory of Racialized Organizations"; Rodgers, "Race in the Labor Market."

28. Bor et al., "Police Killings and Their Spillover Effects on the Mental Health of Black Americans"; Crenshaw et al., "Say Her Name"; Desmond, Papachristos, and Kirk, "Police Violence and Citizen Crime Reporting in the Black Community"; Edwards, Lee, and Esposito, "Risk of Being Killed by Police Use of Force in the United States by Age, Race-Ethnicity, and Sex"; Sewell, "The Illness Associations of Police Violence"; Sewell et al., "Illness Spillovers of Lethal Police Violence"; Sewell and Jefferson, "Collateral Damage."

29. Richeson, "Americans Are Determined to Believe in Black Progress"; Onyeador et al., "Disrupting Beliefs in Racial Progress"; Seamster and Ray, "Against Teleology in the Study of Race."

30. Mills, *The Racial Contract*, 18.

31. The data in this paragraph and the next are from Pew Research Center, "Race in America 2019," https://www.pewresearch.org/social-trends/2019/04/09/race-in-america-2019/.

32. Herman and Chomsky, *Manufacturing Consent*; Bonilla-Silva, *Racism without Racists*.

33. Feagin, *The White Racial Frame*.

34. Kevin Morris, Myrna Pérez, Jonathan Brater, and Christopher Deluzio, "Purges: A Growing Threat to the Right to Vote, July 20, 2018," Brennan Center.

35. Souli, "Does America Need a Truth and Reconciliation Commission?"

36. Jefferson and Ray, "White Backlash Is a Type of Racial Reckoning Too."

37. Mike Huckabee, comments on *The Situation Room with Wolf Blitzer*, CNN, August 18, 2015.

38. SNCC Legacy Project, "To Our Brothers and Sisters of the #BlackLivesMatter Movement."

39. King, *Why We Can't Wait*, 131.

40. Yazdiha, "Toward a Du Boisian Framework of Immigrant Incorporation."

41. Tarrow, *Power in Movement*; Tilly and Tarrow, *Contentious Politics*.

42. Hall, "The Rediscovery of 'Ideology'"; Hall, *Representation*, 26; Hall, "Cultural Identity and Diaspora"; Hall, "Cultural Identity and Diaspora."

43. Foucault, *Power/Knowledge*; Fanon, *Black Skin, White Masks*.

44. Korver-Glenn, "(Collective) Memory of Racial Violence and the Social Construction of the Hispanic Category among Houston Hispanics"; Assmann and Czaplicka, "Collective Memory and Cultural Identity."

45. Assmann and Czaplicka, "Collective Memory and Cultural Identity"; Halbwachs, *On Collective Memory*; Olick, "Collective Memory."

46. Lamont and Fournier, *Cultivating Differences*; Lamont and Molnár, "The Study of Boundaries in the Social Sciences."

47. Simko, Cunningham, and Fox, "Contesting Commemorative Landscapes."

48. Pelak, "Institutionalizing Counter-Memories of the U.S. Civil Rights Movement."

49. Valencia-García, *Far-Right Revisionism and the End of History*.

50. Abrams, *Historical Sociology*; Aminzade, "Historical Sociology and Time"; Mahoney, "Path Dependence in Historical Sociology"; Mahoney, "Comparative-Historical Methodology."

51. Small, "'How Many Cases Do I Need?'"

52. Abbott, "Conceptions of Time and Events in Social Science Methods"; Abell, "Narrative Explanation"; Franzosi, "Narrative Analysis—Or Why (and How) Sociologists Should Be Interested in Narrative"; Gotham and Staples, "Narrative Analysis and the New Historical Sociology."

53. Bloor, *Focus Groups in Social Research*; Krueger and Casey, *Focus Groups*; Morgan, *Focus Groups as Qualitative Research*; Corbin and Strauss, *Basics of Qualitative Research*; Charmaz, *Constructing Grounded Theory*.

Chapter 1

1. Fentress and Wickham, *Social Memory*; Halbwachs, *On Collective Memory*; Olick, "Collective Memory"; Olick and Levy, "Collective Memory and Cultural Constraint"; Sturken, *Tangled Memories*; Conway, "New Directions in the Sociology of Collective Memory and Commemoration."

2. Olick and Robbins, "Social Memory Studies," 112.

3. Zelizer, "Reading the Past against the Grain."

4. Isaac, "Movement of Movements."

5. Daphi and Zamponi, "Exploring the Movement-Memory Nexus."

6. Armstrong and Crage, "Movements and Memory."

7. Conway, *Commemoration and Bloody Sunday*.

8. Jansen, "Resurrection and Appropriation."

9. Alexander et al., *Cultural Trauma and Collective Identity*; Simko, "Marking Time in Memorials and Museums of Terror."

10. Wagner-Pacifici and Schwartz, "The Vietnam Veterans Memorial"; Wagner-Pacifici, "Memories in the Making."

11. Simko, "Marking Time in Memorials and Museums of Terror."

12. Savelsberg, *Knowing about Genocide*.

13. Trouillot, *Silencing the Past*.

14. Assmann, *Shadows of Trauma*.

15. Stein, "Whose Memories?"

16. Savelsberg, *Knowing about Genocide*.

17. Formisano, *Boston against Busing*; Sokol, *There Goes My Everything*.

18. Kruse, *White Flight*, 9.

19. Spong, "John Shelby Spong's Controversial Christian Stance."

20. King, *Where Do We Go from Here*, 101.

21. http://www.thekingcenter.org.

22. Wolfensberger, "The Martin Luther King, Jr. Holiday."

23. Chappell, *Waking from the Dream*, 140.

24. Remarks of Rep. Robert Garcia, Martin Luther King Birthday, *Congressional Record*, 1979.

25. Quoted in Chappell, *Waking from the Dream*.

26. Ibid., 143.

27. "Bill to Honor Rev. King Weakened, Then Pulled from House Consideration," *Congressional Quarterly Weekly Report*, December 8, 1979, 2795.

28. Gomer and Petrella, "Reagan Used MLK Day to Undermine Racial Justice."

29. Chappell, *Waking from the Dream*.

30. Troy, "The Example of Ronald Reagan."

31. Coretta Scott King, Hearing on Proposals for Martin Luther King, Jr. National Holiday, 97th Cong., 2nd sess., February 23, 1982, 11–12.

32. Chappell, *Waking from the Dream*, 152.

33. Ibid., 92–93.

34. Associated Press, "In Snow and Icy Winds, a Nation Honors Dr. King."

35. Ronald Reagan, "Remarks on the Anniversary of the Birth of Martin Luther King, Jr.," January 15, 1983, https://www.reaganlibrary.gov/archives/speech/remarks-anniversary-birth-martin-luther-king-jr.

36. Dewar, "Helms Stalls King's Day in Senate."

37. Ibid.

38. Ibid.

39. Rothman, "How MLK Day Became a Holiday."

40. Robert Rothman, "Congress Clears King Holiday after Heated Senate Debate: Reagan Will Sign the Measure," *Congressional Quarterly Weekly Report*, October 12, 1983, 2175.

41. Smith, *Conservatism and Racism, and Why in America They Are the Same*.

42. Isaacson, "Backing into the Race."

43. Clines, "Reagan's Doubts on Dr. King Disclosed."

44. Herbers, "Reagan's Changes on Rights Are Starting to Have Impact."

45. Gomer and Petrella, "Reagan Used MLK Day to Undermine Racial Justice.

46. Mohr, "Marchers Exhorted to Go after 'Deferred Dreams.'"

Chapter 2

1. Walsh, "Teen Who Recorded George Floyd Video."

2. Donald Trump, Twitter post, April 17, 2020, 11:21 a.m.

3. Papenfuss, "Covid-19 Protesters Just Like Rosa Parks."

4. Quoted in Scott, "The Audacity of Those Comparing 'Open Up' Protesters to Rosa Parks."

5. Ibid.

6. Conway, *Commemoration and Bloody Sunday*; Gongaware, "Collective Memory Anchors"; Gutman, *Memory Activism*; Jansen, "Resurrection and Appropriation."

7. Baldwin and Burrow, *The Domestication of Martin Luther King Jr.*; Bruyneel, "The King's Body"; Dyson, *I May Not Get There with You*; Hall, "The Long Civil Rights Movement and the Political Uses of the Past"; Shelby and Terry, *To Shape a New World*; Terry, "MLK Now"; Theoharis, *A More Beautiful and Terrible History*.

8. Lamont et al., *Getting Respect*; Polletta, *It Was Like a Fever*; Armstrong and Bernstein, "Culture, Power, and Institutions"; Meyer, Whittier, and Robnett, *Social Movements*; Eliasoph and Lichterman, "Culture in Interaction."

9. Goffman, *Frame Analysis*.

10. Snow et al., "Frame Alignment Processes, Micromobilization, and Movement Participation."

11. Saguy, *Come Out, Come Out, Whoever You Are*; Enriquez and Saguy, "Coming out of the Shadows."

12. Tarrow, *Power in Movement*, 118.

13. Oliver and Johnston, "What a Good Idea!"

14. Glenn, "Settler Colonialism as Structure"; Razack, *Race, Space, and the Law*; Roediger, *The Wages of Whiteness*; Robinson, *Black Marxism*; Crenshaw, "Mapping the Margins."

15. Omi and Winant, *Racial Formation in the United States*; Bonilla-Silva, *White Supremacy and Racism in the Post–Civil Rights Era*; Feagin, *Systemic Racism*.

16. Hancock, *The Politics of Disgust*, 4.

17. Bracey, "Toward a Critical Race Theory of State"; Bracey, "Black Movements Need Black Theorizing"; Luna, "'Black Children Are an Endangered Species'"; Nummi, Jennings, and Feagin, "#BlackLivesMatter: Innovative Black Resistance"; Reyes and Ragon, "Analyzing Ethnoracial Mobilization"; Robinson, "(Re)Theorizing Civic Engagement"; Watkins Liu, "The Anti-Oppressive Value of Critical Race Theory and Intersectionality in Social Movement Study."

18. Carbado et al., "Intersectionality: Mapping the Movements of a Theory"; Cho, Crenshaw, and McCall, "Toward a Field of Intersectionality Studies"; Collins, "Learning from the Outsider Within"; Collins and Bilge, *Intersectionality*; Crenshaw, "Mapping the Margins"; Stoetzler and Yuval-Davis, "Standpoint Theory, Situated Knowledge and the Situated Imagination."

19. Collins, "The Difference That Power Makes."

20. Brown et al., "#SayHerName"; Cole, "Coalitions as a Model for Intersectionality"; Luna, "'Truly a Women of Color Organization'"; Roberts and Jesudason, "Movement Intersectionality"; Terriquez, "Intersectional Mobilization"; Terriquez, Brenes, and Lopez, "Intersectionality as a Multipurpose Collective Action Frame"; Verloo, "Intersectional and Cross-Movement Politics and Policies."

21. Armstrong and Bernstein, "Culture, Power, and Institutions."

22. Gurbuz, *Rival Kurdish Movements in Turkey*.

23. Fetner, "Working Anita Bryant"; Meyer and Staggenborg, "Movements, Countermovements, and the Structure of Political Opportunity"; Lo, "Countermovements and Conservative Movements in the Contemporary U.S."; Rohlinger, "Framing the Abortion Debate."

24. Fleming, *Resurrecting Slavery*, 17.

25. Somers, "Narrativity, Narrative Identity, and Social Action"; Halbwachs, *On Collective Memory*; Zerubavel, "Social Memories"; Olick and Robbins, "Social Memory Studies"; Conway, *Commemoration and Bloody Sunday*; Polletta, *It Was Like a Fever*; Simko, *The Politics of Consolation*; Gordon, *Ghostly Matters*; Dixon-Román, "Toward a Hauntology on Data"; Derrida, *Specters of Marx*.

26. Yazdiha, "An Intersectional Theory of Strategic Decisions."

27. Polletta, *It Was Like a Fever*, 143.

28. Bourdieu, *Outline of a Theory of Practice*.

29. Mische, "Projects and Possibilities"; Mische, "Measuring Futures in Action."

30. Tavory and Eliasoph, "Coordinating Futures."

31. Simko, "From Difficult Past to Imagined Future."

32. Foster, *I Don't Like the Blues*; Carrington, *Speculative Blackness*; Butler, *Critical Black Futures*.

33. Strong and Chaplin, "Afrofuturism and Black Panther."

34. Emirbayer and Mische, "What Is Agency?"

35. McAdam, *Political Process and the Development of Black Insurgency*.

36. Bonilla-Silva, *Racism without Racists*; Bonilla-Silva, *White Supremacy and Racism in the Post–Civil Rights Era*; Feagin, *The White Racial Frame*; Feagin, *Systemic Racism*; Feagin and Elias, "Rethinking Racial Formation Theory"; Hall, "The Rediscovery of 'Ideology.'"

37. Gaby and Caren, "The Rise of Inequality."

38. Meyer, *How Social Movements (Sometimes) Matter*.

39. Amenta et al., "The Political Consequences of Social Movements"; Andrews and Caren, "Making the News."

40. Boomgaarden and Vliegenthart, "Explaining the Rise of Anti-Immigrant Parties"; Carlson, "Moral Panic, Moral Breach"; Cook, *Governing with the News*.

41. Mills, "White Ignorance."

42. Bracey et al., "The White Racial Frame"; Mueller, "Racial Ideology or Racial Ignorance?"; Martí, *American Blindspot*.

43. Bonilla-Silva, *Racism without Racists*.

44. Mueller, "Racial Ideology or Racial Ignorance," 142.

45. Proctor and Schiebinger, *Agnotology*.

46. Seamster and Ray, "Against Teleology in the Study of Race"; Richeson, "Americans Are Determined to Believe in Black Progress"; Onyeador et al., "Disrupting Beliefs in Racial Progress."

47. Seidman, "Queer-ing Sociology, Sociologizing Queer Theory"; Altman, *Homosexual*; Escoffier, "Sexual Revolution and the Politics of Gay Identity"; Epstein, "Gay Politics, Ethnic Identity"; Gamson, "Must Identity Movements Self-Destruct?"; Vaid, *Virtual Equality*; Bernstein, "Celebration and Suppression."

48. Greer, "Violence against Homosexuals Rising."

49. Shapiro, "A New 'Common Identity' for the Disabled."

50. Quoted in ibid.

51. Corry, "TV: 'CBS Reports' Examines Black Families."

52. Unger, "Hard-hitting Special about Black Families."

53. MacKenzie, "Former Klansman's Racism Plays Well in New Orleans."

54. Berbrier, "'Half the Battle'"; Hall, "The Long Civil Rights Movement and the Political Uses of the Past."

55. C-SPAN, "State of Black America," January 21, 1992.

56. Edsall, "Rights Drive Said to Lose Underpinnings."

57. Ibid.

58. C-SPAN, "Sister Souljah Moment," June 1992, https://www.c-span.org/video/?c4460582/sister-souljah-moment.

59. Greenberg, "Sister Souljah and the Irrational Rationality of Hate."

60. Dart, "Gays."

61. Hussain, "Class Action."

62. Loose, "Gay Activists Summon Their Hopes, Resolve."

63. Biskupic, "Court Permits Parade Sponsors to Exclude Gays."

64. Prison Activist Resource Center, 1997, Berkeley, CA.

65. Jesse Jackson, "Million Man March," C-SPAN, October 16, 1995, https://www.c-span.org/video/?67630-1/million-man-march.

66. Lester Sloan on *Weekend Edition*, NPR, October 29, 1995.

67. Loose, "Gay Activists Summon Their Hopes, Resolve."

68. Eagle Forum, press release, 1994.

69. Goodstein, "Rockers Lead New Wave of Anti-Abortion Fight."

70. Stammer, "Is Christian Coalition's Conversion Real?"

71. Ibid.

72. Alex Castellanos, Jesse Helms "Hands" political advertisement, 1990.

73. Chan, "A Call to Action, Celebration."

74. Ibid.

75. Kingsbury, "Protests to Hit District."

76. Al-Yousef, "For Arabs and Muslims in America, MLK's Legacy Looms Larger after 9/11."

77. PAL, "Pro-Life Activists Celebrate 8–1 Victory."

78. Bulkeley, "Gay-Rights Activist Hails Today's Openness."

79. AIM, "AIM Report: King's 'Dream' Becomes a Nightmare."

80. Bonilla-Silva, *Racism without Racists*.

81. Bailey, Mummolo, and Noel, "Tea Party Influence"; Parker, *Change They Can't Believe In*; Perrin et al., "Political and Cultural Dimensions of Tea Party Support"; Skocpol and Williamson, *The Tea Party and the Remaking of Republican Conservatism*; Zernike, *Boiling Mad*.

82. Bailey, Mummolo, and Noel, "Tea Party Influence"; Parker, *Change They Can't Believe In*; Perrin et al., "Political and Cultural Dimensions of Tea Party Support"; Skocpol and Williamson, *The Tea Party and the Remaking of Republican Conservatism*; Zernike, *Boiling Mad*.

83. Citizens Committee for the Right to Keep and Bear Arms, "CCRKBA Tells Gun Owners to Circle Aug. 28 for Counter Protest Effort," press release, July 9, 2007.

84. Blackwell, "Second Amendment Freedoms Aided the Civil Rights Movement.

85. "Meet NRA News Commentator Colion Noir," 2013, https://www.youtube.com/watch?v=UKY3scPIMd8&feature=youtube_gdata_player.

86. NRA News, "S2 E14: 'Martin Luther King Jr.," Commentators You Tube show, January 20, 2014.

87. Quoted in Morgan Whitaker, "Nugent: Gun Activists Need to Be Like Rosa Parks," MSNBC News, March 28, 2014.

88. Alexander, *The New Jim Crow*.

89. Bill Quigley, "14 Shocking Facts That Prove the US Criminal Justice System Is Racist," *Open Democracy*, July 27, 2010.

90. King, *Letter from Birmingham Jail*, 2.

91. Quoted in Cineas. "White Rage Won't Just Go Away."

92. Blue, "Buchanan."

93. Braunstein, "The Tea Party Goes to Washington."

94. C-SPAN, *Tea Party Rally against IRS Practices*, vol. 313449-101 (West Front of the Capitol, Washington, DC, 2013).

95. Kaufman, "'Cowboy' Conservative Claims MLK for the Tea Party."

96. Chen, "Phillip Agnew, Dream Defender."

97. Lawyers' Committee for Civil Rights Under Law, "A Unified Statement of Action to Promote Reform and Stop Police Abuse."

98. Foran, "A Year of Black Lives Matter."

99. Bill O'Reilly, "O'Reilly: 'Martin Luther King Would Not Participate in a Black Lives Matter Protest,'" *The O'Reilly Factor* (Fox News, July 11, 2016), http://insider.foxnews.com/2016/07/11/oreilly-mlk-would-not-participate-blm-protest.

100. Alveda King, on *Fox and Friends*, July 3, 2020; Penny Starr, "Alveda King on 'Black Lives Matter'—'From Conception to Natural Death,'" CNS News, January 8, 2015.

101. Caldera, "Fact Check: Democrats Have Condemned Violence Linked to BLM, Antifascist Protests."

102. Murray, "It's 2016 and the Civil Rights Era Hasn't Ended."

103. Remnick, "John Lewis, Donald Trump, and the Meaning of Legitimacy."

104. Donald Trump, Twitter post, January 15, 2017.

105. Dinesh D'Souza, Twitter post, January 14, 2017, 7:28 a.m. https://twitter.com/dineshdsouza/status/820291541872746497.

106. Remnick, "John Lewis, Donald Trump, and the Meaning of Legitimacy."

107. Yang, "Rep. John Lewis on Not Meeting with Trump."

108. Leadership Conference on Civil and Human Rights, "Trump Administration Civil and Human Rights Rollbacks."

109. William Allman, "President Obama Meets Civil Rights Icon Ruby Bridges," White House Blog, July 15, 2011, https://obamawhitehouse.archives.gov/blog/2011/07/15/president-obama-meets-civil-rights-icon-ruby-bridges.

110. Salaky, "Cartoonist Said He Drew DeVos in Iconic Civil Rights Painting to Open a Dialogue."

Chapter 3

1. Sessions, "Faith Inspired MLK Jr. to March for Civil Rights."

2. Benford and Snow, "Framing Processes and Social Movements"; Gamson et al., "Media Images and the Social Construction of Reality"; Schudson, "How Culture Works."

3. Dixon, "Crime News and Racialized Beliefs"; Luna, "'Black Children Are an Endangered Species'"; Mastro et al., "News Coverage of Immigration"; Radoynovska and King, "To Whom Are You True?"; Walker and Stepick, "Valuing the Cause."

4. Andrews, "Moralizing Regulation"; Beisel, "Morals versus Art: Censorship"; Carlson, "Moral Panic, Moral Breach"; Gurbuz, "Performing Moral Opposition"; Luft, "Theorizing Moral Cognition"; Saguy and Gruys, "Morality and Health."

5. Robinson, *Black Marxism*; Roediger, *Working toward Whiteness.*

6. Haney-Lopez, *Dog Whistle Politics*; Hancock, *The Politics of Disgust.*

7. Skarpelis, "Dresden Will Never Be Hiroshima Morality," 200.

8. Espiritu, *Body Counts.*

9. Lazin, "March on Washington Paved Way for Gay Rights Too."

10. Altman, *Homosexual*; Escoffier, "Sexual Revolution and the Politics of Gay Identity"; Epstein, "Gay Politics, Ethnic Identity"; Seidman, "Queer-ing Sociology, Sociologizing Queer Theory"; Gamson, "Must Identity Movements Self-Destruct?"; Vaid, *Virtual Equality*; Bernstein, "Celebration and Suppression."

11. Quoted in Dart, "Gays."

12. Skrentny, *The Minority Rights Revolution.*

13. Dart, "Gays."

14. Archana, "The Crusade for Gay Rights."

15. Quoted in Eleveld, "Obama, Bayard Rustin, and the New LGBT Civil-Rights Movement."

16. Bassichis and Spade, "Queer Politics and Anti-Blackness"; Carbado, "Black Rights, Gay Rights, Civil Rights."

17. Quoted in Dart, "Gays."

18. Quoted in Nagourney, "Gay Rights Movement Shows Clout in Capital."

19. Ibid.

20. Quoted in Schmalz, "March for Gay Rights."

21. Hirshman, *Victory.*

22. Duggan, "The New Homonormativity."

23. Plotz and Newell, "Ralph Reed's Creed."

24. Quoted in Nagourney, "Gay Rights Movement Shows Clout in Capital."

25. Quoted in Dart, "Gays."

26. Quoted in Human Rights Campaign, "Protect It from Whom?"

27. Quoted in Mawyer, "God and the GOP."

28. Quoted in Fulwood, "Christian Coalition Courts Minorities."

29. Quoted in Monroe, "Race to the Right."

30. Quoted in Fulwood, "Christian Coalition Courts Minorities."

31. Ibid.

32. Roig-Franzia, "Bryant Legacy Resurfaces in Fla."

33. Campbell, "It's the 70s Again."

34. Quoted in Paz, "Struggle, Forgiveness."

35. Campbell, "It's the 70s Again."

36. Roig-Franzia, "Bryant Legacy Resurfaces in Fla."

37. Freiberg, "Miami-Dade Ja vu"; McCraw and Brickley, "Miami-Dade County Commission Extends Law Banning Discrimination to Cover Homosexuals."

38. Campbell, "It's the 70s Again."

39. Robinson, "Black Vote Could Decide Final Outcome on Gay Rights."

40. Nielsen, "Between a Frock and a Hard Place."

41. Ross, "Center Appalled by MLK Use in Flier."

42. Quoted in Long, *Martin Luther King Jr.*, 22.

43. Quoted in Ross, "Black Coalition."

44. Nielsen, "Between a Frock and a Hard Place."

45. Quoted in Bell, "Miami-Dade's Gay Rights May Hinge on Black Votes."

46. Quoted in AP Wire, "Petition Drive Set to Begin against Gay Rights Law."

47. Quoted in Bootie Cosgrove-Mather, "Anita Bryant's Battle Is Back," CBS News, June 7, 2007.

48. Canedy, "Miami Sees Challenge on Gay Rights, Again."

49. Quoted in Canedy, "Miami Sees Challenge on Gay Rights, Again."

50. Freiberg, "Miami-Dade Ja vu."

51. Pitts, "Linking King to Anti-gay Effort Is an Outrage."

52. Bell, "Miami-Dade's Gay Rights May Hinge on Black Votes."

53. Quoted in Nielsen, "Between a Frock and a Hard Place."

54. Quoted in Bar-Diaz, "Black Leaders."

55. Quoted in Nielsen, "Between a Frock and a Hard Place."

56. Quoted in Gay Today, "Expose USA's Christian Coalition Petition Frauds Says NGLTF."

57. Long, *Martin Luther King Jr.*

58. Garris, "Martin Luther King's Conservative Legacy."

59. Jones and Engel, *What Would Martin Say?*

60. Baldwin and Burrow, *The Domestication of Martin Luther King Jr.*, 17.

61. Barack Obama, "Transcript of Barack Obama's Victory Speech," November 5, 2008.

62. Gallagher and Brown, "Marriage: $20 Million Strategy for Victory."

63. Eichner et al., "Potential Legal Impact of the Proposed Domestic Legal Union Amendment to the North Carolina Constitution."

64. Jensen, "Final NC Primary Poll."

65. Meadows, "Losing Forward."

66. Wilson, "North Carolina's Gay Marriage Ban Closer to Public Vote."

67. Meno, "North Carolinians to Vote on Anti-LGBT Amendment One Tuesday."

68. Quoted in Sturgis, "NC Lawmakers Pushing Same-Sex Marriage Ban Enlist Help of Gay-Hating Preacher."

69. William Barber, "Rev. Dr William Barber's Open Letter to Clergy Pimping Wedge Issues," reprinted in *TransGriot*, September 14, 2012. The quotes in the following paragraph are from this open letter as well.

70. Quoted in Peter Cassels, "The Black-Gay Divide: A Clash of Race, Religion & Rights," Edge Media Network, February 7, 2012.

71. TFP Student Action, "10 Reasons Why Homosexual 'Marriage' Is Harmful and Must Be Opposed," 2013, https://www.catholichawaii.org/media/223462/10reasonswhyhomosexualmarriageisharmful.pdf.

72. Ladd, "Amendment Sparks Very Deep Emotions."

73. Shapiro, "North Carolina Amendment 1 Divides Gay Rights Movement."

74. Wetzstein, "N.C. Votes to Not Allow Same-Sex Marriage."

75. Stoogenke, "Amendment One Raises Debate about Businesses Choosing N.C."

76. Quoted in Batten, "Duke's Jim Rogers Tees Off on Marriage Amendment."

77. Stewart, "The Potential Price of Intolerance."

78. Quoted in Thomaston, "Equality on Trial."

79. Quoted in Spaulding, "Amendment One Sponsor Now Says He Will Vote against It."

80. Dr. Martin Luther King Jr., "Remaining Awake through a Great Revolution," speech given at the National Cathedral, March 31, 1968.

81. WWAY News, "Gov. Perdue: 'We Look Like Mississippi," May 11, 2012.

82. Quoted in ABC11, "Perdue."

83. NAACP, "NAACP Announces Support for Marriage Equality," press release, May 19, 2012.

84. Martin Luther King Jr., "I Have a Dream," speech, August 28, 1963.

85. Quoted in Caputo, "Social Conservatives."

86. "Brian Brown Stand for Marriage Rally—Utah State Capitol," 2014.

87. McCarthy, "A Generation of LGBTQ Advocates Hopes the Clock Isn't Ticking Backward."

Chapter 4

1. Californians for Population Stabilization, "Many Congressional Leaders Want to Admit 33 Million More Immigrant Workers to Take Jobs, Despite Record Minority Unemployment," January 15, 2014.

2. Cadava, *Standing on Common Ground*; Erll and Nünning, *Cultural Memory Studies.*

3. Smith, *Myths and Memories of the Nation.*

4. Cornell, *A Well-Regulated Militia*; Belew, *Bring the War Home*; Miller-Idriss, *Hate in the Homeland*; Shapira, *Waiting for José.*

5. Gans, "Symbolic Ethnicity: The Future of Ethnic Groups and Cultures in America," 9; Gordon, *Assimilation in American Life.*

6. Abrams, "Performative Citizenship in the Civil Rights and Immigrant Rights Movements"; Pan, *Incidental Racialization.*

7. Bennett, *The Party of Fear*; Perea, *Immigrants Out!*; Higham, *Strangers in the Land*; Newth, "Rethinking 'Nativism'"; Tatalovich, *Nativism Reborn?*

8. Del, "'They See Us Like Trash'"; Kasinitz, "Becoming American, Becoming Minority, Getting Ahead"; Waters and Kasinitz, "Discrimination, Race Relations, and the Second Generation"; Valdez and Golash-Boza, "Towards an Intersectionality of Race and Ethnicity"; Bashi and McDaniel, "A Theory of Immigration and Racial Stratification"; Aranda, "An Ethnoracial Perspective"; Brown and Jones, "Rethinking Panethnicity and the Race-Immigration Divide"; Maghbouleh, *The Limits of Whiteness*; Shams, "Bangladeshi Muslims in Mississippi."

9. Kim, "The Racial Triangulation of Asian Americans"; Selod, *Forever Suspect*; Grewal, *Islam Is a Foreign Country*; Haddad, *Not Quite American?*

10. Glenn, "Constructing Citizenship"; Yuval-Davis, "Intersectionality, Citizenship and Contemporary Politics of Belonging"; Jiménez and Horowitz, "When White Is Just Alright"; Yazdiha, "Toward a Du Boisian Framework of Immigrant Incorporation."

11. Berbrier, "'Half the Battle'"; Bloemraad, Silva, and Voss, "Rights, Economics, or Family?"; Enriquez, "'Undocumented and Citizen Students Unite'"; Johnston and Noakes, *Frames of*

Protest; McCammon, "Beyond Frame Resonance"; Meyer, Whittier, and Robnett, *Social Movements*; Robnett, "Emotional Resonance, Social Location, and Strategic Framing."

12. Van Dyke and McCammon, *Strategic Alliances*; Carastathis, "Identity Categories as Potential Coalitions"; Enriquez, "'Undocumented and Citizen Students Unite'"; Luna, "Marching toward Reproductive Justice."

13. Bloemraad, "Unity in Diversity?"; Hero and Preuhs, "From Civil Rights to Multiculturalism and Welfare for Immigrants."

14. Jones, *The Browning of the New South*.

15. Treitler, *The Ethnic Project*, 6.

16. Zamora and Osuji, "Mobilizing African Americans for Immigrant Rights."

17. Bonilla-Silva, *Racism without Racists*.

18. Shams, "Successful Yet Precarious"; Xu and Lee, "The Marginalized 'Model' Minority"; Lee and Tran, "The Mere Mention of Asians in Affirmative Action"; Zhou and Bankston, "The Model Minority Stereotype and the National Identity Question."

19. Ebert, Liao, and Estrada, "Apathy and Color-Blindness in Privatized Immigration Control."

20. Bennett, *The Party of Fear*; Perea, *Immigrants Out!*

21. Bank Munoz and Wong, "Don't Miss the Bus."

22. Cleeland, "Immigrants Set Out on Their Own Freedom Ride."

23. Ibid.

24. Ibid.

25. Jamison, "Embedded on the Left."

26. Cleeland, "Immigrants Set Out on Their Own Freedom Ride."

27. "Freedom Ride for Immigrant Rights."

28. Jamison, "Embedded on the Left."

29. Atkin, "We Make the Road by Riding."

30. Cleeland, "Immigrants Set Out on Their Own Freedom Ride."

31. Jamison, "Embedded on the Left."

32. Atkin, "We Make the Road by Riding."

33. Quoted in Greenhouse, "Immigrants' Rights Drive Starts."

34. Quoted in Nolan, "Immigrant Workers Freedom Ride."

35. All of the quotes in this paragraph are from Krikorian, "'Immigrant Workers Freedom Ride' Insults All Americans."

36. Quoted in Moser, "900 Immigrant Workers Take Freedom Ride of Their Own."

37. Quoted in Hague, "'Bring Handguns Rifles and Shotguns.'"

38. Leblanc, "Immigrant Workers Freedom Ride"; Moser, "900 Immigrant Workers Take Freedom Ride of Their Own"; Nolan, "Immigrant Workers Freedom Ride."

39. Atkin, "We Make the Road by Riding."

40. Voss and Bloemraad, *Rallying for Immigrant Rights*.

41. Cruz, Margolis, and Mora, "Immigrant Workers Freedom Ride."

42. Luntz, "Respect for the Law & Economic Fairness."

43. Quoted in Garcia, "Undocubus Set to Travel to Democratic National Convention."

44. Quoted in ibid.

45. Bello, "Dignity beyond Voting."

46. Quoted in Saavedra, "Undocubus Tour."

47. Myerson, "Riders of the 'UndocuBus' Have 'No Papers, No Fear.'"

48. Quoted in Costantini, "Hopeful, 'Unapologetic' Art Rebrands the Immigration Movement."

49. Sabate and Benedetti, "No Papers, No Fear."

50. Ramirez Jimenez, "In Admiration."

51. Ruckus, "Undocu-Bus 'No Papers No Fear Ride for Justice,'" https://ruckus.org/undocu-bus-no-papers-no-fear-ride-for-justice/.

52. González, "Undocumented Immigrants Take Cause to Defiant New Level."

53. Quoted in González, "Illegal Migrants across U.S. Taking Protests to Defiant New Level."

54. Gonzalez, "Undocumented Immigrants Take Cause to Defiant New Level."

55. Quoted in Kammer, "Frank Morris Calls Rep. John Conyers 'Blind' to the Negative Effects of Immigration on Workers."

56. Domenico Montanaro, "How the 'Replacement' Theory Went Mainstream on the Political Right," NPR News, May 17, 2022.

Chapter 5

1. CAIR, "CAIR to Mark Juneteenth with Month-Long Photo Journal of Muslim Activists on Alabama Civil Rights Tour," press release, June 19, 2018.

2. CAIR, "CAIR Alabama Civil Rights Tour Photo Journal Project," Facebook photo journal, June 20, 2018.

3. CAIR, "In Their Footsteps: An American Muslim Civil Rights Journey," 2018, https://www.youtube.com/watch?v=zkfCbidBiwQ.

4. CAIR, "CAIR Alabama Civil Rights Tour Photo Journal Project."

5. Bumiller, *The Civil Rights Society*; Evans, *Personal Politics*; Fleming and Morris, "Theorizing Ethnic and Racial Movements in the Global Age Lessons from the Civil Rights Movement"; Shapiro, *No Pity*; Skrentny, *The Minority Rights Revolution*.

6. Guhin, "Colorblind Islam"; Husain, "Moving Beyond (and Back to) the Black-White Binary"; Garner and Selod, "The Racialization of Muslims."

7. Chan-Malik, *Being Muslim*; Jackson, *Islam and the Blackamerican*; Jackson, "Muslims, Islam(s), Race, and American Islamophobia."

8. Downey and Rohlinger, "Linking Strategic Choice with Macro-Organizational Dynamics"; Gamson, *The Strategy of Social Protest*; Jasper, "A Strategic Approach to Collective Action"; Fligstein and McAdam, "Toward a General Theory of Strategic Action Fields."

9. Bernstein, "Identity Politics"; Jasper, "A Strategic Approach to Collective Action"; Jasper, "Strategic Marginalizations, Emotional Marginalities"; Klandermans, van der Toorn, and van Stekelenburg, "Embeddedness and Identity."

10. Jenkins, *Social Identity*; Stryker, Owens, and White, *Self, Identity, and Social Movements*; Tajfel, *Social Identity and Intergroup Relations*; Tajfel and Turner, "The Social Identity Theory of Intergroup Behavior."

11. Einwohner, "Identity Work and Collective Action in a Repressive Context"; Ghaziani, "Post-Gay Collective Identity Construction"; Klandermans, "Identity Politics and Politicized Identities"; Meyer, "Protest and Political Opportunities"; Meyer, Whittier, and Robnett, *Social*

Movements; Owens, Robinson, and Smith-Lovin, "Three Faces of Identity"; Polletta and Jasper, "Collective Identity and Social Movements"; Stryker, Owens, and White, *Self, Identity, and Social Movements*; Taylor and Whittier, "Collective Identity in Social Movement Communities."

12. Du Bois, *The Souls of Black Folk: Essays and Sketches*, 38.

13. Bashi, "Racial Categories Matter Because Racial Hierarchies Matter"; Bashi and McDaniel, "A Theory of Immigration and Racial Stratification"; Treitler, *The Ethnic Project*; Omi and Winant, *Racial Formation in the United States*.

14. Blumer, "Race Prejudice as a Sense of Group Position"; Bobo, "Prejudice as Group Position"; Brown and Jones, "Rethinking Panethnicity and the Race-Immigration Divide"; Omi and Winant, *Racial Formation in the United States*; Valdez and Golash-Boza, "Towards an Intersectionality of Race and Ethnicity"; Maghbouleh, *The Limits of Whiteness*.

15. Brodkin, *How Jews Became White Folks*; Ignatiev, *How the Irish Became White*; Roediger, *Working toward Whiteness*.

16. Valdez and Golash-Boza, "Towards an Intersectionality of Race and Ethnicity"; Gotanda, "'Other Non-Whites' in American Legal History"; Kim, "The Racial Triangulation of Asian Americans"; Lee and Kye, "Racialized Assimilation of Asian Americans"; Nagel, "American Indian Ethnic Renewal"; Smith, "Black Mexicans, Conjunctural Ethnicity, and Operating Identities"; Waters et al., "Segmented Assimilation Revisited"; Zhou and Bankston, "The Model Minority Stereotype and the National Identity Question"; Zhou et al., "Success Attained, Deterred, and Denied."

17. Cainkar, "Fluid Terror Threat."

18. Treitler, *The Ethnic Project*, 10.

19. Okamoto, "Institutional Panethnicity"; Okamoto, "Toward a Theory of Panethnicity"; Okamoto and Mora, "Panethnicity."

20. Sharma, *Hip Hop Desis*.

21. Abraham and Abraham, *Arabs in the New World*; Haddad, *Not Quite American?*; Jamal and Naber, *Race and Arab Americans Before and After 9/11*.

22. Bakalian and Bozorgmehr, *Backlash 9/11*; Khan, "Constructing the American Muslim Community"; Santoro and Azab, "Arab American Protest in the Terror Decade."

23. Bail, "The Fringe Effect"; Cainkar and Maira, "Targeting Arab/Muslim/South Asian Americans"; Haddad, *Not Quite American?*; Jamal and Naber, *Race and Arab Americans Before and After 9/11*; Khan, "Constructing the American Muslim Community"; Qureshi and Sells, *The New Crusades*; Said, *Orientalism*; Yazdiha, "Law as Movement Strategy."

24. Khan, "As a Muslim Republican."

25. "Pete King (NY-03) Takes Money from Mosque Then Calls Them Terrorists," http://migramatters.blogspot.com/2006/09/pete-king-ny-03-takes-money-from.html?m=0.

26. King Watch, "Interview with Dr. Farouque Khan."

27. Quoted in Kolker, "Peter King's Muslim Problem."

28. Auston, "Mapping the Intersections of Islamophobia & #BlackLivesMatter"; Karim, "To Be Black, Female, and Muslim"; Abdul Khabeer, *Muslim Cool*; Khan, "As a Muslim Republican."

29. Khan, "America's Muslims Share Martin Luther King's Dream."

30. Nagel and Staeheli, "'We're Just Like the Irish.'"

31. Gans, "Symbolic Ethnicity and Symbolic Religiosity"; Jamal and Naber, *Race and Arab Americans Before and After 9/11*.

32. Love, *Islamophobia and Racism in America*.

33. Abraham and Abraham, *Arabs in the New World*.

34. Haddad and Ricks, "Claiming Space in America's Pluralism."

35. Unless otherwise noted, the uncited quotes are from my focus groups and fieldwork.

36. Elliott, "Between Black and Immigrant Muslims, an Uneasy Alliance."

37. Swidler, "Culture in Action."

38. Bakalian and Bozorgmehr, *Backlash 9/11*; Disha, Cavendish, and King, "Historical Events and Spaces of Hate."

39. FBI, "FBI Uniform Crime Reporting Program Report."

40. Cainkar and Maira, "Targeting Arab/Muslim/South Asian Americans."

41. Beydoun, *American Islamophobia*, 97.

42. Bail, *Terrified*; Ekman, "Online Islamophobia and the Politics of Fear; Yazdiha, "Law as Movement Strategy."

43. Wan, "Hearings on Muslims Trigger Panic."

44. Elliott, "Between Black and Immigrant Muslims, an Uneasy Alliance."

45. Ibid.

46. Nadel, "For Island's Muslims, a Time to Be Wary."

47. Mian, "Muslim Americans."

48. Hassan, "What Does the Civil Rights Movement Mean for Muslims?"

49. Hooper, "Bar Religious Profiling."

50. Epstein, "Peter King Defends Muslim Hearings."

51. Goldman and Apuzzo, "NYPD Muslim Spying Led to No Leads, Terror Cases."

52. Khan, "Tell Them about the Dream, Barack."

53. "The Muslim Community Rises with Ferguson: From Palestine to Ferguson," Center for Global Muslim Life on Medium, October 17, 2014.

54. Pipes and Chadha, "CAIR: Islamists Fooling the Establishment."

55. Weaselzippers Online Forum, 2014.

56. Schlussel, "Martin Luther King, Jr."

57. Elliott, "Between Black and Immigrant Muslims, an Uneasy Alliance."

58. Latif, "American-Muslims on Black Lives Matter and Anti-Racism Initiatives."

59. Khwaja, "Black Muslim Americans."

60. Suleiman, "Reclaiming Malcolm X's Legacy."

61. Elliott, "Between Black and Immigrant Muslims, an Uneasy Alliance."

62. Stein, "Harlem Mosque Leader Talks Malcolm X Legacy."

63. Muslim ARC and Muslims for Ferguson, "Call for Justice: Joint Letter on American Muslim Solidarity against Police Brutality," January 26, 2015.

64. Du Bois, *The Souls of Black Folk*.

65. Segura, "Trump's Muslim Ban Galvanizes Civil Rights Activists across the American South."

Chapter 6

1. Jacob Pramuk, "Oprah's Globes Speech Sparks 2020 Presidential Speculation," CNBC, January 8, 2018.

2. Tyle, "Oprah Keeps MLK's Dream Alive."

3. Brody, "'The Rape of Recy Taylor.'"

4. Garcia, "The Woman Who Created #MeToo Long before Hashtags."

5. Ibid.; Onwuachi-Willig, "What About #UsToo"; Trott, "Networked Feminism."

6. Quoted in Nyren, "Jane Fonda."

7. Simko, "From Legacy to Memory"; Pelak, "Institutionalizing Counter-Memories of the U.S. Civil Rights Movement"; Ghoshal, "Transforming Collective Memory"; Amadiume et al., *The Politics of Memory*; Chioneso et al., "Community Healing and Resistance through Storytelling."

8. Ghoshal, "Transforming Collective Memory"; Olick, "Collective Memory"; Simko, "From Difficult Past to Imagined Future."

9. David, "Cultural Trauma, Memory, and Gendered Collective Action"; Hershatter, *The Gender of Memory*; Jacobs, "Gender and Collective Memory"; McEwan, "Building a Postcolonial Archive?"; Volo, "The Dynamics of Emotion and Activism."

10. Hershatter, *The Gender of Memory*; Jacobs, "Gender and Collective Memory"; McEwan, "Building a Postcolonial Archive?"

11. Luna and Pirtle, *Black Feminist Sociology*, 8.

12. McEwan, "Building a Postcolonial Archive?"

13. Carbado et al., "Intersectionality: Mapping the Movements of a Theory"; Collins, "Learning from the Outsider Within"; Luna, "Who Speaks for Whom?"; Newman and Newman, *White Women's Rights*; Taylor, *How We Get Free*; Ware, *Beyond the Pale*.

14. Crawford et al., *Women in the Civil Rights Movement*; Glasrud and Pitre, *Southern Black Women in the Modern Civil Rights Movement*; Glymph, "Du Bois's Black Reconstruction and Slave Women's War for Freedom"; Greene, *Our Separate Ways*; Robnett, "African-American Women in the Civil Rights Movement, 1954–1965"; Taylor, *How We Get Free*; Theoharis, *A More Beautiful and Terrible History*.

15. Ransby, "Fannie Lou Hamer's Message Should Be Remembered."

16. Misra, "The Intersectionality of Precarity."

17. Clark, "To Tweet Our Own Cause"; Freelon et al., "How Black Twitter and Other Social Media Communities Interact with Mainstream News"; Graham and Smith, "The Content of Our #Characters"; Harp, Grimm, and Loke, "Rape, Storytelling and Social Media."

18. Purifoy, "A Black Feminist Guide to Electoral Politics in 2020."

19. Baer, "Redoing Feminism"; Freelon et al., "How Black Twitter and Other Social Media Communities Interact with Mainstream News"; Jackson, Bailey, and Welles, *#HashtagActivism*; Schradie, "The Digital Activism Gap"; Tufekci, *Twitter and Tear Gas*.

20. Jackson, Bailey, and Welles, *#HashtagActivism*, xxv.

21. Quoted in Lang, "How the Karen Meme Confronts History of White Womanhood."

22. Goh et al., "Narrow Prototypes and Neglected Victims."

23. Phipps, "White Tears, White Rage"; Johnson, "Ain't I a Woman?"

24. Fessler, "Gloria Steinem's Message to Women and Girls."

25. Quoted in Elber, "Film Depicts Black Lives Matter."

26. Lee, "There Is No #MeToo without Black Women."

27. Lipsitz, "Sexual Harassment Law Was Shaped by the Battles of Black Women."

28. Lindsey, "Black Women Have Consistently Been Trailblazers for Social Change."

29. Lipsitz, "Sexual Harassment Law Was Shaped by the Battles of Black Women."

30. Quoted in Onwuachi-Willig, "What About #UsToo."

31. Lange, "Activists Who Attended the Golden Globes Say Women in Hollywood 'Are Trying to Learn from Us.'"

32. Arkin, "#MeToo, Powerful Speeches Dominate the 75th Golden Globe Awards."

33. Estepa, "Rep. Jackie Speier."

34. "2018: The Year of the Black Woman," Pub. L. No. 47 (2018), *Congressional Record*, https://www.congress.gov/crec/2018/03/19/modified/CREC-2018-03-19-pt1-PgH1688.htm.

35. Roeder, "How Conservative Is Brett Kavanaugh?"

36. McLaughlin, "#MeToo Founder Tarana Burke Says There Is a 'Collective Disappointment and Frustration.'"

37. Kurtz, "Alyssa Milano: Despite Kavanaugh Confirmation, 'I Do Have Hope.'"

38. Mansbridge and Tate, "Race Trumps Gender."

39. Quoted in Goff, "TV Writer Keli Goff."

40. Hobbs, "One Year of #MeToo."

41. James, "Anita Hill."

42. Hamer, "Testimony before the Credentials Committee."

43. Hill, "Let's Talk about How to End Sexual Violence."

44. Ruiz, "Anita Hill on Clarence Thomas, Brett Kavanaugh, and Her New Memoir, 'Believing.'"

45. Marla Reynolds, Twitter post, October 6, 2018.

46. Pieter Hanson, Twitter post, October 8, 2018, 9:36 p.m., https://twitter.com/Thatwasmymom/status/1049518834972020737.

47. Leuci and Francescani, "Camille Cosby on Her Husband's Appeal and the Black Lives Matter and #MeToo Movements."

48. Ransby, "A Black Feminist's Response to Attacks on Martin Luther King Jr.'s Legacy."

49. Lorde, *Sister Outsider*, 223.

50. Gill and Rahman-Jones, "Me Too Founder Tarana Burke."

51. Combahee River Collective, *The Combahee River Collective Statement*; Taylor, *How We Get Free*.

52. Stafford, "On #MeToo Anniversary, Leaders Say Focus Is on Inequality."

53. Lindsey, "Black Women Have Consistently Been Trailblazers for Social Change."

54. "The Van Jones Show: Interview with Oprah Winfrey and Ava DuVernay," CNN, March 11, 2018.

55. Lindsey, "Black Women Have Consistently Been Trailblazers for Social Change."

56. Bennett, "How History Changed Anita Hill."

Conclusion

1. Charles, "The *New York Times* 1619 Project Is Reshaping the Conversation on Slavery."

2. Arnn, Swain, and Spalding, *The 1776 Report*, 5.

3. Ibid., 31.

4. Ibid., 31, 32.

5. "ACLU Statement on Trump Administration's 1776 Commission Report," January 19, 2021.

6. "The ACLU on Fighting Critical Race Theory Bans."

7. Sprunt, "The Brewing Political Battle over Critical Race Theory."

8. Folley, "Bernice King Hits GOP."

9. Bernice King, Twitter post, April 5, 2022, 11:12 a.m., https://twitter.com/BerniceKing/status/1511406522508754945.

10. Josh Mandel, Twitter post, April 5, 2022, 3:41 p.m.

11. Lorde, *Sister Outsider*.

12. Vega, "Protesters Out to Reclaim King's Legacy."

13. Action Ferguson, "Reclaim MLK."

14. ASATA, "Reclaim MLK Day 2018."

15. Tometi and Lenoir, "Black Lives Matter Is Not a Civil Rights Movement."

16. Bennett, "Inheriting the Movement."

17. Barber, "America's Moral Malady."

18. Metzl, *Dying of Whiteness*.

19. Williamson and Fisher, "It's Time for Democrats to Stop 'Clapping for Tinkerbell.'"

20. brown, *Emergent Strategy*, 2.

21. Han, McKenna, and Oyakawa, *Prisms of the People*; Hancock, *Solidarity Politics for Millennials*; Yuval-Davis, "Intersectionality, Citizenship and Contemporary Politics of Belonging."

Methodological Appendix

1. Amenta et al., "All the Movements Fit to Print."

2. Jenkins and Eckert, "Channeling Black Insurgency"; Kerbo and Shaffer, "Lower Class Insurgency and the Political Process"; McAdam and Su, "The War at Home"; Soule and Earl, "A Movement Society Evaluated."

3. Corbin and Strauss, *Basics of Qualitative Research*.

4. Abbott, "Conceptions of Time and Events in Social Science Methods"; Abell, "Narrative Explanation"; Somers, "Narrativity, Narrative Identity, and Social Action."

5. Goffman, *Frame Analysis*.

6. Bloor, *Focus Groups in Social Research*; Johnston, "Verification and Proof in Frame and Discourse Analysis"; Morgan, *Focus Groups as Qualitative Research*; Porta, "Making the Polis."

7. Morales Henry and Weintraub, "#metoo Digital Media Collection."

REFERENCES

Abbott, Andrew. 1990a. "Conceptions of Time and Events in Social Science Methods: Causal and Narrative Approaches." *Historical Methods: A Journal of Quantitative and Interdisciplinary History* 23 (4): 140–50. https://doi.org/10.1080/01615440.1990.10594204.

ABC11. 2012. "Perdue: 'We Look Like Mississippi.'" ABC11 Raleigh-Durham, May 11. http://abc11.com/archive/8657823/.

Abell, Peter. 2004. "Narrative Explanation: An Alternative to Variable-Centered Explanation?" *Annual Review of Sociology* 30 (1): 287–310.

Abraham, Sameer Y., and Nabeel Abraham. 1983. *Arabs in the New World: Studies on Arab-American Communities*. Wayne State University, Center for Urban Studies.

Abrams, Kathryn. 2014. "Performative Citizenship in the Civil Rights and Immigrant Rights Movements." *UC Berkeley Public Law Research Paper* (March): 1–24.

Abrams, Philip. 1982. *Historical Sociology*. Cornell University Press.

"The ACLU on Fighting Critical Race Theory Bans: 'It's about Our Country Reckoning with Racism.'" 2021. *The Guardian*, July 1. http://www.theguardian.com/us-news/2021/jul/01/aclu-fights-state-bans-teaching-critical-race-theory.

Action Ferguson. n.d. "Reclaim MLK." *Ferguson Action* (blog). http://fergusonaction.com/reclaim-mlk/.

Addo, Fenaba R., and William A. Darity. 2021. "Disparate Recoveries: Wealth, Race, and the Working Class after the Great Recession." *Annals of the American Academy of Political and Social Science* 695 (1): 173–92. https://doi.org/10.1177/00027162211028822.

AIM. 2003. "AIM Report: King's 'Dream' Becomes a Nightmare." *Accuracy in Media* (blog), October 1. http://www.aim.org/aim-report/aim-report-kings-dream-becomes-a-nightmare/.

Alexander, Jeffrey C., Ron Eyerman, Bernard Giesen, Neil J. Smelser, and Piotr Sztompka. 2004. *Cultural Trauma and Collective Identity*. University of California Press.

Alexander, Michelle. 2010. *The New Jim Crow: Mass Incarceration in the Age of Colorblindness*. New Press.

Altman, Dennis. 1993. *Homosexual: Oppression and Liberation*. New York University Press.

Al-Yousef, Yousef. 2002. "For Arabs and Muslims in America, MLK's Legacy Looms Larger after 9/11." *IslamiCity* (blog), January 27. https://www.islamicity.org/1689/for-arabs-and-muslims-in-america-mlks-legacy-looms-larger-after-911/.

Amadiume, Ifi, Abd Allah Ahmad Naim, Abdullahi An-Na'im, and Abdullahi An-Na'im. 2000. *The Politics of Memory: Truth, Healing and Social Justice*. Zed Books.

Amenta, Edwin, Neal Caren, Elizabeth Chiarello, and Yang Su. 2010. "The Political Consequences of Social Movements." *Annual Review of Sociology* 36: 287–307.

Amenta, Edwin, Neal Caren, Sheera Joy Olasky, and James E. Stobaugh. 2009. "All the Movements Fit to Print: Who, What, When, Where, and Why SMO Families Appeared in the *New York Times* in the Twentieth Century." *American Sociological Review* 74 (4): 636–56. https://doi.org/10.1177/000312240907400407.

Aminzade, Ronald. 1992. "Historical Sociology and Time." *Sociological Methods & Research* 20 (4): 456–80. https://doi.org/10.1177/0049124192020004003.

Anderson, Carol. 2016. *White Rage: The Unspoken Truth of Our Racial Divide*. Bloomsbury Publishing.

Andrews, Abigail L. 2018. "Moralizing Regulation: The Implications of Policing 'Good' versus 'Bad' Immigrants." *Ethnic and Racial Studies* 41 (14): 2485–2503. https://doi.org/10.1080/01419870.2017.1375133.

Andrews, Kenneth T., and Neal Caren. 2010. "Making the News: Movement Organizations, Media Attention, and the Public Agenda." *American Sociological Review* 75 (6): 841–66. https://doi.org/10.1177/0003122410386689.

Aranda, Elizabeth. 2017. "An Ethnoracial Perspective: Response to Valdez and Golash-Boza." *Ethnic and Racial Studies* 40 (13): 2232–39. https://doi.org/10.1080/01419870.2017.1344264.

Archana, Subramaniam. 1995. "The Crusade for Gay Rights." *Roanoke Times*, March 14.

Arkin, Daniel. 2018. "#MeToo, Powerful Speeches Dominate the 75th Golden Globe Awards." NBC News, January 7. https://www.nbcnews.com/pop-culture/awards/golden-globes-2018-metoo-casts-shadow-over-celebration-movies-tv-n835451.

Armstrong, Elizabeth A., and Mary Bernstein. 2008. "Culture, Power, and Institutions: A Multi-Institutional Politics Approach to Social Movements." *Sociological Theory* 26 (1): 74–99. https://doi.org/10.1111/j.1467-9558.2008.00319.x.

Armstrong, Elizabeth A., and Suzanna M. Crage. 2006. "Movements and Memory: The Making of the Stonewall Myth." *American Sociological Review* 71 (5): 724–51.

Arnn, Larry P., Carol Swain, and Matthew Spalding. 2021. *The 1776 Report*. Encounter Books.

Arnold, Martin. 1964. "CORE Plans Tests: Rights Leaders Praise Passage." *New York Times*, June 20.

ASATA. 2018. "Reclaim MLK Day 2018." *ASATA* (blog), January 25. https://www.asata.org/post/170131971873/reclaim-mlk-day-2018.

Assmann, Aleida. 2016. *Shadows of Trauma: Memory and the Politics of Postwar Identity*. Fordham University Press.

Assmann, Jan, and John Czaplicka. 1995. "Collective Memory and Cultural Identity." *New German Critique* (65): 125–33. https://doi.org/10.2307/488538.

Associated Press. 1982. "In Snow and Icy Winds, a Nation Honors Dr. King." *New York Times*, January 16. https://www.nytimes.com/1982/01/16/us/in-snow-and-icy-winds-a-nation-honors-dr-king.html.

Associated Press (AP) Wire. "Petition Drive Set to Begin against Gay Rights Law." *St. Petersburg Times*, February 4.

Atkin, Jerry. 2005. "We Make the Road by Riding (Se Hace el Camino al Viajar): Stories from a Journal of the Immigrant Workers Freedom Ride—Portland to New York, September 23 to October 4, 2003." *Radical History Review* 1 (93): 200–216.

Auston, Donna. 2016. "Mapping the Intersections of Islamophobia & #BlackLivesMatter: Unearthing Black Muslim Life & Activism in the Policing Crisis." *Sapelo Square* (blog),

August 30. https://sapelosquare.com/2016/08/30/mapping-the-intersections-of-islamophobia-blacklivesmatter-unearthing-black-muslim-life-activism-in-the-policing-crisis/.

Baer, Hester. 2016. "Redoing Feminism: Digital Activism, Body Politics, and Neoliberalism." *Feminist Media Studies* 16 (1): 17–34. https://doi.org/10.1080/14680777.2015.1093070.

Bail, Christopher A. 2012. "The Fringe Effect: Civil Society Organizations and the Evolution of Media Discourse about Islam since the September 11th Attacks." *American Sociological Review* 77 (6): 855–79. https://doi.org/10.1177/0003122412465743.

———. 2016. *Terrified: How Anti-Muslim Fringe Organizations Became Mainstream*. Reprint. Princeton University Press.

Bailey, Michael A., Jonathan Mummolo, and Hans Noel. 2012. "Tea Party Influence: A Story of Activists and Elites." *American Politics Research* 40 (5): 769–804. https://doi.org/10.1177/1532673X11435150.

Bakalian, Anny P., and Mehdi Bozorgmehr. 2009. *Backlash 9/11: Middle Eastern and Muslim Americans Respond*. University of California Press.

Baker, Regina S. 2022. "The Historical Racial Regime and Racial Inequality in Poverty in the American South." *American Journal of Sociology* 127 (6): 1721–81. https://doi.org/10.1086/719653.

Baldwin, Lewis V., and Rufus Burrow. 2013. *The Domestication of Martin Luther King Jr.: Clarence B. Jones, Right-Wing Conservatism, and the Manipulation of the King Legacy*. Wipf and Stock Publishers.

Bank Munoz, Carolina, and Kent Wong. 2004. "Don't Miss the Bus: The Immigrant Workers Freedom Ride." *New Labor Forum* 13 (2): 61–66.

Bar-Diaz, Madeline. 2002. "Black Leaders: Keep Gay Rights." *Sun Sentinel*, August 14. http://articles.sun-sentinel.com/2002-08-14/news/0208130543_1_coretta-scott-king-repeal-king-s-picture.

Barber, William J. 2018. "America's Moral Malady." *The Atlantic*. https://www.theatlantic.com/magazine/archive/2018/02/a-new-poor-peoples-campaign/552503/.

Barnett, Bernice McNair. 1993. "Invisible Southern Black Women Leaders in the Civil Rights Movement: The Triple Constraints of Gender, Race, and Class." *Gender & Society* 7 (2): 162–82. https://doi.org/10.1177/089124393007002002.

Bashi, Vilna. 1998. "Racial Categories Matter Because Racial Hierarchies Matter: A Commentary." *Ethnic and Racial Studies* 21 (5): 959–68. https://doi.org/10.1080/014198798329748

Bashi, Vilna, and Antonio McDaniel. 1997. "A Theory of Immigration and Racial Stratification." *Journal of Black Studies* 27 (5): 668–82.

Bassichis, Morgan, and Dean Spade. 2014. "Queer Politics and Anti-Blackness." In *Queer Necropolitics*. Routledge.

Batten, Taylor. 2012. "Duke's Jim Rogers Tees Off on Marriage Amendment." *Charlotte Observer*, April 13.

Beck, Glenn. 2010. "Glenn Beck: Keynote Address at the Restoring Honor Rally." https://www.americanrhetoric.com/speeches/glennbeckrestoringhonorkeynote.htm.

Beisel, Nicola. 1993. "Morals versus Art: Censorship, the Politics of Interpretation, and the Victorian Nude." *American Sociological Review* 58 (2): 145–62. https://doi.org/10.2307/2095963.

Belew, Kathleen. 2018. *Bring the War Home: The White Power Movement and Paramilitary America*. Harvard University Press.

Bell, Joyce M. 2014. *The Black Power Movement and American Social Work*. Columbia University Press.

Bell, Maya. 2002. "Miami-Dade's Gay Rights May Hinge on Black Votes." *Orlando Sentinel*, August 10. http://articles.orlandosentinel.com/2002-08-10/news/0208100348_1_miami-dade-discrimination-gays-and-lesbians.

Bello, Kimi. 2012. "Dignity beyond Voting: Undocumented Immigrants Cast Their Hopes." *Colorlines* (blog), October 25. https://www.colorlines.com/articles/dignity-beyond-voting-undocumented-immigrants-cast-their-hopes.

Benford, Robert D., and David A. Snow. 2000. "Framing Processes and Social Movements: An Overview and Assessment." *Annual Review of Sociology* 26 (1): 611–39. https://doi.org/10.1146/annurev.soc.26.1.611.

Bennett, Brad. 2021. "Inheriting the Movement: Daughter of Dr. Martin Luther King Jr. Reflects on Message of Nonviolent Social Change." *Southern Poverty Law Center* (blog), January 15. https://www.splcenter.org/news/2021/01/15/inheriting-movement-daughter-dr-martin-luther-king-jr-reflects-message-nonviolent-social.

Bennett, David Harry. 1988. *The Party of Fear: From Nativist Movements to the New Right in American History*. University of North Carolina Press.

Bennett, Jessica. 2019. "How History Changed Anita Hill." *New York Times*, June 17, sec. U.S. https://www.nytimes.com/2019/06/17/us/anita-hill-women-power.html.

Berbrier, Mitch. 1998. "'Half the Battle': Cultural Resonance, Framing Processes, and Ethnic Affectations in Contemporary White Separatist Rhetoric." *Social Problems* 45 (4): 431–50. https://doi.org/10.2307/3097206.

Bernstein, Mary. 1997. "Celebration and Suppression: The Strategic Uses of Identity by the Lesbian and Gay Movement." *American Journal of Sociology* 103 (3): 531–65. https://doi.org/10.1086/231250.

———. 2005. "Identity Politics." *Annual Review of Sociology* 31 (1): 47–74. https://doi.org/10.1146/annurev.soc.29.010202.100054.

Beydoun, Khaled A. 2018. *American Islamophobia: Understanding the Roots and Rise of Fear*. University of California Press.

Biskupic, Joan. 1995. "Court Permits Parade Sponsors to Exclude Gays." *Washington Post*, June 20.

Blackwell, Ken. 2007. "Second Amendment Freedoms Aided the Civil Rights Movement." *Townhall*, February 6. https://townhall.com/columnists/kenblackwell/2007/02/06/second-amendment-freedoms-aided-the-civil-rights-movement-n1409414.

Bloemraad, Irene. 2007. "Unity in Diversity?: Bridging Models of Multiculturalism and Immigrant Integration." *Du Bois Review: Social Science Research on Race* 4 (2): 317–36. https://doi.org/10.1017/S1742058X0707018X.

Bloemraad, Irene, Fabiana Silva, and Kim Voss. 2016. "Rights, Economics, or Family? Frame Resonance, Political Ideology, and the Immigrant Rights Movement." *Social Forces* 94 (4): 1647–74. https://doi.org/10.1093/sf/sov123.

Bloor, Michael. 2001. *Focus Groups in Social Research*. Sage.

Blue, Miranda. 2014. "Buchanan: 'Time to Move On' from Civil Rights Movement." *Right Wing Watch*, February 26. http://www.rightwingwatch.org/post/buchanan-time-to-move-on-from-civil-rights-movement/.

Blumer, Herbert. 1958. "Race Prejudice as a Sense of Group Position." *Pacific Sociological Review* 1 (1): 3–7.

Bobo, Lawrence D. 1999. "Prejudice as Group Position: Microfoundations of a Sociological Approach to Racism and Race Relations." *Journal of Social Issues* 55 (3): 445–72.

Boen, Courtney. 2016. "The Role of Socioeconomic Factors in Black-White Health Inequities across the Life Course: Point-in-Time Measures, Long-Term Exposures, and Differential Health Returns." *Social Science & Medicine* 170: 63–76. https://doi.org/10.1016/j.socscimed.2016.10.008.

Bonilla-Silva, Eduardo. 2001. *White Supremacy and Racism in the Post–Civil Rights Era*. Lynne Rienner Publishers.

———. 2013. *Racism without Racists: Color-Blind Racism and the Persistence of Racial Inequality in America*. Rowman & Littlefield.

Boomgaarden, Hajo G., and Rens Vliegenthart. 2007. "Explaining the Rise of Anti-Immigrant Parties: The Role of News Media Content." *Electoral Studies* 26 (2): 404–17. https://doi.org/10.1016/j.electstud.2006.10.018.

Bor, Jacob, Atheendar S. Venkataramani, David R. Williams, and Alexander C. Tsai. 2018. "Police Killings and Their Spillover Effects on the Mental Health of Black Americans: A Population-Based, Quasi-Experimental Study." *Lancet* 392 (10144): 302–10. https://doi.org/10.1016/S0140-6736(18)31130-9.

Bourdieu, Pierre. 1977. *Outline of a Theory of Practice*. Cambridge University Press.

Bracey, Glenn E. 2015. "Toward a Critical Race Theory of State." *Critical Sociology* 41 (3): 553–72. https://doi.org/10.1177/0896920513504600.

———. 2016. "Black Movements Need Black Theorizing: Exposing Implicit Whiteness in Political Process Theory." *Sociological Focus* 49 (1): 11–27. https://doi.org/10.1080/00380237.2015.1067569.

Bracey, Glenn, Christopher Chambers, Kristen Lavelle, and Jennifer C. Mueller. 2017. "The White Racial Frame: A Roundtable Discussion." In *Systemic Racism: Making Liberty, Justice, and Democracy Real*, ed. Ruth Thompson-Miller and Kimberley Ducey, 41–75. Palgrave Macmillan. https://doi.org/10.1057/978-1-137-59410-5_3.

Braunstein, Ruth. 2015. "The Tea Party Goes to Washington: Mass Demonstrations as Performative and Interactional Processes." *Qualitative Sociology* 38 (4): 353–74. https://doi.org/10.1007/s11133-015-9314-3.

Brodkin, Karen. 1998. *How Jews Became White Folks and What That Says about Race in America*. Rutgers University Press.

Brody, Richard. 2017. "'The Rape of Recy Taylor': An Essential, Flawed Documentary at the New York Film Festival." *New Yorker*, October 3. https://www.newyorker.com/culture/richard-brody/the-rape-of-recy-taylor-an-essential-flawed-documentary-at-the-new-york-film-festival.

brown, adrienne maree. 2017. *Emergent Strategy: Shaping Change, Changing Worlds*. AK Press.

Brown, Hana, and Jennifer A. Jones. 2015. "Rethinking Panethnicity and the Race-Immigration Divide: An Ethnoracialization Model of Group Formation." *Sociology of Race and Ethnicity* 1 (1): 181–91. https://doi.org/10.1177/2332649214558304.

Brown, Melissa, Rashawn Ray, Ed Summers, and Neil Fraistat. 2017. "#SayHerName: A Case Study of Intersectional Social Media Activism." *Ethnic and Racial Studies* 40 (11): 1831–46. https://doi.org/10.1080/01419870.2017.1334934.

Bruyneel, Kevin. 2014. "The King's Body: The Martin Luther King Jr. Memorial and the Politics of Collective Memory." *History & Memory* 26 (1): 75–108.

Bulkeley, Deborah. 2005. "Gay-Rights Activist Hails Today's Openness." *Deseret News*, October 11.

Bumiller, Kristin. 1992. *The Civil Rights Society: The Social Construction of Victims*. Johns Hopkins University Press.

Butler, Philip. 2021. *Critical Black Futures: Speculative Theories and Explorations*. Springer Nature.

Byrd, W. Carson. 2017. *Poison in the Ivy: Race Relations and the Reproduction of Inequality on Elite College Campuses*. Rutgers University Press.

Cadava, Geraldo L. 2013. *Standing on Common Ground*. Harvard University Press.

Cainkar, Louise. 2018. "Fluid Terror Threat." *Amerasia Journal* 44 (1): 27–59.

Cainkar, Louise, and Sunaina Maira. 2005. "Targeting Arab/Muslim/South Asian Americans: Criminalization and Cultural Citizenship." *Amerasia Journal* 31 (3): 1–28.

Caldera, Camille. 2020. "Fact Check: Democrats Have Condemned Violence Linked to BLM, Anti-fascist Protests." *USA Today*, August 13.

Calderone, Michael. 2009. "Fox's Beck: Obama Is 'a Racist.'" *Politico*, July 28.

Campbell, Duncan. 2002. "It's the 70s Again as Pink Voters Fight Plan to Bring Back Anti-Gay Laws." *Guardian*, September 9, sec. World News. https://www.theguardian.com/world/2002/sep/09/usa.gayrights.

Canedy, Dana. 2002. "Miami Sees Challenge on Gay Rights, Again." *New York Times*, September 5. http://www.nytimes.com/2002/09/05/us/miami-sees-challenge-on-gay-rights-again.html.

Caputo, Marc. 2014. "Social Conservatives: Lawsuit Fighting Gay-Marriage Ban Is Like Bull Connor Fighting Civil Rights." *Miami Herald*, February 14.

Carastathis, Anna. 2013. "Identity Categories as Potential Coalitions." *Signs* 38 (4): 941–65. https://doi.org/10.1086/669573.

Carbado, Devon W. 1999. "Black Rights, Gay Rights, Civil Rights." *UCLA Law Review* 47: 1467.

Carbado, Devon W., Kimberlé Williams Crenshaw, Vickie M. Mays, and Barbara Tomlinson. 2013. "Intersectionality: Mapping the Movements of a Theory." *Du Bois Review: Social Science Research on Race* 10 (2): 303–12. https://doi.org/10.1017/S1742058X13000349.

Carlson, Jennifer. 2016. "Moral Panic, Moral Breach: Bernhard Goetz, George Zimmerman, and Racialized News Reporting in Contested Cases of Self-Defense." *Social Problems* 63 (1): 1–20. https://doi.org/10.1093/socpro/spv029.

Carrington, André M. 2016. *Speculative Blackness: The Future of Race in Science Fiction*. University of Minnesota Press.

Chan, Sewell. 2002. "A Call to Action, Celebration." *Washington Post*, January 20.

Chan-Malik, Sylvia. 2018. *Being Muslim: A Cultural History of Women of Color in American Islam*. New York University Press.

Chappell, David L. 2014. *Waking from the Dream: The Struggle for Civil Rights in the Shadow of Martin Luther King, Jr.* Random House.

Charles, J. Brian. 2019. "The *New York Times* 1619 Project Is Reshaping the Conversation on Slavery. Conservatives Hate It." *Vox*, August 20, 2019.

Charmaz, Kathy. 2006. *Constructing Grounded Theory*. Sage.

Chen, Michelle. 2015. "Phillip Agnew, Dream Defender." *In These Times*, January 19. http://inthesetimes.com/article/17543/phillip_agnew_dream_defender.

Chioneso, Nkechinyelum A., Carla D. Hunter, Robyn L. Gobin, Shardé McNeil Smith, Ruby Mendenhall, and Helen A. Neville. 2020. "Community Healing and Resistance through Storytelling: A Framework to Address Racial Trauma in Africana Communities." *Journal of Black Psychology* 46 (2–3): 95–121. https://doi.org/10.1177/0095798420929468.

Cho, Sumi, Kimberlé Williams Crenshaw, and Leslie McCall. 2013. "Toward a Field of Intersectionality Studies: Theory, Applications, and Praxis." *Signs: Journal of Women in Culture and Society* 38 (4): 785–810. https://doi.org/10.1086/669608.

Cineas, Fabiola. 2021. "White Rage Won't Just Go Away." *Vox*, January 27. https://www.vox.com/22243875/white-rage-white-nationalism.

Clark, Meredith. 2014. "To Tweet Our Own Cause: A Mixed-Methods Study of the Online Phenomenon 'Black Twitter.'" University of North Carolina at Chapel Hill Graduate School. https://doi.org/10.17615/7bfs-rp55.

Cleeland, Nancy. 2003. "Immigrants Set Out on Their Own Freedom Ride." *Los Angeles Times*, September 23. http://articles.latimes.com/2003/sep/23/business/fi-ride23.

Clines, Francis X. 1983. "Reagan's Doubts on Dr. King Disclosed." *New York Times*, October 22. https://www.nytimes.com/1983/10/22/us/reagan-s-doubts-on-dr-king-disclosed.html.

Cole, Elizabeth R. 2008. "Coalitions as a Model for Intersectionality: From Practice to Theory." *Sex Roles* 59 (5): 443–53. https://doi.org/10.1007/s11199-008-9419-1.

Collier-Thomas, Bettye, and V. P. Franklin. 2001. *Sisters in the Struggle: African American Women in the Civil Rights-Black Power Movement*. New York University Press.

Collins, Patricia Hill. 1986. "Learning from the Outsider Within: The Sociological Significance of Black Feminist Thought." *Social Problems* 33 (6): S14–32. https://doi.org/10.2307/800672.

———. 2019. "The Difference That Power Makes: Intersectionality and Participatory Democracy." In *The Palgrave Handbook of Intersectionality in Public Policy*, ed. Olena Hankivsky and Julia S. Jordan-Zachery, 167–92. The Politics of Intersectionality. Springer International Publishing. https://doi.org/10.1007/978-3-319-98473-5_7.

Collins, Patricia Hill, and Sirma Bilge. 2016. *Intersectionality*. John Wiley & Sons.

Combahee River Collective. 1977. *The Combahee River Collective Statement: Black Feminist Organizing in the Seventies and Eighties*. Kitchen Table: Women of Color Press.

Conway, Brian. 2010a. *Commemoration and Bloody Sunday: Pathways of Memory*. Springer.

———. 2010b. "New Directions in the Sociology of Collective Memory and Commemoration." *Sociology Compass* 4 (7): 442–53. https://doi.org/10.1111/j.1751-9020.2010.00300.x.

Cook, Timothy E. 1998. *Governing with the News: The News Media as a Political Institution*. University of Chicago Press.

Corbin, J., and A. Strauss. 2008. *Basics of Qualitative Research: Techniques and Procedures for Developing Grounded Theory*. 3rd ed. Sage.

Cornell, Saul. 2006. *A Well-Regulated Militia: The Founding Fathers and the Origins of Gun Control in America*. Oxford University Press.

Corry, John. 1986. "TV: 'CBS Reports' Examines Black Families." *New York Times*, January 25, sec. Arts. https://www.nytimes.com/1986/01/25/arts/tv-cbs-reports-examines-black-families.html.

Costantini, Cristina. 2013. "Hopeful, 'Unapologetic' Art Rebrands the Immigration Movement." ABC News, February 27. https://abcnews.go.com/ABC_Univision/art-rebrands-immigration-reform-movement/story?id=18610975.

Crawford, Vicki L., Jacqueline Anne Rouse, Barbara Woods, and Broadus Butler. 1993. *Women in the Civil Rights Movement: Trailblazers and Torchbearers, 1941–1965*. Indiana University Press.

Crenshaw, Kimberlé. 1990. "Mapping the Margins: Intersectionality, Identity Politics, and Violence against Women of Color." *Stanford Law Review* 43: 1241.

Crenshaw, Kimberlé, Andrea Ritchie, Rachel Anspach, Rachel Gilmer, and Luke Harris. 2015. "Say Her Name: Resisting Police Brutality against Black Women." African American Policy Forum, Center for Intersectionality and Social Policy Studies, Columbia Law School.

Cruz, José A., Dan Margolis, and Elena Mora. 2003. "Immigrant Workers Freedom Ride: A New Movement Is Born." *People's World*, October 10.

Daphi, Priska, and Lorenzo Zamponi. 2019. "Exploring the Movement-Memory Nexus: Insights and Ways Forward." *Mobilization: An International Quarterly* 24 (4): 399–417. https://doi.org/10.17813/1086-671X-24-4-399.

Dart, Bob. 1993. "Gays: President Pivotal to '90s Fight for Rights." *Palm Beach Post*, February 25, sec. A.

David, Emmanuel. 2008. "Cultural Trauma, Memory, and Gendered Collective Action: The Case of Women of the Storm Following Hurricane Katrina." *NWSA Journal* 20 (3): 138–62.

Del, Real Deisy. 2019. "'They See Us Like Trash': How Mexican Illegality Stigma Affects the Psychological Well-Being of Undocumented and US-Born Young Adults of Mexican Descent." In *Immigration and Health*, 19:205–28. Advances in Medical Sociology. Emerald Group Publishing. https://doi.org/10.1108/S1057-629020190000019010.

Derrida, Jacques. 1994. *Specters of Marx: The State of the Debt, the Work of Mourning, and the New International*. Psychology Press.

Desmond, Matthew, Andrew V. Papachristos, and David S. Kirk. 2016. "Police Violence and Citizen Crime Reporting in the Black Community." *American Sociological Review* 81 (5): 857–76. https://doi.org/10.1177/0003122416663494.

Dewar, Helen. 1983. "Helms Stalls King's Day in Senate." *Washington Post*, October 4, A01.

Disha, Ilir, James C. Cavendish, and Ryan D. King. 2011. "Historical Events and Spaces of Hate: Hate Crimes against Arabs and Muslims in Post-9/11 America." *Social Problems* 58 (1): 21–46. https://doi.org/10.1525/sp.2011.58.1.21.

Dixon, Travis L. 2008. "Crime News and Racialized Beliefs: Understanding the Relationship between Local News Viewing and Perceptions of African Americans and Crime." *Journal of Communication* 58 (1): 106–25. https://doi.org/10.1111/j.1460-2466.2007.00376.x.

Dixon-Román, Ezekiel. 2017. "Toward a Hauntology on Data: On the Sociopolitical Forces of Data Assemblages." *Research in Education* 98 (1): 44–58. https://doi.org/10.1177/0034523717723387.

Dolak, Kevin. 2010. "Alveda King Speaks at Glenn Beck's D.C. Rally." ABC News, August 28.

Downey, Dennis J., and Deana Rohlinger. 2008. "Linking Strategic Choice with Macro-Organizational Dynamics: Strategy and Social Movement Articulation." In *Research in Social Movements, Conflicts and Change*, 28:3–38. Emerald Group Publishing. http://www.emeraldinsight.com/doi/abs/10.1016/S0163-786X(08)28001-8.

Du Bois, W.E.B. 1903. *The Souls of Black Folk*. A. C. McClurg.

———. 1907. *The Souls of Black Folk: Essays and Sketches*. A.C. McClurg.

Duggan, Lisa. 2002. "The New Homonormativity: The Sexual Politics of Neoliberalism." In *Materializing Democracy: Toward a Revitalized Cultural Politics*, ed. Russ Castronovo and Dana D. Nelson, 175–94. Duke University Press.

Dyson, Michael Eric. 2000. *I May Not Get There with You: The True Martin Luther King, Jr.* Simon and Schuster.

Ebert, Kim, Wenjie Liao, and Emily P. Estrada. 2020. "Apathy and Color-Blindness in Privatized Immigration Control." *Sociology of Race and Ethnicity* 6 (4): 533–47. https://doi.org/10.1177/2332649219846140.

Edsall, Thomas B. 1991. "Rights Drive Said to Lose Underpinnings." *Washington Post*, March 9. http://www.washingtonpost.com/archive/politics/1991/03/09/rights-drive-said-to-lose-underpinnings/b69e743d-1a8c-4920-9d59-2d90131bbe61/.

Edwards, Frank, Hedwig Lee, and Michael Esposito. 2019. "Risk of Being Killed by Police Use of Force in the United States by Age, Race-Ethnicity, and Sex." *Proceedings of the National Academy of Sciences* 116 (34): 16793–98. https://doi.org/10.1073/pnas.1821204116.

Eichner, Maxine, Barbara Fedders, Holning Lau, and Rachel Blunk. 2011. "Potential Legal Impact of the Proposed Domestic Legal Union Amendment to the North Carolina Constitution." University of North Carolina at Chapel Hill.

Einwohner, Rachel L. 2006. "Identity Work and Collective Action in a Repressive Context: Jewish Resistance on the 'Aryan Side' of the Warsaw Ghetto." *Social Problems* 53 (1): 38–56. https://doi.org/10.1525/sp.2006.53.1.38.

Ekman, Mattias. 2015. "Online Islamophobia and the Politics of Fear: Manufacturing the Green Scare." *Ethnic and Racial Studies* 38 (11): 1986–2002. https://doi.org/10.1080/01419870.2015.1021264.

Elber, Lynn. 2020. "Film Depicts Black Lives Matter, #MeToo as New Feminist Wave." AP News, October 23, sec. Entertainment. https://apnews.com/article/breonna-taylor-race-and-ethnicity-gloria-steinem-feminism-a7e10ecb7a9eb603c9145a78c24ac0df.

Eleveld, Kerry. 2013. "Obama, Bayard Rustin, and the New LGBT Civil-Rights Movement." *The Atlantic*, August 29. http://www.theatlantic.com/politics/archive/2013/08/obama-bayard-rustin-and-the-new-lgbt-civil-rights-movement/279173/.

Eliasoph, Nina, and Paul Lichterman. 2003. "Culture in Interaction." *American Journal of Sociology* 108 (4): 735–94. https://doi.org/10.1086/367920.

Elliott, Andrea. 2007. "Between Black and Immigrant Muslims, an Uneasy Alliance." *New York Times*, March 11. https://www.nytimes.com/2007/03/11/nyregion/11muslim.html.

Emirbayer, Mustafa, and Ann Mische. 1998. "What Is Agency?" *American Journal of Sociology* 103 (4): 962–1023. https://doi.org/10.1086/231294.

Enriquez, Laura E. 2014. "'Undocumented and Citizen Students Unite': Building a Cross-Status Coalition through Shared Ideology." *Social Problems* 61 (2): 155–74. https://doi.org/10.1525/sp.2014.12032.

Enriquez, Laura E., and Abigail C. Saguy. 2016. "Coming out of the Shadows: Harnessing a Cultural Schema to Advance the Undocumented Immigrant Youth Movement." *American Journal of Cultural Sociology* 4 (1): 107–30. https://doi.org/10.1057/ajcs.2015.6.

Epstein, Jennifer. 2011. "Peter King Defends Muslim Hearings." *Politico*, June 13. https://www.politico.com/story/2011/06/peter-king-defends-muslim-hearings-056815.

Epstein, Steven G. 1987. "Gay Politics, Ethnic Identity: The Limits of Social Constructionism." *Socialist Review* 93: 9–54.

Erll, Astrid, and Ansgar Nünning. 2010. *Cultural Memory Studies: An International and Interdisciplinary Handbook.* Walter de Gruyter.

Escoffier, Jeffrey. 1985. "Sexual Revolution and the Politics of Gay Identity." *Socialist Review* 81/82: 119–54.

Espiritu, Yen Le. 2014. *Body Counts: The Vietnam War and Militarized Refugees*. University of California Press.

Estepa, Jessica. 2018. "Rep. Jackie Speier: I Hope Women and Men Wear Black to State of the Union." *USA Today*, January 11.

Evans, Sara Margaret. 1979. *Personal Politics: The Roots of Women's Liberation in the Civil Rights Movement and the New Left*. Random House.

Ewing, Eve L. 2018. *Ghosts in the Schoolyard: Racism and School Closings on Chicago's South Side.* University of Chicago Press.

Fanon, Frantz. 2008. *Black Skin, White Masks*. Grove Press.

Feagin, Joe R. 2006. *Systemic Racism: A Theory of Oppression*. Taylor & Francis.

———. 2010. *The White Racial Frame: Centuries of Racial Framing and Counter-Framing.* Routledge.

Feagin, Joe, and Sean Elias. 2013. "Rethinking Racial Formation Theory: A Systemic Racism Critique." *Ethnic and Racial Studies* 36 (6): 931–60. https://doi.org/10.1080/01419870.2012.669839.

Federal Bureau of Investigation (FBI). 2001. "FBI Uniform Crime Reporting Program Report." https://ucr.fbi.gov/crime-in-the-u.s/2001.

Fentress, James J., and Chris Wickham. 2009. *Social Memory: New Perspectives on the Past*. ACLS Humanities.

Fessler, Leah. 2017. "Gloria Steinem's Message to Women and Girls: Act Like a Cat." *Quartz*, December 8. https://qz.com/1150028/gloria-steinem-on-metoo-black-women-have-always-been-more-feminist-than-white-women/.

Fetner, Tina. 2001. "Working Anita Bryant: The Impact of Christian Anti-Gay Activism on Lesbian and Gay Movement Claims." *Social Problems* 48 (3): 411–28.

Fleming, Crystal Marie. 2017. *Resurrecting Slavery: Racial Legacies and White Supremacy in France*. Temple University Press.

Fleming, Crystal M., and Aldon Morris. 2015. "Theorizing Ethnic and Racial Movements in the Global Age: Lessons from the Civil Rights Movement." *Sociology of Race and Ethnicity* 1 (1): 105–26. https://doi.org/10.1177/2332649214562473.

Fligstein, Neil, and Doug McAdam. 2011. "Toward a General Theory of Strategic Action Fields." *Sociological Theory* 29 (1): 1–26. https://doi.org/10.1111/j.1467-9558.2010.01385.x.

Folley, Aris. 2021. "Bernice King Hits GOP: 'Beyond Insulting' to Misuse MLK's Teachings to Oppose Critical Race Theory." *The Hill* (blog), July 15. https://thehill.com/blogs/blog-briefing-room/news/563113-bernice-king-hits-gop-beyond-insulting-to-use-mlks-teachings-to/.

Foran, Clare. 2015. "A Year of Black Lives Matter." *The Atlantic*, December 31. http://www.theatlantic.com/politics/archive/2015/12/black-lives-matter/421839/.

Formisano, Ronald. 2004. *Boston against Busing: Race, Class, and Ethnicity in the 1960s and 1970s*. Chapel Hill: University of North Carolina Press.

Foster, B. Brian. 2020. *I Don't Like the Blues: Race, Place, and the Backbeat of Black Life*. University of North Carolina Press.

Foucault, Michel. 1980. *Power/Knowledge: Selected Interviews and Other Writings, 1972–1977*. Pantheon Books.

Franzosi, Roberto. 1998. "Narrative Analysis—Or Why (and How) Sociologists Should Be Interested in Narrative." *Annual Review of Sociology* 24 (1): 517–54. https://doi.org/10.1146/annurev.soc.24.1.517.

Fraser, Steve, and Gary Gerstle. 1990. *The Rise and Fall of the New Deal Order, 1930–1980*. Reprint. Princeton University Press.

"Freedom Ride for Immigrant Rights." 2003. *Socialist Worker*, October 3.

Freelon, Dean, Lori Lopez, Meredith Clark, and Sarah Jackson. 2017. "How Black Twitter and Other Social Media Communities Interact with Mainstream News." Knight Foundation. http://knightfoundation.org/features/twittermedia/.

Freiberg, Peter. 2002. "Miami-Dade Ja vu: A Quarter Century after Anita Bryant's 'Save Our Children' Campaign, Miami-Dade Voters Are Again Squaring Off over Gay Rights. " *The Free Library*, September 3. https://www.thefreelibrary.com/Miami-Dade+ja+vu%3a+a+quarter+century+after+Anita+Bryant%27s+%22Save+Our . . . -a090990467.

Fulwood, Sam. 1997. "Christian Coalition Courts Minorities." *Los Angeles Times*, January 31. http://articles.latimes.com/1997-01-31/news/mn-24082_1_christian-coalition.

Gaby, Sarah, and Neal Caren. 2016. "The Rise of Inequality: How Social Movements Shape Discursive Fields." *Mobilization: An International Quarterly* 21 (4): 413–29. https://doi.org/10.17813/1086-671X-21-4-413.

Gaddis, S. Michael. 2015. "Discrimination in the Credential Society: An Audit Study of Race and College Selectivity in the Labor Market." *Social Forces* 93 (4): 1451–79. https://doi.org/10.1093/sf/sou111.

Gallagher, Maggie, and Brian S. Brown. n.d. "Marriage: $20 Million Strategy for Victory." https://ia600301.us.archive.org/11/items/NationalOrganizationForMarriageDocuments/Nom4.pdf.

Gamson, Joshua. 1995. "Must Identity Movements Self-Destruct? A Queer Dilemma." *Social Problems* 42: 390–407.

Gamson, William A. 1975. *The Strategy of Social Protest*. Wadsworth Publishing.

Gamson, William A., David Croteau, William Hoynes, and Theodore Sasson. 1992. "Media Images and the Social Construction of Reality." *Annual Review of Sociology* 18: 373–93.

Gans, Herbert J. 1979. "Symbolic Ethnicity: The Future of Ethnic Groups and Cultures in America." *Ethnic and Racial Studies* 2 (1): 1–20. https://herbertgans.org/wp-content/uploads/2020/09/13-Symbolic-Ethnicity.pdf.

———. 1994. "Symbolic Ethnicity and Symbolic Religiosity: Towards a Comparison of Ethnic and Religious Acculturation." *Ethnic and Racial Studies* 17 (4): 577–92.

———. 2007. "Acculturation, Assimilation and Mobility." *Ethnic and Racial Studies* 30 (1): 152–64. https://doi.org/10.1080/01419870601006637.

Garcia, Sandra E. 2017. "The Woman Who Created #MeToo Long before Hashtags." *New York Times*, October 20, sec. U.S. https://www.nytimes.com/2017/10/20/us/me-too-movement-tarana-burke.html.

Garcia, Uriel J. 2012. "Undocubus Set to Travel to Democratic National Convention." *No Papers, No Fear Ride for Justice* (blog), July 9.

Garner, Steve, and Saher Selod. 2015. "The Racialization of Muslims: Empirical Studies of Islamophobia." *Critical Sociology* 41 (1): 9–19. https://doi.org/10.1177/0896920514531606.

Garris, Carolyn. 2006. "Martin Luther King's Conservative Legacy." *Heritage Foundation* (blog), January 12. http://www.heritage.org/research/reports/2006/01/martin-luther-kings-conservative-legacy.

Gay Today. 2002. "Expose USA's Christian Coalition Petition Frauds Says NGLTF." *Gay Today* (blog), August 20. http://gaytoday.com/events/082002ev.asp.

Ghaziani, Amin. 2011. "Post-Gay Collective Identity Construction." *Social Problems* 58 (1): 99–125. https://doi.org/10.1525/sp.2011.58.1.99.

Ghoshal, Raj Andrew. 2013. "Transforming Collective Memory: Mnemonic Opportunity Structures and the Outcomes of Racial Violence Memory Movements." *Theory and Society* 42 (4): 329–50. https://doi.org/10.1007/s11186-013-9197-9.

Gill, Gurvinder, and Imran Rahman-Jones. 2020. "Me Too Founder Tarana Burke: Movement Is Not Over." BBC News, July 9, sec. Newsbeat. https://www.bbc.com/news/newsbeat-53269751.

Glasrud, Bruce A., and Merline Pitre. 2013. *Southern Black Women in the Modern Civil Rights Movement.* Texas A&M University Press.

Glenn, Evelyn Nakano. 2011. "Constructing Citizenship: Exclusion, Subordination, and Resistance." *American Sociological Review* 76 (1): 1–24. https://doi.org/10.1177/0003122411398443.

———. 2015. "Settler Colonialism as Structure: A Framework for Comparative Studies of U.S. Race and Gender Formation." *Sociology of Race and Ethnicity* 1 (1): 52–72. https://doi.org/10.1177/2332649214560440.

Glymph, Thavolia. 2013. "Du Bois's Black Reconstruction and Slave Women's War for Freedom." *South Atlantic Quarterly* 112 (3): 489–505. https://doi.org/10.1215/00382876-2146431.

Goff, Keli. 2019. "TV Writer Keli Goff: The Complexity of #MeToo for Black Women (Guest Column)." *Hollywood Reporter* (blog), February 14. https://www.hollywoodreporter.com/lifestyle/lifestyle-news/tv-writer-keli-goff-complexity-metoo-black-women-guest-column-1186005/.

Goffman, Erving. 1974. *Frame Analysis: An Essay on the Organization of Experience.* Harvard University Press.

Goh, Jin X., Bryn Bandt-Law, Nathan N. Cheek, Stacey Sinclair, and Cheryl R. Kaiser. 2021. "Narrow Prototypes and Neglected Victims: Understanding Perceptions of Sexual Harassment." *Journal of Personality and Social Psychology* 122 (5): 873–93. https://doi.org/10.1037/pspi0000260.

Goldman, Adam, and Matt Apuzzo. 2012. "NYPD Muslim Spying Led to No Leads, Terror Cases." Associated Press, August 21. https://www.ap.org/ap-in-the-news/2012/nypd-muslim-spying-led-to-no-leads-terror-cases.

Gomer, Justin, and Christopher Petrella. 2017. "Reagan Used MLK Day to Undermine Racial Justice." *Boston Review*, January 15.

Gongaware, Timothy B. 2010. "Collective Memory Anchors: Collective Identity and Continuity in Social Movements." *Sociological Focus* 43 (3): 214–39. https://doi.org/10.1080/00380237.2010.10571377.

González, Daniel. 2012a. "Illegal Migrants across U.S. Taking Protests to Defiant New Level." *Arizona Republic*, September 20. http://www.azcentral.com/news/articles/2012/09/13/20120913illegal-migrants-us-protests-defiant-new-level.html.

———. 2012b. "Undocumented Immigrants Take Cause to Defiant New Level." *USA Today*, September 22.

Goodstein, Laurie. 1998. "Rockers Lead New Wave of Anti-Abortion Fight." *New York Times*, January 21.

Gordon, Avery. 1997. *Ghostly Matters: Haunting and the Sociological Imagination*. University of Minnesota Press.

Gordon, Milton M. 1964. *Assimilation in American Life*. Oxford University Press.

Gotanda, Neil. 1985. "'Other Non-Whites' in American Legal History: A Review of 'Justice at War.'" Ed. Peter Irons. *Columbia Law Review* 85 (5): 1186–92. https://doi.org/10.2307/1122468.

Gotham, Kevin Fox, and William G. Staples. 1996. "Narrative Analysis and the New Historical Sociology." *Sociological Quarterly* 37 (3): 481–501.

Graham, Roderick, and 'Shawn Smith. 2016. "The Content of Our #Characters: Black Twitter as Counterpublic." *Sociology of Race and Ethnicity* 2 (4): 433–49. https://doi.org/10.1177/2332649216639067.

Greenberg, Paul. 1992. "Sister Souljah and the Irrational Rationality of Hate." *Chicago Tribune*, June 19. http://articles.chicagotribune.com/1992-06-19/news/9202240214_1_context-moral-rationality.

Greene, Christina. 2005. *Our Separate Ways: Women and the Black Freedom Movement in Durham, North Carolina*. University of North Carolina Press.

Greenhouse, Steven. 2003. "Immigrants' Rights Drive Starts." *New York Times*, September 25, sec. U.S. http://www.nytimes.com/2003/09/25/us/immigrants-rights-drive-starts.html.

Greenwald, Robert. 2010. "Glenn Beck Is Not Martin Luther King Jr." *Huffington Post*, August 25.

Greenwood, Brad N., Rachel R. Hardeman, Laura Huang, and Aaron Sojourner. 2020. "Physician-Patient Racial Concordance and Disparities in Birthing Mortality for Newborns." *Proceedings of the National Academy of Sciences* 117 (35): 21194–200. https://doi.org/10.1073/pnas.1913405117.

Greer, William R. 1986. "Violence against Homosexuals Rising, Groups Seeking Wider Protection Say." *New York Times*, November 23, sec. U.S. http://www.nytimes.com/1986/11/23/us/violence-against-homosexuals-rising-groups-seeking-wider-protection-say.html.

Grewal, Zareena. 2014. *Islam Is a Foreign Country: American Muslims and the Global Crisis of Authority*. New York University Press.

Guhin, Jeffrey. 2018. "Colorblind Islam: The Racial Hinges of Immigrant Muslims in the United States." *Social Inclusion* 6 (2): 87–97. https://doi.org/10.17645/si.v6i2.1422.

Gurbuz, Mustafa. 2007. "Performing Moral Opposition: Musings on the Strategy and Identity in the Gülen Movement." In *Muslim World in Transition: Contributions of the Gülen Movement*, ed. Ihsan Yilmaz et al., 104–17. Leeds Metropolitan University Press.

———. 2016. *Rival Kurdish Movements in Turkey*. Amsterdam University Press.

Gutman, Yifat. 2017. *Memory Activism: Reimagining the Past for the Future in Israel-Palestine*. Vanderbilt University Press.

Haddad, Yvonne Yazbeck. 2004. *Not Quite American?: The Shaping of Arab and Muslim Identity in the United States.* Baylor University Press.

Haddad, Yvonne Yazbeck, and Robert Stephen Ricks. 2009. "Claiming Space in America's Pluralism: Muslims Enter the Political Maelstrom." In *Muslims in Western Politics.* Indiana University Press.

Hague, Jim. 2003. "'Bring Handguns Rifles and Shotguns': Controversial NB Radio Host Responds to Planned Rally Which Draws Attention of FBI State Police." *Hudson Reporter,* September 5. http://hudsonreporter.com/pages/full_story/push?article--Bring+handguns-+rifles+and+shotguns-+Controversial+NB+radio+host+responds+to+planned+rally-+which+draws+attention+of+FBI-+State+Police%20&id=2392858.

Halbwachs, Maurice. 1992. *On Collective Memory.* University of Chicago Press.

Hall, Jacquelyn Dowd. 2005. "The Long Civil Rights Movement and the Political Uses of the Past." *Journal of American History* 91 (4): 1233–63. https://doi.org/10.2307/3660172.

Hall, Stuart. 1982. "The Rediscovery of 'Ideology': Return of the Repressed in Media Studies." In *Culture, Society, and the Media,* 56–90. Routledge.

———. 1990. "Cultural Identity and Diaspora." In *Identity: Community, Culture, Difference,* ed. J. Rutherford, 222–37. Lawrence & Wishart.

———, ed. 1997. *Representation: Cultural Representations and Signifying Practices.* Sage.

Hamer, Fannie Lou. 1964. "Testimony before the Credentials Committee." https://americanradioworks.publicradio.org/features/sayitplain/flhamer.html.

Han, Hahrie, Elizabeth McKenna, and Michelle Oyakawa. 2021. *Prisms of the People: Power & Organizing in Twenty-First-Century America.* University of Chicago Press.

Hancock, Ange-Marie. 2004. *The Politics of Disgust: The Public Identity of the Welfare Queen.* New York University Press.

———. 2013. *Solidarity Politics for Millennials: A Guide to Ending the Oppression Olympics.* Palgrave Macmillan.

Haney-Lopez, Ian. 2014. *Dog Whistle Politics: How Coded Racial Appeals Have Wrecked the Middle Class.* Oxford University Press.

Harp, Dustin, Josh Grimm, and Jaime Loke. 2018. "Rape, Storytelling and Social Media: How Twitter Interrupted the News Media's Ability to Construct Collective Memory." *Feminist Media Studies* 18 (6): 979–95. https://doi.org/10.1080/14680777.2017.1373688.

Hassan, Nabeed. 2011. "What Does the Civil Rights Movement Mean for Muslims?" *Muslim Matters,* March 3.

Herbers, John. 1982. "Reagan's Changes on Rights Are Starting to Have Impact; Reagan's First Year Last of Six Articles." *New York Times,* January 24.

Herman, Edward S., and Noam Chomsky. 2010. *Manufacturing Consent: The Political Economy of the Mass Media.* Random House.

Hero, Rodney E., and Robert R. Preuhs. 2006. "From Civil Rights to Multiculturalism and Welfare for Immigrants: An Egalitarian Tradition across the American States?" *Du Bois Review: Social Science Research on Race* 3 (2): 317–40. https://doi.org/10.1017/S1742058X0606022X.

Hershatter, Gail. 2014. *The Gender of Memory: Rural Women and China's Collective Past.* University of California Press.

Higham, John. 2002. *Strangers in the Land: Patterns of American Nativism, 1860–1925.* Rutgers University Press.

Hill, Anita. 2019. "Let's Talk about How to End Sexual Violence." *New York Times*, May 9. https://www.nytimes.com/2019/05/09/opinion/anita-hill-sexual-violence.html.

Hill, Theon E. 2017. "Sanitizing the Struggle: Barack Obama, Selma, and Civil Rights Memory." *Communication Quarterly* 1–23. https://doi.org/10.1080/01463373.2016.1275728.

Hirshman, Linda. 2012. *Victory: The Triumphant Gay Revolution*. HarperCollins.

Hobbs, Allyson. 2018. "One Year of #MeToo: The Legacy of Black Women's Testimonies." *New Yorker*, October 10. https://www.newyorker.com/culture/personal-history/one-year-of-metoo-the-legacy-of-black-womens-testimonies.

Hobsbawm, Eric. 1983. *The Invention of Tradition*. Cambridge University Press.

Hooper, Ibrahim. 2009. "Bar Religious Profiling." *USA Today*, October 26, sec. NEWS.

Human Rights Campaign. 2004. "Protect It from Whom?" Human Rights Campaign Foundation. https://assets2.hrc.org/files/assets/resources/AnnualReport_2004.pdf.

Husain, Atiya. 2017. "Moving Beyond (and Back to) the Black-White Binary: A Study of Black and White Muslims' Racial Positioning in the United States." *Ethnic and Racial Studies* 42 (4): 589–606.

Hussain, Pat. 1997. "Class Action: Bringing Economic Diversity to the Gay and Lesbian Movement." In *Homo Economics: Capitalism, Community, and Lesbian and Gay Life*, ed. A. Gluckman and B. Reed, 65–71. Routledge.

Ignatiev, Noel. 2008. *How the Irish Became White*. 1st ed. Routledge.

Isaac, Larry. 2008. "Movement of Movements: Culture Moves in the Long Civil Rights Struggle." *Social Forces* 87 (1): 33–63.

Isaacson, Walter. 1983. "Backing into the Race." *Time*, October 24.

Jabbari, Jason, and Odis Johnson. 2020. "The Collateral Damage of In-School Suspensions: A Counterfactual Analysis of High-Suspension Schools, Math Achievement and College Attendance." *Urban Education*. https://doi.org/10.1177/0042085920902256.

———. 2021. "The Process of 'Pushing Out': Accumulated Disadvantage across School Punishment and Math Achievement Trajectories." *Youth & Society*. https://doi.org/10.1177/0044118X211007175.

Jackson, Sarah J., Moya Bailey, and Brooke Foucault Welles. 2020. *#HashtagActivism: Networks of Race and Gender Justice*. MIT Press.

Jackson, Sherman A. 2005. *Islam and the Blackamerican: Looking toward the Third Resurrection*. Oxford University Press.

———. 2011. "Muslims, Islam(s), Race, and American Islamophobia." In *Islamophobia: The Challenge of Pluralism in the 21st Century*. Oxford University Press.

Jacobs, Janet. 2008. "Gender and Collective Memory: Women and Representation at Auschwitz." *Memory Studies* 1 (2): 211–25. https://doi.org/10.1177/1750698007088387.

Jamal, Amaney A., and Nadine Christine Naber. 2008. *Race and Arab Americans Before and After 9/11: From Invisible Citizens to Visible Subjects*. Syracuse University Press.

James, Joy. 1991. "Anita Hill: Martyr Heroism & Gender Abstractions." *Black Scholar* 22 (1/2): 17–20.

Jamison, Angela. 2005. "Embedded on the Left: Aggressive Media Strategies and Their Organizational Impact on the Immigrant Worker Freedom Ride." Department of Sociology, University of California, Berkeley. https://escholarship.org/uc/item/8m18r30r.

Jansen, Robert S. 2007. "Resurrection and Appropriation: Reputational Trajectories, Memory Work, and the Political Use of Historical Figures." *American Journal of Sociology* 112 (4): 953–1007. https://doi.org/10.1086/508789.

Jasper, James. 2004. "A Strategic Approach to Collective Action: Looking for Agency in Social-Movement Choices." *Mobilization: An International Quarterly* 9 (1): 1–16. https://doi.org/10.17813/maiq.9.1.m112677546p63361.

———. 2010. "Strategic Marginalizations, Emotional Marginalities: The Dilemma of Stigmatized Identities." In *Surviving against Odds: The Marginalized in a Globalizing World*, ed. D. Singha Roy, 29–37. Manohar Publishers.

Jefferson, Hakeem, and Victor Ray. 2022. "White Backlash Is a Type of Racial Reckoning Too." *FiveThirtyEight*, January 6. https://fivethirtyeight.com/features/white-backlash-is-a-type-of-racial-reckoning-too/.

Jenkins, J. Craig, and Craig M. Eckert. 1986. "Channeling Black Insurgency: Elite Patronage and Professional Social Movement Organizations in the Development of the Black Movement." *American Sociological Review* 51 (6): 812–29. https://doi.org/10.2307/2095369.

Jenkins, Richard. 2008. *Social Identity*. Taylor & Francis.

Jensen, Tom. 2012. "Final NC Primary Poll." *Public Policy Polling* (blog), May 6. http://www.publicpolicypolling.com/main/2012/05/final-nc-primary-poll.html.

Jiménez, Tomás R., and Adam L. Horowitz. 2013. "When White Is Just Alright: How Immigrants Redefine Achievement and Reconfigure the Ethnoracial Hierarchy." *American Sociological Review* 78 (5): 849–71. https://doi.org/10.1177/0003122413497012.

Johnson, Karani. 2018. "Ain't I a Woman?" *Random Lengths News* (blog), April 5. https://www.randomlengthsnews.com/2018/04/05/aint-i-a-woman/.

Johnston, Hank. 2002. "Verification and Proof in Frame and Discourse Analysis." In *Methods of Social Movement Research*, 62–91. University of Minnesota Press.

Johnston, Hank, and John A. Noakes. 2005. *Frames of Protest: Social Movements and the Framing Perspective*. Rowman & Littlefield.

Jones, Clarence B., and Joel Engel. 2008. *What Would Martin Say?* Reprint. Harper Perennial.

Jones, Jennifer A. 2019. *The Browning of the New South*. University of Chicago Press.

Kammer, Jerry. 2013. "Frank Morris Calls Rep. John Conyers 'Blind' to the Negative Effects of Immigration on Workers." Center for Immigration Studies. https://cis.org/Kammer/Frank-Morris-Calls-Rep-John-Conyers-Blind-Negative-Effects-Immigration-Workers.

Karim, Jamillah A. 2006. "To Be Black, Female, and Muslim: A Candid Conversation about Race in the American Ummah." *Journal of Muslim Minority Affairs* 26 (2): 225–33. https://doi.org/10.1080/13602000600937655.

Kasinitz, Philip. 2008. "Becoming American, Becoming Minority, Getting Ahead: The Role of Racial and Ethnic Status in the Upward Mobility of the Children of Immigrants." *Annals of the American Academy of Political and Social Science* 620 (1): 253–69. https://doi.org/10.1177/0002716208322880.

Kaufman, Scott. 2015. "'Cowboy' Conservative Claims MLK for the Tea Party until Liberals Stop Bringing Up Race." *Raw Story*, January 19. http://www.rawstory.com/2015/01/cowboy-conservative-claims-mlk-for-the-tea-party-until-liberals-stop-bringing-up-race/.

Kerbo, Harold, and Richard Shaffer. 1992. "Lower Class Insurgency and the Political Process: The Response of the U.S. Unemployed, 1890–1940." *Social Problems* 39 (2): 139–54.

Khabeer, Su'ad Abdul. 2016. *Muslim Cool*. New York University Press. http://nyupress.org/books/9781479894505/.

Khan, Faroque A. 2001. *Story of a Mosque in America*. Cedar Graphics.

———. 2016. "As a Muslim Republican, I Can't Vote Trump." *Newsday*. https://www.newsday.com/opinion/as-a-muslim-and-republican-i-ve-been-a-victim-of-donald-trump-s-candidacy-1.12107118.

Khan, M. A. Muqtedar. 2003. "Constructing the American Muslim Community." In *Religion and Immigration: Christian, Jewish, and Muslim Experiences in the United States*, ed. Yvonne Yazbeck Haddad, Jane I. Smith, and John L. Esposito. Rowman Altamira.

Khan, Taimur. 2013a. "America's Muslims Share Martin Luther King's Dream." *National News*, August 25. https://www.thenationalnews.com/world/the-americas/america-s-muslims-share-martin-luther-king-s-dream-1.654569.

———. 2013b. "Tell Them about the Dream, Barack . . . the Muslim Dream." *The National*, August 26.

Khan, Zeba. 2015. "American Muslims Have a Race Problem." *Al Jazeera*, June 16. http://america.aljazeera.com/opinions/2015/6/american-muslims-have-a-race-problem.html.

Khwaja, Maria. 2016. "Black Muslim Americans: The Minority within a Minority." *Fair Observer*, February 22. http://www.fairobserver.com/region/north_america/black-muslim-americans-the-minority-within-a-minority-34590/.

Kim, Claire Jean. 1999. "The Racial Triangulation of Asian Americans." *Politics & Society* 27 (1): 105–38. https://doi.org/10.1177/0032329299027001005.

King, Martin Luther, Jr. 1964. *Why We Can't Wait*. New American Library.

———. 1967. *Where Do We Go from Here: Chaos or Community?* Harper & Row.

———. 2018. *Letter from Birmingham Jail*. Penguin Modern.

King Watch. 2006. "Interview with Dr. Farouque Khan of the Islamic Center of Long Island." *Peter King Watch* (blog), September 22. http://kingwatch.blogspot.com/2006/09/interview-with-dr-farouque-khan-of.html.

Kingsbury, Alex. 2003. "Protests to Hit District." *GW Hatchet* (blog), January 16. https://www.gwhatchet.com/2003/01/16/protests-to-hit-district/.

Klandermans, Bert, Jojanneke van der Toorn, and Jacquelien van Stekelenburg. 2008. "Embeddedness and Identity: How Immigrants Turn Grievances into Action." *American Sociological Review* 73 (6): 992–1012. https://doi.org/10.1177/000312240807300606.

Klandermans, P. G. 2014. "Identity Politics and Politicized Identities: Identity Processes and the Dynamics of Protest." *Political Psychology* 35 (1): 1–22. https://doi.org/10.1111/pops.12167.

Kolker, Robert. 2011. "Peter King's Muslim Problem." *New York Magazine*, March 4, 2011.

Korver-Glenn, Elizabeth. 2015. "(Collective) Memory of Racial Violence and the Social Construction of the Hispanic Category among Houston Hispanics." *Sociology of Race and Ethnicity* 1 (3): 424–38. https://doi.org/10.1177/2332649215576757.

———. 2021. *Race Brokers: Housing Markets and Segregation in 21st Century Urban America*. Oxford University Press.

Krikorian, Mark. 2003. "'Immigrant Workers Freedom Ride' Insults All Americans." *National Review Online*, October 3.

Krueger, Richard A., and Mary Anne Casey. 2009. *Focus Groups: A Practical Guide for Applied Research*. Sage.

Kruse, Kevin M. 2007. *White Flight: Atlanta and the Making of Modern Conservatism*. Princeton University Press.

Kurtz, Judy. 2018. "Alyssa Milano: Despite Kavanaugh Confirmation, 'I Do Have Hope.'" *The Hill*, October 9.

Ladd, Susan. 2012. "Amendment Sparks Very Deep Emotions." *Greensboro News & Record*, February 11. http://www.greensboro.com/news/amendment-sparks-very-deep-emotions/article_f544b24b-bbcf-52f7-b51c-b7e580d5ec95.html.

Lamont, Michèle, and Marcel Fournier. 1992. *Cultivating Differences: Symbolic Boundaries and the Making of Inequality*. University of Chicago Press.

Lamont, Michèle, and Virág Molnár. 2002. "The Study of Boundaries in the Social Sciences." *Annual Review of Sociology* 28: 167–95.

Lamont, Michèle, Graziella Moraes Silva, Jessica Welburn, Joshua Guetzkow, Nissim Mizrachi, Hanna Herzog, and Elisa Reis. 2016. *Getting Respect: Responding to Stigma and Discrimination in the United States, Brazil, and Israel*. Princeton University Press. https://doi.org/10.1515/9781400883776.

Lang, Cady. 2020. "How the Karen Meme Confronts History of White Womanhood." *Time*, July 6. https://time.com/5857023/karen-meme-history-meaning/.

Lange, Ariane. 2018. "Activists Who Attended the Golden Globes Say Women in Hollywood 'Are Trying to Learn from Us.'" *BuzzFeed News*, January 9. https://www.buzzfeednews.com/article/arianelange/activists-golden-globes-times-up.

Latif, Imam Khalid. 2016. "American-Muslims on Black Lives Matter and Anti-Racism Initiatives." *Arab America*, July 19.

Lawyers' Committee for Civil Rights Under Law. 2014. "A Unified Statement of Action to Promote Reform and Stop Police Abuse." August 18. http://signup.lawyerscommittee.org/p/dia/action3/common/public/?action_KEY=10281.

Lazin, Malcolm. 2013. "March on Washington Paved Way for Gay Rights Too." CNN, August 28. https://www.cnn.com/2013/08/28/opinion/lazin-march-on-washington-gay-rights/index.html.

Leadership Conference on Civil and Human Rights. 2017. "Trump Administration Civil and Human Rights Rollbacks." https://civilrights.org/trump-rollbacks/.

Leblanc, J. 2003. "Immigrant Workers Freedom Ride: A New Movement Is Born." *People's World* (blog), October 10. http://www.peoplesworld.org/article/immigrant-workers-freedom-ride-a-new-movement-is-born/.

Lee, Jennifer C., and Samuel Kye. 2016. "Racialized Assimilation of Asian Americans." *Annual Review of Sociology* 42 (1): 253–73. https://doi.org/10.1146/annurev-soc-081715-074310.

Lee, Jennifer, and Van C. Tran. 2019. "The Mere Mention of Asians in Affirmative Action." *Sociological Science* 6 (September): 551–79. https://doi.org/10.15195/v6.a21.

Lee, Shanon. 2018. "There Is No #MeToo without Black Women." *Healthline*, February. https://www.healthline.com/health/black-women-metoo-antirape-movement.

Leuci, Santina, and Chris Francescani. 2020. "Camille Cosby on Her Husband's Appeal and the Black Lives Matter and #MeToo Movements." ABC News, June 23.

Lindsey, Treva. 2020. "Black Women Have Consistently Been Trailblazers for Social Change: Why Are Black Women So Often Relegated to the Margins?" *Time*, July 22. https://time.com/5869662/black-women-social-change/.

Lipsitz, Raina. 2017. "Sexual Harassment Law Was Shaped by the Battles of Black Women." *The Nation*, October 20. https://www.thenation.com/article/archive/sexual-harassment-law-was-shaped-by-the-battles-of-black-women/.

Lo, C.Y.H. 1982. "Countermovements and Conservative Movements in the Contemporary U.S." *Annual Review of Sociology* 8 (1): 107–34. https://doi.org/10.1146/annurev.so.08.080182.000543.

Long, Michael G. 2012. *Martin Luther King Jr., Homosexuality, and the Early Gay Rights Movement: Keeping the Dream Straight?* Palgrave Macmillan.

Loose, Cindy. "Gay Activists Summon Their Hopes, Resolve." *Washington Post*, April 18.

Lorde, Audre. 2007. *Sister Outsider: Essays and Speeches*. Crossing Press.

Love, Erik. 2017. *Islamophobia and Racism in America*. New York University Press.

Luft, Aliza. 2020. "Theorizing Moral Cognition: Culture in Action, Situations, and Relationships." *Socius* 6 (January). https://doi.org/10.1177/2378023120916125.

Luna, Zakiya T. 2010. "Marching toward Reproductive Justice: Coalitional (Re)Framing of the March for Women's Lives." *Sociological Inquiry* 80 (4): 554–78. https://doi.org/10.1111/j.1475-682X.2010.00349.x.

———. 2016. "'Truly a Women of Color Organization': Negotiating Sameness and Difference in Pursuit of Intersectionality." *Gender & Society* 30 (5): 769–90. https://doi.org/10.1177/0891243216649929.

———. 2017a. "'Black Children Are an Endangered Species': Examining Racial Framing in Social Movements." *Sociological Focus* 51 (3): 238–51.

———. 2017b. "Who Speaks for Whom? (Mis)Representation and Authenticity in Social Movements." *Mobilization: An International Quarterly* 22 (4): 435–50. https://doi.org/10.17813/1086-671X-22-4-435.

Luna, Zakiya, and Whitney Pirtle. 2021. *Black Feminist Sociology: Perspectives and Praxis*. Routledge.

Luntz, Frank. 2005. "Respect for the Law & Economic Fairness: Illegal Immigration Prevention." Maslansky Strategic Research. https://kipdf.com/luntz-maslansky-strategic-research_5afaea228ead0e758d8b461d.html.

MacKenzie, Colin. 1989. "Former Klansman's Racism Plays Well in New Orleans." *Globe and Mail*, March 7.

Maghbouleh, Neda. 2017. *The Limits of Whiteness: Iranian Americans and the Everyday Politics of Race*. Stanford University Press.

Mahoney, James. 2000. "Path Dependence in Historical Sociology." *Theory and Society* 29 (4): 507–48. https://doi.org/10.1023/A:1007113830879.

———. 2004. "Comparative-Historical Methodology." *Annual Review of Sociology* 30: 81–101.

Mansbridge, Jane, and Katherine Tate. 1992. "Race Trumps Gender: The Thomas Nomination in the Black Community." *PS: Political Science and Politics* 25 (3): 488–92. https://doi.org/10.2307/419439.

Martí, Gerardo. 2019. *American Blindspot: Race, Class, Religion, and the Trump Presidency*. Rowman & Littlefield.

Massey, Douglas, and Nancy A. Denton. 1993. *American Apartheid: Segregation and the Making of the Underclass*. Harvard University Press.

Mastro, Dana, Riva Tukachinsky, Elizabeth Behm-Morawitz, and Erin Blecha. 2014. "News Coverage of Immigration: The Influence of Exposure to Linguistic Bias in the News on Consumer's Racial/Ethnic Cognitions." *Communication Quarterly* 62 (2). http://www.tandfonline.com.libproxy1.usc.edu/doi/abs/10.1080/01463373.2014.890115.

Mawyer, Martin. 1993. "God and the GOP; Will We on the Christian Right Go Wrong?" *Washington Post*, September 26. http://www.lexisnexis.com.libproxy.lib.unc.edu/lnacui2api/api/version1/getDocCui?lni=3S7T-84P0-0088-P3R8&csi=8411&hl=t&hv=t&hnsd=f&hns=t&hgn=t&oc=00240&perma=true.

McAdam, Doug. 1982. *Political Process and the Development of Black Insurgency, 1930–1970*. University of Chicago Press.

McAdam, Doug, and Yang Su. 2002. "The War at Home: Antiwar Protests and Congressional Voting, 1965 to 1973." *American Sociological Review* 67 (5): 696–721. https://doi.org/10.2307/3088914.

McCammon, Holly. 2009. "Beyond Frame Resonance: The Argumentative Structure and Persuasive Capacity of Twentieth-Century U.S. Women's Jury-Rights Frames." *Mobilization: An International Quarterly* 14 (1): 45–64. https://doi.org/10.17813/maiq.14.1.yr2671812325362v.

McCarthy, Ellen. 2022. "A Generation of LGBTQ Advocates Hopes the Clock Isn't Ticking Backward." *Washington Post*, May 20.

McCraw, Maggie, and Ellen Brickley. 1999. "Miami-Dade County Commission Extends Law Banning Discrimination to Cover Homosexuals." *The Militant*, January 11. http://www.themilitant.com/1999/631/631_16.html.

McEwan, Cheryl. 2003. "Building a Postcolonial Archive? Gender, Collective Memory and Citizenship in Post-Apartheid South Africa." *Journal of Southern African Studies* 29 (3): 739–57. https://doi.org/10.1080/0305707032000095009.

McGee, Ebony Omotola. 2021. *Black, Brown, Bruised: How Racialized STEM Education Stifles Innovation*. Harvard Education Press.

McLaughlin, Kelly. 2018. "#MeToo Founder Tarana Burke Says There Is a 'Collective Disappointment and Frustration' in the US Following Brett Kavanaugh's Supreme Court Confirmation." *Insider*, October 12. https://www.insider.com/metoo-tarana-burke-says-there-is-a-collective-disappointment-and-frustration-in-the-us-following-brett-kavanaughs-supreme-court-confirmation-2018-10.

Meadows, Laura. 2015. "Losing Forward: An Ethnographic Study of the LGBT Movement in North Carolina." University of North Carolina at Chapel Hill. http://gradworks.umi.com/37/03/3703868.html.

Meno, Mike. 2012. "North Carolinians to Vote on Anti-LGBT Amendment One Tuesday." *American Civil Liberties Union* (blog), May 7. https://www.aclu.org/blog/north-carolinians-vote-anti-lgbt-amendment-one-tuesday.

Metzl, Jonathan M. 2019. *Dying of Whiteness: How the Politics of Racial Resentment Is Killing America's Heartland*. Basic Books.

Meyer, David S. 2004. "Protest and Political Opportunities." *Annual Review of Sociology* 30 (1): 125–45. https://doi.org/10.1146/annurev.soc.30.012703.110545.

———. 2021. *How Social Movements (Sometimes) Matter*. Wiley.

Meyer, David S., and Suzanne Staggenborg. 1996. "Movements, Countermovements, and the Structure of Political Opportunity." *American Journal of Sociology* 101 (6): 1628–60.

Meyer, David S., Nancy Whittier, and Belinda Robnett. 2002. *Social Movements: Identity, Culture, and the State.* Oxford University Press.

Mian, Rashed. 2013. "Muslim Americans: Behind the Veil of a Religion under Attack." *Long Island News from the Long Island Press* (blog), April 27. https://www.longislandpress.com/2013/04/27/muslim-americans-behind-the-veil-of-a-religion-under-attack/.

Miller-Idriss, Cynthia. 2020. *Hate in the Homeland: The New Global Far Right.* Princeton University Press.

Mills, Charles W. 1997. *The Racial Contract.* Cornell University Press.

———. 2007. "White Ignorance." In *Race and Epistemologies of Ignorance,* ed. Shannon Sullivan and Nancy Tuana, 11–38. State University of New York Press.

Mische, Ann. 2009. "Projects and Possibilities: Researching Futures in Action." *Sociological Forum* 24 (3): 694–704. https://doi.org/10.1111/j.1573-7861.2009.01127.x.

———. 2014. "Measuring Futures in Action: Projective Grammars in the Rio + 20 Debates." *Theory and Society* 43 (3–4): 437–64. https://doi.org/10.1007/s11186-014-9226-3.

Misra, Joya. 2021. "The Intersectionality of Precarity." *Contemporary Sociology* 50 (2): 104–8. https://doi.org/10.1177/0094306121991073a.

Mohr, Charles. 1988. "Marchers Exhorted to Go after 'Deferred Dreams.'" *New York Times,* August 28.

Monroe, Ann. 1997. "Race to the Right." *Mother Jones,* May 1997. http://www.motherjones.com/politics/1997/05/race-right.

Morales Henry, Pablo, and Jennifer Weintraub. 2020. "#metoo Digital Media Collection—Twitter Dataset." Harvard Dataverse, V1. https://doi.org/10.7910/DVN/2SRSKJ.

Morgan, David L. 1997. *Focus Groups as Qualitative Research.* Sage.

Morris, Aldon. 2015. *The Scholar Denied: W.E.B. Du Bois and the Birth of Modern Sociology.* University of California Press.

Moser, Bob. 2003. "900 Immigrant Workers Take Freedom Ride of Their Own." *Southern Poverty Law Center Intelligence Report,* December 31. https://www.splcenter.org/fighting-hate/intelligence-report/2003/900-immigrant-workers-take-freedom-ride-their-own.

Mueller, Jennifer C. 2020. "Racial Ideology or Racial Ignorance? An Alternative Theory of Racial Cognition." *Sociological Theory* 38 (2): 142–69. https://doi.org/10.1177/0735275120926197.

Murray, Cecil. 2016. "Op-Ed: It's 2016 and the Civil Rights Era Hasn't Ended." *Los Angeles Times,* August 7.

Myerson, J. A. 2012. "Riders of the 'UndocuBus' Have 'No Papers, No Fear.'" *In These Times,* September 5. http://inthesetimes.com/uprising/entry/13779/riders_of_the_undocubus_have_no_papers_no_fear.

Nadel, Laurie. 2005. "For Island's Muslims, a Time to Be Wary." *New York Times,* September 4, sec. N.Y./Region. https://www.nytimes.com/2005/09/04/nyregion/nyregionspecial2/for-islands-muslims-a-time-to-be-wary.html.

Nagel, Caroline R., and Lynn A. Staeheli. 2005. "'We're Just Like the Irish': Narratives of Assimilation, Belonging and Citizenship amongst Arab-American Activists." *Citizenship Studies* 9 (5): 485–98. https://doi.org/10.1080/13621020500301262.

Nagel, Joane. 1995. "American Indian Ethnic Renewal: Politics and the Resurgence of Identity." *American Sociological Review* 60 (6): 947–65. https://doi.org/10.2307/2096434.

Nagourney, Adam. 1993. "Gay Rights Movement Shows Clout in Capital." *USA Today,* April 23, sec. News.

Newman, Louise Michele, and Louise M. Newman. 1999. *White Women's Rights: The Racial Origins of Feminism in the United States*. Oxford University Press.

Newth, George. 2021. "Rethinking 'Nativism': Beyond the Ideational Approach." *Identities* 1–20. https://doi.org/10.1080/1070289X.2021.1969161.

Nielsen, Kirk. 2002. "Between a Frock and a Hard Place." *Miami New Times*, August 15. http://www.miaminewtimes.com/news/between-a-frock-and-a-hard-place-6349930.

Nolan, Robert. 2003. "Immigrant Workers Freedom Ride." *Gotham Gazette*, July 16. http://www.gothamgazette.com/index.php/civil-rights/1895-immigrant-workers-freedom-ride.

Nummi, Jozie, Carly Jennings, and Joe Feagin. 2019. "#BlackLivesMatter: Innovative Black Resistance." *Sociological Forum* 34 (S1): 1042–64. https://doi.org/10.1111/socf.12540.

Nyren, Erin. 2017. "Jane Fonda: People Are Paying Attention to Weinstein's Accusers Because They're 'Famous and White.'" *Variety*, October 27. https://variety.com/2017/biz/news/jane-fonda-harvey-weinstein-famous-white-victims-1202600709/.

Odoms-Young, Angela M. 2018. "Examining the Impact of Structural Racism on Food Insecurity: Implications for Addressing Racial/Ethnic Disparities." *Family & Community Health* 41: S3–6. https://doi.org/10.1097/FCH.0000000000000183.

Okamoto, Dina G. 2003. "Toward a Theory of Panethnicity: Explaining Asian American Collective Action." *American Sociological Review* 68 (6): 811–42. https://doi.org/10.2307/1519747.

———. 2006. "Institutional Panethnicity: Boundary Formation in Asian-American Organizing." *Social Forces* 85 (1): 1–25. https://doi.org/10.1353/sof.2006.0136.

Okamoto, Dina, and Cristina G. Mora. 2014. "Panethnicity." *Annual Review of Sociology* 40: 219–39.

Olick, Jeffrey K. 1999. "Collective Memory: The Two Cultures." *Sociological Theory* 17 (3): 333–48. https://doi.org/10.1111/0735-2751.00083.

Olick, Jeffrey K., and Daniel Levy. 1997. "Collective Memory and Cultural Constraint: Holocaust Myth and Rationality in German Politics." *American Sociological Review* 62 (6): 921–36. https://doi.org/10.2307/2657347.

Olick, Jeffrey K., and Joyce Robbins. 1998. "Social Memory Studies: From 'Collective Memory' to the Historical Sociology of Mnemonic Practices." *Annual Review of Sociology* 24 (1): 105–40. https://doi.org/10.1146/annurev.soc.24.1.105.

Oliver, Pamela E., and Hank Johnston. 2000. "What a Good Idea! Ideologies and Frames in Social Movement Research." *Mobilization: An International Quarterly* 4 (1): 37–54.

Omi, Michael, and Howard Winant. 1994. *Racial Formation in the United States: From the 1960s to the 1990s*. Psychology Press.

Onwuachi-Willig, Angela. 2018. "What About #UsToo: The Invisibility of Race in the #MeToo Movement." *Yale Law Journal Forum* 128: 105.

Onyeador, Ivuoma N., Natalie M. Daumeyer, Julian M. Rucker, Ajua Duker, Michael W. Kraus, and Jennifer A. Richeson. 2020. "Disrupting Beliefs in Racial Progress: Reminders of Persistent Racism Alter Perceptions of Past, but Not Current, Racial Economic Equality." *Personality and Social Psychology Bulletin*, August. https://doi.org/10.1177/0146167220942625.

Owens, Ann. 2020. "Unequal Opportunity: School and Neighborhood Segregation in the USA." *Race and Social Problems* 12 (1): 29–41. https://doi.org/10.1007/s12552-019-09274-z.

Owens, Timothy J., Dawn T. Robinson, and Lynn Smith-Lovin. 2010. "Three Faces of Identity." *Annual Review of Sociology* 36 (1): 477–99. https://doi.org/10.1146/annurev.soc.34.040507.134725.

PAL. 2003. "Pro-Life Activists Celebrate 8–1 Victory." *Pro-Life Action League* (blog), June 15. https://prolifeaction.org/2003/2003v22n2celebration/.

Pan, Yung-Yi Diana. 2017. *Incidental Racialization: Performative Assimilation in Law School.* Temple University Press.

Papenfuss, Mary. 2020. "Covid-19 Protesters Just Like Rosa Parks, Says White House Adviser Stephen Moore." *Huffington Post,* April 18.

Parker, Christopher S. 2013. *Change They Can't Believe In: The Tea Party and Reactionary Politics in America.* Princeton University Press.

Paz, Diane Urbani de la. 2020. "Struggle, Forgiveness: 'Dear Anita Bryant' to Stream This Week." *Peninsula Daily News,* August 7. https://www.peninsuladailynews.com/entertainment/struggle-forgiveness-dear-anita-bryant-to-stream-this-week/.

Pelak, Cynthia Fabrizio. 2015. "Institutionalizing Counter-Memories of the U.S. Civil Rights Movement: The National Civil Rights Museum and an Application of the Interest-Convergence Principle." *Sociological Forum* 30 (2): 305–27. https://doi.org/10.1111/socf.12164.

Perea, Juan F. 1997. *Immigrants Out!: The New Nativism and the Anti-Immigrant Impulse in the United States.* New York University Press.

Perrin, Andrew J., Steven J. Tepper, Neal Caren, and Sally Morris. 2014. "Political and Cultural Dimensions of Tea Party Support, 2009–2012." *Sociological Quarterly* 55 (4): 625–52. https://doi.org/10.1111/tsq.12069.

Perry, Brea L., Brian Aronson, and Bernice A. Pescosolido. 2021. "Pandemic Precarity: COVID-19 Is Exposing and Exacerbating Inequalities in the American Heartland." *Proceedings of the National Academy of Sciences* 118 (8): e2020685118. https://doi.org/10.1073/pnas.2020685118.

Phipps, Alison. 2021. "White Tears, White Rage: Victimhood and (as) Violence in Mainstream Feminism." *European Journal of Cultural Studies* 24 (1): 81–93. https://doi.org/10.1177/1367549420985852.

Pipes, Daniel, and Sharon Chadha. 2006. "CAIR: Islamists Fooling the Establishment." *Middle East Quarterly* (Spring 2006): 3–20.

Pitts, Leonard. 2002. "Linking King to Anti-gay Effort Is an Outrage." *Chicago Tribune,* August 5.

Plotz, David, and Jim Newell. 1997. "Ralph Reed's Creed." *Slate,* May 4. http://www.slate.com/articles/news_and_politics/assessment/1997/05/ralph_reeds_creed.html.

Polletta, Francesca. 2009. *It Was Like a Fever: Storytelling in Protest and Politics.* University of Chicago Press.

Polletta, Francesca, and James M. Jasper. 2001. "Collective Identity and Social Movements." *Annual Review of Sociology* 27 (1): 283–305. https://doi.org/10.1146/annurev.soc.27.1.283.

Porta, Donatella. 2005. "Making the Polis: Social Forums and Democracy in the Global Justice Movement." *Mobilization: An International Quarterly* 10 (1): 73–94. https://doi.org/10.17813/maiq.10.1.vg717358676hh1q6.

Proctor, Robert, and Londa L. Schiebinger. 2008. *Agnotology: The Making and Unmaking of Ignorance*. Stanford University Press.

Purifoy, Danielle. 2020. "A Black Feminist Guide to Electoral Politics in 2020." *Scalawag*, October 6. https://scalawagmagazine.org/2020/10/black-feminism-roundtable/.

Qureshi, Emran, and Michael A. Sells. 2003. *The New Crusades: Constructing the Muslim Enemy*. Columbia University Press.

Radoynovska, Nevena, and Brayden G. King. 2019. "To Whom Are You True? Audience Perceptions of Authenticity in Nascent Crowdfunding Ventures." *Organization Science* 30 (4): 781–802. https://doi.org/10.1287/orsc.2018.1253.

Ramirez Jimenez, Mari Cruz. 2012. "In Admiration: Learning about the Civil Rights Movement" *No Papers No Fear Ride* (blog), August 16.

Ransby, Barbara. 2016. "Fannie Lou Hamer's Message Should Be Remembered." *Progressive.org*, October 6. https://progressive.org/%3Fq%3Dnode/188985/.

———. 2019. "A Black Feminist's Response to Attacks on Martin Luther King Jr.'s Legacy." *New York Times*, June 3, sec. Opinion. https://www.nytimes.com/2019/06/03/opinion/martin-luther-king-fbi.html.

Ray, Victor. 2019. "A Theory of Racialized Organizations." *American Sociological Review* 84 (1): 26–53. https://doi.org.10.1177/0003122418822335.

Razack, Sherene. 2002. *Race, Space, and the Law: Unmapping a White Settler Society*. Between the Lines Publishing.

Remnick, David. 2017. "John Lewis, Donald Trump, and the Meaning of Legitimacy." *New Yorker*, January 15. https://www.newyorker.com/news/news-desk/john-lewis-donald-trump-and-the-meaning-of-legitimacy.

Reyes, Daisy Verduzco, and Kathleen Ragon. 2018. "Analyzing Ethnoracial Mobilization." *Sociology Compass* 12 (10): e12629. https://doi.org/10.1111/soc4.12629.

Rich, Peter, Jennifer Candipan, and Ann Owens. 2021. "Segregated Neighborhoods, Segregated Schools: Do Charters Break a Stubborn Link?" *Demography* 58 (2): 471–98. https://doi.org/10.1215/00703370-9000820.

Richeson, Jennifer A. 2020. "Americans Are Determined to Believe in Black Progress." *The Atlantic*, July 27. https://www.theatlantic.com/magazine/archive/2020/09/the-mythology-of-racial-progress/614173/.

Roberts, Dorothy, and Sujatha Jesudason. 2013. "Movement Intersectionality: The Case of Race, Gender, Disability, and Genetic Technologies." *Du Bois Review: Social Science Research on Race* 10 (2): 313–28. https://doi.org/10.1017/S1742058X13000210.

Robinson, Andrea. 2002. "Black Vote Could Decide Final Outcome on Gay Rights." *Miami Herald*, July 1.

Robinson, Candice C. 2019. "(Re)Theorizing Civic Engagement: Foundations for Black Americans Civic Engagement Theory." *Sociology Compass* 13 (9): e12728. https://doi.org/10.1111/soc4.12728.

Robinson, Cedric J. 1983. *Black Marxism: The Making of the Black Radical Tradition*. Zed.

Robnett, Belinda. 1996. "African-American Women in the Civil Rights Movement, 1954–1965: Gender, Leadership, and Micromobilization." *American Journal of Sociology* 101 (6): 1661–93. https://doi.org/10.1086/230870.

———. 2004. "Emotional Resonance, Social Location, and Strategic Framing." *Sociological Focus* 37 (3): 195–212.

Rodgers, William M. 2019. "Race in the Labor Market: The Role of Equal Employment Opportunity and Other Policies." *RSF: The Russell Sage Foundation Journal of the Social Sciences* 5 (5): 198–220. https://doi.org/10.7758/RSF.2019.5.5.10.

Roeder, Oliver. 2018. "How Conservative Is Brett Kavanaugh?" *FiveThirtyEight* (blog), July 17. https://fivethirtyeight.com/features/how-conservative-is-brett-kavanaugh/.

Roediger, David R. 1999. *The Wages of Whiteness: Race and the Making of the American Working Class*. Verso.

———. 2006. *Working toward Whiteness: How America's Immigrants Became White: The Strange Journey from Ellis Island to the Suburbs*. Basic Books.

Rohlinger, Deana A. 2002. "Framing the Abortion Debate: Organizational Resources, Media Strategies, and Movement-Countermovement Dynamics." *Sociological Quarterly* 43 (4): 479–507. https://doi.org/10.1111/j.1533-8525.2002.tb00063.x.

Roig-Franzia, Manuel. 2002. "Bryant Legacy Resurfaces in Fla." *Washington Post*, September 7. https://www.washingtonpost.com/archive/politics/2002/09/07/bryant-legacy-resurfaces-in-fla/e7b951f0-b6f9-4b25-8192-0d2409ec21ac/.

Romano, Renee Christine, and Leigh Raiford. 2006. *The Civil Rights Movement in American Memory*. University of Georgia Press.

Ross, Karl. 2002a. "Black Coalition: Repeal Gay-Rights Section." *Miami Herald*, June 15.

———. 2002b. "Center Appalled by MLK Use in Flier." *Miami Herald*, August 2.

Rothman, Lily. 2015. "How MLK Day Became a Holiday." *Time*, January 19.

Royster, Deirdre A. 2003. *Race and the Invisible Hand: How White Networks Exclude Black Men from Blue-Collar Jobs*. University of California Press.

Ruiz, Michelle. 2021. "Anita Hill on Clarence Thomas, Brett Kavanaugh, and Her New Memoir, 'Believing.'" *Vogue*, September 28. https://www.vogue.com/article/anita-hill-believing.

Saavedra, Mariella. 2012. "Undocubus Tour: No Papers, No Fear." *America's Voice* (blog), July 30. http://americasvoice.org/blog/undocubus-tour-no-papers-no-fear/.

Sabate, Albert, and Ana Maria Benedetti. 2012. "No Papers, No Fear: Undocumented Protesters Arrive at DNC." *Fusion*, September 3. http://thisisfusion.tumblr.com/post/30799811289/riding-for-justice.

Saguy, Abigail C. 2020. *Come Out, Come Out, Whoever You Are*. Oxford University Press.

Saguy, Abigail C., and Kjerstin Gruys. 2010. "Morality and Health: News Media Constructions of Overweight and Eating Disorders." *Social Problems* 57 (2): 231–50. https://doi.org/10.1525/sp.2010.57.2.231.

Said, Edward W. 1979. *Orientalism*. Vintage Books.

Salaky, Kristin. 2017. "Cartoonist Said He Drew DeVos in Iconic Civil Rights Painting to Open a Dialogue." *Talking Points Memo*, February 15. talkingpointsmemo.com/news/glenn-mccoy-explains-devos-cartoon.

Santoro, Wayne A., and Marian Azab. 2015. "Arab American Protest in the Terror Decade: Macro- and Micro-Level Response to Post-9/11 Repression." *Social Problems* 62 (2): 219–40. https://doi.org/10.1093/socpro/spv004.

Savelsberg, Joachim J. 2021. *Knowing about Genocide: Armenian Suffering and Epistemic Struggles*. University of California Press.

Schlussel, Debbie. 2013. "Martin Luther King, Jr.: Muslim Extremists Continue to Hijack Pro-Israel Civil Rights Leader's Name Like It's a Plane." www.Debbieschlussel.com (blog),

January 21. http://www.debbieschlussel.com/58562/martin-luther-king-jr-muslims-continue-to-hijack-pro-israel-civil-rights-leaders-name-like-its-a-plane/.

Schmalz, Jeffrey. 1993. "March for Gay Rights; Gay Marchers Throng Mall in Appeal for Rights." *New York Times*, April 26, sec. U.S. http://www.nytimes.com/1993/04/26/us/march-for-gay-rights-gay-marchers-throng-mall-in-appeal-for-rights.html.

Schradie, Jen. 2018. "The Digital Activism Gap: How Class and Costs Shape Online Collective Action." *Social Problems* 65 (1): 51–74. https://doi.org/10.1093/socpro/spx042.

Schudson, Michael. 1989. "How Culture Works: Perspectives from Media Studies on the Efficacy of Symbols." *Theory and Society* 18 (2): 153–80. https://doi.org/10.2307/657530.

Scott, Eugene. 2020. "The Audacity of Those Comparing 'Open Up' Protesters to Rosa Parks." *Washington Post*, May 1. https://www.washingtonpost.com/politics/2020/05/01/problems-with-holding-up-open-up-protesters-legacy-rosa-parks/.

Seamster, Louise, and Victor Ray. 2018. "Against Teleology in the Study of Race: Toward the Abolition of the Progress Paradigm." *Sociological Theory*, December. https://doi.org/10.1177/0735275118813614.

Segura, Liliana. 2017. "Trump's Muslim Ban Galvanizes Civil Rights Activists across the American South." *Intercept*, February 1.

Seidman, Steven. 1994. "Queer-ing Sociology, Sociologizing Queer Theory: An Introduction." *Sociological Theory* 12 (2): 166–77. https://doi.org/10.2307/201862.

Selod, Saher. 2018. *Forever Suspect: Racialized Surveillance of Muslim Americans in the War on Terror*. Rutgers University Press.

Sessions, Jeff. 2017. "Faith Inspired MLK Jr. to March for Civil Rights." *The Federalist*, July 13. https://thefederalist.com/2017/07/13/heres-the-speech-jeff-sessions-delivered-to-christian-first-amendment-lawyers/.

Sewell, Abigail A. 2017. "The Illness Associations of Police Violence: Differential Relationships by Ethnoracial Composition." *Sociological Forum* 32 (S1): 975–97. https://doi.org/10.1111/socf.12361.

Sewell, Abigail A., and Kevin A. Jefferson. 2016. "Collateral Damage: The Health Effects of Invasive Police Encounters in New York City." *Journal of Urban Health* 93 (1): 42–67. https://doi.org/10.1007/s11524-015-0016-7.

Sewell, Alyasah Ali, Justin M. Feldman, Rashawn Ray, Keon L. Gilbert, Kevin A. Jefferson, and Hedwig Lee. 2021. "Illness Spillovers of Lethal Police Violence: The Significance of Gendered Marginalization." *Ethnic and Racial Studies* 44 (7): 1089–1114. https://doi.org/10.1080/01419870.2020.1781913.

Shams, Tahseen. 2015. "Bangladeshi Muslims in Mississippi: Impression Management Based on the Intersectionality of Religion, Ethnicity, and Gender." *Cultural Dynamics* 27 (3): 379–97. https://doi.org/10.1177/0921374014548281.

———. 2019. "Successful Yet Precarious: South Asian Muslim Americans, Islamophobia, and the Model Minority Myth." *Sociological Perspectives*, December. https://doi.org/10.1177/0731121419895006.

Shapira, Harel. 2017. *Waiting for José: The Minutemen's Pursuit of America*. Princeton University Press.

Shapiro, Joseph P. 1988. "A New 'Common Identity' for the Disabled." *Washington Post*, March 29. https://www.washingtonpost.com/archive/lifestyle/wellness/1988/03/29/a-new-common-identity-for-the-disabled/1560359a-2b64-48d2-b9a1-b701d198a452.

———. 1994. *No Pity: People with Disabilities Forging a New Civil Rights Movement*. Random House.

Shapiro, Lila. 2012. "North Carolina Amendment 1 Divides Gay Rights Movement." *Huffington Post*, May 9, sec. Queer Voices. http://www.huffingtonpost.com/2012/05/08/north-carolina-amendment-1-gay-rights-movement_n_1501501.html.

Sharma, Nitasha Tamar. 2010. *Hip Hop Desis: South Asian Americans, Blackness, and a Global Race Consciousness*. Duke University Press.

Shelby, Tommie, and Brandon M. Terry. 2018. *To Shape a New World: Essays on the Political Philosophy of Martin Luther King, Jr.* Harvard University Press.

Simko, Christina. 2015. *The Politics of Consolation: Memory and the Meaning of September 11*. Oxford University Press.

———. 2018. "From Difficult Past to Imagined Future: Projective Reversal and the Transformation of Ground Zero." *Poetics* 67 (April): 39–52. https://doi.org/10.1016/j.poetic.2017.12.002.

———. 2020. "Marking Time in Memorials and Museums of Terror: Temporality and Cultural Trauma." *Sociological Theory* 38 (1): 51–77. https://doi.org/10.1177/0735275120906430.

———. 2021. "From Legacy to Memory: Reckoning with Racial Violence at the National Memorial for Peace and Justice." *Annals of the American Academy of Political and Social Science* 694 (1): 157–71. https://doi.org/10.1177/00027162211011604.

Simko, Christina, David Cunningham, and Nicole Fox. 2022. "Contesting Commemorative Landscapes: Confederate Monuments and Trajectories of Change." *Social Problems* 69 (3): 591–611. https://doi.org/10.1093/socpro/spaa067.

Sisk, Richard. 2010. "Glenn Beck: America Is Wandering in the Dark." *New York Daily News*, August 28.

Skarpelis, Anna. 2020. "Dresden Will Never Be Hiroshima: Morality, the Bomb and Far-Right Empathy for the Refugee." In *Far-Right Revisionism and the End of History: Alt/Histories*, 199–219. Routledge.

Skocpol, Theda, and Vanessa Williamson. 2012. *The Tea Party and the Remaking of Republican Conservatism*. Oxford University Press.

Skrentny, John D. 2004. *The Minority Rights Revolution*. Belknap Press.

Slaughter-Acey, Jaime C., Devon Sneed, Lauren Parker, Verna M. Keith, Nora L. Lee, and Dawn P. Misra. 2019. "Skin Tone Matters: Racial Microaggressions and Delayed Prenatal Care." *American Journal of Preventive Medicine* 57 (3): 321–29. https://doi.org/10.1016/j.amepre.2019.04.014.

Small, Mario Luis. 2009. "'How Many Cases Do I Need?': On Science and the Logic of Case Selection in Field-Based Research." *Ethnography* 10 (1): 5–38. https://doi.org/10.1177/1466138108099586.

Smith, Anthony D. 1999. *Myths and Memories of the Nation*. Oxford University Press.

Smith, Robert C. 2010. *Conservatism and Racism, and Why in America They Are the Same*. State University of New York Press.

Smith, Robert Courtney. 2014. "Black Mexicans, Conjunctural Ethnicity, and Operating Identities: Long-Term Ethnographic Analysis." *American Sociological Review* 79 (3): 517–48. https://doi.org/10.1177/0003122414529585.

Smitherman, Geneva. 1995. *African American Women Speak Out on Anita Hill-Clarence Thomas*. Wayne State University Press.

SNCC Legacy Project. 2016. "To Our Brothers and Sisters of the #BlackLivesMatter Movement." *Huffington Post*, August 4.

Snow, David A., and Robert D. Benford. 1992. "Master Frames and Cycles of Protest." In *Frontiers in Social Movement Theory*. Yale University Press.

Snow, David A., E. Burke Rochford, Steven K. Worden, and Robert D. Benford. 1986. "Frame Alignment Processes, Micromobilization, and Movement Participation." *American Sociological Review* 51 (4): 464–81. https://doi.org/10.2307/2095581.

Sokol, Jason. 2007. *There Goes My Everything: White Southerners in the Age of Civil Rights, 1945–1975*. Reprint. Vintage.

Somers, Margaret R. 1992. "Narrativity, Narrative Identity, and Social Action: Rethinking English Working-Class Formation." *Social Science History* 16 (4): 591–630. https://doi.org/10.2307/1171314.

Soule, Sarah, and Jennifer Earl. 2005. "A Movement Society Evaluated: Collective Protest in the United States, 1960–1986." *Mobilization: An International Quarterly* 10 (3): 345–64. https://doi.org/10.17813/maiq.10.3.730350353753l022.

Souli, Sarah. 2020. "Does America Need a Truth and Reconciliation Commission?" *Politico*, August 16. https://www.politico.com/news/magazine/2020/08/16/does-america-need-a-truth-and-reconciliation-commission-395332.

Spaulding, Pam. 2012. "Amendment One Sponsor Now Says He Will Vote against It (and Lies about His Past Support of It)." *Shadowproof* (blog), April 26. https://shadowproof.com/2012/04/26/amendment-one-sponsor-now-says-he-will-vote-against-it-and-lies-about-his-past-support-of-it/.

Spong, John Shelby. 2007. "John Shelby Spong's Controversial Christian Stance." August 31. https://www.abc.net.au/local/stories/2007/08/31/2020226.htm.

Sprunt, Barbara. 2021. "The Brewing Political Battle over Critical Race Theory." *NPR: Morning Edition*, June 21. https://www.npr.org/2021/06/02/1001055828/the-brewing-political-battle-over-critical-race-theory.

Stafford, Kat. 2020. "On #MeToo Anniversary, Leaders Say Focus Is on Inequality." AP News, October 15, sec. Virus Outbreak. https://apnews.com/article/virus-outbreak-race-and-ethnicity-politics-violence-tarana-burke-72e676703031b02a862d070380ab39ee.

Stammer, Larry. 1997. "Is Christian Coalition's Conversion Real?" *Los Angeles Times*, March 1.

Stein, Arlene. 1998. "Whose Memories? Whose Victimhood? Contests for the Holocaust Frame in Recent Social Movement Discourse." *Sociological Perspectives* 41 (3): 519–40. https://doi.org/10.2307/1389562.

Stein, Isaac. 2014. "Harlem Mosque Leader Talks Malcolm X Legacy." *Chicago Maroon*, February 28. http://chicagomaroon.com/18677/news/harlem-mosque-leader-talks-malcolm-x-legacy/.

Stewart, James B. 2012. "The Potential Price of Intolerance—Common Sense." *New York Times*, May 11. http://www.nytimes.com/2012/05/12/business/same-sex-marriage-bans-are-bad-for-business-common-sense.html.

Stoetzler, Marcel, and Nira Yuval-Davis. 2002. "Standpoint Theory, Situated Knowledge and the Situated Imagination." *Feminist Theory* 3 (3): 315–33. https://doi.org/10.1177/146470002762492024.

Stoogenke, Jason. 2012. "Amendment One Raises Debate about Businesses Choosing N.C." WSOC-TV. https://www.wsoctv.com/news/local/amendment-one-raises-debate-about-businesses-choos/329682241/.

Stovall, David Omotoso. 2016. *Born Out of Struggle: Critical Race Theory, School Creation, and the Politics of Interruption*. State University of New York Press.

Strong, Myron T., and K. Sean Chaplin. 2019. "Afrofuturism and Black Panther." *Contexts* 18 (2): 58–59. https://doi.org/10.1177/1536504219854725.

Stryker, Sheldon, Timothy Joseph Owens, and Robert W. White. 2000. *Self, Identity, and Social Movements*. University of Minnesota Press.

Sturgis, Sue. 2011. "NC Lawmakers Pushing Same-Sex Marriage Ban Enlist Help of Gay-Hating Preacher." *Facing South*, September 12. https://www.facingsouth.org/2011/09/nc-lawmakers-pushing-same-sex-marriage-ban-enlist-help-of-gay-hating-preacher.html.

Sturken, Marita. 1997. *Tangled Memories*. University of California Press.

Suleiman, Imam Omar. 2018. "Reclaiming Malcolm X's Legacy." *Muslim Matters*, June 1. https://muslimmatters.org/2018/06/01/reclaiming-malcolm-xs-legacy/.

Swidler, Ann. 1986. "Culture in Action: Symbols and Strategies." *American Sociological Review* 51 (2): 273–86. https://doi.org/10.2307/2095521.

Tajfel, Henri. 2010. *Social Identity and Intergroup Relations*. Cambridge University Press.

Tajfel, Henri, and John C. Turner. 1986. "The Social Identity Theory of Intergroup Behavior." *Psychology of Intergroup Relations* 5: 7–24.

Tarrow, Sidney. 1998. *Power in Movement: Social Movements and Contentious Politics*. Cambridge University Press.

Tatalovich, Raymond. 2014. *Nativism Reborn?: The Official English Language Movement and the American States*. University Press of Kentucky.

Tavory, Iddo, and Nina Eliasoph. 2013. "Coordinating Futures: Toward a Theory of Anticipation." *American Journal of Sociology* 118 (4): 908–42. https://doi.org/10.1086/668646.

Taylor, Keeanga-Yamahtta. 2017. *How We Get Free: Black Feminism and the Combahee River Collective*. Haymarket Books.

Taylor, Verta, and Nancy E. Whittier. 1992. "Collective Identity in Social Movement Communities: Lesbian Feminist Mobilization." In *Frontiers in Social Movement Theory*, ed. A. D. Morris and C. M. Mueller, 104–29. Yale University Press.

Terriquez, Veronica. 2015. "Intersectional Mobilization, Social Movement Spillover, and Queer Youth Leadership in the Immigrant Rights Movement." *Social Problems* 62 (3): 343–62. https://doi.org/10.1093/socpro/spv010.

Terriquez, Veronica, Tizoc Brenes, and Abdiel Lopez. 2018. "Intersectionality as a Multipurpose Collective Action Frame: The Case of the Undocumented Youth Movement." *Ethnicities* 18 (2): 260–76. https://doi.org/10.1177/1468796817752558.

Terry, Brandon M. 2018. "MLK Now." *Boston Review*, September 10. http://bostonreview.net/forum/brandon-m-terry-mlk-now.

Theoharis, Jeanne. 2018. *A More Beautiful and Terrible History: The Uses and Misuses of Civil Rights History*. Beacon Press.

Thomas-Lester, Avis, Hamil R., Harris, and Krissah Thompson. 2010. "Sharpton's 'Reclaim the Dream' Event Brings Thousands to Honor MLK." *Washington Post*, August 28.

Thomaston, Scottie. 2012. "Equality on Trial." *Equality on Trial* (blog), April 26. http://www.equalityontrial.com/2012/04/26/sponsor-of-anti-gay-amendment-1-in-north-carolina-abandons-it-will-vote-against-it/.

Tilly, Charles. 1978. *From Mobilization to Revolution*. Addison-Wesley.

Tilly, Charles, and Sidney Tarrow. 2015. *Contentious Politics*. Oxford University Press.

Tomaskovic-Devey, Donald, and Dustin Avent-Holt. 2018. *Relational Inequalities: An Organizational Approach*. Oxford University Press.

Tometi, Opal, and Gerald Lenoir. 2015. "Black Lives Matter Is Not a Civil Rights Movement." *Time*, December 10. http://time.com/4144655/international-human-rights-day-black-lives-matter/.

Treitler, Vilna Bashi. 2013. *The Ethnic Project: Transforming Racial Fiction into Ethnic Factions*. Stanford University Press.

Trott, Verity. 2021. "Networked Feminism: Counterpublics and the Intersectional Issues of #MeToo." *Feminist Media Studies* 21 (7): 1125–42. ttps://doi.org/10.1080/14680777.2020.1718176.

Trouillot, Michel-Rolph. 1995. *Silencing the Past: Power and the Production of History*. Beacon Press.

Troy, Gil. 2016. "The Example of Ronald Reagan." *New York Times*, November 10.

Tufekci, Zeynep. 2017. *Twitter and Tear Gas: The Power and Fragility of Networked Protest*. Yale University Press.

Tyle, Trevor. 2018. "Oprah Keeps MLK's Dream Alive with Powerful Golden Globes Speech." *Oakland Post* (blog), January 16. https://oaklandpostonline.com/20357/opinion/opinion-oprah-keeps-mlks-dream-alive-with-powerful-golden-globes-speech/.

Unger, Arthur. 1986. "Hard-hitting Special about Black Families." *Christian Science Monitor*, January 23.

Vaid, Urvashi. 1995. *Virtual Equality: The Mainstreaming of Gay and Lesbian Liberation*. Anchor Books.

Valdez, Zulema, and Tanya Golash-Boza. 2017. "Towards an Intersectionality of Race and Ethnicity." *Ethnic and Racial Studies* 40 (13): 2256–61. https://doi.org/10.1080/01419870.2017.1344277.

Valencia-García, Louie Dean. 2021. *Far-Right Revisionism and the End of History: Alt/Histories*. Taylor & Francis Limited.

Van Dyke, Nella, and Holly J. McCammon, eds. 2010. *Strategic Alliances: Coalition Building and Social Movements*. University of Minnesota Press.

Vega, Tanzania. 2015. "Protesters Out to Reclaim King's Legacy, but in Era That Defies Comparison." *New York Times*, January 17.

Verloo, Mieke. 2013. "Intersectional and Cross-Movement Politics and Policies: Reflections on Current Practices and Debates." *Signs: Journal of Women in Culture and Society* 38 (4): 893–915. https://doi.org/10.1086/669572.

Vilda, Dovile, Rachel Hardeman, Lauren Dyer, Katherine P. Theall, and Maeve Wallace. 2021. "Structural Racism, Racial Inequities and Urban-Rural Differences in Infant Mortality in the US." *Journal of Epidemiology Community Health* 75 (8): 788–93. https://doi.org/10.1136/jech-2020-214260.

Volo, Lorraine de. 2007. "The Dynamics of Emotion and Activism: Grief, Gender, and Collective Identity in Revolutionary Nicaragua." *Mobilization: An International Quarterly* 11 (4): 461–74. https://doi.org/10.17813/maiq.11.4.q21r3432561l21t7.

Voss, Kim, and Irene Bloemraad. 2011. *Rallying for Immigrant Rights: The Fight for Inclusion in 21st Century America*. University of California Press.

Wagner-Pacifici, Robin. 1996. "Memories in the Making: The Shapes of Things That Went." *Qualitative Sociology* 19 (3): 301–21. https://doi.org/10.1007/BF02393274.

Wagner-Pacifici, Robin, and Barry Schwartz. 1991. "The Vietnam Veterans Memorial: Commemorating a Difficult Past." *American Journal of Sociology* 97 (2): 376–420. https://doi.org/10.1086/229783.

Walker, Edward T., and Lina Stepick. 2020. "Valuing the Cause: A Theory of Authenticity in Social Movements." *Mobilization: An International Quarterly* 25 (1): 1–25. https://doi.org/10.17813/1086-671X-25-1-1.

Walsh, Paul. 2020. "Teen Who Recorded George Floyd Video Wasn't Looking to Be a Hero, Her Lawyer Says." *Star Tribune*, June 11.

Wan, William. 2011. "Hearings on Muslims Trigger Panic." *Washington Post*, January 24.

Ware, Vron. 2015. *Beyond the Pale: White Women, Racism, and History*. Verso Books.

Waters, Mary C., and Philip Kasinitz. 2010. "Discrimination, Race Relations, and the Second Generation." *Social Research: An International Quarterly* 77 (1): 101–32.

Waters, Mary C., Van C. Tran, Phillip Kasinitz, and John Mollenkopf. 2010. "Segmented Assimilation Revisited: Types of Acculturation and Socioeconomic Mobility in Young Adulthood." *Ethnic and Racial Studies* 33 (7): 1168–93.

Watkins Liu, Callie. 2018. "The Anti-Oppressive Value of Critical Race Theory and Intersectionality in Social Movement Study." *Sociology of Race and Ethnicity* 4 (3): 306–21. https://doi.org/10.1177/2332649217743771.

Wetzstein, Cheryl. 2012. "N.C. Votes to Not Allow Same-Sex Marriage." *Washington Times*, May 8.

Williamson, Vanessa, and Dana R. Fisher. 2022. "It's Time for Democrats to Stop 'Clapping for Tinkerbell.'" *The Nation*, June 10. https://www.thenation.com/article/politics/democrats-clapping-tinkerbell/.

Wilson, Jason Carson. 2011. "North Carolina's Gay Marriage Ban Closer to Public Vote." *Equally Wed*. https://equallywed.com/north-carolinas-gay-marriage-ban-closer-to-public-vote/.

Wolfensberger, Don. 2008."The Martin Luther King, Jr. Holiday: The Long Struggle in Congress." Presented at "The Martin Luther King, Jr. Holiday: How Did It Happen?" January 14. Woodrow Wilson International Center for Scholars.

Xu, Jun, and Jennifer C. Lee. 2013. "The Marginalized 'Model' Minority: An Empirical Examination of the Racial Triangulation of Asian Americans." *Social Forces* 91 (4): 1363–97. https://doi.org/10.1093/sf/sot049.

Yang, Allie. 2018. "Rep. John Lewis on Not Meeting with Trump: Martin Luther King Jr. 'Would Have Taken the Same Position I Did.'" ABC News, January 15.

Yazdiha, Hajar. 2014. "Law as Movement Strategy: How the Islamophobia Movement Institutionalizes Fear through Legislation." *Social Movement Studies* 13 (2): 267–74. https://doi.org/10.1080/14742837.2013.807730.

———. 2020. "An Intersectional Theory of Strategic Decisions: Muslim American Immigrants and the Dilemmas of Policing." *Mobilization: An International Quarterly* 25 (4): 475–92. https://doi.org/10.17813/1086-671X-25-4-475.

———. 2021. "Toward a Du Boisian Framework of Immigrant Incorporation: Racialized Contexts, Relational Identities, and Muslim American Collective Action." *Social Problems* 68 (2): 300–320. https://doi.org/10.1093/socpro/spaa058.

Yuval-Davis, Nira. 2007. "Intersectionality, Citizenship and Contemporary Politics of Belonging." *Critical Review of International Social and Political Philosophy* 10 (4): 561–74. https://doi.org/10.1080/13698230701660220.

Zamora, Sylvia, and Chinyere Osuji. 2014. "Mobilizing African Americans for Immigrant Rights: Framing Strategies in Two Multi-racial Coalitions." *Latino Studies* 12: 424–48. https://doi.org/10.1057/lst.2014.47.

Zelizer, Barbie. 1994. "Reading the Past against the Grain: The Shape of Memory Studies." *Critical Studies in Mass Communication* 12 (2): 214–39.

Zernike, Kate. 2010a. "Where Dr. King Stood, Tea Party Claims His Mantle." *New York Times*, August 27.

———. 2010b. *Boiling Mad: Inside Tea Party America*. Macmillan.

Zerubavel, Eviatar. 1996. "Social Memories: Steps to a Sociology of the Past." *Qualitative Sociology* 19 (3): 283–99. https://doi.org/10.1007/BF02393273.

Zhou, Min, and Carl L. Bankston. 2020. "The Model Minority Stereotype and the National Identity Question: The Challenges Facing Asian Immigrants and Their Children." *Ethnic and Racial Studies* 43 (1): 233–53. https://doi.org/10.1080/01419870.2019.1667511.

Zhou, Min, Jennifer Lee, Jody Agius Vallejo, Rosaura Tafoya-Estrada, and Yang Sao Xiong. 2008. "Success Attained, Deterred, and Denied: Divergent Pathways to Social Mobility in Los Angeles's New Second Generation." *Annals of the American Academy of Political and Social Science* 620 (1): 37–61.

INDEX

Page numbers in *italics* indicate figures and tables.

A NOTE ON THE TYPE

This book has been composed in Arno, an Old-style serif typeface in the classic Venetian tradition, designed by Robert Slimbach at Adobe.

Printed in the USA
CPSIA information can be obtained
at www.ICGtesting.com
JSHW020229051224
74788JS00008B/169

9 780691 246475

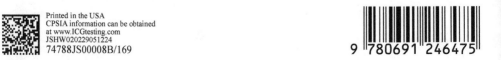